Crossing boundaries

An analysis of Roman coins in Danish contexts

Contents

Foreword 9

Acknowledgements 11

Chapter 1 • Introduction 13
    1.1 The legal background 13
    1.2 Finding – recording – collecting 13
    1.3 Roman coins as archaeological artefacts – the history of research and interpretation 16
    1.4 Coins and other Roman finds in Denmark 20
    1.5 Approaching the finds 21

Chapter 2 • The area 23
    2.1 Introduction 23
    2.2 Denmark between the Early Roman and the Early Germanic Iron Ages ... 24
    2.3 Danish Iron Age chronology 25
    2.4 Roman coins and Scandinavian chronology 27

Chapter 3 • The material 29
    3.1 Introduction 29
    3.2 Is the material representative? 31
    3.3 Coins and the metal detector 32
    3.4 Survey finds and excavation finds 34
    3.5 Differences in find density 34
    3.6 Hoards and single finds 35
    3.7 Reassembling a scattered hoard 36
    3.8 The importance of the metal detector 37
    3.9 Denominations 39

Chapter 4 • Geographical distribution of coin finds – the coins in their regional contexts ... 41
- 4.1 Sealand ... 41
- 4.2 Funen ... 47
- 4.3 Jutland ... 50
  - 4.3.1 Northern Jutland and the Limfjord area ... 51
  - 4.3.2 Eastern Jutland ... 54
  - 4.3.3 Central, western and southern Jutland ... 55

Chapter 5 • Context types ... 57
- 5.1 Coins found in graves ... 57
  - 5.1.1 Sealand ... 57
  - 5.1.2 Funen ... 61
  - 5.1.3 Jutland ... 63
  - 5.1.4 Possible grave finds? ... 63
  - 5.1.5 Geographical distribution of coins in graves ... 64
  - 5.1.6 Chronological distribution of coins found in graves ... 65
  - 5.1.7 The meaning of the coin in the grave ... 66
  - 5.1.8 Charon's fee? ... 67
  - 5.1.9 "Münzersatz" ... 68
  - 5.1.10 Summary ... 69
- 5.2 Isolated depositions ... 71
  - 5.2.1 The weapon sacrifices ... 71
  - 5.2.2 Denarius hoards from moors and wetland areas ... 76
  - 5.2.3 Other denarius finds from wetland areas ... 83
  - 5.2.4 Mixed hoards ... 86
  - 5.2.5 Gold hoards ... 87
  - 5.2.6 Single finds of Ancient gold coins ... 91
- 5.3 Settlements ... 94
  - 5.3.1 Gudme, Lundeborg and the surrounding area ... 94
  - 5.3.2 Three sites with denarius hoards ... 105
  - 5.3.3 Other settlements with denarius finds ... 108
  - 5.3.4 Hacksilber hoards from settlements ... 115
  - 5.3.5 Settlements with other Roman denominations ... 116

Chapter 6 • Coins. Denominations and striking periods ... 121
- 6.1 Denarii ... 121
  - 6.1.1 Finds of Republican and Julio-Claudian denarii (until AD 68) ... 121
  - 6.1.2 Post-Neronian denarii ... 125
  - 6.1.3 The chronological distribution of Antonine coinages ... 126
  - 6.1.4 Chronological composition of closed finds with several denarii ... 129
  - 6.1.5 Single finds in dated contexts ... 135
  - 6.1.6 Single finds of denarii from detector sites ... 135
  - 6.1.7 Barbarian denarii ... 135
- 6.2 Siliquae ... 138
- 6.3 Roman gold coins ... 144
  - 6.3.1 Aurei and solidi until AD 395 ... 144
  - 6.3.2 The Barbarian imitations of aurei and early solidi ... 148
  - 6.3.3 The Roman 4th century medallions ... 149
  - 6.3.4 Imitations of Constantinian medallions and other 4th century coins ... 152

Crossing boundaries

An analysis of Roman coins in Danish contexts

Vol. 1: Finds from Sealand, Funen and Jutland

Helle W. Horsnæs

PNM
Publications of the National Museum
Studies in Archaeology and History Vol. 18

Copenhagen 2010

Publications from the National Museum, Studies in Archaeology and History Vol. 18
Crossing boundaries
An analysis of Roman coins in Danish contexts
Vol. 1: Finds from Sealand, Funen and Jutland
Helle W. Horsnæs

Copyright © The National Museum of Denmark and the author
All rights reserved

Cover design by Christine Clemmensen
Typesetting by ansats@provinsen
Produced by Støvring Bogfremstilling
Printed by Clemenstrykkeriet

Published by The National Museum of Denmark
Royal Collection of Coins and Medals
12 Frederiksholms Kanal, DK-1220 Copenhagen K

On commission at University Press of Southern Denmark

ISBN: 978-87-7602-133-7.

Funded by:
Dr. Margrethe II's Arkæologiske Fond
Elisabeth Munksgaards Fond
Lillian og Dan Finks Fond
Advokat Axel Ernst's og Frøken Alfrida Ernst's Legat til Fremme af Numismatisk Forskning i Danmark
Den Hielmstierne-Rosencroneske Stiftelse
Farumgaard-Fonden

Cover: Roman denarius struck during the reign of Antoninus Pius in the name of his deceased wife Faustina Major (dead 141 AD). *Roman Imperial Coinage* type 351, with ten occurrences the most commonly registered type from Sealand, Funen and Jutland. This coin is one of four specimens of this type from the Præstemosen Hoard, Gudme. Photo John Lee/Danish National Museum.

	6.3.5 Late Roman solidi	154
	6.3.6 A 6th century triens	156
	6.3.7 Bracteates and Roman coins	156
	6.3.8 Gold – Summary	157
6.4	Base metal coins	160
6.5	Antoniniani	162
6.6	Roman Provincial coins and Alexandrian coins	166
6.7	Geographical distribution of mints	166
6.8	Reworked coins	167
	6.8.1 Denarii	167
	6.8.2 Siliquae	169
	6.8.3 Gold coins	169
	6.8.4 Pierced or looped base metal coins	170
	6.8.5 Coin rings	171
	6.8.6 Clipped coins	172
	6.8.7 Cut coins	172

Chapter 7 • Find patterns in other parts of Barbaricum ... 173
- 7.1 South of Denmark ... 173
  - The Netherlands ... 173
  - Germany ... 174
  - Poland ... 175
  - Bohemia, Northern Austria and Slovakia ... 175
- 7.2 North of Denmark ... 176
  - Norway ... 176
  - Mainland Sweden ... 176
  - Öland, Gotland and Bornholm ... 176
  - Finland ... 177

Chapter 8 • Synthesis ... 179
- 8.1 From mint to soil – how to get there? ... 180
- 8.2 Romans in Southern Scandinavia? ... 182
- 8.3 Sailing the North Sea? ... 183
- 8.4 The Amber Routes ... 183
- 8.5 The distribution of Roman coins in Western Denmark ... 185
- 8.6 The period of influx ... 186
- 8.7 An international network ... 186
- 8.8 The routes to Denmark ... 187
- 8.9 The meaning of the Roman coins in the Danish Iron Age context ... 188

Indices ... 191

Abbreviations ... 203

Bibliography ... 205

Foreword

The Roman coins found within the area of modern Denmark form the empirical basis of the present study. It is my intention to present and discuss the coins as archaeological artefacts. The provenance and context of the individual coin are regarded as parameters of equal importance for the interpretation of the find as the numismatic evidence inherent in the coin. Initially more weight is put on answering the "how, when and why" regarding the Roman coins in the local context and the import of the Roman coins into the Danish Iron Age cultures, than the "how, when and why" regarding the export of the coins from the Roman Empire. The latter questions will mostly be touched on in the last part of the book, where I will attempt to compare the evidence from Denmark with finds from other parts of Barbaricum.

The present work takes as its starting point the area today under Danish jurisdiction. The modern Danish area is convenient to study as an entity, because for many centuries the same legislation has been used over this area. Finds have been collected under the Danish treasure trove law for centuries, and during the last decades the employment of the metal detector has changed the volume of finds drastically. It is therefore of great importance to consider Denmark with its legislation apart from for example Sweden, where the use of metal detectors is forbidden. The archaeological finds, however, do not allow a balanced overview over the whole area. This has induced me to divide the study into two parts of which the present part 1 covers Jutland, Funen and Sealand with adjacent islands and with mentions of neighbouring areas.

The relatively small island Bornholm is situated in the middle of the Baltic Sea. In many respects the archaeology of Bornholm is more closely connected to Baltic cultures than to Denmark, and it is clear that the finds of Roman coins from Bornholm also differ from those presented here.[1] Part 2 of the study therefore will be dedicated to the Roman coin finds from Bornholm and the island's pivotal role in the Baltic area. It is hoped that it will be possible to write part 2 during my planned research leave in 2011.

The book is based on as many finds as possible, but I cannot claim my find lists to be comprehensive. Distribution maps and statistics were made in spring 2008, and they have not been updated with more recent finds. I have attempted to update relevant parts with finds made later in 2008, but no additions were made after 2008. Nor will there be consistency in the figures given in the various counts and diagrams. I have always included as much material as possible, but in cases where relevant information of a coin is lacking or not obtainable it has been left out: in cases where a coin can be assigned to an emperor but not to a specific issue, it is included in diagrams based on reigns but not in those where more specific infor-

---

1 Horsnæs *forthcoming A*; Horsnæs 2009.

mation was needed. When possible, I have inserted information about old finds that are no longer extant. In these cases information on weights are normally completely lacking, descriptions often provide the denomination and the emperor depicted on the coin, and depending on the degree of accuracy of the description it may or may not enable an attempt at identifying the type or issue of the coin. Old archaeological finds are often notorious for their lack of precise information on the find circumstances, but in the case of coin finds the "magic of money" often seems to have preserved more information than usual.

Today, amateur archaeologists undertaking metal detector surveys provide us with the majority of new finds of Roman coins. These coins are protected by the Danish *danefæ* legislation, and must be handed in to the National Museum. Coins found during archaeological excavations are also often handed in to the National Museum for identification. These coins are the ones most likely to have a well-known and fully described archaeological context, and I am greatly indebted to all my colleagues who have generously shared their knowledge of coin finds and contexts with me.

It was from the outset decided to write the book in English to enable non-Danish readers to get an idea of the finds from our area, and to evaluate the Danish results in relation to other areas in Europe, in particular to other areas in Barbaricum, from Scotland to the Black Sea area. Therefore the distribution maps have mostly been kept to the large-scale overview of the material. For more detailed maps I refer to the maps of the individual sites in http://www.dkconline.dk .

This book is certainly not intended to be the "last nail in the coffin" on the vast and many-sided theme of Roman coins in Barbarian contexts. On the contrary it is my hope that it will be an invitation to my colleagues to cross the artificial boundaries between the scholarly fields of archaeology, ancient history and numismatics and develop upon and argue against my ideas, while new finds and better data may widen the discourse.

Acknowledgements

The book has benefited greatly from fruitful discussions, good advice and practical help from a lot of friends and colleagues. I owe sincere thanks to all of them. They are far too many to mention them all, but I would like to express my special gratitude to the many colleagues in local museums throughout Denmark, whom I have been pestering with my inquiries. Special thanks also to Josefine Franck Bican who made all the distribution maps and Maria Louise Storm Svendsen who helped with photography and other practicalities.

Ted Buttrey, Anne Marie Carstens, Jørgen Steen Jensen and Michael Märcher read and commented on earlier versions of the manuscript and last, but certainly not least, Gitte Tarnow Ingvardson and Richard Reece read the whole manuscript. They all corrected numerous errors and made valuable suggestions that improved the final version. The manuscript was finished in December 2008 and only minor updates were made since then.

The publication of the book was only possible through generous support from Dr. Margrethe II's Arkæologiske Fond, Elisabeth Munksgaards Fond, Lillian og Dan Finks Fond, Advokat Axel Ernst's og Frøken Alfrida Ernst's Legat til Fremme af Numismatisk Forskning i Danmark, Den Hielmstierne-Rosencroneske Stiftelse, and Farumgaard-Fonden.

If I have been able to see further than others, it is because I have stood on the shoulders of giants.
Sir Isaac Newton

CHAPTER 1
Introduction

"EX ANTIQVO TESAVRO…"

1.1 The legal background

The Danish treasure trove legislation goes back to the *Jyske Lov* confirmed by king Valdemar II in 1241, where it was stipulated that "If any man finds silver or gold in barrows or after the plough, or by any other means, the King shall have it".[2] In the *Sjællanske Lov* from the 13th century ownerless valuables found in the soil are for the first time called *danefæ*. The word originally meant "dead ownerless property", and the expression is still used today where the word is used to designate all Danish treasure trove.

In a public notice of 1752 "old coins" were specifically mentioned as part of the treasures that should be handed over to the king, and it was noted not only that the finder should have a reward equal to the value of the find, but also that "anyone who dares conceal that which is found shall be subject to rightful punishment". The present legislation, from 2001, still preserves the core elements of the Medieval laws, namely that "Objects of the past, including coins found in Denmark, of which no one can prove to be the rightful owner, shall be treasure trove (*danefæ*) if made of valuable material or being of a special cultural heritage value".[3]

The material found and handed in to the king was originally an income of gold and silver for the king, but the cultural value of the objects eventually became a more and more prominent part of the collection. In the nineteenth century, archaeological considerations of saving the country's historical heritage definitively superseded the fiscal purpose of the law. The *danefæ* were sent either to the Royal Coin Cabinet, created as a separate body in 1780, or to the Museum of Nordic Antiquities, founded in 1807.

The legislation regarding treasure trove has been in force for several hundred years with only slight modifications, and has covered all the area which is today Denmark. This continuity in legislation means that finds from all parts of modern Denmark have been treated in the same manner throughout the whole period where finds have been collected and noted, and it facilitates comparative studies of finds within Denmark. All the Roman coins discussed in the present work are declared treasure trove and therefore property of the Danish state.

1.2 Finding – recording – collecting

Collecting of archaeological artefacts only gradually became the major issue for the legislation, but in some cases we gather knowledge of finds that are no longer preserved, and we learn that in spite of the legislation many finds were never handed in to the au-

---

2 *Jyske Lov*, volume 2, article 112, quoted after Moesgaard 1999/2002.
3 Museum Act – ACT no. 473 of 07/06/2001, Chapter 9.30: http://www.kulturministeriet.dk/sw4497.asp.

thorities. Letters and memoirs reveal that even state officials, whom one should have expected to know better, kept coins for their own collections. Nobility in fact seems to have had some right to act in this way. A decree from Viborg *landsting* in 1556 stipulated that noblemen could keep *danefæ*, but only when found in fenced in areas.

The legend of a unique, curious gold medal reads: EX ANTIQVO TESAVRO FRVTO IN ARVO LVNDEBORG FIONVM SVMVS A 1585 (*Fig. 1*).[4] It reveals that an ancient treasure had been ploughed up in the field of Lundeborg on the island of Funen in or shortly before 1585, and that the gold had been re-used for one, or more likely several [SVMVS], medals of this kind.

The area of Lundeborg and Gudme, both close to Hesselagergård, are among the most important sites of Iron Age Denmark, with numerous finds, among other things the Broholm treasure that is one of the largest gold hoards from Iron Age Denmark. The medal is the earliest evidence of finds of a gold treasure in this area.[5]

Fig. 2. Ironically, the earliest find with known provenance that still exists is not a Roman coin, but a uniface imitation of a Late Roman solidus found at Kinbjerg in northern Jutland in 1670 (see *Fig. 3*). Drawing of the Kinbjerg imitation, from Thomas Bartholin, Acta medica et philosophica Hafniensa, vol. III, ann. 1674-1675, obs. XXIX p. 60f. (reproduced after Galster 1936, 9).

Fig. 1. The Lundeborg medal weighs 12.01 g, equivalent to between two and three Roman gold coins, but we do not know how many medals were cast from the ancient treasure, nor can we decide whether the treasure consisted of Roman coins and/or of other gold objects. The medal carries the initials and coat-of-arms of Niels Friis and his wife Wibeke Gyldenstjerne, who owned the Hesselagergård manor from 1570. Scale 2:1. Photo National Museum of Denmark.

4 Kromann & Jensen 1993.
5 The first finds included in the present study are: the imitation of a Late Roman solidus from Kinbjerg (Galster 1936, 9-11; see section 6.3.5), a silver coin with "a similar image" found inside a human skull at Lille Næstved (Galster 1936, 30, see section 5.1.1, where the interpretation of the coin as a denarius is questioned) and a denarius struck by Antoninus Pius from Viborg area (Galster 1936, 41, see section 4.3.1 and Chapter 8).

Fig. 3. The Kinbjerg coin imitation, obverse and reverse. Scale 2:1. Photo MLSS.

Clearly, the *danefæ* legislation could be put into use when authorities wanted it to be so. One of the earliest and best illustrated examples is the recovery of the Råmose Hoard found on western Sealand.

In July 1782 rumours of a find of a large hoard of ancient coins had reached Copenhagen. The prime minister Ove Høegh-Guldberg, himself a keen collector of coins, took action and demanded an inquiry. It turned out that peasants had found old silver coins while digging for peat in the Råmose. The find evidently created a silver rush where several other peasants took part and the finds were sold to local officers, a gold-smith *et alii*. Høegh-Guldberg requested that the local authorities should demand the coins for the King and that they should interrogate the original finders as to the find circumstances. We therefore know that the coins from the Råmose Hoard were found concentrated in an area of 3 x 1½ *alen* (i.e. 1.90 x 0.95 m) from *c*. 23.5 cm depth downwards, and that there were no traces of "wood, iron or pottery" in the area. The fact that the coins were re-collected from several finders and buyers and arrived in Copenhagen in several consignments resulted in some uncertainty as to the total number of coins from the find. Prof. Abraham Kall, who had been appointed to undertake the scientific research on the coins, left a manuscript of which only part is preserved. Here it is noted that the find consisted of 388 coins, and that the latest coin of the find was struck in 188 AD. Prof. Kall had studied the coins in his home, and after his death a total of 428(!) coins were handed back to the Royal Coin Cabinet. On that occasion the director of the Coin Cabinet, Chr. Ramus, made a summary list of the coins from the hoard. He noted that the find included coins from the period from Tiberius to Marcus Aurelius. Perhaps the hoard was not complete when handed back to Ramus, as it seems difficult to imagine that either of the two gentlemen should mistake a Marcus Aurelius (161-180 AD) for a Commodus (180-192) or vice versa.[6]

The "Medaille Cabinet" was part of the King's "Kunstkammer"[7] until the late 18th century. In 1780 it was decided to transfer the coin collection to the Rosenborg Castle, remaining the property of the King.[8] The collection is known through a series of inventories, the oldest of which from 1673. From this early period it is not possible to identify individual coin finds. They were collected – and kept – as a coin cabinet, not as an archaeological collection. Therefore the finds followed the fate of other coins in the Cabinet: provenances were lost, and the coins themselves were exchanged for other types or better examples, or even melted down. Unfortunately this also became the fate of the Råmose Hoard. Although some of the denarii in The Royal Collection of Coins and Medals may originate from this hoard it cannot be proved beyond doubt. In reality what we have left of the hoard are an incomplete manuscript and a summary list of the finds – and they are not in agreement. This loss is of course irreparable and a warning not to discard objects or information that may seem meaningless in our present context.

Thus literary sources have provided us with some knowledge about coin finds from the 17th and 18th century, but we can rarely connect this information with the actual coins themselves.

After the Period of Enlightenment and the French revolution the bourgoisie community grew and gave rise to the formation of Nation States throughout Europe. The political development of course had parallels in science. During the 19th century there was a growing awareness of the importance of archaeological finds interacting with a growing concern for the past of the Nation. The Register of Finds (or Find

---

6 Kromann 1995. To be able to use the Råmose Hoard for statistics the list of finds made by Chr. Ramus in 1800 and long considered the most reliable evidence for the composition of the hoard, was used in the present work.
7 Gundestrup 2001.
8 Horsnæs 2009b, with reference to previous research on the history of the collection.

Protocol: FP) of the Royal Coin Cabinet was initiated in 1801, and in particular since the directorship of P.O. Brøndsted in the 1830's coin finds were continously listed in the Protocol and kept in the Cabinet. With the Constitution of 1849 the Royal collections became property of the State, but the coin collection remained in the Rosenborg Castle until 1867, when it was transferred to its present address in the *Prince's Palace* that already housed other collections. In 1892 the National Museum was founded, based on the collections housed in the *Prince's Palace*. The treasure trove legislation still ensures that all coin finds from Denmark should be registered in The Royal Collection of Coins and Medals. The coins remain, as all *danefæ*, property of the State, and are kept in the National Museum if not deposited in one of the many local archaeological museums of Denmark.

1.3 Roman coins as archaeological artefacts – the history of research and interpretation

The 19th century saw the rise of the *corpora*, and lists of finds of Roman (or rather "Ancient") coins from Denmark and/or Northern Europe were published. The Swedish archaeologist Oscar Montelius provided one of the first lists of finds from Denmark, Norway and Sweden in his overview of Nordic Iron Age,[9] and some years later the Danish numismatist Peter Chr. Hauberg presented a similar list.[10] Montelius' aim was a cultural history of the Nordic areas and he used the coin finds as his prime dating evidence.

Hauberg took a purely numismatic view. He concluded that denarii were the most commonly found type of Roman coins and among these, coins struck in the period from Nero to Septimius Severus dominated. Contrary to this, contemporary aurei and bronze coins were rare, while a number of solidi minted after the reform of Constantine the Great were noted.

Already in those days there was a clear pattern in the geographical distribution of finds. The majority of coins were found in Southern Scandinavia, i.e. Denmark and Scania, and on the Baltic islands: Gotland, Öland and Bornholm. The solidi finds could be divided into two well-defined groups: coins minted before the division of the Empire were found mainly on Funen, while the Late-Roman solidi, post-dating 395 AD, were found on the Baltic islands.

The work of the Swedish historian Sture Bolin (*Fynden av romerska mynt i det fria Germanien. Studier i romersk och äldre germansk historie*) from 1926 was a major landmark in the research of Roman coins in Barbaricum, and of Roman-Barbarian contacts in general.[11] His aim was a comprehensive study, formulated as the conclusion of his 2nd chapter in which he had put forward his critique of previous research: "what do the finds of Roman and Byzantine coins in Germania and Scandinavia teach us?".[12] To achieve his aims he first undertook a survey of the "coin finds and coin relations within the Roman Empire", secondly he discussed the "political relations within Germania" as known to us through *classical literature* (my italics). He based himself on the totality of the finds, underlining that a discussion of the finds from a single country or of a single type would not suffice. Consequently his book included not only 70 pages on Roman coinage, but also 150 pages with lists of coin finds from Germania and another 70 pages with lists of Roman coin hoards from within the empire. The main part of his book on "Germania and its coin finds" covered chapters 8-14, where the introductory chapter 8 described the literary sources to a history of Roman-Germanic connections. A very important part of his work was a thorough analysis of the composition of the coin hoards from Germania (Chapter 10), where he used two main parameters: the latest coin of the hoard and the chronological distribution of coins within the hoard.

Bolin parted from the assumption that an increased number of coin hoards reflected crisis and war in the area in question. For example, the many denarius hoards ending with Marcus Aurelius that Bolin had noted throughout Germania were according to him related to the Marcomannic Wars (166-180 AD). The evidence of the coin hoards also led him to conclude that the crisis created by the Marcomannic Wars had affected not only the Danube area, but even the greater part of Germania. His use of

---

9   Montelius 1869.
10 Hauberg 1894.

11 Bolin 1926.
12 Bolin 1926, 20; my translation.

the Marcomannic Wars as an explanatory model for the interpretation of the coin finds has had a major impact on archaeological research even till our days.

The coin hoards ending with coins struck during the reigns of Commodus (180-192) to Septimius Severus (193-211) *and* deposited during the same periods, were according to Bolin very rare. In the majority of cases he believed it was not possible to date the deposition of the hoard, and he therefore did not dare to relate this particular group of hoards with historical events, but later finds were, again, related to historical events known from Roman sources.

Scandinavia presented a more complicated picture to Bolin, as he dismissed both the Roman literary sources that did not mention areas as far north and the later sagas as reliable sources. Among the archaeological finds he abstained from the use of un-datable material, and was left with only the Roman coins![13] The coin finds revealed a period of crisis throughout Scandinavia in the 4th century, a major crisis on Öland in 450-490 AD, a crisis on Bornholm in 475-525 AD, and a period of crisis ending around 560 AD on Gotland.

Bolin concluded that coins came to Barbaricum as part of a continuous trade pattern as well as a result of wars. The finds reflected crisis rather than wealth. However, he did not doubt that the coins mainly had a monetary function, even as far from the Empire as for example Gotland.

In spite of Bolin's warnings that the material should be studied as a whole, since his days the majority of studies have been concentrated either on a specific area or a specific coin type.

In the 1940's Niels Breitenstein initiated a series of articles with lists of finds from Denmark,[14] a series that was concluded and extended with Jørgen Balling's articles on Jutland and southern Sweden.[15] These articles were comprehensive and thus included and reviewed old finds already mentioned by e.g. Hauberg. Anne Kromann updated the Danish material until *c.* 1980.[16] In 1986 she summarized the finds,[17] and in a symposium in Ravello 1990 she discussed the function of the Roman coin finds from Denmark.[18] In the 1980's and until her premature death in 1996 Kromann also published a number of articles on the many finds that the new detector archaeology produced.

The coin finds from Denmark have been listed in the Annual reports of the Royal Coll. of Coins and Medals published in the *Nordisk Numismatisk Årsskrift* (*Nordic Numismatic Journal: NNÅ*) and 1984-2002 in the *Arkæologiske Udgravninger i Danmark* (*Archaeological Excavations in Denmark: AUD*). The recent Danish material was included in a study of the function and circulation of the Roman coins from North-western Barbaricum including Denmark.[19] The conclusions stressed the regional and chronological variations in the material within the area.

Since the 1990's a number of minor articles dealing with specific Danish finds, and shorter summaries of the find situation and possible interpretations have been published.[20]

Sweden has yielded a considerably larger number of Roman coins than Denmark. The Swedish finds have been the starting point for a number of studies. Joan Fagerlie presented her study of Late Roman and Byzantine solidi found in Sweden and Denmark in 1967. The work included a catalogue of all finds from Denmark and Sweden,[21] but discussed mainly the finds from the Baltic islands (Öland, Gotland and Bornholm). Fagerlie concluded that a continuous stream of coins flowed northwards during the century 450-550 AD. At first Öland acted as the main import

---

13 Bolin 1926, 249.
14 Breitenstein 1942; 1943; 1944 and 1946.
15 Balling 1962 and 1966.
16 Kromann 1983-84.

17 Kromann 1990.
18 A Danish version of the paper was published posthumously as Kromann 1999.
19 Korthauer 1998. The work is an unpublished *Magisterarbeit*, and I owe my sincerest thanks to Carsten Korthauer for access to this thorough and inspiring work.
20 Summary of find situation in Horsnæs 2003b, for a more interpretative article see Horsnæs 2005. Articles on individual finds will be referred to in connection with the find in question.
21 Only one solidus from this period has been found in Norway. It is mounted in a beaded rim, and it was found in a grave in Hamre (Sogn & Fjordane region) in 1889, cf. Skaare 1976, find no. 120, pl. I.6.

area whence the coins were redistributed to other parts of Scandinavia, but after a major catastrophe in 476/477 AD, the stream to Öland was interrupted and redirected towards Gotland. The majority of the Late Roman and Byzantine solidi were found on the Baltic islands (Öland, Gotland and Bornholm), and consequently the finds from mainland Sweden as well as the relatively low number of finds from Denmark were treated secondarily as coins redistributed from the Baltic islands.[22] Fagerlie's work with its good type catalogue and quite comprehensive find lists has proved fundamental for all subsequent work of Late Roman solidi in Scandinavia. Only in 1994, some of her mint attributions, in particular regarding the non-Imperial issues, were changed by J.P.C. Kent.[23]

A number of Swedish scholars have also made thorough investigations on Roman coin finds from Scandinavia. Majvor Östergren made a contextual analysis of the coin finds (denarii and solidi) from Gotland, concluding that the overwhelming majority of the coins (hoards as well as single finds) must have been deposited in settlements and more precisely inside the houses.[24] Working more specifically with the solidi, Fagerlie's monograph was followed up by Ola Kyhlberg[25] and Frans Herschend.[26] Kyhlberg and Herschend alike are deeply influenced by "new archaeology" in their extensive use of statistics and quantitative analyses, and they are focusing on metrology.[27] Kyhlberg used the Helgö finds as a basis for an analysis of the solidi in Scandinavia. He suggested that the solidus hoards had been formed on the Continent, and they were brought from the coasts of Poland and Eastern Germany to Mainland Sweden (in practise, Helgö in the Mälar area, the main subject of his study), to Öland and to Bornholm. Gotland was, contrary to the view of Fagerlie, a secondary receptor, and Western Denmark was regarded a peripheral area only rarely receiving solidi. He suggested that many of the coins originated from payments made by Leo I to the Ostrogoths in 461 AD, while the secondary/late inflow to Gotland was due to trade and piracy. A large part of the gold found on Öland and Gotland is in the form of solidi, while the Mälar area has yielded large and heavy gold hoards but relatively few solidi. Kyhlberg argued that the gold from the Mälar area in great extent derived from melted down solidi.

Fagerlie's and her followers' work and conclusions have been summarized and criticized by Metcalf,[28] who argued for a less rigid interpretation of the evidence, and questioned some of Fagerlie's major conclusions.

In 1981 and 1988 Lennart Lind published a catalogue and an analysis, respectively, of finds of denarii in Sweden.[29] Lind recognized the difficulties encountered when attempting to apply a strictly numismatic approach to a material found that far from the area of monetary circulation, yet his study is basically a numismatic single type study that by and large disregard both finds of other denominations and other archaeological evidence as a whole.

Lind criticised Bolin, whom he accused of a circular argument: having departed from the idea that the Germanic peoples (contrary to the Slavic ones) were on a level of civilisation that allowed them a certain degree of monetarization, Bolin only made a thorough catalogue of the coin finds from the area which he believed was inhabited by German tribes, while areas east of modern Germany (except northern Poland) were almost neglected.

The majority of the finds, *c.* 6000 of the more than 7000 Roman denarii from Sweden, were found on Gotland. This of course means that Lind concentrated on the many finds from Gotland. It was, however, noted how the coins from Mainland Sweden and Öland were often less worn than the coins from Gotland. Lind also to some degree recognized the division of the hoards with denarii from the period 69-193 AD into hoards with "early" and "late" composition, and the seeming preponderance of hoards with "early" composition in the western part of Barbaricum, including Denmark and Mainland Sweden.

Lind explained the great similarities between the denarii from a number of hoards in Gotland and

---

22 Fagerlie 1967.
23 Kent 1994 = *RIC* X.
24 Östergren 1981.
25 Kyhlberg 1980; 1983;1986.
26 Herschend 1980; 1983; 1991.
27 The metrological approach still seems to enjoy some popularity in Sweden, see e.g. Fischer 2008.

28 Metcalf 1995.
29 Lind 1981 and 1988. Some critical comments are presented by a.o. Kromann 1989 and Talvio 1992.

Central/Eastern Europe by the coins having a common origin in the treasury of Rome. He argued that they had been withdrawn from circulation by the emperor in the period after *c.* AD 220, and kept in the treasury awaiting re-use. Instead they had been used in the mid/late 3rd century AD to pacify Gothic tribes who redistributed the coins by internal barter trade. This would explain the distribution of similarly composed hoards over a vast geographical area from the Danube to northern Black Sea coasts, and to the Baltic coasts. His argumentation rests heavily on the similarities between the hoards with so-called "late" composition on the one hand and – on the other hand – the composition of 45485 of the 81044 coins from the Reka Devnia hoard from Bulgaria (i.e. inside the Roman Empire), as well as on the presence of the relatively rare issues of the short-lived reign of Didius Julianus in AD 193. He argued that both an "eastern" route (east of the Carpathians) and a "western" route were used, the two routes converging somewhere in the Vistula basin.

According to Lind trade in the Baltic area in this period would have followed the coastline, not reaching the isolated island of Gotland. He maintained that Gotland (as well as Bornholm) in this period were peripheral pirates' nests, and he argued that the majority of the denarii from Gotland had been brought there as the result of a single raid on an unidentified site in the Vistula mouth, and suggested the same explanation for Bornholm.

Lind was less specific about the routes of the hoards with "early" composition, and in general of the denarii from Western Denmark and Mainland Sweden. He hesitantly mentioned the possibility that denarii may have come from Northern Germany through Denmark to Sweden, while it was not impossible that the coins from Öland derived from Gotland.

To these major studies of the Swedish material should be added a number of coin lists adding new material to the above mentioned,[30] and specific attention should be drawn to the recent investigations of the central place at Uppåkra near Lund in southern Sweden.[31]

Other studies have analysed the Roman coins finds from the areas immediately south of Denmark. The corpus project *Die Fundmünzen der Römischen Zeit* (*FMRZ*) was initiated in the Bundesrepublik Deutschland in 1960.[32] Since then the project has published volumes on all the now reunited German *Länder*, and the project has been extended to cover also a number of other European countries including both areas that were once a part of the Roman Empire as well as areas outside the Limes: The Netherlands, Luxembourg, Austria, Hungary, Slovenia, Croatia and Poland. Furthermore other local initiatives have been taken to publish lists of finds of Ancient/Roman coins, adding greatly to the volume of material now available. The *Fundmünzen* series has been published continuously to our days with only minor changes and additions to the original set-up. However, the sheer volume of the material today makes the use of printed coin lists very time-consuming, and, more importantly, the lists do not provide up-to-date information, in spite of the fact that some supplementary volumes have appeared. In order to facilitate access to information on new finds the Fundmünzen der Antike has set up a new project "*INTERFACE – INTERnetportal: Finds of Ancient Coins in Europe*" to form an internet based common platform with search tools making national find databases available.[33]

A problem regarding availability of information is the fear of plundering of archaeological sites by metal detectorists, which means that information on newly discovered sites is deliberately not published. These sites remain unknown not only to the public, but also to the scholarly world, or they can be discussed only in general terms.

The *FMRZ* project is integrated into the *Fundmünzen der Antike* (*FdA*) project that employs the basic collection of the material in the *FMRZ* to a series of syntheses in the form of collected works or monographs published in the *Studien zu Fundmünzen der*

---

30 Westermark 1980; Westermark & Wiséhn 1983; 1984 and 1989; Stjernquist 1983.
31 On the coin finds from Uppåkra, see Silvegren 1999 and 2002. The homepage of the Uppåkra project provides updated information and bibliographical references on the site: http://www.uppakra.se/
32 On the background for the project, see Hans Gebhart & Konrad Kraft: Einführung in das Gesamtwerk, in: *FMRZ Deutschland, Abt. I Bayern, 1. Oberbayern*, 1960, 7-26.
33 Further information http://www.fda.adwmainz.de

Antike (SFMA). This series includes two of the most important works for the present study.

Frank Berger's study of the coin finds from northwestern Germany was published as *SFMA* 9.[34] This work takes as its basis the coins published in the *FMRZ Deutschland* VI.3-6, VII and the western part of Sachsen-Anhalt.[35] The coins are basically treated as Roman objects, and the division into chapters is based on the date of issue of the individual coins: Celtic coins, Roman coins until 14 AD, the time from Tiberius until 235 AD, the 3rd century, the 4th century, and finally Late Antique coin finds. The basic question, however, is asked from a local perspective: What was the significance of the Roman coins in ancient Northwest Germany? The discussions are focused on three periods: the period of Roman presence in the area (until *c.* AD 16), the denarius finds of the late 2nd century, and the gold and copper coins of the 4th-5th centuries.[36]

Aleksander Bursche's study of *Later Roman – Barbarian contacts* in the *SFMA* 11 covers the area delimited by the River Oder, the Baltic Sea until the port Liepaya and south towards the Carpathian and Sudetes Mountains.[37] He defined the geographical limits of his research area by the archaeological cultures that occupied the areas, and the chronological limits were set by the coins struck between 193 and 395 AD. As indicated by the German subtitle *Ein Beitrag zur Geschichte der Beziehungen zwischen Rom und den Barbaren im 3. und 4. Jh. n.Chr.* Bursche used the coins as sources for a history of cross-cultural contacts in the 3rd and 4th centuries AD. Bursche has also published a large number of articles on denarius finds in Barbaricum[38] and on the significance of Roman coin finds in Barbaricum in general,[39] as well as important works of the Roman 4th century gold medallions,[40] and Nordic bracteates.[41]

The Roman coin finds from Poland are in the process of being published. A first volume on Mazovia and Podlachia appeared in 1979,[42] and a volume on Little Poland followed suit in 1985.[43] In 2001 Ciołek's catalogue of finds in Pomerania appeared (in Polish), and an updated version including 50 new finds appeared in 2007 (in German).[44] A volume covering the finds from Silesia appeared in late 2008.[45]

The volume of Roman coins in Barbaricum is vast: tens of thousands of coins spread over a vast area, inhabited by peoples that have left behind objects belonging to a multitude of archaeological cultures. Bolin's urge – as stated in 1926 – to study the material in its entity is simply not done by a single person. Therefore initiatives as the INTERFACE mentioned above are extremely important, and so is the international collaboration between scholars from all Barbaricum.

1.4 Coins and other Roman finds in Denmark

As has been described, the traditional approach to the study of Roman coin finds in Barbaricum has focussed on the striking periods of the coins, and it has often been based on a primary division of the material into single finds and hoards. It has been discussed when and how the coins travelled north, and Roman political history as well as the Roman policies towards the Barbarians, as reflected in the written sources, have been used to explain the many coin finds outside the Empire. The chronological distribution within a hoard has been analysed and differences in the distribution between various hoards

---

34 Berger 1992. See also review article: Bursche 1994.
35 The latter based on the coin lists in Laser 1980, now republished as FMRD XIII (by Laser and Stribrny).
36 Berger 1992, 19-21. While the first of these three periods has little relevance for the present study, Berger's results on the two latter periods will be discussed below.
37 Bursche 1996.
38 E.g. Bursche 1993.
39 E.g. Bursche 2002.
40 Bursche 1998 (not available to the present author), summarized in Bursche 2001. See also Bursche 1999 and 2003b.
41 Bursche 2007.
42 Kubiak 1979.
43 Kunisz 1985.
44 Ciołek 2001 and 2007.
45 Ciołek 2008. Unfortunately the volume appeared too late to be fully considered in the present work.

have been interpreted as indications that these hoards arrived in Barbaricum at various points of time as a result of different known political events. The coins have normally been treated by numismatists, often with a background in studies of Classics. Indeed, the Roman coins from Barbaricum are in many studies related to a Roman context rather than the local one.

It is significant that the coins have often been considered apart from other types of objects, and although they represent the numerically largest group of imported objects in the Danish Iron Age contexts, they have rarely been analysed in this context. Symptomatically, Ulla Lund Hansen in her monumental work on Roman imports in the Nordic countries refrained from a discussion of the Roman coin finds. The coins from burials were mentioned, but coins were not discussed as an individual artefact group in line with other Roman finds.[46]

A few attempts to discuss the Roman coins in their Danish find contexts have, however, been made by Svend Nielsen and Eliza Fonnesbech-Sandberg. In a number of articles from the late 1980's, Nielsen attempted to bridge the traditional gap between numismatists and archaeologists.[47] In the papers he argued for a contextual approach to the coin finds, and for an awareness of the many different uses of coins as artefacts in a non-monetary Iron Age society. Yet, he was convinced that the finds from Lundeborg and Dankirke were the result of the use of coins as money under special conditions.

Fonnesbech-Sandberg first approached the coins from a metrological point of view. Although she criticized previous metrological studies and demonstrated that it is very hard to identify any single weight module within the Danish gold hoards from the Early Germanic Iron Age, she still did not doubt that some weight system existed and suggested that it was based on the weight of the Roman solidus.[48] She developed her ideas on the function of Roman coins in Denmark in an in-depth survey of the coin finds, including many important observations.[49] She employed Kromann's division of denarius finds into "early" and "late" compositions, an idea originating in the work of Bolin, to argue that the majority of coins imported during the Roman Iron Age (including most denarius finds) were also deposited during that phase. She furthermore believed that most finds – also single finds – were the result of deliberate depositions, and that the multiple finds from Dankirke and Lundeborg were ploughed-up hoards. She argued that the coins were not used as money, but they were a by-product in the Roman-Germanic or Germanic-Germanic trade, and she believed that the Roman coins in some cases were used as "special purpose money".

The works of Nielsen and Fonnesbech-Sandberg have been important sources of inspiration for the present study, but since the publication of these articles the number of coins found in Denmark has more than doubled, and the interpretations offered now are in many aspects different from the ones presented by Nielsen or Fonnesbech-Sandberg.

1.5 Approaching the finds

The present study relies heavily on the empirical basis, namely the coins. It is inspired by the post-modern focus on the individual. The individual coin should in the first interpretative level be seen in its proper context. Secondly it should be discussed in relation to other coins in similar contexts and to similar coins in other contexts.

I believe that the finds might be reflections of a number of different phenomena that must be analysed individually before a coherent history of this part of Danish Iron Age culture can be constructed, instead of starting from the assumption that Roman coin finds in a given part of Barbaricum is evidence for *one* act.

Roman coins obviously have a special potential. Contrary to most other archaeological artefacts of the period their place and date of manufacture can often be pinpointed with great precision. This is of course of great advantage, but this easy access to production details also seems to have created a barrier in the studies that many scholars have been unable to cross. Instead of focussing on the production date and the mint, the present work takes as its starting point the find context of the coins and attempts an analysis of the meaning and function of the imported Roman coins in their new context. Consequently more

---

46 Lund Hansen 1987, in particular 229.
47 Nielsen 1986; 1987-88 (published in 1992); 1989.
48 Fonnesbech-Sandberg 1987.
49 Fonnesbech-Sandberg 1989 and 1990b.

weight has been put on an analysis of the deposition circumstances than on the production circumstances. The place and time of the production of the coins are considered a starting point for a story, where the most important parts are the period in which the coins were in use, and the function of the coins in the non-monetary context of Danish Iron Age cultures.

An archaeological material can be classified in many different ways – and so can a numismatic material. In a study of coins as archaeological finds it is desirable to find a way of classifying the coins in a way that takes both the numismatic and the archaeological properties into account. This is not easy.[50]

The situation has become even more complicated within the last decades, as detector archaeology has given a number of finds where the traditional distinction between hoard and single find has been blurred, and requires an extra interpretative level. The ideal situation, where one or more coins are found in an untouched primary context during a controlled archaeological investigation, is rarely seen in real life.

The Roman coin finds from Denmark are presented in three chapters that form the main part of the present work: in Chapter 4 an overview of the geographical distribution of the coin finds in the three major regions Sealand, Funen and Jutland is presented. In Chapter 5 the question of context types is approached and in Chapter 6 the coins are discussed on nominal level.

---

50 Cf. Lind 1988, 17.

CHAPTER 2

The area

2.1 Introduction

Modern Denmark forms a very convenient area for study and analysis because coin finds have been identified and provenanced in the same way over the whole area. But it is important not to narrow down the geographical area, but also include a discussion of coin finds from neighbouring areas.

Archaeological material, indeed archaeological "cultures" in general, do not comply with modern political borders. Therefore it is not possible to consider all modern Denmark as one entity existing already in the Iron Age, nor is it possible to make a research into Roman coin finds from Barbaricum looking at only one tiny area.

It has been decided to exclude the island of Bornholm from the present study. Bornholm takes a special place, both as regards to the huge number of Roman coins found on this relatively small island, and as regards to the material culture of Bornholm itself. Culturally, Iron Age Bornholm clearly belongs in a Baltic context, and must – as the Swedish islands of Öland and Gotland – be seen in relation to this area, whereas the remaining parts of modern Denmark is more closely related to the areas immediately to the south, east, north and – perhaps – to the west of Denmark.[1]

Southern Sweden (Scania, Halland and Blekinge) is another area that needs special consideration. The area was part of the Danish realm until 1658, when it was lost to Sweden, and it is in many respects: archaeologically, culturally, topographically and geographically, linked as closely to Denmark as to the remaining parts of modern Sweden. The cultural connections across Øresund in the Iron Age has recently been investigated within the project "Öresund – barriär eller bro?".[2] The studies undertaken within the project have shown that in particular the agrarian landscapes of south-western Scania must have had close connections with eastern Sealand. This of course calls for an assessment of the Roman coin finds from southern Sweden in line with the Danish find. Yet, because of the very different legislations of the two countries, it is not possible to make direct comparisons between them. Metal detecting is strictly forbidden in Sweden, which means that except for a few sites, in particular the important centre at Uppåkra where metal detectors have been used intensively in connection with the modern archaeo-

---

1 On coin finds from Bornholm see preliminary overviews in Horsnæs 2009 and (*Forthcoming*) "Roman coins from Bornholm – a preliminary overview", in Anna Bitner Wroblewska & Ulla Lund Hansen (eds.): *Papers from the "Network Denmark-Poland. Archaeology and cultural heritage. Contacts across the Baltic in the Iron Age (500 BC–1000 AD)"*.

2 Carlie 2008.

logical investigations and excavations, some types of find will be underrepresented in the archaeological material from southern Sweden in comparison with the Danish material. It has therefore been decided to discuss the finds from southern Sweden on the same level as other finds from neighbouring states.

Place names and areas are described by their modern names, as are archaeological cultures. References to areas by the name of an ancient tribe, that according to one or more written sources inhabited the area, are avoided, as none of these areas can be defined with any degree of certainty.

One will find the use of the term "Southern Scandinavia" in many archaeological texts. This use of "Southern Scandinavia" normally covers modern Denmark and southern Sweden. Often Bornholm is included into the term Southern Scandinavia, but in the present work this is not the case.

2.2 Denmark between the Early Roman and the Early Germanic Iron Ages

The majority of the Roman coins have been found in contexts that can be dated within the archaeological phases B-D in Denmark, in the periods most commonly referred to as the Early Roman, Late Roman and the Early Germanic Iron Ages. In absolute dates these phases covers the years from the beginning of our era to *c.* AD 550. During the last decades these periods have been studied by two groups of Danish archaeologists that to some degree can be seen as representatives of the two Universities with schools of Danish archaeology. The pivotal figure of the Copenhagen school is Ulla Lund Hansen, whose work is based on thorough empirical analyses of artefact types and their chronological and geographical distributions. Her main publications are concentrating on the Roman imports in Scandinavia[3] and on the Iron Age of Sealand,[4] and they have both generated a lot of related studies by younger scholars. The work is always integrated into a larger, European, setting, and takes in close collaboration with colleagues in Sweden, Poland and Germany.

The Århus school with which the present professor of archaeology in Olso University, Lotte Hedeager, should be counted, is far more inspired by Anglo-Saxon paradigms inspired by social anthropology and figures such as Hodder, Shanks and Tilley. Important initiatives from the Århus school are Lotte Hedeager's dissertation[5] and for example seminars on "The organisation of societies and regional variation".[6] It should, however, be underlined that there is no sharp division line between these two groups of scholars. There are some fluctuations between the groups, and representatives of both groups have often contributed to the same collective works.

The recent research combines to suggest an interpretation of the Danish Iron Age as a period of marked changes from small and relatively closed, local entities governed by petty chieftains towards a growing social differentiation, with larger regional groupings and the coming of small states that eventually entered the European scene as tribes governed by "kings". It is commonly maintained that the process was speeded up – if not triggered – by the Roman expansion far into Germanic areas during the reign of Augustus, and by the subsequent growing contact between Barbaricum and the more complex societies of the Mediterranean region. One should, however, not forget that from the very beginning of the Iron Age (and even before) we have examples of exclusive single imports,[7] and this trend continues. Some chieftains, as for example the man buried in the "princely" grave at Hoby, on the island Lolland south of Sealand, had access to some of the finest tableware of his days: two Roman relief bowls of Campanian manufacture, comparable to the finds of the Boscoreale Hoard. The events of the Varus defeat in AD 9 may give a possible historical explanation of this kind of find. The Germanic chief Ariminus (Hermann) was not only a nobleman of Germanic descent, but he had also crossed over culturally and served, with the rank of a Roman knight, in the Roman army. We must therefore imagine a society where the greater part of the population lived within a very restricted local community, but where a small number of individuals had long distance

---

3 Lund Hansen 1987.
4 Lund Hansen 1995.

5 Hedeager 1990.
6 Fabech & Ringtved 1991 (my translation of title).
7 See for example Riis 1959.

connections, with a possibility of cross-cultural elite intermarriage.

Within the centuries following the beginning of our era the elite burials present a growing number of Roman luxury imports. In the Early Roman Iron Age many of the imports are of unique or very rare types, while the Late Roman Iron Age is characterized by a larger number of mass-produced types and/or objects imported for secondary use as raw materials. The imported Roman objects are direct and easily visible evidence for Roman influence. But other types of evidence should also be noted. Changes in the settlement pattern may reflect new ways of working the fields and/or new crops. New types of plants and animals provide new possibilities and create new demands. Finally the exchange of knowledge and ideology should be mentioned, although these types of inspiration may be very hard to detect archaeologically.

The Roman import has played an enormous role in the study of the Danish Iron Age, but it is certainly not the only foreign influence detectable in the Danish material. Throughout the Roman Iron Age there is also evidence for relations with other parts of Barbaricum. There are interesting parallels to the Danish material in the burials of Thüringen, there are examples of jewellery with close parallels in the Cernachov culture of south-eastern Europe, and among the glass objects found in Denmark should be counted both Roman and Pontic imports. The study of the south-eastern connections certainly suffered through the years of the Cold War, but it is now becoming more and more prominent. From the later part of the Late Roman and from the Early Germanic Iron Ages also the connections with the up-coming Frank and the Gothic kingdoms should be mentioned.

The major areas under consideration in this volume are Sealand with adjacent islands, Funen with adjacent islands, and Jutland. It must be stressed that although these areas go through the same general cultural development, they are not identical. The strict geographical division of the material into these three blocks has a tendency to hide the fact that the limits of the archaeological cultures do not follow the same lines as the modern administrative divisions of the country. In fact, the Belts and Øresund that today delimit the administrative units may in the Iron Age have been communication routes rather than barriers. But for practical reasons the modern units will be maintained in the presentation of the material.

2.3 Danish Iron Age chronology

The Roman coins are most often found in contexts that belong to the chronological phases Early Roman Iron Age, Late Roman Iron Age and Early Germanic Iron Age. The first two phases are normally described as period B (Early Roman Iron Age) and period C (Late Roman Iron Age), both with subdivisions. The Early Germanic Iron Age is also known as Migration Period, or period D.

The chronological system commonly employed today for Iron Age Barbaricum is based on the work of Eggers (1955). His work has been used by, discussed and refined by numerous scholars working with northern Europe, most important are the works by Godłowski (1970) for Continental Europe and Lund Hansen (1976 and 1987) for Southern Scandinavia. Ulla Lund Hansen also provided a full discussion of previous works on the chronological studies of Southern Scandinavia and presented a diagram that illustrates the various opinions.[8] Her own chronology was based on a two-step evaluation of the Danish Iron Age burials with Roman imports. First a relative chronology was built up based on fibula and pottery of local manufacture; secondly a seriation of the same burials with Roman import was undertaken. She followed previous scholars in dividing the material into an Early Roman Iron Age (period B) and a Late Roman Iron Age (period C), and subdivided the phases according to the appearance of new phase defining "Leittypen". She defined the early part of period B as a transitional period, where a number of characteristics from the previous Pre-Roman Iron Age (period A) lived on alongside the appearance of new phase defining types (Eggers types 24 and 131 and Almgren types II 24 and III 45). The transition from period B to period C was defined by the disappearance of fibulae of Almgren type V and the appearance of Almgren type VII. Transitions from one to another archaeologically defined phase are rarely clear-cut, and Lund Hansen thus operated with a transitional phase B2/C1a, and she also had to acknowledge that

---

[8] Lund Hansen 1987, 30 fig. 10.

she had little material from the latest part of period C (period C3). The absolute chronology applied to the phases was based on the Roman imports and on the Continental material related to events known from the Roman history.

Chronology is the backbone of all archaeological research, and as such the chronological systems that we employ to handle the finds will always be subject to discussions and critical reviews. In spite of the wide acceptance of the chronological framework suggested by Ulla Lund Hansen, her work is no exception to this rule. It has been pointed out that it is mainly based on burials from Sealand, and that this material is not wholly compatible with the finds from Jutland. Therefore Ethelberg suggested some minor adjustments of the absolute dates.[9] Large numbers of burials are known from Funen, but they are in the main cremation burials and less richly equipped than the contemporary burials from Sealand. Few of them therefore qualified to be used in Lund Hansen's seriation. In the case of Funen, Albrectsen had already built up a local chronology based on the local pottery types found in the burials. His phases are termed phase I-III, and they are in the main comparable to the Lund Hansen phases.

Furthermore, as pointed out by Lund Hansen herself, there is a lack of burials from period C3 in her matrix of the Late Roman Iron Age, where burials from C1b dominate. This problem is caused by her methodology. Her matrix is built up on burials with Roman imports, but the use of Roman imports in burials falls dramatically in period C3.

There are a number of problems in the correlation of the Southern Scandinavian and Continental relative chronology in the sense that high status objects that appear in burials assigned to phase C1b in Sealand are found on the Continent in burials dated in phase C2, in particular in the burials from the Hassleben-Leuna complex.[10] Ethelberg attempted to solve the problem by allowing for a 10-year overlap between Sealand period C1b and Continental C2, but he still saw Sealand as a very important centre playing a leading role in the development. One of the

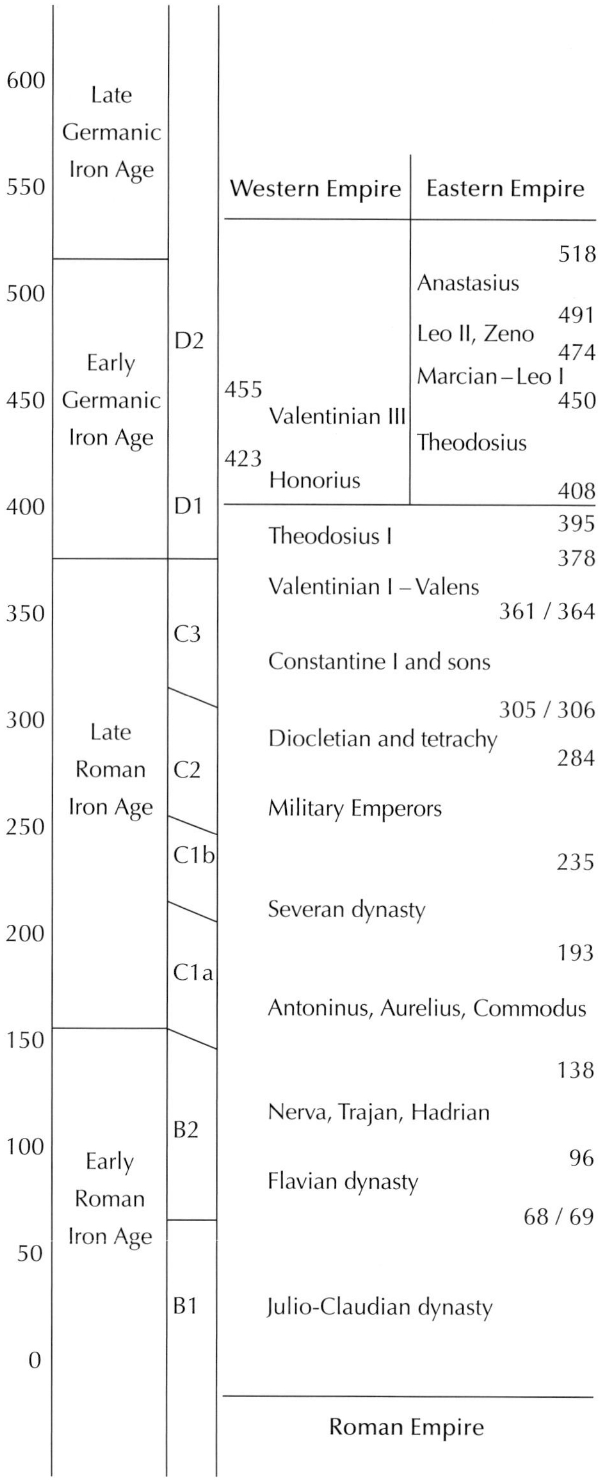

Fig. 4. Chronological table: Danish Iron Age (after Jørgensen et al. 2003), Roman emperors and dynasties (simplified). Drawing Dennis Støvring.

---

9 Ethelberg 2000, 39-43.
10 Lund Hansen 1987, 205; Ethelberg 2000; Grane 2007, 118-125.

main problems is whether we should accept Ethelberg's theory that a number of highly prestigious – and technically complicated – objects were developed and mainly produced in Sealand. If not it seems inevitable that period C1b in Denmark (Sealand?) should be somewhat longer in absolute years, and that the Danish periods C2 and C3 consequently must be a bit shorter than normally suggested.

Not only do the number of imports in burials fall during the later part of period C, but also the number of burials decline. Burials dated in period D are rare, and they are normally extremely poor. Therefore the chronology of period D has to be built up on other criteria, namely the typological development of objects and the stylistic development of ornaments.[11] This leads to more loosely defined periods and the lack of subdivisions of the Early and Late Germanic Iron Ages. It seems that it is today generally accepted to date the transition from period C to period D *c.* AD 375,[12] and the transition from Early to Late Germanic Iron Age is normally placed in the first half or at the middle of the 6th century AD.

2.4 Roman coins and Scandinavian chronology

The production date of a Roman coin can in many cases be given within a year. This is often the case for the denarii from the late 1st until the early 3rd centuries that are the most abundant Roman type found in Barbaricum. Coin finds are of major importance for the absolute dates of the archaeological phases throughout Iron Age Barbaricum. It must, however, be kept in mind that the coin can only provide a *post quem* date for the assemblage in which it is found. There are many examples that a coin is considerably older than the remaining finds from an assemblage.

In the present work the context of the coin finds are as important as the coin finds themselves. I have in particular searched for independently dated contexts in order to discuss not only the coins, but also the period that they were in use in Southern Scandinavia and the roles that they played in this foreign geographic as well as cultural context. In this connection is it very important to avoid the circular arguments on the chronology.

Scrutinizing chronology may sometimes seem a never-ending academic waste of time. Yet precision in chronological matters is of outmost importance for any type of historical research that will venture into not only the "when", but also the much more interesting "how" and "why". The absolute dates of the Danish Iron Age phases are of major importance for the correlations of the Danish material with the material from Continental Barbaricum and ultimately with Rome. Throughout the present work I have repeated the dates proposed by the archaeologists working with the finds in question unless otherwise indicated. A coin is regarded to be in use (or in circulation, but not in the monetary sense of the word) from the earliest possible production date until it was deposited. In many cases the deposition date cannot be established with greater precision than "after the production date".

It must be kept in mind that it is always dangerous to use relative and absolute chronologies side by side. We are sometimes dealing with context dates that are placed within different sub-phases by different specialists. It should also be kept in mind that several of the sub-phases are very short – in reality equivalent to one generation only – and that they are wholly based on stylistic developments of artefact types. Furthermore, the absolute chronology of Danish Iron Age is based on imported objects – that are often themselves dated by stylistic analysis in the production area – in combination with assumptions on longevity of types and number of finds from each phase.[13] Any change in the assignment of a particular find from one phase to another, or more dramatically a change of the absolute date of a phase, will have great consequences for the interpretation of the find in relation to other finds and/or historical events.

---

11 Axboe 2004, 223-245.
12 Axboe 2004, 218-222 points out that the Nordic imitations of Roman medallions, based on Roman prototypes struck during the reigns of Constantine through Valens are found in independently dated contexts from period C3. Therefore the transition from C3 to D can hardly be placed much earlier than 375 AD.

13 As summarized in Ethelberg 2000, 42.

CHAPTER 3

The material

3.1 Introduction

The empirical basis for the present work is a database covering ideally all finds of Roman coins from present-day Denmark. This database is based on previous collections of the Danish material presented by Montelius, Bolin, Galster, Hauberg, Breitenstein, Balling and most recently Kromann, covering the period of finds up to *c*. 1980. To the coin finds published by these authors are added the finds from the last 25 years. Amateur archaeologists surveying with metal detectors found the majority of these coins, and the finds have been handed in to the National Museum of Denmark according to the *danefæ* legislation. My knowledge of finds from recent archaeological excavations is often due to the generosity of the individual excavators, to whom my sincerest thanks.

Furthermore I have inserted a very small number of old coin finds that for one reason or another had been overlooked. In most cases I was made aware of these finds in conversations with colleagues from local museums around Denmark. I am greatly indebted to all who helped me fill in the lacunae in the database.[1]

The book does not contain a catalogue of coins. Instead there are references to the individual coin by its site number and inventory number. The site number refers to the site registration made by The National Cultural Heritage Agency and available in *Fund og Fortidsminder* on www.dkconline.dk. Here all sites are numbered with a 6-digit code by their position according to the old administrative division of Denmark[2] in "amt", "herred" and "sogn" (county, district (or shire) and parish), and with a serial number (sb no.) of each site within the parish (*Fig. 5*). In some cases – mostly old finds – the site has not yet been registered in the *Fund og Fortidsminder*. They have been listed with the 6-digit parish code without sb no. Most of the coins belong to The Royal Collection of Coins and Medals in the Danish National Museum and carry the inventory number of the Find Protocol (FP) of this collection. Other coins have entered the Department of Prehistoric Archaeology of the Danish National Museum (inventory numbers preceded by "NM I"). A minor number of coins are in the holdings of local museums, the name of which precedes the inventory number. Furthermore there

---

1 The database was originally intended as a draft for a numismatic corpus in line with the German "Fundmünzen der Antike"-project. With the present increase in finds due to detector archaeology a printed catalogue of finds makes little sense. It is hoped that it will be possible to make the database available for further studies in an Internet based version.

2 Later administrative reforms are not reflected in the archaeological use of this division.

Crossing boundaries

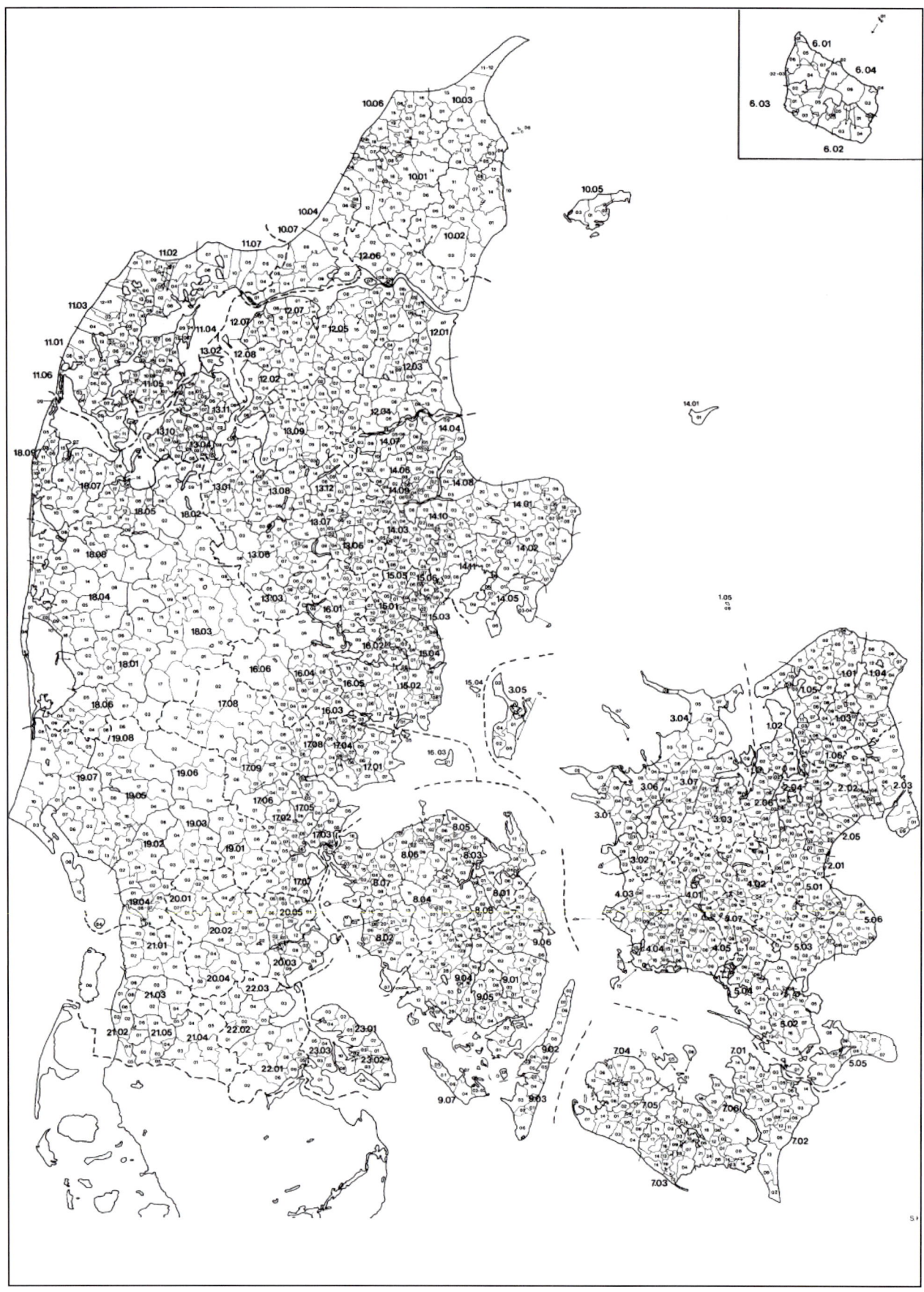

Fig. 5. The administrative division of Denmark employed in archaeological registration (after Lund Hansen 1995, 19).

are references to entries in Breitenstein, Balling or Kromann, and to recent and/or important discussions of the site in the archaeological literature.

The coins are classified according to *Roman Imperial Coinage* (*RIC*) vols. I-X. For the coins issued between 31 BC and AD 69 *RIC* vol. I, 2nd edition 1984 is used unless otherwise indicated, while the 2nd edition (2007) of vol. II, part 1 appeared too late to be taken into consideration. Type numbers are, however, only indicated when relevant for the discussion.

3.2 Is the material representative?

The traditional and uniform Danish legislation has ensured that coin finds from the whole country have been treated in the same manner. It is therefore easy to compare coin finds from various parts of the country.

Coin finds were first regarded as a means to improve the country's finances, and only later the coins were seen as objects of interest. This interest shifted from a purely collector's point of view to a more cultural historical and archaeological approach during the 19th century.

Since the 1830s the Find Protocol (FP) in The Royal Collection of Coins and Medals has been filled in according to guidelines that are comparable, and it has been possible to make an assessment of the number of finds decade by decade. The diagram (*Fig. 6*) illustrates the number of finds registered in the Find Protocols in the period 1840-2009. By find is here indicated a separate entry – i.e. any number of coins, from one to several thousands of coins, handed in to the authorities at one single occasion. To clarify the development, finds of coins from all periods of history have been included in this diagram. It has been noted that the increased cultivation of marginal soils around the middle of the 19th century, followed by the use of improved ploughs, brought to light in particular many gold hoards in the second half of the

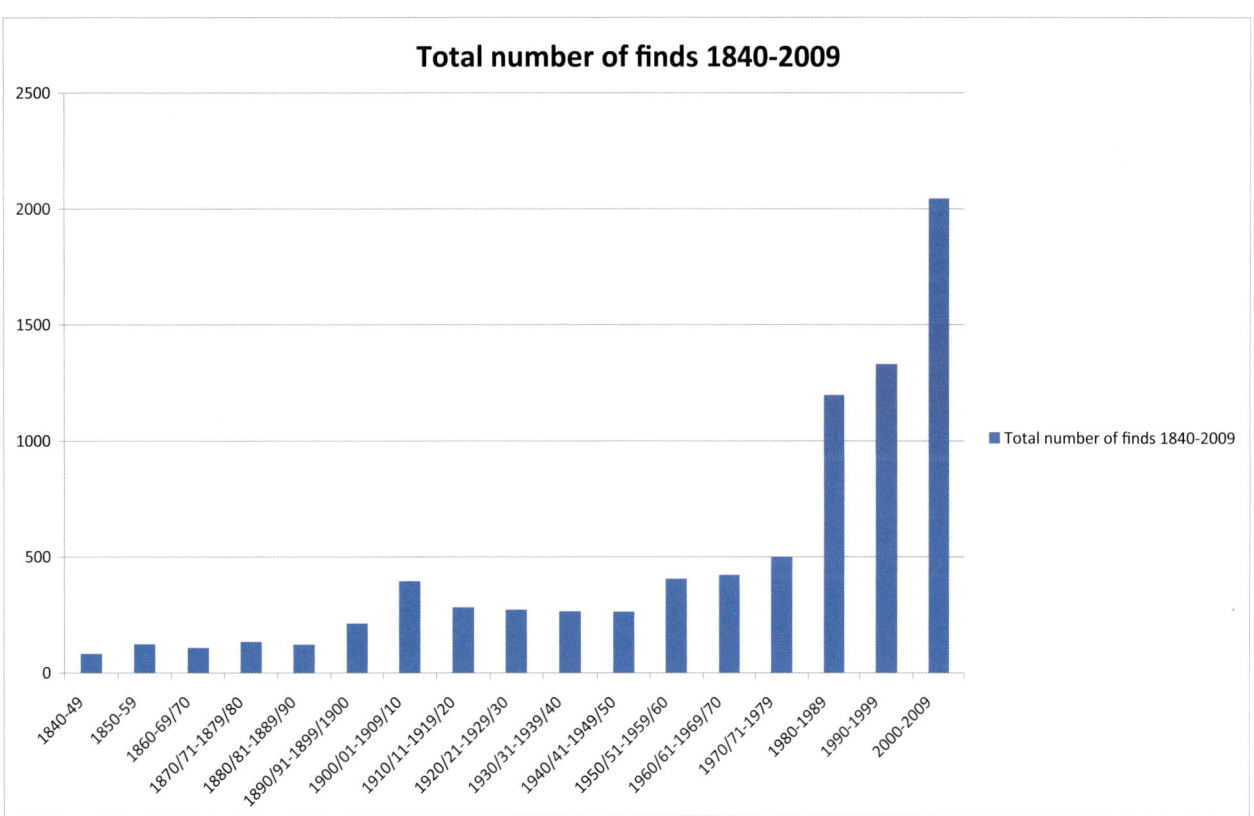

Fig. 6. The total number of finds registered by The Royal Coll. of Coins and Medals 1840-2009. A find may contain a single coin, a series of coins found in the same survey/excavation, or a coin hoard.

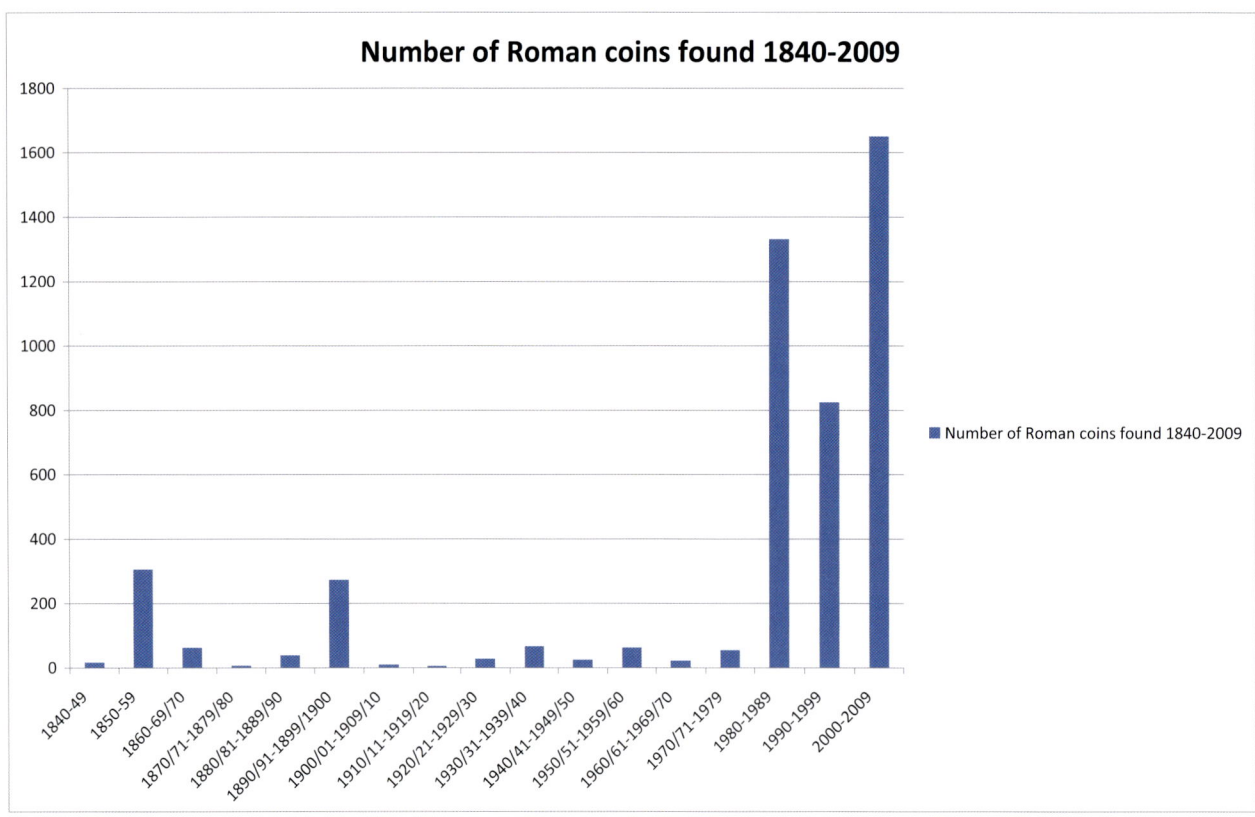

Fig. 7. Total number of Roman coins found in Denmark per decade 1840-2009.

19th century.[3] This tendency is hard to detect in the diagram, as it illustrates only the registration after 1840, but an evaluation of the Find Protocols from the first half of the century actually indicates that the number of finds rises around the mid-19th century.

During most of the 19th century a little more than a hundred finds were registered during each decade, a number that was more than doubled at the turn of the century. After the 2nd World War an administrative circular claimed that all soil from excavations in and around old churches should be sieved for small finds. This decision yielded a rise in the number of finds, as did the growing number of professional excavations in general.

3.3 Coins and the metal detector

A dramatic rise in the number of finds can clearly be seen in the years from *c.* 1980 onwards. This is due to detector archaeology. In Denmark the use of metal detector by amateurs is legal on all private areas, provided of course that the owner of the area permits it. Areas with monuments already defined as "*fredede fortidsminder*" (i.e. cultural heritage) are protected by law. After an initial phase of discussions and anxiety among professional archaeologists, the use of metal detector is today appreciated as a powerful and useful tool to recover material from the plough soil. The metal detector is regularly used also during archaeological excavations to reveal possible finds of fragile metal objects, before the archaeologist starts digging the area, and thereby it is possible to employ an excavation strategy taking possible finds of fragile material into consideration.

The combination of the conservative *danefæ* legislation, a historical awareness among most amateur detectorists, and a good and close collaboration on local level between museum and amateur archaeologists has ensured a unique research material. During the 140 years from 1840 to 1979 a total of 991 Roman coins were found in Denmark, while in the 25-year period from 1980 to 2004 alone 3498 Roman coins have been registered.

---

3 Henriksen & Horsnæs 2004.

The material

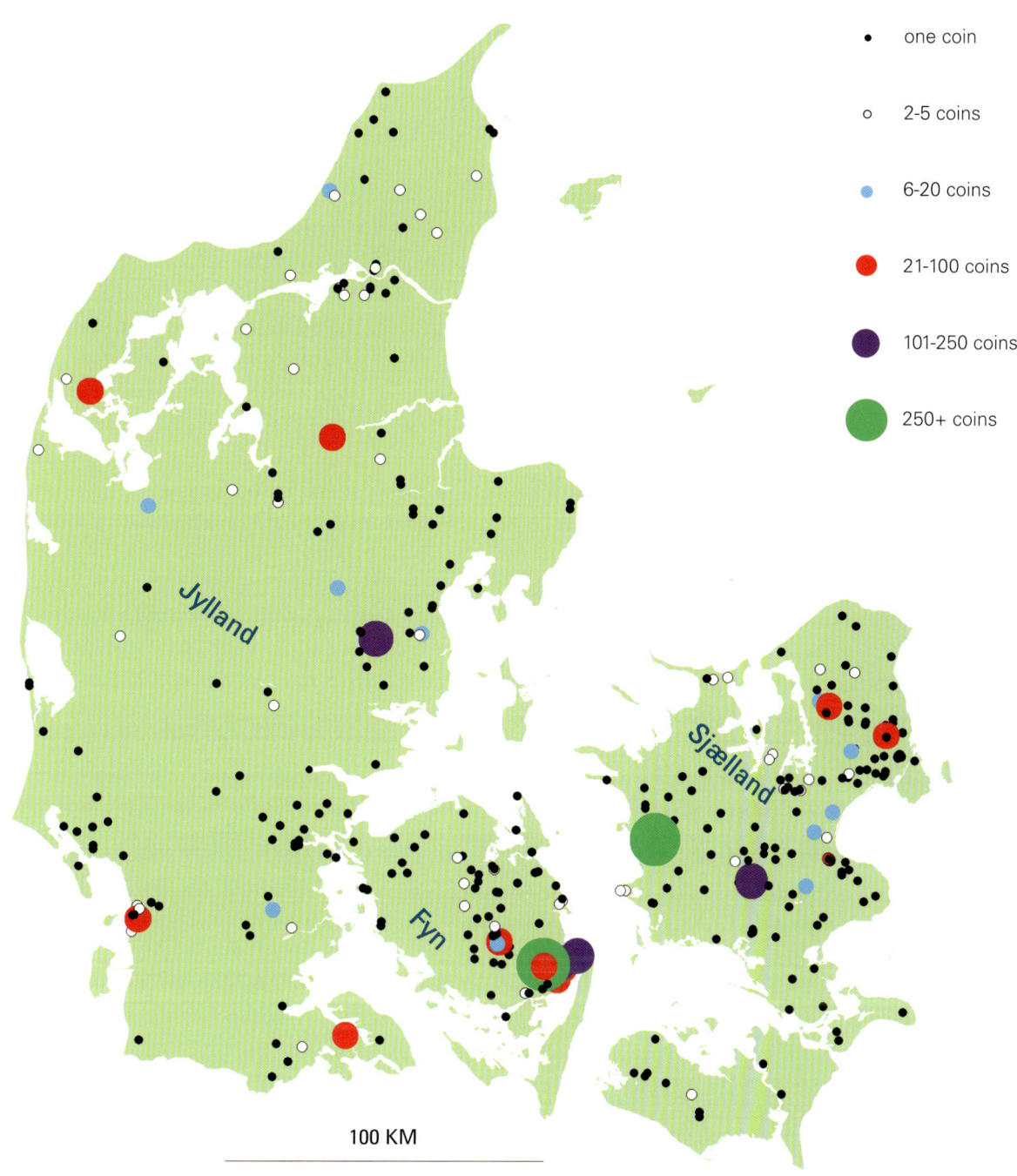

Fig. 8. Distribution of Ancient coins in Denmark. All types and nominations. Map Josefine Franck Bican.

This means that since c. 1980 between 125 and 150 Roman coins have been found each year. Considering the relatively small size of Denmark this growth in material is enormous.[4] Poland is a country that is many times bigger than Denmark and extremely large denarius hoards have been found.[5] But until recently only a couple of new finds were registered each year.[6] Right now, this picture seems to be changing, as professional archaeologists have started employing

---

4   A similar growth in material is seen also in the Netherlands, see Bazelmans 2003.

5   Bursche 2002.
6   I thank Dr. Renata Ciołek, Warsaw University, for this information.

the metal detector, and this means that denarii are being discovered on settlement sites regularly.[7] The considerable change in volume of material in Denmark since regular use of metal detectors was initiated as well as the discovery of wholly new context types makes it impossible to make direct comparison between finds from Denmark and finds from other countries with different treasure trove legislation and different view upon the use of metal detectors.

The Roman coins found in Denmark now amount to almost 5000 coins. Of them *c.* 2380 were found on the island of Bornholm, and therefore will be only touched on in this study. The remaining *c.* 2700 coins are not evenly distributed, neither geographically nor chronologically.

A simple map showing the overall distribution of coins immediately reveals striking differences in the density of finds. The areas with the highest density of finds all contain finds of one or more hoards or coins from a weapon sacrifice (Illerup, Nydam). The central place in Gudme and the secondary sites pertaining to this site, in particular the port-of-trade at Lundeborg in south-eastern Funen, take a special place with a total of more than 1200 coins, almost half the number of coins from the study area (section 5.3.1).

3.4 Survey finds and excavation finds

Various parameters must be taken into consideration when evaluating the effects of post-depositional processes on archaeological objects, in particular objects in plough soil and objects in layers suffering from heavy corrosion.[8]

There is no guarantee that the finds from the plough soil are of the same types as the finds from the underlying cultural layers – on the contrary. The finds from the plough soil belong to the cultural layers that are no longer to be found, and they can thereby provide us with information on an occupational period that is later than the one identified by an excavation on the same site. In cases of ploughed-up hoards this may be even more pronounced. A hoard would often have been concealed beneath for example a floor level, i.e. it was dug down below an occupation layer. This layer would have been hit by the plough and destroyed before the hoard was destroyed. Therefore we may often see that in cases of a ploughed up hoard positioned in connection with a building, this building would only be identified by the fill representing the lowest part of the posts.

While we may often assume that the finds from the plough layer is situated close to the original deposition, this may not always be the case. Small objects such as coins may be moved a considerable distance from their original deposition spot by ploughing. The evidence from the Smørenge Hoard from Bornholm is clear. The bottom of the original deposition was identified during excavation, and the majority of the coins ascribed to the hoard were found clustered around the original deposition, but a few coins were carried up to 50 m away.

3.5 Differences in find density

Even though we can boast a uniform legislation throughout Denmark, and we have been lucky to avoid great natural disasters or destructions in war, there are great differences in the find density throughout the country. Can this be interpreted as a reflection of a pre-historical situation?

We have to take into consideration also the differences in activity among the amateur detectorists. Some areas have many detectorists that are well organised in amateur archaeologists associations. They may have very close relations to the local museums, to whom they report observations, and the amateurs volunteer to take part in professional investigations. In other areas there are no detectorists, or the local museum has not had the possibility to invest time and money in creating the ideal collaboration with detectorists.

A distribution map based on addresses of amateur archaeologists[9] not surprisingly showed some correspondence to the distribution of recent metal finds:[10]

---

7 Personal information from Dr. Mateucz Bogucki summer 2008.
8 Paulsson 1999.

9 Grønnegård 1997, fig. 5.
10 Henriksen 2006, fig. 2 based on data from *Fund og Fortidsminder* March 2003 – note that this map is based on data collected six years after the distribution

a number of addresses around and west of Copenhagen is reflected in a considerable number of sites found by detector in this area, and a dense cluster of detectorists with addresses in Aalborg is responsible for the large number of sites around Aalborg. A comparison between the map showing the distribution of sites with treasure trove found with detector (until 2003) and the distribution map of Roman coin finds (2008) reveals that although there are some differences that may reveal differences in the density of the distribution of Roman coins in Denmark in general, the similarities between the maps are striking: Areas of Jutland with few finds of Roman coins are in fact some of the areas with few detector finds in general, and the same applies to smaller areas in Funen and Sealand.[11]

An often mentioned but nonetheless extremely important factor when dealing with material retrieved by amateur archaeologists is the strengthening effect of detector finds: If something has been found, more will be found on the same spot! It has been shown that systematic surveys tend to give a larger distribution of artefacts than the unsystematic one, and it is therefore important to check what seem to be clusters of finds registered after unsystematic surveys.[12]

But to be fair, amateurs are not the only bees swarming around the honey pot. Rich (or published!) archaeological sites tend to become richer and take a sometimes unwarranted place in the archaeological literature, while unknown sites of equal importance may only be discovered by pure chance.

In the beginning the provenance of a detector find was given as within a specific field, but from early in the 1980's some local museums actively trained amateur detectorists to measure their finds within the field by using a simple metric coordinate system, based on fixed points along the borders of the field. This foresight greatly enhanced the scientific potential of the finds, and made it easier to identify ploughed up hoards. With the introduction of cheap and easily operational GPS systems an increasing number of detectorists are now giving the position of each individual find with GPS coordinates, gradually increasing the precision of the information available.

3.6 Hoards and single finds

A hoard is defined as a group of objects deposited as one single act. A hoard can consist of any type of material or objects, but the present work will deal mainly with hoards of objects made of valuable materials, and – of course – in particular with hoards containing Roman coins. The Roman coins may be only part of the hoard or combined with other types of artefacts, as e.g. the case of Hacksilber hoards including siliquae. Other hoards consist solely of coins, and some of these hold coins of one denomination only, as for example the majority of denarius hoards.

In the numismatic world the word "hoard" is the common terminology for a find consisting of two or more coins. The expression was used to avoid the large assemblage of coins in a hoard distorting a statistical picture of the distribution of coins. It has been suggested that when dealing with base metal coinage the word "hoard" should be used only in cases where five or more coins have been found together. In the case of Denmark, where Roman base metal coins are very rare, this way of distinguishing is hardly relevant.

Other scholars have suggested that a single gold coin might be seen as a hoard, because its intrinsic value would be far higher than a number of silver coins. In these cases the expression hoard is used not only to avoid counting many coins from a single find as separate entities, but it takes on a more "classic" meaning, namely that of a hoard being something very valuable.

Within the Roman Empire an aureus would be worth 25 denarii, but we can only guess at the "exchange rate" outside the Empire, let alone the special status that the coins may have had as an imported exotic object. It does, however, seem safe to assume

---

map of addresses of amateur detectorists, collected by Grønnegård.
11 Henriksen 2006, 218. The differences are for example the two clusters around Copenhagen and Aalborg that are not fully reflected by the Roman coin finds, but as many of the sites located in these areas are dated mainly to the Medieval period, this need not have a bearing on the present discourse. A closer analysis ought to be made of sites with material from the Iron Ages in general in relation to sites with finds of Roman coins, but this has been deemed outside the scope of the present work.
12 Paulsson 1999, 52.

that gold was highly priced, and that the deposition of a single aureus was a deposition of considerable value and therefore hardly incidental.

The word "hoard" is used here to designate any functional deposition of more than one coin. Only in a second instance will it be proposed to interpret the deposition as a sacrifice, hidden treasure, raw material, or plain loss.

Any child would be able to describe the traditional hoard (or treasure). This is the type of find encountered in numerous cartoons and films: a box of gold and jewellery or a chest of (gold!) coins. These types of finds do appear in serious archaeological literature as well, but more often only a part of the original deposition is recovered. Either the container has rotten away or the original deposition has been scattered by forces of nature, animals or human intervention. In the past a number of coins found on the same site were normally interpreted as a disturbed hoard. But the experience gained from detector archaeology over the last decades has warned us that in particular when dealing with the large and complex settlement areas great care must be taken to distinguish between scattered hoards and series of single finds.[13] The extensive use of metal detectors has yielded a large number of single finds that are never-the-less not coins that were deposited (or lost) one by one, but a coin hoard that has been disturbed by agricultural works, and scattered into plough-soil. In any of these finds the individual "single" finds must therefore be analysed closely to reveal if they, and in that case how many of them, are true single losses and if not, how many derive from scattered hoards. This analysis must be based on exact information on the find spot, measured with as great precision as possible. The scattered hoards are normally found within a restricted area, and the pattern of the scatter itself together with information on ploughing and other earth works of the area may give information as to where the hoard was originally deposited. Analysis of wear and corrosion of the coins may yield additional evidence that in cases can show that coins found within a rather small area still may be divided into a number of single finds and coins deriving from a hoard.

3.7 Reassembling a scattered hoard

A cluster of near-contemporary objects appearing within a restricted area may be indicative of a single deposition that has been disturbed by the plough. The single type coin hoards found on sites with no other finds are easy to recognize. Good examples of these are the Orup Hoard from Sealand and the Præstemosen Hoard from the periphery of Gudme (see below). In both cases the hoard had been totally ploughed up, but the lack of other finds indicates that a hoard had been deposited. Hoards may be more difficult to identify if other contemporary objects appear in the same area, as is the case with the large detector sites. The plough had hit both the Gudme III Hoard (*Fig. 72*) and the Smørenge Hoard from Bornholm, and parts of the hoards had been scattered. Yet, excavations succeeded in locating the bottom of the original deposition *in situ*, proving beyond doubt that the coins were deposited as hoards. The number of times a field has been ploughed and harrowed after the hoard is first disturbed of course is of importance. The distribution of for example the Smørenge Hoard[14] is far "denser" than the distribution of the Orup Hoard (*Fig. 31*).[15] While the Smørenge Hoard had probably been disturbed only a few years before the (first) excavation of the hoard, the Orup Hoard must have been hit at least 50 years before excavation.

When a number of coins have been found in stacks or bundles still sticking together we clearly deal with coins that have been preserved in soil for a long time together, and it would be absurd not to regard them as a single deposition. In other cases it is possible to suggest that coins that share the same characteristic surface corrosion may belong to a single deposition.[16] Still, in particular when it comes to a smaller number of coin finds from a single site, it may be very hard to conclude whether all coins came from one deposition or are the result of a series of losses.[17]

---

13 Horsnæs 2006b.

14 Kromann & Watt 1984, fig. 4.
15 Roland & Horsnæs 2004, fig. 7.
16 Horsnæs 2006b discusses the possible implications.
17 Interpretations of the finds at Dankirke and Katrinelund were attempted by Bjerg 2007.

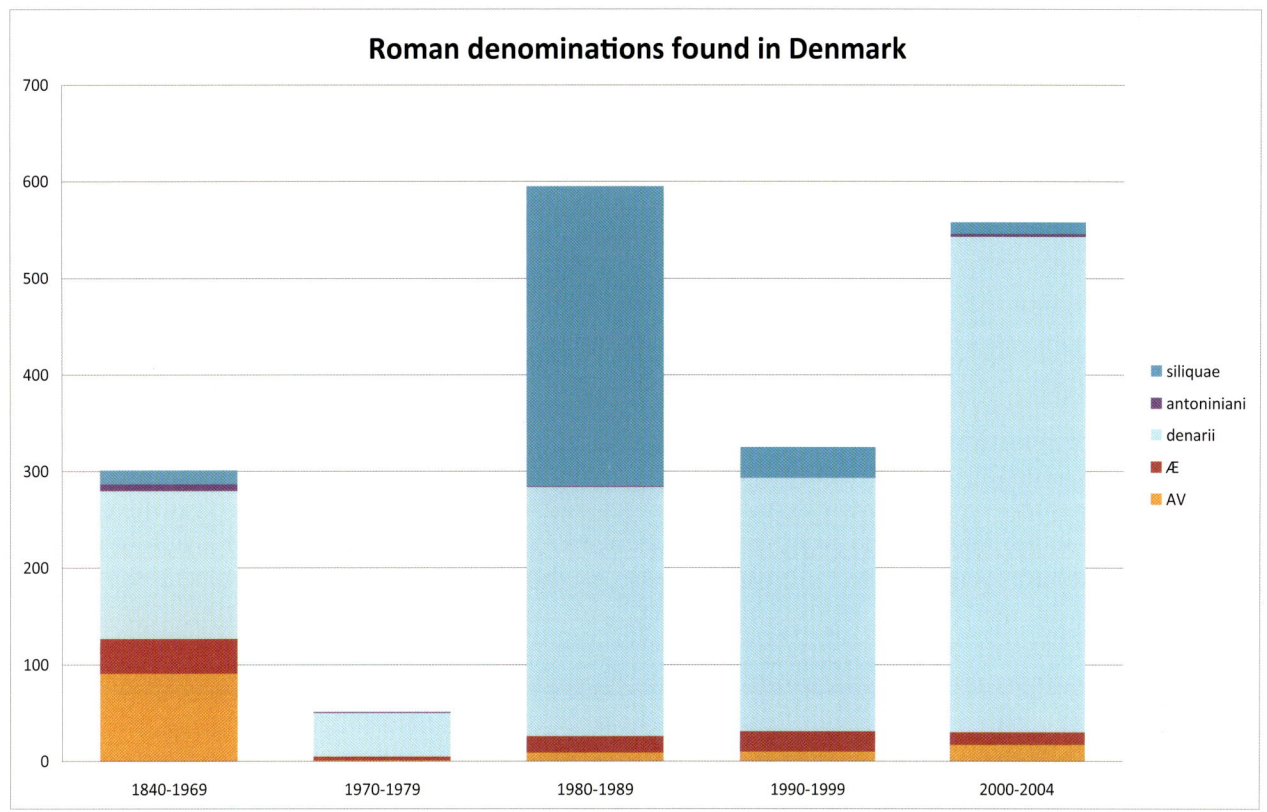

Fig. 9. Finds of Roman coins in Denmark in the periods: 1840-1969, 1970-1979, 1980-1989, 1990-1999 and 2000-2004. The coins are divided into base metal coins, denarii, antoniniani, gold coins. The diagram reveals the changes in the find pattern conditioned by the metal detector.

3.8 The importance of the metal detector

The use of the metal detector has increased the volume of metal finds considerably. But it has not only increased the number of finds. It has also changed the types of finds that are recovered, and it has revealed context types that were either totally unknown or badly represented before.

The percentage of finds of gold coins has decreased considerably since the introduction of the metal detector (*Fig. 9*). Many of the old finds of gold coins were made by farmers working the land manually or while walking behind a plough drawn by horses. The gold was easily visible when walking in the fields. A closer look at the recent gold finds reveals an even more interesting picture: of the 17 gold coins found in 2000-2004, 10 came from the Boltinggård Hoard. The first finds of this hoard appeared already in 1867, and three gold coins were found in the period 1888-1916. A fourth coin was found with detector in 1987, a fifth in 1994, and after the sixth coin was found in early 2004, an excavation of the area revealed the last coins, some of which were found still *in situ*.[18] Also the Brangstrup Hoard and the very large Broholm Hoard were originally found in the 19th century, and they have both yielded more gold coins as a result of detector surveys of the old find spots: Three coins were added to the Brangstrup Hoard in the 1990's[19] and a fourth in 2004.[20] Thus a considerable number of recent finds of gold coins were made as the result of targeted surveying of a site already yielding gold hoards in the 19th century.

The bronze coins would have been less visible when working the fields, but still a considerable number was found in the period from 1840. These coins are only rarely found during modern detector surveys, although they are extremely common within

---

18   Henriksen & Horsnæs 2004 and 2006.
19   FP 5005; Henriksen 1992a.
20   FP 6829; Horsnæs 2004.

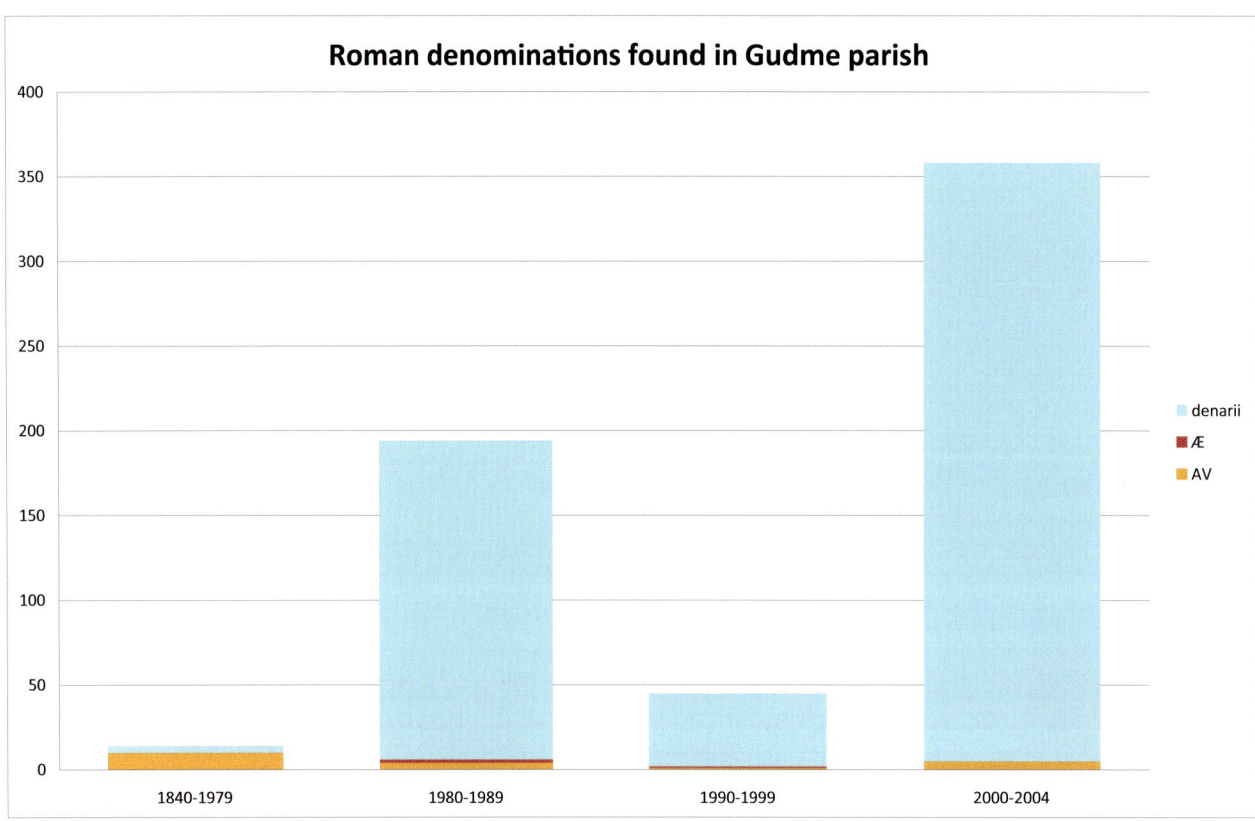

Fig. 10. The changes in the find pattern in Gudme parish, note the many early finds of gold coins in comparison to the number of denarii.

the Roman Empire and quite easy to find with a detector. Indeed, when found, a strikingly large number of the bronze coins come from sites with occupation from the Viking or Medieval Periods.

The relative decrease in number of gold finds, and the enormous increase in number of denarius finds become even more evident when looking at the Gudme district/parish (*Fig. 10*). This area, well-known for its many archaeological finds since the late 19th century, yielded only a relatively low number of denarii until the large detector surveys started.[21] Clearly gold is so much easier to see in the surface than silver that we must expect many sites with known gold finds to yield also silver artefacts and coins, if surveyed by the use of metal detector. We must therefore conclude that denarii are easily underrepresented in an area where the detector has not been used.[22]

The use of the metal detector has also provided new context types. The vast majority of the recently found coins are from only two sites: Gudme and Lundeborg, both within Gudme district. But even not considering these two sites, denarius finds from settlements plays a very important role (see below: List of denarius finds from settlements. Note that the year of the first find is very often after 1980).

---

21 Breitenstein 1942 described four denarii and 17 solidi from Gudme parish. A similar situation is found in Ibsker parish, Bornholm. The area has been known for gold finds since the 16th century, but the first three denarii were found in the mid-20th century. Since the late 1970's amateur archaeologists with detectors have found almost 650 denarii.

22 The siliquae finds have not been included in the diagram. The majority of the siliquae from Denmark were found as a single hoard in Gudme, and this hoard would distort the general picture provided by the other finds. (Cf. below on *Siliquae*).

3.9 Denominations

Normally it is quite easy to identify the denomination of a Roman coin and the well-preserved coins can be dated accurately thanks to type catalogues as the *RIC*. The preservation of the coin, however, is not always perfect. Still, when the portrait of the emperor can be recognized the date of production can be given with greater precision than most other archaeological artefacts. When a coin is only known from verbal description, the possibility to identify the denomination and type is wholly dependent on the expertise of the original registration of the coin. The initial classification of the Roman coins from Denmark thus follows the normal classification according to denomination.

Silver coins are normally divided into denarii, quinarii, antoniniani and siliquae. By far the overwhelming majority of the Roman coins found in Denmark are denarii that make up for 74 % of the total number of coins. Republican and Julio-Claudian denarii are relatively rare finds from Denmark. The number of finds rises quite suddenly with the issues of the Civil Wars in AD 68-69, and there is a considerable number of coins struck during the reign of Vespasian. Coins struck during the period from the Flavian to the Antonine dynasties are the most commonly found ones, but there are also several Severan denarii. The post-Severan period is represented by few finds only.

Only two quinarii have been found, both during circumstances that make it unlikely that they have ever belonged to an Iron Age context. The first is an Augustan silver quinarius from Thorsager, where it was found close to the station (*Fig. 11*). It was initially believed that the coin had been found on Funen, but this information was corrected by Balling.[23] The second quinarius was struck by Trajan. It was found in Holmslands Klit, the dunes west of Ringkøbing, in an area were numerous Late Medieval and Premodern coins have been found.[24] Some Barbarian

Fig. 11. The Augustan quinarius from Thorsager. Scale 2:1. Photo HWH.

imitations of gold coins have been labelled quinarii. I have decided to treat them with the imitations of Roman aurei, as we cannot be certain whether the imitation consciously attempted to follow the Roman weight system.

Also antoniniani are relatively rare. They were officially meant to be double denarii and as such silver coins, but their silver content dropped quickly. The debasement came so fast that the antoninianus obviously never gained any confidence outside the Empire, and in fact the find pattern of the antoniniani in Denmark is so closely comparable to that of the base metal coinage, that it has been decided to treat them here among the latter group.

Siliquae are not common, and the overwhelming majority of the Danish finds have been made at Gudme. A smaller number of siliquae have been found in three hack-silver hoards, in connection with burials or as single finds.

Gold coins are divided into aurei, early solidi, and solidi from the divided empire. A total of 124 gold coins and medallions struck before the division of the Roman Empire in AD 395 have been found in Denmark.[25] The coins struck after AD 395 are represented by only 42 Late Roman and Early Byzantine coins. The overwhelming majority of the gold coins have been found on Funen, in particular in a number of hoards, but there are a number of significant single finds from both Sealand and Jutland. A very large part of the gold coins – both coins from hoards and single finds – are pierced and/or looped, clearly indicating a secondary use as amulet/jewellery.

A number of the so-called Barbarian imitations of Roman coins have been found in Denmark. This

---

23 141109 sb 188: FP 1452 = NM I C17847: Augustus *RIC* 2nd ed. 276 (c. 29-27 BC); Breitenstein 1943, 1 no. I; Balling 1962, 10 no. 4.

24 180404 sb 10: FP 4514.1: Trajan *BMC* 24 or later; *AUD* 1987, 220. On other coin finds from Holmslands Klit, see Eriksen 2000.

25 Including ten Barbarian gold imitations of Roman coins.

group comprises imitations of denarii, siliquae, aurei, solidi and medallions, in short: imitations of all denominations struck in valuable metals. It is deemed important to focus on the imitations as a source for information on exchange routes and patterns within Barbaricum.

In connection with the Roman gold coins also the Nordic bracteates should be mentioned. They are from the outset clearly influenced by the Roman gold coins and medals and contemporary with them.

A final group is made up of all Roman base metal coinage, no matter which denomination was intended. As noted above the restricted number of antoniniani found in Denmark has been included in this group.

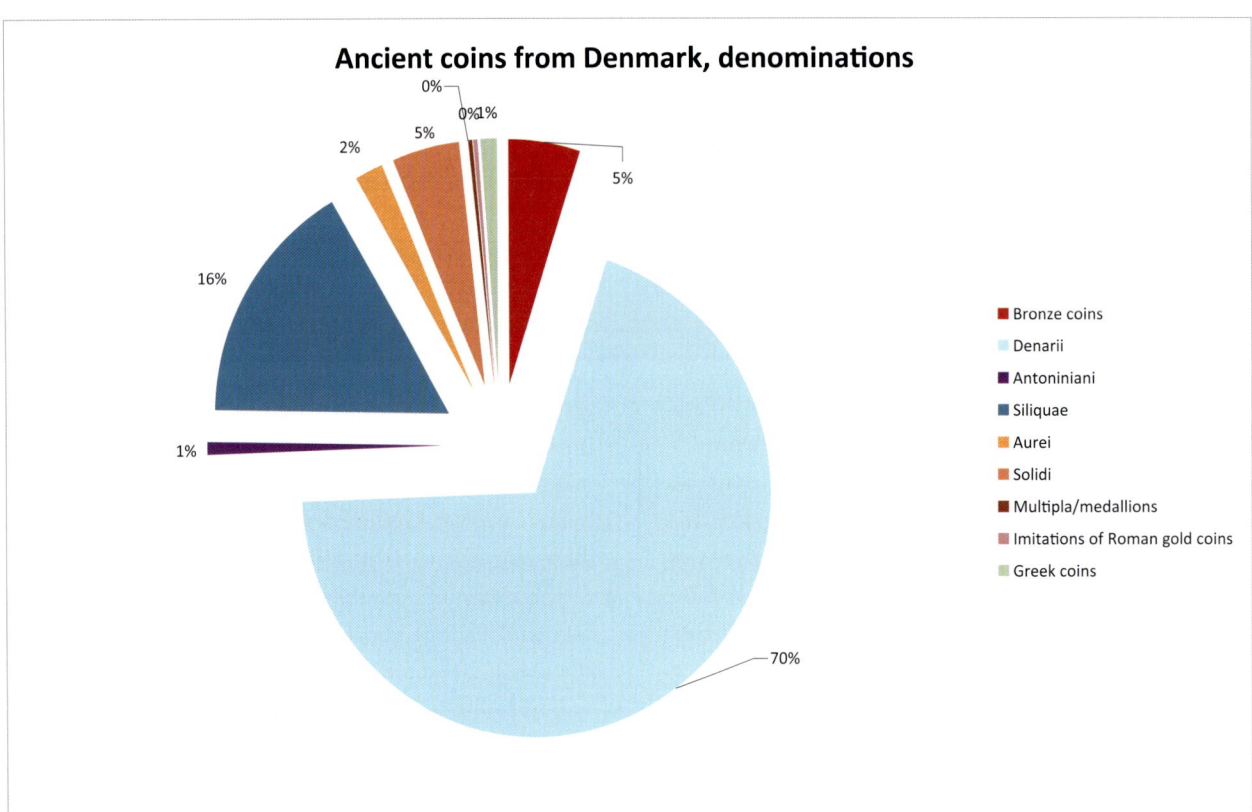

Fig. 12. Distribution of denominations of coin finds from Denmark (excl. Bornholm).

CHAPTER 4

Geographical distribution of coin finds – the coins in their regional contexts

Roman coins have not been found in equal numbers throughout Denmark. Some areas have evidently received far larger numbers of coins than others, and there are clusters of coins in particular types of contexts. It has therefore been decided initially to discuss the geographical distribution of the coins with a view to the special characteristics of the areas in question, and secondly to analyse a number of particular contexts types that have been found in various areas.

4.1 Sealand

With *c.* 800 registered Roman coins from *c.* 150 sites Sealand, with the southern islands of Møn, Lolland and Falster, is the second largest area in Denmark when it comes to the number of coin finds. Considering that 530 of these coins derive from the four denarius hoards from Lærkefryd, Bagsværd, Råmosen and Orup, the large number of sites indicates that the majority of the remaining *c.* 270 coins were single finds. Roman coins in general are quite evenly distributed throughout Sealand. "Empty" areas can mostly be explained as areas with forests and/or extensive wetlands that have inhibited building activity (ancient and/or modern). Some of the areas with many finds, for example the triangle between the Copenhagen, Roskilde and Køge areas, are today subject to intensive building activity due to the urban growth of major Copenhagen, and many rescue excavations have been undertaken. The many excavations have revealed a dense scatter of Roman coins, but there are differences worth noting from one area to another. West of Copenhagen very large areas have been uncovered with evidence of dense occupation throughout the Iron Age, but in spite of the many thousands post holes, pits etc. only a handful of Roman coins have been discovered. In the Roskilde area only denarii have been found, most of them as single finds. In the Køge area there is a number of sites with multiple finds of denarii, but it is important to note that also in the outskirts of Køge vast excavations of Iron Age settlements with remains of numerous buildings have yielded no coin finds at all.[1]

The base metal coins have a distribution that at first sight seems quite odd. There is a relatively high number of finds in and around Copenhagen. Probably this distribution pattern can be related to modern import of Roman coins as souvenirs or collectors' items (*Fig. 86*).[2]

An analysis of the settlement pattern on Sealand has revealed that areas situated 1-10 km from the coastline were more densely settled than other areas in the Early Roman to Early Germanic Iron

---

1 Excavations at Køge Transportcenter, information from Sv.Å. Tornbjerg.
2 Horsnæs 2006a; see also below.

Fig. 13. Hørup. The black soil area indicating the settlement site is clearly visible in the foreground. On the top of the hill building remains have been identified. Photo HWH.

Ages. Coastal areas became more densely settled in the Late Germanic Iron Age with the appearance of a considerable number of landing places.[3] Likewise there seems to have been little interest in establishing settlements along streams and rivers.[4]

Sealand has yielded relatively more denarius hoards than Funen and Jutland, and more than half the Roman coins from Sealand derive from one denarius hoard, the Råmosen Hoard. Smaller denarius hoards together make up for another 25 % of the material. The denarius hoards are not mixed with other issues, or other artefact types, and most of them have been found in areas with few or no other finds (sections 5.2 and 6.1.4).

Only the Lærkefryd Hoard in north-eastern Sealand may be related to other Iron Age finds from the area. Among these should be mentioned two finds of a denarius at Sperrestrup Mose (Moor) only *c.* 2.5 km south of Lærkefryd. The first find cannot be pinpointed more exactly then "Sperrestrup Mose" (the coin was a single find during peat cutting),[5] while the other was a detector find from 1992.[6] Both coins are

---

3 Rindel 2002. For the landing places see Ulriksen 1998.
4 Contrary to what was the case in contemporary southern and western Jutland, Rindel in Fabech & Ringtved: Settlement and landscape 1999, 79-99.

---

5 010306 sb 106: FP 1168.
6 010306 sb 34: FP 5162.

denarii struck during the reign of Antoninus Pius. Also a Viking Age hoard is known from this area. More important in the present context is the workshop area at Hørup, situated less than 5 km northwest of the Lærkefryd site.[7]

In the densely populated areas around and north of Copenhagen a remarkable number of single finds of Roman base metal coins has been found. This must be due to the fact that bronze coins have been collected through centuries, and many of them have probably been imported quite recently as collector's items or tourist souvenirs. These relatively cheap coins have not been thoroughly searched for when lost by collectors, indeed many stories are being told between collectors about practical jokes often involving the tossing of cheap Roman bronze coins over a fence, hoping that someone would believe that he was about to make a spectacular find.[8]

Around Roskilde only denarii have been found, most of them as single finds, but in a few cases more than one coin has appeared on a site. Glim parish has yielded a total of six denarii. One denarius was found in Glim together with a Medieval copper coin,[9] three came from an area just east of Glim,[10] one from a field south of Glim,[11] and one was found in Øm-Gammeltoft c. 1.5 km west-southwest of Glim and close to Lejre.[12] At Lejre a denarius was found before 1882, but its exact find spot was not recorded.[13] A republican denarius was found during excavations at Gammel Lejre (Old Lejre), together with among other things a Dorestad coin. They were found in connection with a pile of burnt stone including material accumulated over the period c. 500-1000 AD. In the Herthadal (Hertha Valley), close to Ledreborg Castle west of Lejre, two denarii struck by Trajan and Commodus have been found. No other finds were recorded.[14]

North of Ledreborg, at Lindholm "site 2" in Gevninge parish a single denarius has been found.[15] Similarly, a single denarius was found by detector at Højbjerggård in Gevninge 15 km northwest of Glim.[16] In all cases these denarii were found by detector reconnaissance and other material from the sites include a wide chronological range, from the Iron Age through the Medieval Period. From the large Vindinge cemetery east of Roskilde there is a single burial with a denarius re-used as part of the jewellery (*Fig. 22*).[17]

Between Roskilde and Copenhagen very large areas have been uncovered with evidence of dense occupation throughout the Iron Age, but in spite of the many thousands post holes, pits etc. only a handful of Roman coins have been discovered. Among these are four denarii, all single finds from archaeological investigations of Iron Age sites.[18] A fifth denarius, struck by Trajan, was found in the garden of the Vridsløselille Prison without context.[19] Also one siliqua[20] and one Barbarian imitation of an aureus[21] have been found in this general area. The two last were reworked into pendants and they were both found as part of the jewellery in an elite burial. The already mentioned seven denarii from Ledøje, possibly deriving from a hoard, and the single find from the same area come from an area only a few km north of the cluster of finds from the Tåstrup area.

---

7   Sørensen 2000 and 2006a.
8   Section 6.4; Horsnæs 2006a.
9   020402 sb 24: FP 4642.1.
10 020402 sb 41: FP 5287.1 and 5991.1.
11 020402 sb 22: FP 7824.
12 020402 sb 43: FP 6636.1.
13 020601 without sb no., NM I inv. C 4815; Breitenstein 1946, no. 18.
14 020601 sb 106: FP 3573.1-2; Kromann 1995, 349 no. 37.1-2.

15 020603 sb 87, FP5196; Kromann 1995, 349 no. 30.
16 020409 sb 19: FP 4708; Kromann 1995 349 no. 13.
17 020512 sb 4: Roskilde Museum inv.no. ROM 555/83. Kromann 1995, 349 no. 39A. For more recent excavations on the site see Høj 2005.
18 020204 sb 10 (Vissinge Vest): Kroppedal Museum inv.no. SØL 1061 struck by Vespasian.
    020205 sb 19 (Hyldager): FP 5124; Kromann 1995, 349 no. 18.
    020208 sb 29 (Ishøj): Kroppedal Museum inv.no. SØL 1042, the denarius was struck by Commodus for Crispina.
    020215 sb 25 (Vallensbæk Nordmark): FP 6358; *AUD* 2001, 236.
19 020202 sb 24: FP 2962; Kromann 1983-84, 104 no. 31.
20 020213 sb 20: FP 5164; Kromann 1995, 350 no. 59.
21 020213 sb 41: FP 6095; *AUD* 1999, 265 and 279 fig. 28.

Only one denarius has been found closer to the centre of Copenhagen, namely a denarius found between Brønshøj and Husum in 1914.[22]

In the Køge area there is a number of sites with multiple finds of denarii. The Østervang site 8 km northwest of Køge is another specialized workshop site, where excavations have uncovered the remains of more than 50 buildings, and the rich detector finds include 11 denarii.[23]

Ellebækgård *c.* 4 km to the north-northwest of Køge has yielded detector finds from the Early Roman Iron Age to the Medieval Period, and excavations have shown that the area was settled from the Early Roman Iron Age to the end of the Viking Age. Among the coin finds are five Roman denarii, ranging from Vespasian to Commodus, as well as three Frankish coins, two dirhams, an imitation of a dirham, and an Early Medieval penning.[24]

At Solrød, *c.* 10 km north of Køge, another cluster of denarii have been found. 12 denarii come from two areas north of Solrød, Ejrebækgård north[25] and Kirsebærhaven south[26] of the Ejrebæk (Ejre Stream). Other objects from the Medieval period have been found in the area, but there is so far no evidence of settlement from the Iron Age other than the coins. A denarius has also been found immediately south of Solrød, in an area with a number of finds, including coins, from the Medieval period.[27]

The Himlingøje centre is well known for the very rich elite burials found not only at Himlingøje itself, but also in a number of other sites around Himlingøje.[28] One of the rich burials at Himlingøje itself contained a denarius that was re-used as a central element in the long necklace of the buried lady,[29] and a denarius was found with detector at Himlingøje/Nytofte.[30] Another denarius was found in a burial site at Gunnerupgård Mark already in 1817[31] and not far from this a Late Roman solidus was found on a field in Herfølge Mark in 1859.[32]

Toftegård between Valløby and the Tryggevælde Å (Stream) and *c.* 7 km south-southeast of Køge is a detector site that has yielded a number of finds from the Iron Age to the Medieval Period, among other things a single denarius.[33] At Store Tårnby, also close to the Tryggevælde Å, but 2.5 km southeast of Valløby, another denarius was found in 1930.[34] This site is 3 km north of Varpelev, where an elite burial among other things contained a looped aureus struck by Probus,[35] and at Bjælkerup, southeast of Varpelev, a single denarius was found on a field in 1881.[36]

In Central Sealand single finds of denarii have been made at Slimminge Mark halfway between Køge and Ringsted in 1943,[37] at Cirkelhusene (Ringsted),[38] at Gammel Kærup,[39] and at Bringstrup.[40] The latter is a detector site with finds dating from the Iron Age to

---

22 020306 sb 412: FP 1405; Breitenstein 1946, 10 no. 6.
23 020103 sb 16: FP 6159, 6188, 6189, 6538, 6770, 6771 and 6832; Tornbjerg 2002.
24 020105 sb 36: FP 5721.1, 6158, 6187, 6539.1 and 6560.1; Tornbjerg 2003.
25 020510 sb 37: FP 5161, 5555 and 5792, a total of eight denarii.
26 020510 sb 28: FP 5123, 5167 and 5557, a total of four denarii.
27 020510 sb 31: FP 6687.1.
28 Lund Hansen 1995.

29 050105 sb 29: FP 2236; Kromann 1983-84, 104 no. 30; Lund Hansen 1995, 155 and Kromann 1995, 349 no. 6.
30 050105 sb 25: FP 6262.
31 050104 sb 58: NM I XCIII-XCVI; Breitenstein 1946, 15-16 no. 21; Kromann 1995, 349 no. 27.
32 050104 without sb no., NM I C18617; Breitenstein 1946, 25-26 no. 38 and fig. 21.
33 050111 sb 36: FP 5556.
34 050110 sb 16: FP 1746; Breitenstein 1946, 14-15 no. 19.
35 050613 sb 8: NM I C 3067; Breitenstein 1946, 16-17 no. 24 and fig. 3.
36 050610 without sb no., NM I C 4412; Breitenstein 1946, 10-11 no. 8.
37 050103 sb 16: FP 2098; Breitenstein 1946, 11 no. 10.
38 040213 sb 64: FP 5860.
39 040213 sb 69: FP 6990. A site with evidence of more than 70 buildings distributed in three groups around a cemetery with 11 burials was excavated at Kærup only *c.* 1 km north of Gammel Kærup in 2007. The material is dated in the Late Roman Iron Age. Excavation presented by Lehne Christensen in paper given at Kroppedal Museum 29/04/08.
40 040203 sb 2: FP 5985.1.

Fig. 14. Denarius from Slimminge Mark. Scale c. 2:1. Photo Lennart Larsen/National Museum of Denmark.

Fig. 15. Denarius from Assenhøj, Aversi. Scale 2:1. Photo HWH.

the Medieval Period, while the coin from Gammel Kærup has been found with material from the Medieval period or perhaps even later. A single denarius was also found in grave H of the Nordrup cemetery c. 6 km southeast of Gammel Kærup.[41] The already mentioned Orup Hoard was excavated c. 10 km south of Ringsted, and only a couple of km east of Orup a single denarius was found at Aversi.[42]

This general area is surrounded by a small number of finds of siliquae and gold coins. Both Høsten Torp and a settlement at Engelsborg have yielded Hacksilber hoards including siliquae. The greater hoard, found at Høsten Torp southeast of Ringsted, consisted of 4.453 kg of silver including eight siliquae.[43] A single find of a looped Constantinian solidus was made at Kværkeby northeast of Ringsted.[44] These finds were all made between Tyrstrup Sø (Lake) southwest of Ringsted and the lakes at Haraldsted and Gyrstinge north of Ringsted. Two denarii, both struck for Diva Faustina Major, were reported found in Skee-Tåstrup a bit north of these lakes, probably in the 1890's, but they were never handed in, and their present whereabouts is unknown.[45]

Situated topographically in the same area are a small number of gold coins. A Leo I solidus was found in 1868 on Assentorp Mark northwest of the Gyrstinge Sø (Lake),[46] and west of the Sorø Sø (Lake) two gold coins were found. One is a Burgundian triens imitation found on the Late Medieval castle mounds at Rollerup,[47] and the other is a looped solidus struck by Crispus Caesar found while ploughing in Haldagerlille.[48] These gold coins are found without any other indication of human presence, or – in the case of the Rollerup find – on a site that was only settled in a period much later than the coin date.

In western Sealand, a number of sites situated as pearls on a string have yielded denarii. The southernmost of these sites is Neble where denarii have been found on two distinct sites. In the first area detector surveys have yielded mainly Medieval and later material as well as a single denarius,[49] while the second area apart from a single denarius (*Fig. 16*) has yielded finds from Roman Iron Age through to the Viking Age, including Viking Age silver hoards.[50] Close to Slagelse a denarius was found on a field belonging to

---

41 040211 sb 17, NM I C 4823.
42 050701 sb 7: FP 5531.
43 040205 sb 5: FP 1830; Breitenstein 1946, 22-23 no. 36.

44 040210 without sb no.: FP 99; Breitenstein 1946, no. 31 and fig. 7.
45 040206 without sb no.; Galster 1924, 187 no. 7 referring to unpublished note by Chr. Jørgensen.
46 040112 sb 445: FP 304; Breitenstein 1946, 26-27 no. 41.
47 040312 sb 36 and 58: FP 1484; Breitenstein 1946, 27 no. 42; Tomasini 1964, 229 no. 400 (where the coin is erroneously described as part of a hoard).
48 040506 sb 4: FP 355; Breitenstein 1946, 19 no. 29 and fig. 6.
49 040301 sb 101: FP 4475; Kromann 1995, 349 no. 33.2.
50 040301 sb 105: FP 4586.1; Kromann 1995, 249 no. 33.2. Bendixen *et al.* 1990.

Idagård before 1873,[51] and another on Asbjerggård.[52] Further north the large Råmose Hoard has already been mentioned. At Laurvig c. 5 km north-northeast of the moor a denarius was found,[53] while on the eastern shore of Tissø, c. 11 km north of Råmosen, a denarius was found at Selschausdal manor in 1868.[54] The recent excavation of a chieftain's centre on the western shore of Tissø must now be taken into consideration while evaluating this find, although it should be stressed that the finds from Tissø are dated in the Late Germanic Iron Age and Viking Age.

Fig. 16. Denarius from Neble. Scale 2:1. Photo MLSS.

There are few finds of Roman coins from north-western Sealand. Two sites between Holbæk and Kalundborg have yielded denarii, one was found in connection with a burial at Bennebo Mark,[55] the other is a single denarius found in a moor at Mørkøv in 1887.[56] The exact find spot of the denarius from Mørkøv is unknown, but the two sites are situated perhaps no more than 1 km apart. A richly equipped burial at Nyrup has yielded the only Roman coins from this part of Sealand: two siliquae and one solidus.[57]

Finds are also sparse in southern Sealand. A gold medallion struck by Valentinian I was found in 1768 in "Fakse Mark on property belonging to the University".[58] A bit to the south of Fakse, not far from the sea, the investigations at Tyrstrup have yielded a denarius,[59] and on the southern coast of Sealand, at Klinteby, a 1st century aureus struck by Titus was found in 1939.[60] A denarius struck by Antoninus Pius was found during the excavation in Farvergade in the centre of the Medieval town of Næstved south of Ringsted. It came from a layer dated in the Early Germanic Iron Age.[61] Also an aureus, struck during the reign of Marcus Aurelius, was found during excavations in Næstved. The aureus was found in a context dated in the 14th century, but the presence of Iron Age phases in central Næstved clearly indicates that the aureus may have come from an Iron Age context that had been disturbed during the Medieval period.[62] The last coin from Sealand to be mentioned is a denarius mounted in a bronze frame that was re-used as pendant in an elaborate necklace in a burial on the Skovgårde cemetery.[63]

The three islands south of Sealand have each yielded a low number of finds. Three of a total of four gold coins, two from Møn[64] and one – a one-sided solidus imitation – from Strangegården on Falster[65] have been found in coastal areas without context. Two denarii have been found on the island Falster,

---

51 040313 without sb no.: NM I C 1612; Breitenstein 1946, 11 no. 9.
52 040302 without sb no.: FP 3718; Kromann 1983-84, 104 no. 33.
53 030211 without sb no.: FP 3572; Kromann 1983-84, 104 no. 32.
54 030202 sb 54: NM I C 295; Breitenstein 1946, 13 no. 14.
55 030710 sb 1: NM I 16388; Breitenstein 1946, 11-12 no. 11.
56 030708 without sb no.: NM I C 5831; Breitenstein 1946, 15 no. 20.
57 030405 sb 100.

---

58 050302: NM I 8511; Breitenstein 1946, 21-22 no. 35 and fig. 10.
59 050302 sb 36: FP 5992; Møller Hansen & Staal 1996; Staal 1997, 30.
60 040509 sb 71: FP 1993; Breitenstein 1946, 9-10, no. 5 and fig. 2.
61 050707 sb 29: Næstved Museum inv.no. NÆM 81/100 + 86/200; Petersen 1987, 180 and fig. 10.
62 050707 sb 53: FP 6060; Larsen 1996, 18-23, spec. 22.
63 050212 sb 27: Sydvestsjællands Museum inv.no. SMV 7021x1209; Ethelberg 2000.
64 Færgegården 050505 sb 163: FP 2072; Breitenstein 1946, 24-25 no. 37, and Magleby 050604 sb 5: NM I C 5510; Breitenstein 1946, 20 no. 32 and fig. 8. A third gold coin has ben found on Møn, but there are no details as to the exact find spot: FP 652; Breitenstein 1946, 9 no. 4 and fig. 1.
65 Strangegården. 070110 sb 65: FP1733; Breitenstein 1946, 21 no. 34.

Geographical distribution of coin finds

but there is no further indication of the find spot,[66] and four have been found on Lolland. Among the latter, two of the denarii were found at Erikstrup in an area that has been cultivated only from c. 1830 onwards, and it is possible that they came from the same field as some Iron Age gold jewellery (Fig. 40).[67] The third denarius was found on a field in Søllested,[68] while the fourth, a Republican denarius, was a detector find from Kohave.[69] The composition of the Ancient coins from the southern islands is quite curious. Among the 14 coins noted, only four are the most commonly found 2nd century denarii. Instead there are five Roman bronze coins, two Republican denarii, a Pre-Roman Greek coin and a Roman Provincial coin, as well as the odd solidus imitation from Strangegården.

4.2 Funen

Funen has yielded by far the largest number of Roman coins from Denmark, a total of 1383 coins, but the many coins present a picture that to a great extent varies from that of Sealand. The coins have been found in a relatively restricted number of sites. The majority of coin finds are concentrated in south-eastern Funen, where the central place Gudme and its port-of-trade Lundeborg are situated (section 5.3.1).[70] Central Funen has yielded a number of important finds of gold coins, but the remaining part of the island is only partly affected by the Gudme centre. The minor sites around Odense can to some degree be compared with the workshop sites of Sealand, while the western part of Funen is empty both as regards to coin finds and as regards to other Roman imports. The same applies to the islands south of Funen. Except for a Barbarian aureus imitation from Tåsinge, not a single Roman coin has been found there. The situation in Langeland in particular is in striking contrast to the obviously lively occupation of the island and its close proximity to Lundeborg.

Two gold hoards containing Constantinian coins have been found at Brangstrup[71] and Boltinggård[72] close to Ringe, and a single find of a pierced Constantinian solidus was made in a garden in Ringe parish.[73] At Rynkebygård north of Ringe town a hoard consisting of five Late Roman solidi was found during peat-cutting in 1848, and Ringe parish has yielded several other gold finds that can be dated in the Late Roman or Early Migration period.[74] On the contrary few denarii have been found in this central part of Funen. A cemetery with +200 burials from the Roman and Early Germanic Iron Age has been excavated at Bregentved, 3 km from Boltinggård and Brangstrup and just west of the modern town

Fig. 17. Solidus imitation from Strangegården. Scale 2:1. Photo HWH.

---

66 FP 468; Breitenstein 1946, 28 no. 2.
67 070321 sb 19: NM I C 3660-3661; Breitenstein 1946, 8-9 no. 3. See also below p. 84-85.
68 050512 without sb no.: FP 3052a; Kromann 1983-84, 106 no. 35.
69 070403 sb 37: FP 6480; Horsnæs & Schilling 2002.

70 A series of publications of the many surveys and excavations in Gudme since 1980 is in preparation.
71 090108 sb 19. Henriksen 1992; Horsnæs 2004.
72 090108 sb 13. Henriksen & Horsnæs 2004 and 2006.
73 090108 sb 125: FP 242. The coin was of the same type as a coin from the Brangstrup Hoard and was therefore exchanged. Its present whereabouts is unknown. Breitenstein 1942, 86, VI.
74 Albrectsen 1960; Henriksen & Horsnæs 2004, 141.

of Ringe.⁷⁵ In one of the latest graves a woman was buried with a small necklace consisting of glass and amber beads and a pierced denarius subaeratus struck for Marcus Aurelius Caesar.⁷⁶ It is suggested that a contemporary settlement is situated west of the cemetery, at the Ringe Golfbane (Golf Course), where among other things a denarius has been found during detector surveys.⁷⁷

North of Ringe the parishes of Nørre-Søby, Nørre-Lyndelse and Årslev have yielded several gold finds, among which there are two coins. One is a looped Barbarian imitation of an aureus found in the very rich Årslev grave (cf. below);⁷⁸ the other is an isolated find of a solidus struck by Valentinian I (364-375 AD) in Arles.⁷⁹ A fragment of the rim is broken off; perhaps a loop was once fastened here.

Kværndrup parish south of Ringe has yielded two gold coins and a denarius. A looped Barbarian imitation of an aureus was found in 1861 while harrowing a field at Kværndrup at the creek at Falle Mølle (Mill).⁸⁰ Excavations in the area have revealed a series of Iron Age settlements with evidence of workshop activities,⁸¹ and a settlement area that produced a denarius found with detector (*Fig. 18*).⁸² A single find of a denarius has been made at Hillerslev west-southwest of Ringe.⁸³ A medallion with traces of a loop struck by Constantius II Caesar in 323-337 AD was found in a small wood at Trunderup northeast of Kværndrup.⁸⁴ The two gold coins cannot be directly related to the other finds, but the settlement remains at Kvændrup certainly testifies to Iron Age occupation in the general area.

Fig. 18. Denarius from Falle Mølle. Scale 2:1. Photo Svendborg og Omegns Museer.

Also the parishes of Stenstrup and Krarup have yielded finds of gold coins without contexts. The coin from Stenstrup was a solidus struck by Constantine I at Nicomedeia in 335-337 AD.⁸⁵ A boy found it in 1774 while harrowing a field in Hundtofte. Rumours said that a similar coin had previously been found on the same area. The coin from Krarup is a looped Barbarian imitation of an aureus. It was found in 1935 while digging close to a well in Tange.⁸⁶ In a field not far away a small bucket formed gold pendant has been found.

West of Ringe parish, in Sallinge, a Theodosius II solidus, which was both looped and mounted in a frame, was found while ploughing in 1863. Later on, the same field has yielded a number of "urns", none of which, however, has been retrieved archaeologically. The find spot is on a field bordering the Køllenbjerg Moor.⁸⁷

The finds closer to modern Odense seem to be of a different character. Extensive settlement areas with evidence of workshop activities have been excavated at Seden and Lundsgård, and both sites have yielded denarii. The sites are only *c.* 1 km apart and they are contemporary.⁸⁸ Similar settlement material, as well

---

75 Henriksen 1989 and 1992b.
76 090108 sb 11: FP 5072. Cf. below on coins in graves.
77 090108 sb 160: FP 7565.
78 090619 sb 4.
79 080806 sb 18. FP 745; Breitenstein 1943, 15-16 XXV.
80 090506 sb 7. FP 229; Breitenstein 1943, 10 XVI.
81 Thomsen 1998.
82 090506 sb 51. Report of the excavation in http://www.svendborgmuseum.dk/images/stories/Arkaeologi/Rapporter/som_01347_bygherre_opsat.pdf
83 090411 sb 74: FP 3968; Kromann 1983-84, 71 no. 12.
84 090506 sb 32: FP 639; Breitenstein 1943, 12-14, XXI, fig. 16.

---

85 090511 sb 22; Breitenstein 1943, 11 XIX. The coin was lost.
86 090416 sb 36: FP 1977; Breitenstein 1943, 9 XIV.
87 090411 sb 1: NM I C 21307; Breitenstein 1943, 16 XXVI, fig. 19; Fagerlie 1967, find 195, cat. 210.
88 Seden 080809 sb 7: FP 5983, Antonine or Severan denarius; Lundsgård 080811 sb 25: FP 5805, four denarii from Trajan to Marcus Aurelius; Toruplund SV 080811 sb 44: FP 6843, a denarius struck by Antoninus Pius; Henriksen 2000.

as three 2nd century denarii, was found at Troelsegård west of Odense.[89] These sites are clearly production sites, and among other things extensive production of flax has been taking place at Seden.

Northwest of Odense are three very important finds. At Næsby a looped 5th century solidus has been found in a garden close to the Stavis Å (Stream),[90] and 5 km to the northwest a looped 4th century medallion with traces of decoration on gold granulation was found in 1908 in a garden in the village of Allese.[91] A bracteate has been found few km to the north-west of Allese,[92] and at a similar distance west of Allese is the find spot of the important Vimose weapon sacrifice (section 5.2.1).

Outside the areas already described a number of coins have been found as single finds without any archaeological context. A 4th century solidus has been found at Rørup,[93] a pierced imitation of an aureus comes from Brenderup,[94] and a looped 4th century solidus was found at Gamby,[95] all single finds from north-west Funen. A similar single find this time of a pierced 3rd century aureus was made in 1777 in Ørbæk on eastern Funen.[96]

A pierced 5th century solidus was found on Midskov at the narrowest point of the entrance to the Odense Fjord.[97] At a similar strategic point south of Funen, at Vornæs Skov on the north-western coast of Tåsinge at the Svendborg Sund, a looped imitation of an aureus was found.[98] In the shallow waters off the shore of Vornæs Skov a Germanic gold necklace was recovered in 1861, and the two gold finds may be related.[99] Also in a coastal position is the gold hoard from Slipshavn Skov. The latest material of the hoard dates the deposition *c.* 500 AD, but it also includes two Roman aurei: a Valerian and a Diocletian.[100]

Among the gold coins there is also a single Tiberian aureus from Rørbæk that by some scholars has been related to a burial (section 5.1.4).

Denarii have been found in a number of burials. The female inhumation burial from Bregentved has already been mentioned. Furthermore, one denarius comes from a rich inhumation burial at Hågerup,[101] and it is possible that two denarii from Skrillinge Mark and Fjeldsted may have been related to cremation burials.[102] The evidence for these, however, is not decisive. The cremation burials from Møllegårdsmarken at Gudme have yielded both denarii and gold coins (section 5.1.2).

A denarius from Rorslev may be related to a settlement with workshop area from the Roman Iron Age, comparable to the sites around Odense. The coin was found in a pit with a gold spiral finger ring, a fragment of terra sigillata pottery and a glass sherd. No systematic investigation of the site has been undertaken.[103] Another one, from Rabenslyst Nordøst, was found on a field with black soil that may indicate a prehistoric settlement, together with an Iron Age belt fitting.[104]

At Fangel two denarii, both struck during the reign of Trajan, have been found. One was found on "Fangel Mark" in the early 19th century, while the

---

89   080409 sb 51: FP 6791.
90   080406 sb 18: NM I 7610/93. A Visigothic imitation of Valentinian III. Henriksen 1994b.
91   080301 sb 3: NM I DNF 3/08. Constantius II, Antiochia.
92   080301 sb 17: NM I DNF 6/08.
93   080717 sb 19; Breitenstein 1943, 15 XXIII. The coin no longer exists.
94   080703 sb 63: FP 141; Breitenstein 1943, 10-11 XVII.
95   080604 sb 49: FP 2067; Breitenstein 1943, 11-12 XX, fig. 15.
96   090618 sb 39: BP 217; Breitenstein 1943, 6 XII fig. 8.
97   080108 sb 80: FP 1166; Breitenstein 1943, 17-18 XXVII.
98   090507 sb 78: FP 110; Breitenstein 1943, 9-10 XV. The coin had been pierced, but the hole has been filled in prior to the mounting of the loop.

---

99   401561 sb 5: NM I 19697.
100   090611 sb 71: FP 3749; Kromann 1983-84, 73 no. 18 and FP 4359; *AUD* 1985, 158.
101   090403 sb 34: NM I C23248-23259; Breitenstein 1943, 3 V; Albrectsen 1968, 123 and 297, plate 26; Lund Hansen 1987, 426.
102   080712 sb 62: NM I C5846; Breitenstein 1943, 6 X, from Skrillinge Mark. 080705 sb 35: FP 1132, Breitenstein 1943, 5 VIII; Albrectsen 1968, 26 and 297, from Fjeldsted.
103   080506 sb 19: FP 3331 (now lost); Kromann 1983-84, 72 no. 15; Henriksen 1998, 14 and fig. 9.
104   090601 sb 78: FP 6149; *AUD* 2000, 298 (fragment).

Fig. 19. Trajanic denarius from Fangel. In private possession. Scale 2:1. Photo Jørgen Nielsen/Odense Bys Museer.

other one was the only surviving part of a small silver hoard found in the 1890's.[105] The other contents of this assumed hoard are not known (section 5.2.2.2).

Two denarii have been found in circumstances that do not a priori exclude that they are the first finds from an Iron Age site: One was found during agricultural work at Flødstrup before 1938,[106] the other was found in Skårup on a field sloping down towards the Vejstrup Å (Stream).[107]

The provenance of remaining single finds of denarii is either so badly recorded that the coins can be related to the parish only,[108] or the coins have most likely been found in secondary positions.[109]

A number of Roman bronze coins from Funen have already been mentioned above. There is, furthermore, a bronze coin found in connection with the ruins of the Dalum monastery, and therefore possibly from a Medieval context.[110]

The last coins to be mentioned are four Roman bronze coins from Odense,[111] Assens (two coins)[112] and Skårup.[113] In all cases the find circumstances indicate that these coins must have been deposited long after the Iron Age.

4.3 Jutland

Roman coins are found sparsely across Jutland. The number is somewhat lower than in the other regions of Denmark, to date only *c.* 550 coins. A general geographical pattern has long been visible: Sites with Roman coins were concentrated on the eastern coast of Jutland, with some finds around Aalborg and around and north of Limfjorden, as well as some finds on the south-western coast. The large heath areas in midwestern Jutland are almost void of finds. Detector archaeology has not changed this general pattern. Although the number of sites has grown from 65 to more than 100 since 1962, the "new" sites tend to fall within the same geographical areas. In particular the many detector amateurs around Aalborg have had a considerable influence with more than 10 new sites, and most recently the annual "detector rallies" in Thy (northwest of Limfjorden) are producing numerous "new" sites. These are cases where the number of detectorists has been of importance.

There are clear differences in the distribution of denominations. The majority of the finds are, as usual, denarii. There are few finds with very large numbers of coins, the largest being the weapon sacrifices in Illerup Ådal (201 coins) and Nydam Mose (56 coins), but there is also a number of minor denarius hoards (Hvornum Kær, Ginderup, Dankirke East and West), a Hacksilber hoard with siliquae (Simmersted Moor), a gold hoard including two Late Roman solidi (Års), and a bracteate hoard with a Late Roman solidus (Apholm). Denarii are found in most

---

105 080405 sb 35: The coin found in 1819 was registered as NM I CXIX, but was lost before 1943. It was described as having traces of gilding. The second find was registered and photographed by Odense Bys Museer (OBM 8759), it is presently in private possession; *AUD* 2001, 243.
106 090605 sb 55: FP 1968; Breitenstein 1943, 6 XI.
107 090510 sb 117: FP 3460; Kromann 1983-84, 72 no. 14.
108 080710 sb 37: a lost denarius from Wedelsborg; 080609 sb 55: NM I C7775; Breitenstein 1943, 5 IX, from Moderup.
109 090610 sb 152: FP 1432; Breitenstein 1943, 4 VI, from Nyborg (probably in secondary position); 090513 without sb no.: FP 6772 found in a garden that is known to have had soil brought in.

110 080404 sb 30: FP 2657; Horsnæs 2006a, cat.no. 44.
111 080407 sb 206: FP 3571; Horsnæs 2006a, cat.no. 73.
112 080201 sb 9: FP 1681 and sb 22: FP 1179; Horsnæs 2006a, cat.nos. 93 and 72b.
113 090510 without sb no.: FP 3643; Horsnæs 2006a, cat.no. 94.

areas where Roman coins have been discovered, in contrast to the other denominations. Almost half the gold coins are found concentrated along the Lille Bælt coast, while the remaining finds are scattered throughout Jutland. This distribution may be related to the many gold coins found on Funen.

There are relatively many bronze coins and antoniniani, and they have been found scattered over most of Jutland. Some are from probably modern contexts – finds from urban areas and finds from areas that are most unlikely to have been settled/occupied in Pre-modern times – some are without doubt from Viking Age contexts (Ribe, Okholm, Stavnsager) or Medieval sites, and finally there are a few bronze coins that most likely derive from Iron Age sites. The latter tend to be found in areas with many denarius finds as well. As is the case in Funen and Sealand, detector sites with mainly Latest Iron Age, Viking Age and Medieval finds are sometimes yielding a single or a few Roman bronze coins. Some bronze coins have been found in connection with Medieval churches and/or monasteries.

No centres *a par* with Gudme have been identified, yet there are a number of Iron Age settlements with Roman coin finds. Many denarii are found in northern Jutland. Other clusters of sites have been found around Skanderborg in eastern Jutland and Ribe in south-western Jutland. The largest number of denarii derives from the weapon sacrifices in the moors at Illerup and Nydam, and a good parallel for these is the Thorsberg find just across the border in Northern Germany. The weapon sacrifice at Ejsbøl on the other hand yielded no denarii, but two bronze coins and an aureus.

4.3.1 Northern Jutland and the Limfjord area

The densest cluster of sites with Roman coin finds in Jutland is the area around Aalborg. The vast detector areas west of Aalborg have yielded a large number of finds mainly dated in the Medieval period, but there are also at least four Roman coins from the Nørholm area:[114] one 2nd cent. sestertius and one siliqua,[115] one looped Constantinian bronze coin,[116] one denarius[117] and from the Sønderholm area a very worn coin with a relatively large copper content that however seems to be identifiable as a second denarius.[118] Another detector area with many finds from various periods from the Late Roman Iron Age to the Medieval Period is Drastrup immediately to the southwest of Aalborg, where five denarii have been found.[119] The Bejsebakken site, with numerous detector finds from the Iron Age to the Medieval Period, has yielded two denarii. Excavations of 50.000 m² have uncovered the main part of the settlement area with a total of 42 long houses and 350 *Grubenhäuser*, the majority of which have been dated in the Germanic Iron Age. The site is interpreted as a small permanent settlement, occasionally visited by traders and craftsmen. The Roman denarii were both detector finds and came from two places within the Bejsebakken that are situated at some distance.[120]

A site with Medieval coin finds and one Ancient (unidentified Greek or Roman) bronze coin has been identified at Sønder Tranders Church, southeast of Aalborg.[121] A few km to the north, on the Nørre Tranders Church hill, a single denarius was found in 1890.[122]

The important archaeological area, Lindholm Høje, at Nørre Sundby across the Limfjord just

---

114 120508 sb 54 *et al*. Poulsen 2008 has discussed the finds from Nørholm and the methodological problems regarding the Medieval coins finds from the site.
115 FP 5576.1-2; *AUD* 1995, 270 from sb 54.
116 FP 6700.3 (without sb no.).
117 FP 7167, from sb 51.
118 120511 sb 144: FP 7722.
119 120504 sb 16, Roman denarii dated from Hadrian to Marcus Aurelius: FP 5709 and 5710 (*AUD* 1997, 250), 6126, 6226 and 6237 (*AUD* 2000, 299). The coin finds have often been registered with the location "Skelagervej", but should in reality be labelled "western part of Bejsebakken". South of Bejsebakken the Sofiendal area has yielded other Medieval finds (sb 62) including coins (sb 62). On Bejsebakken see Nielsen 2002.
120 120506 sb 51 (Prehistoric finds), sb 56 (Medieval finds), sb 57 and 61 (coin finds). The Roman denarii are FP 4257.1 (Trajan; *AUD* 1985, 159) found on the original sb 64 and FP 4659 (Marcus Aurelius for Divus Antoninus; *AUD* 1989, 217) found on the original sb 56. On the site in general see J.N. Nielsen 2002.
121 120113; Ancient bronze coin FP 6702.19.
122 120108 sb 67: FP 576 (= NM I C 6658).

north of Aalborg has been known for more than a century. Several areas have been investigated among other things the Lindholm Høje cemetery (excavated in the 1950's) with more than 600 burials from the Late Roman Iron Age to the Viking Age.[123] Hvorup in the northern part of the area has yielded detector finds from Iron Age and Viking Period, including one Trajanic denarius,[124] and in the southern part of the area an extensive site with numerous Medieval coin finds has yielded three denarii, one Vespasian and two Septimius Severus.[125]

The common denominator of the Aalborg sites is the settlement continuity from the Late Roman Iron Age throughout the later Prehistoric periods and into the Medieval period. Bejsebakken and Lindholm Høje, situated on moraine hills on each side of the Limfjord, together controlled traffic from east to west, a position that they must have had since the Roman Iron Age. The sites at Nørholm and Sønder Tranders are both situated in a less strategic position, and they seem to have grown only in the later part of the Prehistoric phase. The Drastrup site is situated only few km south of the Bejsebakken complex, and may be seen in relation to this.

Lastly a single find of an antoninianus struck by Probus should be mentioned. The coin was found "while gardening in the outskirts of Aalborg". No more precise location can be given, but it is of course possible that it should be related to one of the now identified sites.[126]

A unique hoard consisting of Republican and early Imperial denarii as well as a single Neronian aureus was found deposited in connection with a house in the Ginderup settlement in Thisted county (section 5.3.2).[127] This area has so far given few other finds of Roman objects, but the most recent detector surveys from this area seem to indicate a more widespread finds pattern. The Vestervig Kirke site has now yielded two denarii, and in 2008 a second Nero aureus

Fig. 20. Coins from Øster Vandet. Scale c. 1:1. Photo John Lee/National Museum of Denmark.

from this county was found at the site.[128] Furthermore the Øster Vandet site, with among other things 10 denarii, was discovered in 2007/08 (*Fig. 20*).[129]

Several other sites in northern Jutland have yielded more than one denarius: North of the Limfjord are six sites with more than one denarius and five sites with a single find of a denarius.

Two denarii were found in 1962 in a field belonging to Overgård *c.* 1.5 km west of Torslev. No other Iron Age finds have been registered at this point, but *c.* 1 km north-west of Overgård is an area with traces of old field systems visible from the air.[130] In this part of northern Jutland Roman coins are otherwise rare.

Directly north of the Aalborg cluster more sites have been identified. Two sites have been found quite close to one another in Saltum parish. Two denarii were found at Torpet.[131] In 1985 a fragment of a Hadrian denarius was handed in with a modern coin[132] and in 2004 an unidentified, partly melted denarius came from the same site.[133] Here no other

---

123 120607 sb 20 designates the total area. The cemetery was published by Ramskou 1976.
124 120607 sb 14: FP 4628; *AUD* 1988, 201.
125 120608 sb 11. The denarii are FP 4165, 4376 (*AUD* 1986, 175) and 5420.
126 120108: FP 2155.
127 Bjerg 2007, 41-56.

128 110612 sb 419: FP 7524.10 and 7751 (denarii). The aureus has not yet been inventorized.
129 110213 sb 56.
130 100707 sb 96 and (fieldsystem) sb 89.
131 100406 sb 77.
132 FP 4557.
133 FP 7008.

finds are recorded, but at Lille Norge less than 2 km to the northwest of Torpet a large detector site with finds from Roman Iron Age to Medieval period has been identified.[134] Among the coin finds are seven denarii and three coins from the Medieval period:[135]

A single find of a Vespasian denarius was made while digging a trench for a drain pipe along a road in Stenum,[136] east/northeast of Saltum. The denarius was found in the soil from the trench probably dug up from *c.* 1 m depth. No other finds were noted at that time, but there are traces of Iron Age material at Skelgården *c.* 2 km west of Stenum.[137]

Three denarii have been found at Vester Mellerup[138] in an area close to a previous find of settlement and jewellery from the Roman Iron Age,[139] and immediately east of an area with traces of prehistoric field systems visible from the air.[140] This site was surrounded by wetlands even into the 18th century.

Stentinget at Klokkerholm has yielded two denarii.[141] The finds were made with detector on a hill north of Klokkerholm along with many other finds dating from the Early Roman Iron Age to the Medieval period. Trial excavations have produced graves (both inhumations and cremations) as well as *Grubenhäuser* and other settlement traces. At Ørum, southeast of Klokkerholm, a single denarius[142] was found with detector not far from the find spot of a gold bracteate[143] in an area where traces of old field systems are visible from the air,[144] and at Hjallerup Mose, southeast of Ørum, two denarii were found on the surface around 1921, probably dug up from a ditch.[145] The find spot of these coins have not been precisely located.

A settlement was located and partly excavated in 1986 and 1994/5 at Ejstrup north of Voldstrup church. The excavations revealed longhouses, *c.* 50 *Grubenhäuser* and remains of several fences dating from the Late Germanic and Viking Ages. After the excavations metal detector surveys have revealed a number of finds, among which were eight coins. Two of them were Roman denarii, struck by Domitian and Hadrian respectively, the remaining were dating from the 9th cent. to 1538.[146]

Further to the north there are three sites around Hjørring each with a single find of a denarius. Northeast of Hjørring is Gaarestrup where trial excavations in 1989 have uncovered part of a settlement area from Late Germanic Iron Age,[147] and subsequent surveys of the area have revealed finds from a chronologically broader spectre, among which eight Medieval coins and a single denarius struck during the reign of Septimius Severus.[148] The area is situated along the Liver Å (Stream), and across the stream are numerous finds from a larger settlement area of the Late Germanic and Viking Ages.[149] A denarius struck by Hadrian was found in 1921 by a man from Ugilt while ploughing a field. It is not certain whether the field was at the village of Ugilt or just somewhere in the parish of Ugilt southeast of Hjørring.[150] The last single find was an Antoninus Pius denarius, dug up "somewhere in Hjørring".[151]

Denarius finds are less densely distributed south of Limfjorden. The most important find is Malle Langhøj Syd. In 1938 Hatt undertook the first excavations at Malle Degnegård, and the area was investigated again in 1980.[152] Trial excavations at Malle Langhøj Syd, *c.* 100 m south of Hatt's excavations, in 2001 revealed more traces of an Iron Age settlement, and

---

134 100406 sb 78.
135 FP 5990.1-2 and 6231.1-5; Medieval period FP 6231.6-8.
136 100111 sb 20: FP 2301; Balling 1962, 38-39 no. 25.
137 100111 sb 11.
138 100106 sb 183: FP 5375.1-2; *AUD* 1994, 257 and FP 5984; *AUD* 1999, 276.
139 Norling-Christensen 1942.
140 100106 sb 71.
141 100205 sb 164: FP 5012.1-2; *AUD* 1991, 228.
142 100215 sb 50: FP 5046, *AUD* 1991, 228.
143 100215 sb 36.
144 100215 sb 39.
145 100203 sb 383: FP 1553; Balling 1962, 47 no. 44.1-2 and fig. 6.

---

146 100214 sb 150 and sb 175: FP 5849.1-8; *AUD* 1986, 93-94 and Michaelsen 1989-1990 (on sb 150); *AUD* 1994, 156-157 and 1995, 161 (on sb 175); *AUD* 1998, 291 (coin finds).
147 100612 sb 86, *AUD* 1989, 149.
148 100612 sb 77: FP 5275.1-7 and 6280 (Medieval coins) and FP 5276 (denarius), *AUD* 1993, 252.
149 100614 sb 46.
150 100617 sb 92: FP 1508; Balling 1962, 45 no. 36.
151 Kromann 1983-4, 62 no. 4.
152 120707 sb 23; Hatt 1938; Nielsen 1980.

detector finds made during the excavations include two denarii, both however found out of context.[153]

The only other finds from Aalborg county (excluding the sites in the Aalborg area treated above) are two single finds, one from Illerknoppen in Alsted parish[154] and another from Ejstrup in St. Brøndum parish,[155] but none of them can with certainty be related to other finds.

Further to the south the westernmost site with denarius finds is Ryde Mølle with two denarii and four Roman bronze coins. At Toftum, *c.* 14 km west of Viborg, two denarii have been found in connection with a settlement with traces of houses as well as material dating from the Early Roman Iron Age to the Germanic Iron Age.[156] On a plateau rising abruptly above Kvosted Å (Stream) detector surveys in early 2008 have yielded three denarii and a sestertius. The site is situated *c.* 14 km northwest of Viborg as the crow flies, but more importantly in this connection is probably its position less than 2 km from Hjarbæk Fjord, which is part of the Limfjorden, on a well protected area surrounded by three streams. Other detector finds from the area include material dated to the Germanic Iron Age until the Medieval period.[157] This find casts new light on the isolated find in 1955 of a denarius struck by Hadrian on the beach "near Hjarbæk" only *c.* 4 km from the Kvosted site.[158] Two other single finds are known from Viborg county: a now lost denarius struck by Antoninus Pius was found in 1693 in a moor "close to Viborg"[159] and at Gudenåen close to Bjerringbro a fragmented Vespasian denarius was found with detector in 1988.[160] None of the single finds can be pinpointed geographically.

A denarius hoard consisting of 23 coins has been found at Hvornum Kær (section 5.2.2 and *Fig. 37*). Djursland has yielded two single finds of denarii. The first is a Marcus Aurelius from Ryomgård Skov, where settlement material but no structural remains have been identified from Late Pre-Roman Iron Age as well as from the Late Iron Age (*Fig. 21*).[161] The other denarius, struck by Trajan, was found in 1942 on the surface in a market garden in Grenå, where Late Medieval coins had previously been found. However, it cannot be excluded that soil has been brought into the market garden to improve the natural soil conditions; therefore this denarius may be regarded as in secondary position.

4.3.2 Eastern Jutland

The most important Roman coin find in eastern Jutland is the Illerup Ådal weapon sacrifice, but although situated physically in eastern Jutland, we cannot know whence the warriors, whose equipment was sacrificed, came. Therefore this find will be treated below, in connection with the Roman coins from other weapon sacrifices from Danish/Nordic moors (section 5.2.1).

The Katrinelund settlement *c.* 10 km east-northeast of Silkeborg has yielded no less than seven Roman denarii, ranging in time from Otho to Commodus. The settlement was excavated in 1985 and 1987. It stretches over more than 400 m developing from a Late Roman Iron Age phase in the eastern part of the excavated area to the Early Germanic Iron Age in the western part.[162] All denarii were found in plough soil in the western area, i.e. the area settled in the Early Germanic Iron Age. The first denarius was found during the excavations,[163] while the remaining six denarii were found during detector surveys in the years following the excavations (*Fig. 61*).[164] It has been suggested that the denarii might represent a ploughed up hoard, but the find circumstances do not support this view. The coins were found in plough soil, indeed the majority were found after the excavations, where the soil heaps have been moved

---

153 120707 sb 64, see also sb 67 for an overall view of the area: FP 6275; Bjerg 2007, 81-83.
154 120201: FP 6294. The denarius was allegedly found southwest of sb 54; *AUD* 2001, 245.
155 120312: FP 3014; Kromann 1983-84, 62 no. 3.
156 130110 sb 106: FP 6236, *AUD* 2000, 300-301 (coins) and 2001, 147 (excavation).
157 130114 sb 147-148: FP 7794-95.
158 130816 sb 157: FP 2451; Balling 1962, 44-45, no. 35.
159 130815 without sb no.; Galster 1936, 41; Balling 1962, 47-48 no. 45. Cf. also Chapter 8.
160 130702 without sb no.: FP 4630, *AUD* 1988, 201. Only half the coin is preserved.

161 141011 sb 70: FP 6637.
162 160115 sb 198; Bjerring Jensen in Hertz 1987, 318-319; *AUD* 1985, 112 no. 274.
163 FP 4333; *AUD* 1985, 162.
164 FP 4639.1-2, 4678.1, 4788.1-2, 5145.1.

Fig. 21. The denarius from Ryomgård Skov has a high copper content, and it is badly preserved. Marcus Aurelius, reverse Provindentia, struck 161-162. FP 6637. Scale 2:1. Photo HWH.

around by heavy machinery, and we might as well interpret them as a series of single finds. Yet, it must be underlined that they were all found in connection with the part of the settlement dated in the Early Germanic Iron Age, and although sporadic finds from the Roman Iron Age have been made in this area, a deposition date for the denarii in the beginning of phase D is the more likely.[165]

A denarius hoard consisting of eight coins as well as a single find of a denarius were found at Testrup Teglværk, c. 14 km east of Skanderborg (*Fig. 38*). Single finds have been made on five other sites in the area around Skanderborg.[166] A Trajan denarius was found around 1850 while working the fields of Rathlousdal, c. 18 km southeast of Skanderborg.[167] In the mid-19th century Rathlousdal Manor owned extensive areas and the exact find spot therefore cannot be pinpointed. A Vespasian denarius was found 1949 on a field in Sim c. 10 km northwest of Skanderborg. The same field has later yielded pottery and a burnt down house dated in the Early Roman Iron Age.[168] Also a denarius struck by Marcus Aurelius for Commodus Caesar may originally derive from Sim. The coin was found in a garden in Ry only 5 km west of Sim, but it is known that soil had been brought in from Sim.[169] Also a field in Hem, on the south bank of Mossø c. 7 km south of Sim, has yielded a single denarius, but the exact find spot is not recorded. Lastly a denarius was found in the garden belonging to the farm "Fredens Hjem" near Ejer Bavnehøj. No other Iron Age finds are recorded from the immediate vicinity.[170]

4.3.3 Central, western and southern Jutland

The central part of Jutland is completely void of denarius finds. The two most important finds from the southernmost part of Jutland are the coins from the weapon sacrifices at Ejsbøl[171] and Nydam[172] (cf. below). Few single finds have been made in the bottom of the East Jutland fjords across the Lille Bælt from Funen. One find of a denarius of Antoninus Pius from Magstrup parish (formerly Maugstrup) northwest of Haderslev is mentioned in a description of the parish from 1775 as found on "Stevnhøj, a heathen *tingsted* (place where the court sits)" situated west of Magstrup town.[173] Another early find is from Volmerstoft on the Nyhus Lake at the bottom of the Flensborg Fjord on the border between Denmark and Germany, where a Trajanic denarius was found before 1860 at the foot of a longish hill. The name Volmerstoft appears on a *Generalstabskort* from 1858 and is identical with the farm Oldemorstoft or Valdemarstoft. The exact find spot within this farm cannot be pinpointed.[174]

On the western coast of southern Jutland, close to Ribe, a number of prominent sites seem to herald the later importance of the area, and a considerable number of these sites have yielded Roman coins. A Republican denarius struck by Gaius Porcius Cato in 137-134 BC was found on Ulhøj (today Ulvehøj) north of Vester Vedsted. Several surface finds from the area date the site to the Late Roman and Early Germanic Iron Ages, and there seems to be no reason to believe that the coin has been lost/deposited

---

165 Bjerg 2007, 77-80. Also nine Medieval coins (FP 4678.2-3, 4788.3-4, 5145.2, 5345, 5740.2-3, 5741) and one dirham (FP 5740.1) have been found in Katrinelund, all, however, outside the area with the denarius finds.
166 150406 sb 36: Dnf. 11/06 (hoard) and C 14079; Balling 1962, 42-44 and 48.
167 150210 without sb no.; C 6657; Balling 1962, 40 no. 28.
168 160203 sb 216: FP 2269; Balling 1962, 38 no. 24.

169 FP 3841; Kromann 1983-84, 63 no. 6.
170 160507 without sb no.; FP1729; Balling 1962, 45 no. 38.
171 200302 sb 19.
172 230304 sb 30.
173 200205 without sb no; Galster 1937, 85.
174 220102 without sb no.; lost, Balling 1962, 41 no. 30.

on the site before the Late Roman Iron Age.[175] Two denarii were found at Skanet Bro in a soil deposit belonging to the Highway Authority together with some pottery fragments and some iron that, however, were not collected by the finder. These denarii must be regarded as found in secondary contexts and cannot be taken as evidence for Prehistoric activities on the site.[176]

In Gammel Hviding three Roman coins have been found.[177] Two of the coins were denarii, and they were found in the north-western part of an area,[178] where extensive remains of a settlement with several houses covering the period from Pre-Roman Iron Age to Early Roman Iron Age were located. There are furthermore detector finds from the Late Roman and Early Germanic Iron Age, but only a few pits can be dated in this phase. From the 8th century the area is resettled. The third coin was found already in 1923 on a field in the eastern part of the area.[179] The denomination of the coin is not recorded, and the coin was never handed in to the authorities. Later air reconnaissance of the area has shown traces of a probable settlement, and ploughed up pottery seems to indicate a date for this settlement in the Late Roman / Early Germanic Iron Age.

In older literature the find of a denarius in an urn at Ribe has been mentioned.[180] In reality, this find could have been made anywhere near Ribe, where there is so far no evidence of occupation in the Roman or Early Germanic Iron Ages. As we shall see Roman coins are only rarely found in connection with burials in Denmark, which should call for caution when using this information.

The last single find of a Roman denarius to be mentioned is a worn Trajanic denarius from Holmslands Klit, the thin isthmus closing Ringkjøbing Fjord off from the North Sea. The denarius was one of at least 70, mostly Medieval and Pre-modern, coins from various areas of Holmsland Klit found within a short period.[181] Not far from this group of coins, an unusual find of a quinarius (also struck by Trajan) has been made.[182] Also this area has yielded many other coin finds from various periods. What today is a continuous isthmus closing Ringkøbing Fjord, was at least until the 17th century a line of islands, controlling the entrance to Ringkøbing Fjord, and the finds from the area south of Sønder Haurvig have been interpreted as the remains of an anchorage situated on one of these islands at the entrance to the Fjord. The vast majority of the finds are, however, from the Medieval period, and the two Roman coins are in themselves not enough to postulate the presence of an Iron Age settlement on the site.[183]

---

175 190411 sb 26: FP 1819, Balling 1962, 6 no. 1 (Sydenham 417). Jensen 1998, vol. 2, 123 no. 15-807. I thank Claus Feveile for additional information on the site.
176 190408 sb 7: FP 3046, Kromann 1983-84, 63 no. 7.
177 210103 sb 109.
178 In sb 57: FP 6283.1, *AUD* 2001, 247, and in sb 85: FP 7136.1 (unpubl.).
179 sb 4.
180 190406 without sb no.; Balling 1962, 70 with reference to Aarbøger for Nordisk Oldkyndighed 1875, 39.
181 180404 sb 18: FP 4051.57.
182 180404 sb 10: FP 4514.1 and RIM 6713; *AUD* 1987, 220.
183 Eriksen 2000.

CHAPTER 5

Context types

The find contexts of the Roman coins from Denmark are of major importance for the understanding of the use of the coins. First of all the contexts, and the dating of them, are the only means to date the deposition more closely than the *post quem* date provided by the coins themselves. Secondly the contexts are of prime importance if we are to achieve an understanding of the functions of the coins within the local society.

The Roman coins from Denmark have been found in a number of different contexts. The most important finds in this connection are the relatively small number of coins found *in situ* with datable material. These are the coins from archaeologically dated contexts such as graves, weapon deposits, mixed hoards, and finally a very small number of the many coins from settlements.

The majority of the coins are detector finds that have normally been found out of primary contexts. The importance of the evidence drawn from the detector finds, however, cannot be neglected. The coins of course still provide a *post quem* date, and the range of dates of other finds from the same site gives a hint as to the possible period of use of the coins. Moreover, the coins from the detector sites can often be inserted into debates of the function of the coins within the settlement and of the settlement hierarchy.

5.1 Coins found in graves

Coins found in graves constitute a relatively low number of finds, but the group is of outmost importance. The single graves provide chronological evidence about the deposition date of the coins. Furthermore this particular context type can give evidence both about the ritual connected with the burial and the possible meaning of the coin in this connection, and about the more profane daily use of the coins in the Iron Age society.[1] Unfortunately the burials with coins are not evenly distributed throughout the country, by far the largest number has been found in Sealand, fewer in Funen, and only one – perhaps two coins – found in Jutland is related to the funerary sphere.

5.1.1 Sealand

The most recent find of a coin in a grave was excavated at Brøndsager in 1997-98.[2] A *c.* 12 years old boy was buried with rich grave goods including among many other things two Roman glass vessels, a snake

---

1 The graves with coin finds have been listed several times: Nielsen 1987-88; Lund Hansen 1995, 240; Ethelberg 2000, 90-91.
2 020213 sb 34: FP 6095; Mahler 1999, 34-35; Fonnesbech-Sandberg 2004; Fonnesbech-Sandberg 2004b, in particular p. 99.

Fig. 22. Reconstruction of the necklace from Stålmosegård, Vindinge. Scale c. 1:1. Photo Roskilde Museum.

head gold ring, a gaming board with glass pieces. The looped coin, a Barbarian imitation of an aureus, was part of a small necklace also containing three beads of bronze, one of amber and two of glass. Two contemporary graves were found, one was the burial of an adult male, the other of a girl of one and a half years. This small family plot was situated in an area with settlement remains, and the boy's grave actually cuts a building from the transition between the Early and Late Roman Iron Age. The grave goods from the burial as a whole are dated in C2 (traditionally dated 250/260-310/320 AD) and even in the earlier part of the phase,[3] but it should be noted that the aureus imitation may date *c.* 300 AD or even in the early 4th century, thus providing the grave with a *t.p.q.* later than the date suggested here. Houses that are regarded to be contemporary with the burials were found some 200 m to the north of the cemetery.

At Torstorp Vesterby, not far from Brøndsager, eight graves were excavated in 1989. It is assumed that the burials are connected to a single farm that can be followed in many phases through centuries.[4] Seven of the burials were childrens' graves; the last was the burial of an adult of *c.* 25 years. The adult's grave goods consisted among other things of a Roman glass vessel and a silver fibula, and a long three-rowed necklace consisting of 482 beads indicates that the buried person was a woman. A looped siliqua struck in Nicomedeia during the reign of Constantius II (340-351 AD) was part of the necklace. The burial was dated in period C3 (310/320 – *c.* 375 AD).

At Stålmosegård/Vindinge close to Roskilde more than 100 graves dating from the Late Roman Iron Age and Early Migration Period have been unearthed in several excavation campaigns in 1971-2004.[5] In 1988 an extremely rich female grave was excavated.

---

3 Fonnesbech-Sandberg 2004b, 100: "C2 probably early part".

4 020207 sb 20: FP 5164; Fonnesbech-Sandberg 1990, in particular 56-59; Mahler 1999, 40.

5 020512 sb 4: ROM inv. no. 555/83; *AUD* 1988, 101; Kromann 1995, 349 no. 39A; Birkebæk 1997, 30-31 (photo); Høj 2005.

Context types

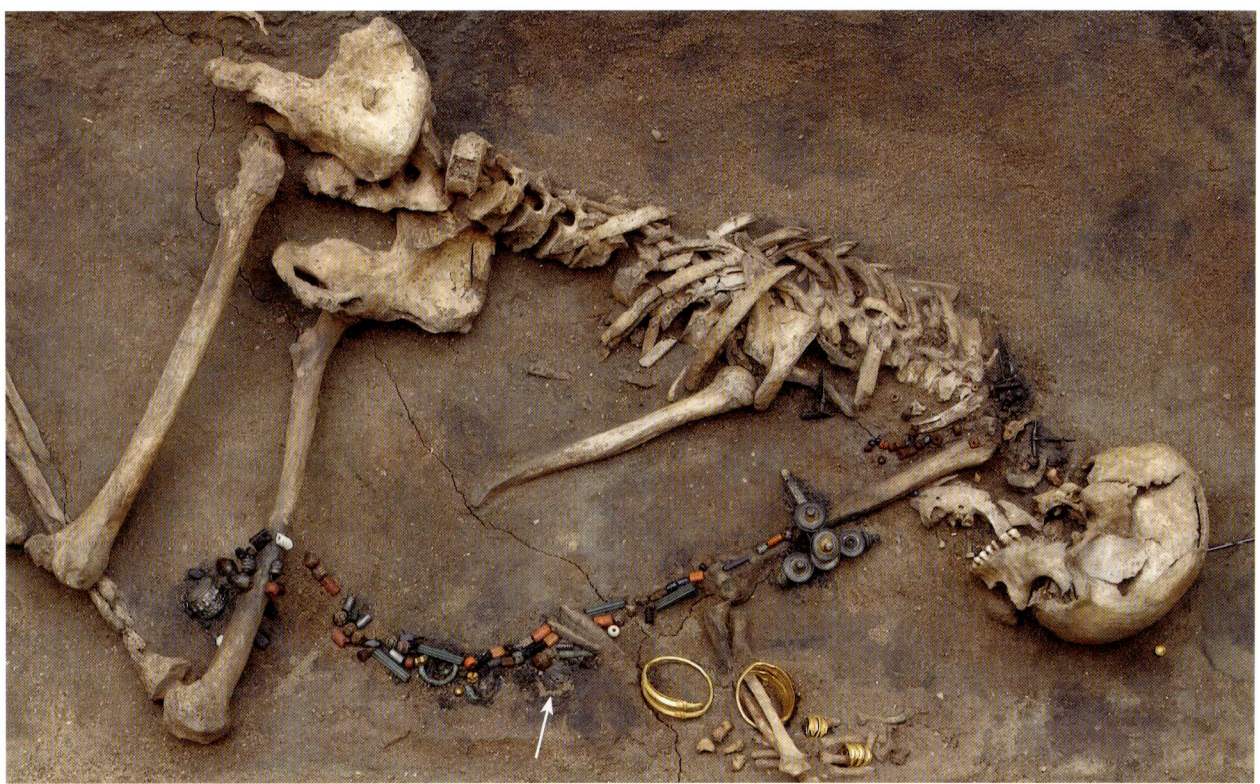

Fig. 23. Himlingøje grave 1949-2. The position of the denarius is indicated by an arrow. Photo John Lee/National Museum of Denmark.

She carried a necklace with four or five rows with a total of more than 300 beads of glass and amber attached to fibulas. Among the beads was a denarius struck for Commodus Caesar during the reign of Marcus Aurelius. Another important feature of the rows of beads was a small ring of bronze to which two amber beads and an imported bladdernut (*staphylea*) was attached.

A cemetery consisting of 18 female burials was excavated at Skovgårde in southern Sealand in 1988. All the burials took place within the period from 200/210 to 260/270 AD, and they are richly furnished. A denarius struck under Hadrian and mounted in a bronze frame with a loop was part of the long necklace of the woman buried in Grave 209. This outstanding grave also contained a large rosetta fibula with a Runic inscription found on the breast of the deceased.[6]

The famous Himlingøje cemetery consists of at least 13, and perhaps up to 20 burials. It is commonly interpreted as the cemetery of a princely dynasty. The graves have extremely rich grave goods including a large number of Roman imports, many of which are unique. Grave 1949-2 was recovered in 1949 and taken as a whole to the National Museum where it is presently exhibited. The deceased woman was 35-55 years old at the time of death. She was lying on her left side with the grave goods – Roman glass and bronze vessels – collected at her feet and her personal objects including among other things gold ornaments, fibulas, one of which is a rosetta fibula with a Runic inscription, a hair pin and jewellery *in situ*. Her large necklace included a denarius stuck by Titus (79-81 AD). The coin was pierced below the head of the emperor.[7] The burial is dated in period C1b (*c.* 210/20-250/60 AD).

---

6   050212 sb 27: SMV inv. no. 7021x1209; *AUD* 1988, 108; Ethelberg 2000, 89 and *passim*.

7   050105 sb 11 and sb 29: FP 2236; Lund Hansen 1995, 152-158 (catalogue) and *passim*, the obverse of the coin is illustrated (**laterally reversed**) on fig. 4:28.

Nine graves were excavated in 1873-1882 at Nordrup.[8] The cemetery yielded very rich graves equipped with among other things painted circus beakers and gaming pieces. An Antoninus Pius denarius struck in 159-160 AD was found in Grave H (excavated 1882), which in comparison with the other burials held less prominent objects: a silver fibula, two thin gold rings, a bone comb, a Hemmoor bucket, and three ceramic jars. The body was lying in supine position, oriented north/south with the head in the southern end of the grave. The coin was found next to the comb below the left knee of the deceased, who – based on the grave goods – was probably an adult male. The burial was dated in period C1b (*c.* 210/20-250/60 AD).

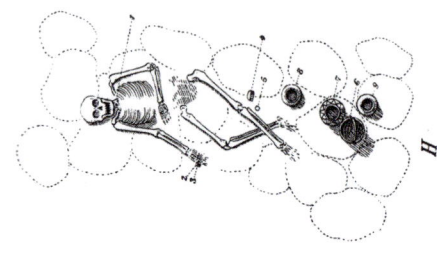

Fig. 24. Nordrup grave H, excavation plan and section. The denarius was found next to a bone comb at the left knee. It is marked as no. 5 on the plan. After Petersen 1890, fig. 6.

In 1874 a burial of a *c.* 30 years old, frail woman was recovered in Nyrup, close to Nykøbing Sjælland on the north-western tip of Sealand. Finds include pottery, a wooden bucket, a Roman glass vessel, gold and silver jewellery, and a very large number of beads: 734 of glass and 484 of amber. There were furthermore three coins, one solidus and two siliquae. They were probably all looped.[9] The skeleton was probably in supine position with the head in the southern end of the grave. The coins were found in the centre of the grave, where also the majority of the beads were situated, the many beads, however, extended towards the feet of the deceased. It seems possible to interpret the coins as part of a lavish necklace of a type similar to the ones from Torstorp, Stålmosegård, Skovgårde and Himlingøje. The Nyrup burial plays a considerable role in the discussion of Iron Age chronologies as it is considered *the* (only) "Leitfund" for Egger's period C3 (310/20-375 AD).[10]

Grave "a" was the richest burial in the Varpelev cemetery excavated in 1876-77. The remains of an adult male were found lying supine in a long grave lined with stones. At each end of the grave were rich grave goods including a number of Roman imports, the best known of which is a glass vessel mounted in silver with a Greek inscription. The man wore gold finger rings, one of which was a snake head finger ring, and a gold necklace (or a large bracelet) was found on his chest together with a gold dress pin. A looped aureus struck under Probus (276-282 AD) was found at his right ear.[11] The deposition is traditionally dated in period C2, but also a date in period C3 has been suggested. The latter date seems preferable in light of not only some of the grave goods that seem to be more closely related to a C3 milieu, but also the coin may paradoxically point in this direction, as other 3rd century aurei have mainly been found in 4th century contexts.[12]

A rich burial with Roman artefacts was unearthed at Bennebo Mark in Holbæk county in 1857. The body was described as lying supine with the head to the south. On the second day of the excavation a denarius struck by Antoninus Pius (145-147 AD) was found 20 *tommer* (inches, *c.* 42 cm) east of the body.

---

8   040211 sb 17: NM I C4823; Petersen 1890-1903; Breitenstein 1946, 13 no. 15; Kromann 1995, 358 Taf. 13:II, no. 23.

9   030405 sb 100: NM I C1975-1996, coins are nos. C1975-76; Engelhardt 1877, 370-372. Bibliography in Lund Hansen 1987, 411.

10 Lund Hansen 1987, 31.

11 050613 sb 8: NM I C 3067; Engelhardt 1877, 350-359; Jørgensen *et al.* 2003, 396 no. 4.14.

12 Lund Hansen 1987; Grane 2007, 182 dated the burial in period C2, but noted the many "first occurences" in the deposition.

Fig. 25. Grave goods from Varpelev grave "a". Photo Kit Weiss/National Museum of Denmark.

The grave goods, including among other things a spiraliform gold finger-ring, silver fibulas and Roman bronze vessels, were not gender characteristic, and skeletal remains were reburied and thus cannot yield any information on the sex of the deceased.[13] The burial was dated in period C1b (*c.* 210/20-250/60 AD).

In 1818 the Queen, represented by count Molkte, donated a number of objects to Museet for Nordiske Oldsager, the forerunner of the National Museum. The objects were found together with skeletons at Gunnerupgård Mark in Herfølge parish. There can be no doubt that the finds came from a number of destroyed burials from the Late Roman Iron Age, but only high status finds were handed in and these finds hint that only a selection of the grave goods from each grave was saved. More humble objects (for example pottery) were probably discarded. The objects from grave 2 included a Roman bronze basin, bronze fittings from a wooden bucket, some amber beads, a rectangular piece of glass mosaic, and a denarius struck for Lucius Verus.[14] The position of the objects within the grave was not noted. The ensemble is dated in period C1b-C2 (*c.* 210/20-310/20 AD).

Thomas Bartholin in 1689 made one of the earliest descriptions of a coin found in connection with human remains. The coin was mentioned after a note on the Kinbjerg coin, a uniface gold coin imitation of a Late Roman solidus (*Figs. 2-3*), and compared to this coin: "as regards the image, I have a silver coin [only] slightly dissimilar, found in a human skull at Little Næstved". This coin has been interpreted as a Roman denarius,[15] but the image on the Kinbjerg coin is an *en face* representation of the emperor, which has no parallels among Roman silver coins. I therefore find it more likely that Bartholin's silver coin was not a denarius, but a somewhat later (Medieval or Early Renaissance?) coin.

5.1.2 Funen

To date 2023 burials have been excavated in the vast cemetery at Møllegårdsmarken.[16] All burials, except eight, were cremations. In the majority of the burials (1169) the cremated remains were found within an urn. As a general rule, relatively few objects were found in the graves at Møllegårdsmarken, and many graves had no grave goods at all. The most common grave goods were beads (normally of glass), combs, fibulas, knives and jewellery, in short personal objects. Among the grave goods local objects prevail, but 106 of the graves contained a total of 170 imported objects, from the earliest phases many bronze

---

13 030710: NM I 16388; Lund Hansen 1976; Kromann 1995, 358 Taf. 13:II, 19.
14 050104 sb 58: NM I inv. no. XCVI (1817); *Antiquariske Annaler* III, 1820, 370, XCVI; the coin should be handed over to a representative of the Coin Cabinet in 1820, but there is no trace of it in the The Royal Coll. of Coins and Medals, cf. Breitenstein 1946, 15-16.

15 Galster 1936, 30, followed by Breitenstein 1946, 27-28.
16 Site 090107 sb 156. Albrectsen 1971.

containers, ladles and sieves, while the Late Roman periods II and III yielded only glass, a couple of sigillata vases and in four of the urn burials a Roman coin was found:

- Grave 1503, urn burial dated in per. III, contained a piece of stamped silver foil and a denarius struck in 159-160 AD. The bones were identified as an adult woman (*adultus*).[17]
- Grave 1715, urn burial dated in per. III, contained a worn denarius struck for Faustina Minor, the bones were identified as an elderly person (*senilis*) of unidentified sex.[18]
- Grave 1755, urn burial dated in per. II or III, contained a set of pincers, an ear pick, and a much worn denarius struck for Faustina Major. Sex and age of the deceased could not be determined on basis of the bones.[19]
- Grave 1796a, urn burial dated per. II, contained remains of a bone comb, six melted fragments of a bronze vase/jar of unidentified type, and an aureus struck during the reign of Caracalla. A fragment above the head of the emperor on the aureus from Møllegårdsmarken grave 1796a has been broken off, and it has been suggested that the coin may have been looped. None of the other coins – all denarii – were reworked.

Apart from the coins found inside the urns, the Møllegårdsmarken cemetery has yielded three single finds of denarii and fragments of two(?) solidi (*Fig. 26*), all found out of contexts.[20] The function of these coins in the cemetery is of course extremely difficult to establish: it is possible that they once were deposited in now disturbed burials, but they may also be seen as remains of post-burial sacrifices, or they were simply accidentally lost by persons visiting the cemetery.

Fig. 26. Fragments of solidi from Møllegårdsmarken. Scale 2:1. Photo Jørgen Nielsen/Odense Bys Museer.

The Bregentved cemetery in Central Funen was discovered in 1912, and 55 cremation graves were excavated. In 1988-1991 the remaining parts of the cemetery were investigated, and a total of almost 200 graves have now been excavated. The cemetery presents a horizontal stratigraphy extending downhill from the highest point of the cemetery, where a rich male burial dated *c.* AD 100 was situated. The majority of the graves were cremations, but at the periphery of the cemetery 22 inhumation graves were situated. Among them, the relatively short (length 1.55 m) Grave LØ contained a burial equipped with a jar and an iron knife. Three amber beads and a denarius with a drilled hole were found within an area of *c.* 30 cm across, and they probably made up a necklace. Furthermore some eyes and hooks of silver were found. They were probably used for the dress, as was a bronze fibula.[21]

A very rich male grave was found in Hågerup in 1932. It was partly excavated by laymen. It was a large grave, lined with stones and with remains of a wooden coffin. The skeleton was lying on its right side with the head in the southern end of the grave, facing northeast. The grave goods included a large number of Roman imports among which was a Roman gold finger-ring with an onyx gem, a silver bowl, and arrow heads. Under the upper part of the right lower jaw was a gold spiral. A denarius, struck in 137 AD for L. Aelius Caesar, was placed at – or perhaps in – the mouth of the deceased.[22] The burial is nor-

---

17 FP 2897.3.
18 FP 2897.2.
19 FP 2961.
20 FP 4564; *AUD* 1988, 198 (denarius, Vespasian). FP 7436.1 (Republican denarius, Crawford 1974, 511/3 = Sydenham 1952, 1344-1345) and FP 7436.2 (unidentified Imperial denarius). OBM 872x4621: fragments of one or more Late Roman solidi; Horsnæs 2009, 257 no. 11b.

---

21 FP 5072, site 090108 sb 11. Henriksen 1989 (on the cemetery in general); *AUD* 1991, 151 find no. 152; *AUD* 1992, 251; Henriksen 1992.
22 NM I C23248-23259 and DNF 30/32-38/32, the coin is no. 34/32, site 090403-34. On the position of

mally dated in period C1b (*c.* 210/20-250/60 AD),[23] but it also has parallels in Leuna 1917-2[24] dated in C2 (*c.* 250/60-310/20), and a number of the imported objects (silver spoon (cochlear) and bowls and the signet ring) are normally found in C2 contexts.

The double grave at Årslev was found in 1820.[25] Two skeletons were found next to each other only 2 *alen* (*c.* 1.25 m) apart. The extremely rich grave goods, including Roman imports as well as gold jewellery from non-Roman areas of south-eastern Europe, were all found with the westernmost skeleton. A physician in Odense examined the skeletal remains of this burial and described them as probably from an adult female, while the remains of the other individual were never examined. The jewellery as well as a Barbarian imitation of an aureus and a rock crystal /quartz ball inscribed with the Greek word ΑΒΛΑΘΑΝΑΛΒΑ[26] were all found at the head or breast of the deceased. The dating of the Årslev burial has been debated. Lund Hansen placed the Årslev burial as the typologically latest deposition in her phase C2 (*c.* 250/60-310/20).[27] In a specialized study of the burial Storgaard dated it in period C3 (*c.* 310/20-375),[28] but he later revised his view and argued for a date in period D, in absolute years no earlier than the last quarter of the 4th century, and he quoted parallels for the find in south-eastern European period D2a (dated 400/410-420/430 AD).[29] The close connections to the Brangstrup Hoard (*t.p.q.* 336 AD, but possibly deposited sometime later) and the exquisite hoard from Simleul-Silvanei, seems to favour a dating of the burial in the second half of the 4th century i.e. late in period C or early in period D.

5.1.3 Jutland

A grave from period B1/B2a with a coin was found in Bæk in southern Jutland. The dead person was buried in a north/south oriented trunk coffin, lined and covered with stones. Around the grave was an empty zone, which again was enclosed by a circular or oval stone paving. Clearly no small effort was taken to construct this tomb. In the eastern end of the grave were a jar and a bowl, and in the western end a single spur. In the middle of the grave, at the southern side, was a Roman aureus struck in Lyons in AD 36/37 during the reign of Tiberius. Other fragments of pottery and a fragment of a bronze pin were found in the store layer above the grave.[30] The dead man belonged to the higher level of the community, as evidenced by the monumental tomb, as well as by the presence of the spur and the coin.

5.1.4 Possible grave finds?

Apart from these examples of coins found in or in close connection with the burial, there are a number of coins found on sites from where grave finds are reported, but where the connection between the coin and the grave cannot be ascertained.

At Bringstrup between Ringsted and Slagelse in Sealand a denarius was found by an amateur detectorist working in connection with an archaeological investigation. The coin was struck by Marcus Aurelius for Lucilla. Also two fibulas as well as some Medieval coins were retrieved, while the excavation yielded only remains of a pit containing Bronze Age pottery. The investigation took place in an area where – according to tradition – "Queen Beren's grave" had once been found.[31] It seems that this legend has sprung from the actual find of a rich burial from the Roman Iron Age, no further remains of this were, however, discovered.[32]

Burials from the Roman Iron Age have been found at Englerup southwest of Ringsted at several instances. The burials in general seem to have been

---

the coin, cf. Protocol of NM I.
23 Lund Hansen 1987; Ethelberg 2000.
24 Werner 1989, 123.
25 NM I 8571, site 090619-4. Mackeprang 1940; Albrectsen 1968, 79-80, 301, 316; Storgaard 1990.
26 The inscription is interpreted as a variation of the seemingly meaningless palindrome ΑΒΛΑΝΑΘΑΝΑΛΒΑ that is connected to Gnostic circles. Mackeprang 1940, 94; Imer 2007, 71; Pentz 2007.
27 Bemmann 2006, 29.
28 Storgaard 1990.
29 Storgaard 1997.

30 200206 sb 215: FP 2217; Korthauer 1995-96.
31 Queen Berengaria, second wife to Valdemar II, died 1220/21 and was buried in the church of Sct. Bendt, Ringsted.
32 040203 sb 2: FP 5985.1 (denarius) and FP 5985.2-4 (Danish Medieval coins struck by Erik of Pomerania and Erik Menved).

quite poor containing only few grave goods.³³ The Hadrianic denarius found by an amateur detectorist in an area southwest of the burials can only with some caution be related to the cemetery.³⁴

Similarly a denarius found together with an English coin (Edward the Confessor)³⁵ some hundred meters from an Iron Age cemetery at Egholm-Nord in northern Sealand, can only be tentatively related to the burials. Again the burials seemed quite poor, and they were badly destroyed. The excavator dated them in the Roman Iron Age, perhaps in the Early Roman Iron Age.³⁶

Funen has also yielded a number of examples where Roman coins might have been related to funerary contexts. A denarius struck in 175-176 AD was among several objects bought by the Fyns Stiftsmuseum in 1907. The objects came from a number of burials, probably including both cremations and inhumations, from Fjelsted Mark. The objects as a whole should be dated in the Late Roman Iron Age, and it is quite possible that the coin originated from one of these disturbed graves.³⁷

A denarius struck for Lucius Verus came to the National Museum in 1887. It was allegedly found in Skrillinge Mark, but having passed through several owners in the area, the exact find spot is unknown.³⁸ In the same period several graves from the Roman Iron Age were excavated in the area, and more recently settlement remains from the Early Roman Iron Age have been investigated.³⁹ The area was certainly occupied in the Roman Iron Age, and the coin find is therefore not surprising, yet it cannot with certainty be ascribed to either of the known archaeological areas.

After the excavation of a Roman Iron Age cemetery at Holmeløkken in 1861, a denarius struck in 96-97 AD was found in 1865 during construction work c. 20-30 *alen* (c. 12-18 m) from the foot of the hillock with the cemetery.⁴⁰

While digging the miller's garden in Rørbæk in 1859 an unusually early aureus struck during the reign of Tiberius was found. Digging deeper the workers found a burial without any grave goods. Locally the site was known to have yielded human bones that were reburied in the local churchyard already in the middle of the 18ᵗʰ century. The topographical situation, as well as the description of the grave, may indicate that the burials should be dated in the Viking Age or even later, and the presence of the Early Imperial aureus may be a coincidence.⁴¹

A Roman coin has also been mentioned in relation to a find of what was previously interpreted as cremation burials in Hviding in southern Jutland.⁴² Later investigations in the area have however demonstrated that it was intensively occupied both during the Iron Age and in the Medieval period, and two denarii as well as a larger number of Viking Age and Medieval coins have now been found.⁴³ It thus seems that also the first mentioned find of a Roman coin may have been related to a settlement area, rather than a cemetery.

A denarius was allegedly found in an urn at Ribe. The coin is no longer extant, and it is not possible to verify this report.⁴⁴

5.1.5 Geographical distribution of coins in graves

The graves with coin finds are rare in Denmark. The certain finds are concentrated on Sealand, with 10 graves, and Funen with seven graves. There are, however, important differences in the burial customs between these two regions.

The dominant inhumation rite in Sealand provides

---

33 040214 sb 25: Nationalmuseet, Danske Afd., Danmarks Oldtid (Beretningsarkiv). Journalnr: 4947/83.
34 040214 sb 49: FP 7096.
35 010304 sb 41: FP 6488.
36 010304 sb 40.
37 080705 sb 35: FP 1132; Breitenstein 1946, 5 no. VIII; Albrectsen 1968, 26 no. 14.
38 080712 sb 62: NM I C5846.
39 Graves in site 080712-4, the settlement remains were found c. 1 km south of the cemetery.

40 080803 sb 8: FS inv. 899-912; Faber 1868, 346; Albrectsen 1968, 68-69 no. 39.
41 Dept. of Prehistory inv. 18380, site 090605-10. Description of find circumstances in letter from 1859, now in topographical archive of NM I. Breitenstein 1943, 2, no. II.
42 210103 sb 4. The coin is only known from a general description.
43 210103 sb 109.
44 *Aarbøger for Nordisk Oldkyndighed* 1875, 39. The find was regarded as doubtful by Balling 1962, 70.

good information on the nature and distribution of the grave goods. The burials are normally aligned north-south, often with the head in the southern end of the grave. Women were often lying on the side in slightly contracted position, while men were buried in supine position. Graves with coin finds are found in small family plots or even as single graves, with the female burial in the larger cemetery of Stålmosegård as a notable exception. It is important to note that coins have been found in only a very small part of the total number of burials. In 1995 *c.* 100 graves with high-status Roman imports were known in Sealand, among a much larger total of burials dated in period C – yet only 10 burials have yielded coins, and these burials are also by other standards considered among the richest elite burials from Roman Iron Age Denmark. It seems safe to conclude that a coin was not just anyone's possession.

The much larger cemeteries of Funen have yielded hundreds of cremation burials from Roman Iron Age. Inhumation is rarely used, but the rite gradually became more popular towards the end of the Roman Iron Age, as evidenced by for example the Bregentved cemetery, where the latest burials are inhumations. Four of the graves with coins are from Møllegårdsmarken. This is the greatest concentration of coins from graves in Denmark, but with a total of 2023 graves the ones with a coin make up only 0.2 %. The cremation burials are generally "poorer" in their expression than the inhumation burials and they cannot be compared directly to them. The inhumation burials from Hågerup and in particular the Årslev grave are, however, as their counterparts in Sealand among the absolute elite burials of their time, while the Bregentved burial is a bit unusual in this aspect.

The grave from Bæk, southern Jutland is unique. It is the only documented burial from Jutland containing a coin. A considerable number of large cemeteries have been excavated in Jutland, and we might have expected at least a couple of them to hold a Roman coin. Yet, there is none. Why were coins not deposited in graves in Jutland? The question is probably a wrong one: looking at the Continental burials, the number of graves including a coin among the grave gifts is extremely low, so we should not expect coins to be found in burials in Jutland (or for that matter in Denmark in general) at all.

The Bæk grave is by far the earliest grave from Denmark with a coin, and the Tiberian aureus is a very uncommon type seen in relation to other coin finds from Denmark. The coin was not pierced, nor mounted in any way, and there is thus no evidence that it was used as a personal ornament. Its position in the grave suggests that it was either held in the hand or carried in a purse at the belt. It is, however, comparable to the other graves from Denmark with a coin in its undisputed membership of an elite level.

Although not considered a primary study area, it should be noted that Bornholm has yielded three graves, where a total of six coins have been found: four denarii in the same grave from Rævekulebakke, dated C1b/C2 (*c.* 210/20-310/20 AD),[45] one from Slusegård, grave 33,[46] and one from Grødbygård, grave 354,[47] the two latter both dated in C1b (*c.* 210/20-250/60 AD). In two cases the coins were found with male burials, in the third (Slusegård, grave 33) the sex of the deceased could not be identified. In the Rævekulebakke grave the four coins were found lying at the hips of the deceased, in a black spot, probably remains of a textile cloth or purse. In the boat grave Slusegård 33 the coin was similarly placed at the hips, while in Grødbygård 354 the coin was situated on the breast, probably wrapped in textile.[48]

5.1.6 Chronological distribution of coins found in graves

Normally, the coins provide a certain *t.p.q.* for the graves in which they were found, but this is certainly not the same as an exact date of the burial. It is important to note that the other material from the grave can give additional information on the deposition date that can narrow down the possible date of the burial.

With the one exception from Jutland already noted, all the coins were found in graves that can be dated in the periods C1b-C3 and perhaps early period D, i.e. within the years *c.* 210/220 to 400 AD. In Sealand 3rd and 4th century burials are almost equally

---

45 FP 4435, site 060205-198. AUD 1986, 170.
46 BMR inv. no. 948x345, site 060205-1. Klindt-Jensen 1978, 35-37; Crumlin Petersen 1991, 113-114 and 215.
47 FP 4365, site 060205-205. *AUD* 1985, 157; Jørgensen 1987, 81.
48 I am grateful to L.H. Lutz for unpublished information on the graves from Bornholm.

represented, while the burials with a coin in Funen seem to be mainly from the 4th century. In most cases some time has lapsed between the production of the coin and its deposition in a grave in Denmark, but there are a few notable exceptions, where the coin may be near contemporary with the burial.[49]

In all areas the amount of grave goods is decreasing throughout the Roman Iron Age. After the end of the Roman Iron Age a change in burial customs took place. Few Germanic Iron Age graves are known from Denmark (Bornholm being an important exception).

5.1.7 The meaning of the coin in the grave

To interpret the meaning of the coin it is important to note its physical position in the grave, its relation to other grave goods, and the relation between graves with coin finds and those without. In many cases, in particular when it comes to old finds, we do not have the information necessary, and only part of the material can be used for analysis.

It is often useful to distinguish between the personal objects belonging to the deceased and indicating the social status, age or gender of the person and the gifts that were placed in the grave either as sacrifices for the dead person or for deities taking care of the dead or as equipment to be used by the dead *en route* or in the next life.

We may often distinguish gifts/sacrifices positioned at the head or the feet of the deceased or along the sides of a wide grave, from personal objects found on/at the body itself. Coins may belong to either of these groups, but in the case of the coins found as part of a necklace or in a purse, the most likely interpretation is to see them as part of the personal belongings, rather than as part of the ritually deposited grave goods.

But objects that are connected with death rituals need not be found inside the grave proper. Sacrifices could also be thrown into the graves during the filling in of soil immediately after the burial, or sacrifices could be made a shorter or longer period of time after the burial either on the grave or in the cemetery among the graves.[50] This might explain some of the "uncertain" finds of coins related to grave finds, but in general the nature of the information on the find circumstances of these coins is not precise enough to allow for any conclusions.

Coins in burials seem not to be gender specific. There are seven female burials, and one (the Årslev grave) that is most probably female, compared to five male burials. In parts of Sealand there seem to be a tendency that men were buried in supine position, while women were lying on their side in slightly contracted position.[51] If this rule could be applied to the grave at Bennebo Mark it would indicate that is was a sixth male burial. Yet the evidence is not unambiguous: the skeleton in the Nyrup grave was probably lying in supine position on its back, but the grave goods indicate that it was female, and at the time of the recovery a physician described the skeleton as female.

In no less than five of the 18 graves considered (Torstorp, Stålmosegård, Nyrup, Himlingøje and Skovgårde), the coin constitutes an important and centrally placed element in a long prestigious necklace, otherwise consisting of numerous – in the case of the Nyrup grave more than 1000 – beads of glass and amber. These female graves are all from Sealand, and they must be considered to belong to the absolute elite of the society. The Bregentved grave from Funen may be considered a parallel on a less elevated social level. In the Årslev grave the looped aureus imitation was found with the other pieces of jewellery at the head or the breast of the deceased, and we must interpret it as part of this rich equipment. The last female burial, and the only one with a coin that was not reworked, was the cremation burial at Møllegårdsmarken grave 1503.

The male burials present a more varied picture in respect to the female burials. In two cases a looped gold coin was found at the head: Varpelev and Brøndsager. This may indicate that a man (or boy: the deceased in the Brøndsager grave was only 12 years old) might have carried a single or few, very

---

49 Diagram in Nielsen 1987-88, 153 fig. 2, note, however, that the production date of the Barbarian aureus imitation in the Årslev grave is not ascertained, and the date of the Årslev grave as a whole is debated. To his diagram should be added the recent finds from Torstorp Vesterby and Brøndsager.

50 On depositions outside the grave see Henriksen 1989 with references to parallels from Northern Germany.
51 Boye 2004, 47.

valuable items in a short necklace, contrary to the lavish female jewellery.

In three cases the coin was found next to the body. The coin was lying close to a comb in the male grave at Nordrup. In this case the coin might have been positioned in a purse in a manner comparable to the purses from the Illerup weapon sacrifice (cf. below), and the three graves from Bornholm mentioned above. In the two other cases the information on the find circumstances are too general to allow for specific interpretations: in the burial from Bennebo Mark we only know that is was found *c. 20 inches* east of the body, and in the somewhat earlier grave from Bæk the coin was found in the middle of the grave close to the long side.

The cremation burials present special problems. The sex could be determined only of one of the burials. None of the coins have traces of fire, which may indicate that the coin was not put on the pyre with the body, but was placed in the urn after the cremation as a grave gift. This seems to be supported by the fact that the three denarii were not reworked.[52] The fourth coin – an aureus – was fragmented, and it has been assumed that a loop was broken off, but strictly speaking there is no trace of a loop preserved.

5.1.8 Charon's fee?

The coins in the Danish graves are regularly described as Charon's fee. This suggestion, although widespread, needs to be thoroughly re-considered. During the last decades several scholars dealing with the classics have discussed the obolus of Charon. Today there seems to be a general tendency to discard this explanatory model in favour of a more differentiated view on coins in burial contexts based on the great variety in ritual practises as evidenced by the archaeological material.[53]

The figure of Charon is pivotal. He belongs in ancient Greek mythology, where he is the ferryman, who sails the souls of the dead across the river Styx to the Underworld. He was, however, never a prominent figure in the eschatology of the Classical world, neither in the archaeological or iconographic material, nor in the Greek literary sources. The Roman literary sources regarding Charon are somewhat more common. In both Greek and Roman literary sources, however, two important notions emerge: Charon's fee was low, and it should be paid with a coin placed in the mouth. But we may wonder whether the literary sources reflect a common practise or even a common belief. Stevens noted that the context of the sources mentioning the notion of paying a fee to Charon is often critical or satirical: Charon is for example found in the Greek comedies or in the verses of of the Roman poet Juvenal.[54]

The archaeological material reveals that in ancient Greece and the Greek *apoikiai* throughout the Mediterranean coins were first found in burials in the 5th century BC, and finds of coins only become less rare in burials of the 4th century BC and later. Even then coins were only deposited in a minority of graves, normally less than 10 % of the burials in a Greek cemetery.[55]

In the Roman Imperial Period coins were part of everyday economic transactions, at least within the urban areas of the Empire, as can be deduced from the coin finds in Pompei. Thus we might expect a larger percentage of burials with a coin. This is also the case, but the number of burials with one or more coins rarely rose above 50 % in one cemetery. There are clear regional differences in the popularity of the rite within the various parts of the northern provinces, and – perhaps more important – there is a tendency that the percentage of graves with a coin along the Limes area is higher in the Roman *castella* than in the hinterland settlements. This should indicate that the habit of depositing coins in burials only occasionally penetrated into the originally Gallic or Germanic communities.[56]

Even though coins were sometimes placed in

---

52 The fact that the coin is not reworked does not in itself exclude that it was carried in a necklace or similar. The reworking of the coin from the Skovgårde cemetery seems not to have altered the coin. Mountings made in other materials may have disappeared completely.

53 Grinder-Hansen 1991; Stevens 1991; Thüry 1999. Parise in Preface of *Caronte. Un obolo per l'Aldilá* 1995.

54 Stevens 1991.

55 For good summaries of various Greek regions see: *Caronte. Un obolo per l'Aldilá* 1995; important observations also in Benassai 1998.

56 Rasbach 1999.

a burial, it can only rarely be shown to be inserted deliberately into the mouth of the deceased. Old excavation reports are not always specific, and the interpretation of coins in graves in the Roman area is made difficult by the prevailing use of cremation burials. In a few cases the position in the urn or even the fact that it is partly melted indicates that the coin actually followed the dead on the pyre.[57] A number of recently excavated Roman cemeteries with a considerable number of inhumation burials have, however, shown that although a number of coins have appeared in the graves, they were rarely in the mouth.

One example is a cemetery consisting of 72 inhumation burials from the 4th century, excavated in Sierentz, close to Mulhouse on the left bank of the Upper Rhine. One or more coins were found in 19 graves. The coins were low denominations (Æ3 or Æ4), but in many cases more than one coin was found in a burial. In four cases one or two coins were found on the eyes, in seven cases near the head, but in the remaining cases the coins were found in positions that could hardly be connected with the traditional view of Charon's fee.[58] Recent investigations are revealing much differentiated coin use depending on the status of a site, even within very small areas of the Limes zone.[59] It seems likely that the coins in the burials in the northern Roman Provinces reflect the ordinary coin use in these areas, and therefore burials with coins would be more common in areas with intensive coins use than in other areas.

In a recent article Bemmann has collected and analysed the material from 263 burials from Central and Northern European Barbaricum, where one or more coins have been found.[60] One of his interesting results is the demonstration that until c. 450 AD there is a broad area along the Barbarian side of the Limes where no coin graves have been found. It is tempting to see this as yet another example of particular cultural habits along the border zone: this is the area without finds of Roman luxury goods, but with finds of *terra* sigillata pottery that is otherwise rare in Barbaricum, and from a numismatic point of view it is a zone with some evidence of a quasi monetary economy.[61]

Bemmann's mapping of the finds point out the chronological differences from area to area. First of all graves with a coin are extremely rare in the Early Imperial period (= Period B1). Apart from the burial at Bæk, only five burials are known, two from the Vistula basin and three from Mähren. During period B2/C1 the number of finds is growing, but the number is not peaking until period C1b and C2 with a considerable number of finds in Sachsen-Anhalt and Thüringen and a minor number in Pommern. In periods C3 to D2 (in this connection: c. 300-450 AD) the majority of the finds are from the Elbe-Weser region (Niedersachsen, Bremen and Nordrhein-Westfalen), and there are finds from Norway and Gotland, two areas previously not touched at all by this use. The change in north-western Barbaricum may be related to the usage in Gaul and Belgium, where coins for the dead are found from the 1st century onwards, but with a significant rise in numbers in the 4th-5th centuries.[62]

Not surprisingly, the spatial and chronological distribution of the coin graves follows the pattern of Roman imports as well. This can be seen in the shift from Sealand to Funen in Denmark, in the peak in Thüringen in C2 and in Northwest Germany in C3-D2

5.1.9 "Münzersatz"

Bemmann concluded that coins may have been used as some sort of Charon's fee in a number of burials of the Hassleben-Leuna Group dated in period C2. In all other areas coins are found only rarely in the burials, or they are positioned in a manner not to support the theory of its function as Charon's fee. But while there is no good evidence for the use of a coin as Charon's fee in Danish Iron Age society, Boye has made a case for considering fragments of gold or glass – by Bemmann termed a *Münzersatz* – found in the mouth of the deceased to be a kind of payment.[63] Bemmann has accepted this theory for

---

57 Rasbach 1999.
58 Dumez *et al.* 1999; more examples in Stevens 1991, 225-226.
59 E.g. Kemmers 2008.
60 Bemmann 2006. The article does not consider finds from the areas Cernjachov/Sintana de Mures culture, nor the material from the "Sarmatian" areas.
61 Hedeager 1978 on bronze coins along the Limes.
62 Böhme 1974.
63 Boye 2002a and b.

the Danish area (in practise Sealand), but notes that there are no good parallels in Continental Europe for a similar usage. It is however possible that the sometimes very small pieces of glass or gold may have been overlooked in earlier excavations, and it will be interesting indeed, to see whether Boye's suggestions may have an impact on the finds in future cemetery excavations on the Continent. It certainly seems that a growing awareness of the possibility of finding a *Münzersatz* has led to a growing number of finds in Denmark in the last couple of years.

The question now is, what is the *Münzersatz*? Is it indeed inspired by the Graeco-Roman notion of payment to the ferryman? In this case we will have to consider carefully, how this idea may have travelled north, and how it was transformed on its way. The usage of a coin in the burials of the Hassleben-Leuna complex may have played a crucial role here. It may however be seen as problematic for this interpretation that the evidence for some similar usage in Sealand with the use of traditional dating of the Sealand phases may be a bit earlier. Bemmann explains this apparent dichotomy as a result of the dominating cremation rite in Central Germany until period C2. The cremation burials antedating period C2 might have held a Charon's fee, but archaeological evidence of it does not exist, and would not easily be revealed.

What then became the meaning of the *Münzersatz* rite? In the Graeco-Roman world the payment to the ferryman was considered ridiculously low, and although a small piece of glass may seem a humble payment, it was not. Glass was a luxury item in Iron Age Denmark, as were the small pieces of gold. Could we instead be witnessing an "indigenous" Scandinavian development only faintly inspired by the hearsay of foreign rituals? How would an eschatology involving a payment to someone on the way to the next world fit into Scandinavian beliefs? It seems plausible that the idea of putting something into the mouth of the deceased may have come to Denmark – perhaps in some transformed manner – through contacts with for example the Germanic cultures in modern Türingen. If the object should be used as a payment, it at least presupposes a belief that someone should be paid for some service, as for example to carry the (soul of the) deceased somewhere. This implication has not been fully discussed, only hinted at by Bemmann arguing that the use of paying a ferryman: "sich ... in die Konzeption der germanischen Jenseitsvorstellungen einfügen liess."[64]

In one case, the Hågerup grave, the coin was found in a position that makes it probable that is was originally placed in the mouth of the deceased. The grave goods of the Hågerup burial reveals close contacts with the continent, but it still seems difficult to connect it with the Mediterranean notion of Charon, even considering that the idea of paying a fee to Charon need not be based on a thorough knowledge on Roman eschatology on part of the Danish Iron Age communities. Thus for the time being it seems safer to avoid the expression "Charon's fee" in Danish Iron Age archaeology in favour of a more neutral terminology.

5.1.10 Summary

The analysis has revealed that coins are rarely found in Danish Iron Age burials. The majority are from Sealand, where they are quite evenly distributed through the periods C1b to C3, and where they are invariably found in burials of very high status, generally with other imported luxury items. The majority of the coins from Danish burials are reworked into jewellery, and the coin is often an important element of the lavish necklaces worn by the women of the aristocracy. It may be argued that men (or boys) could wear a coin in a smaller necklace. The number of burials is of course far too restricted to allow for definite conclusions, but it seems important to note that the majority of the coins were silver (denarii and siliquae), but the two cases with a male necklace were gold. The only female burial with a gold coin in Sealand is the Nyrup burial whose necklace, by number of beads as well as by number of coins, is far superior to any other.

In Funen the burials with a coin seems slightly later, except from the Hågerup grave, which is in many aspects peculiar to the general picture of burials in Funen. The number of grave goods in the cremation burials is in general far smaller than in the inhumations of Sealand, and the female burial from Bregentved may reflect this pattern. The Årslev burial(s) is unique in many aspects.

In other cases the position of the coin in the grave seems to indicate that it was part of the personal

---

64 Bemmann 2006, 29.

List of burials with coin finds

site no		grave	denomination	sex	re-worked	position of coin	coin t.p.q.	date of grave				
								Ethelberg 2000	Lund Hansen 1987	Bemmann 2006	Eggers	other
020213	34	Brøndsager	gold imit.	m	looped	necklace	-					C2[65]
020213	20	Torstorp Vesterby	siliqua	f	looped	necklace	351	C3		C3		
020512	4	Stålmosegård, Vindinge	denarius	f	looped, Æ	necklace	180	C3		C3		
030405	100	Nyrup	2 siliquae, solidus	f	looped, all	necklace??	340	C3	C3	C3	C3	
030710		Bennebo Mark	denarius	m/f	-	20 tommer (inches) east of the body	161	C1b	C1b			
040211	17	Nordrup graveH	denarius	m	-	next to the comb below the left knee	160	C1b	C1b			
050104	58	Gunnerupgård Mark	denarius	?	-	-	169	C1b-C2	C1b-C2			
050105	29	Himlingøje grave 1949-2	denarius	f	pierced	necklace	81	C2	C1b			
050212	27	Skovgårde grave 209	denarius	f	mounted	necklace	138	C1b				
050613	8	Varpelev grave a	aureus	m/f	looped	at right ear	282	C2	C2		C2	t.p.q. 340
060203	1	Slusegård grave 33	denarius	m/f	-	at the hips	98	C1b	C			
060205	205	Grødbygård grave 354	denarius	m	-	on the breast	117	C1b				
060205	198	Rævekulebakke	4 denarii	m	-	at the hips	223			C2		C1b2-C2[66]
080705	35	Fjeldsted, burial?	denarius	?	-	-	176	-	C			
080712	62	Skrillinge Mark, burial?	denarius	-	-	-	163	-				
080803	8	Holmeløkken, burial?	denarius	-	-	-	97	-				
090104	156	Møllegårdsmarken grave 1503	denarius	f	-	cremation	160	C3	C	C3		
090104	156	Møllegårdsmarken grave 1715	denarius	-	-	cremation	176	C3	C	C3		
090104	156	Møllegårdsmarken grave 1755	denarius	-	-	cremation	161	C2	C			
090104	156	Møllegårdsmarken grave 1796a	aureus	-	looped?	cremation	213	C3	C2			
090108	11	Bregentved 1	denarius, subaeratus	f	pierced	necklace?	161	C3		C3		
090403	34	Hågerup	denarius	m	-	at or in mouth	138	C1b	C1b		C2	
090605	10	Rørbæk, burial ?	aureus	-	-	-	37	-	-			-
090619	4	Årslev	gold imit.	f?	looped	at head or breast	-		C2	C3	C2	C3[67]
200206	215	Bæk (Kærgård)	aureus		-	in fill above grave	37			B1		B1/B2a[68]

equipment as well, placed in a purse hanging from the belt. Yet, it cannot be excluded that the coins may have been deposited in the grave as part of the burial ritual. In this case the coin would be interpreted in line with the remaining grave goods such as drinking cups, game boards etc.

65 Fonnesbech-Sandberg 2004.
66 L.H. Lutz, personal communication 2002.
67 Storgaard 1990.
68 Korthauer 1995-96.

Thus in the majority of the cases the coin should probably be seen as a personal object that followed the deceased in the afterlife, rather than part of a ritual. This does not exclude that the coins during lifetime were worn as magic apotropaic amulets.

Chronologically the coin graves point out that 2nd century denarii were present in Denmark at least from period C1b and that they were still in use (above ground!) at least into period C3 (i.e. during the period 210/20-375 AD). Only two 3rd century coins have been found in Danish Iron Age graves. One is from the Varpelev grave. The burial is normally dated in period C2 (250/60-310/20 AD), but a date in period C3 (310/20-375 AD) certainly cannot be excluded, and may indeed be preferable (see also below on gold coins). The other comes from Møllegårdsmarken grave 1796a, dated in period C3 (310/20-375 AD). The latest coins from Danish graves are the siliquae and the solidus from Torstorp Vesterby (*t.p.q.* 351 AD) and Nyrup (*t.p.q.* 340 AD). Both burials belong to period C3 (traditionally dated 310/20-375 AD). The aureus imitations found in the Brøndsager and Årslev graves were possibly produced in the early 4th century (see also below).

5.2 Isolated depositions

5.2.1 The weapon sacrifices

The weapon sacrifices make up a specific sub-group of ritual deposits on moors. More than 20 moors with Iron Age weapon sacrifices are known from Southern Scandinavia,[69] but coins have only been found in a few of them. The largest number of coins was found in the Illerup Deposit A, followed by Nydam, Thorsberg and Skedemosse. Ejsbøl has yielded three coins, and in the Vimose two coins have been found.[70] Two of the sites, Thorsberg and Skedemosse, are situated outside Denmark, in Schleswig (Germany) and on Öland (Sweden) respectively.

5.2.1.1 *Illerup*

Illerup is by far the most important find. Not only because of the high number of coins, 198 denarii including four Barbarian imitations and a sestertius, but also because the excavations were meticuously recorded, and the results of the excavations are being presented in modern publications.[71] The finds from Illerup appeared as a result of drainage of the moor area in 1950, and since then 40,000 m² have been excavated. Three deposits, Illerup A to C, have been found. Illerup A is the largest deposition, and it is the only one that contains coins. Apart from the coins the deposit consists of weaponry, horses' equipment and the warriors' personal equipment. The objects have been deliberately destroyed before they were thrown overboard from a boat.

The coins were found among the personal objects, and they must have been carried in purses hanging from the belt. Thus the coins are not *one* hoard, but a considerable number of smaller coin "hoards" and single finds that all have been deposited at a single moment.[72]

The latest denarii from the deposit were struck during the reign of Commodus. These coins of course provides a *t.p.q.* for the sacrifice as a whole, but the very good preservation of wooden objects have allowed for dendrochronological analysis of the oak used for the shields of the sacrifice. The trees providing the wood have been felled in the period from 164 AD until "after *c.* 205 AD". The sacrifice therefore must have taken place in the early 3rd century. The combined evidence from the coins and the dendrochronological analysis of Illerup deposition A is of major importance as it tells us that the types sacrificed in Illerup were definitely in use in the early 3rd century, and it gives a rare possibility to get a glimpse of the Roman coins "in action".

As mentioned the coins were found among other

---

69 Jørgensen *et al.* 2003 *passim*; distribution map in Ilkjær 2003, Fig. 1.
70 Horsnæs 2003a.

71 In the series *Illerup Ådal*. Summary of the excavation results in Ilkjær 2000. See also http://www.illerup.dk/ (Danish and German versions), including among other things lists of articles on the find, many of which can be downloaded.
72 Kromann 1991; Ilkjær 1993. A publication of the coins from Illerup is under preparation by Aleksander Bursche, who generously provided me with a list of his type identifications of the coins.

Fig. 27. The weapon sacrifice at Illerup during excavation. Photo Moesgård medielab.

objects belonging to the warriors' private equipment. Many of the coins were single finds, while others were found in small groups. The largest group contains 28 denarii that must have been deposited in a leather purse or the like. It was found in the area –6/60 that also contained 42 other coins (single finds or coins found in smaller groups), as well as one of the most luxurious outfits from Illerup. It is therefore possible to suggest that the coins must have belonged to the elite sphere also in relation to the sacrifice at Illerup.

To whom did the sacrificed weapons belong? This is one of the important discussions of the weapon sacrifices. The moors were often used for a number of successive sacrifices, and there must have been a living memory of the sacrifices and the sacredness of the site. It therefore seems most likely that peoples living in the area performed the sacrifices. Whether the moors were sacred on a local or on a regional level is however hard to tell. Whether the battle that resulted in the taking of the booty that eventually ended up at the sacrifice took place in an area close to the moor, or it took place further away and the booty was brought "home" for sacrifice is debated. The original owners of the military equipment may have come from another place. Ilkjær has suggested that the losing part in the case of the Illerup A sacrifice was definitely made up of (mostly) Scandinavian warriors. Spears, lances and shields were of northern manufacture and most of the sacrificed tinderboxes are of a type found in Scandinavia and the northern coasts of modern Germany. However, the combs from the sacrifice are mainly of a type found in western Sweden and Norway, and Ilkjær therefore suggests that the warriors came from this area.

This is a very interesting and highly convincing argument. Yet, it poses some problems in the interpretation of the Roman coins from the sacrifice. Both Norway and western Sweden have yielded a very low number of Roman coins: in all Norway only 10-15 denarii have been found. Did warriors originating from western Sweden/Norway come to the Continent, where they acquired the coins along with sword blades and other specialized equipment? Did this happen only once – in a case where the "Norwegian" warriors did not make it back to their homes? If there had been a larger number of expeditions from "Norway" to the Continent – and back – we might expect more coins to have been found in those areas, considering that the number of coins from the Illerup find alone is 20 times bigger than the number of denarii from Norway/western Sweden.

5.2.1.2 Nydam

The second largest find of coins in the weapon sacrifices is the 56 denarii from Nydam. Nydam is best known by the find of the extraordinarily large and well-preserved boat made of oak tree, now in Schloss Gottorp. Next to the oak timber boat was also a smaller and shattered oak boat and a pine-wood boat. The excavations started in 1859 and were – considering their time – quite well documented. The boats were found in 1863, but shortly after the excavations were interrupted due to the war between Denmark and Prussia.[73]

The majority of the coins were found during Conrad Engelhardt's excavations in the 1860's.[74] The exact location of the finds were not pinpointed, but it is possible to see in which areas the coins were found, and it is evident that – as is the case in Illerup – the coins were found as a number of small assemblages, that were all part of one larger sacrifice. It is impor-

---

73 Wiell 2003, with references to earlier works.
74 Engelhardt 1865; Bemmann & Bemmann 1998.

Fig. 28. Denarii from the weapon sacrifice at Nydam. Group of 18 coins found east of the pine-wood boat. Scale c. 1:1. Photo John Lee/National Museum of Denmark.

tant to note that no less than four examples of type and even die identical coins have been identified among the coins from Nydam, but unfortunately we do not know whether they belonged to the same find groups:

- Two Antoninus Pius (RIC 162, struck 148-149 AD), type identical[75]
- Two Marcus Aurelius (RIC 23, struck 161 AD), type identical[76]
- Two Marcus Aurelius (RIC 171, struck 166-167 AD), type identical[77]
- Four Antoninus Pius (RIC 27, struck 139 AD). This group of coins is regarded to be die identical contemporary imitations struck somewhere outside the Empire (see below).

During re-investigations in Nydam in the 1990's another 19 denarii were found.[78] One was found on the site of the large oak boat, while the remaining 18 denarii were found just east of the pine-wood boat together with material that had probably slid from the boat (*Fig. 28*). The excavator suggests that the coins had been kept in a chest on the boat and that the assemblage was therefore deposited at the same time as the boat in the beginning of the 4th century. All the coins from Nydam come from the area labelled Nydam I, and also the coins from Engelhardt's excavation were found with objects that can be dated *c.* 300 AD. The 18 denarii from the new assemblage are dated in the period from AD 72/73 to 198/200 and the chronological distribution of them is comparable with the coins found during Engelhardt's excavation.

5.2.1.3 Thorsberg

Conrad Engelhardt also excavated the Thorsberg weapon sacrifice.[79] He found 37 denarii, and it has been possible to identify nine coins found together with the famous silver helmet (or mask) and 10 coins found in the so-called area M.[80] The Thorsberg sacrifice probably took place in the 3rd century AD.

After Engelhardt's excavation the Museum in Flensburg has received 24 denarii, an aureus and a sestertius that all were provenanced as found in the moor. Yet, a number of these coins differ from the denarii found during Engelhardt's excavation in the moor, and it is possible that the coins were only registered with this provenance because of the previous coin finds from the moor. It therefore seems preferable to exclude the later incoming coins from discussions of the weapon sacrifice.

5.2.1.4 Skedemosse

The weapon sacrifice at Skedemosse on the Swedish island Öland was investigated in the 1960's. The main part of the offerings took place in the period 200-500 AD. 10 badly preserved denarii were found in the moor, and among them eight were found within a relatively limited area that also yielded remains of an elite belt. The chronological distribution in the find ranges from Titus to Caracalla (79-217).[81]

5.2.1.5 Ejsbøl

Ejsbøl Mose was first investigated in 1955-1964. 1400 artefacts were excavated in 1700 m^2 in two main areas, Ejsbøl Nord (north) and Ejsbøl Syd (south). A single Barbarian imitation of a denarius was found in Ejsbøl Nord. It is pierced and may have been part of the horse equipment that was found with it. The material from Ejsbøl Nord in general is dated in period C2 ("around 300 AD").[82]

In the 1990's renewed investigations took place in an area somewat south of the previously excavated areas.[83] The new investigations revealed six different complexes, labelled Ejsbøl A-F. Ejsbøl C contained richly decorated fittings from a belt including a fitting for the end of a thong with a decoration made of a piece of gold foil pressed over a coin struck for Marcus Aurelius Caesar (i.e. coin *t.p.q.* 139 AD, when the first coins were struck for Aurelius Caesar),[84] 14 pieces of gold from originally at least four hacked up neckrings (altogether 576 g of gold), and an aureus struck for Diva Faustina Major (coin *t.p.q.* 141 AD). The coin was pierced twice. It seems that this ensemble has been deliberately taken away from other of-

---

75 Balling 1962, 30 nos. 8-9.
76 Balling 1962, 31 nos. 18-19.
77 Balling 1962, 31 nos. 21-22.
78 Jørgensen & Petersen 2003.
79 Engelhardt 1863. A re-evaluation of the material from Thorsberg was made 2005-2008 in the project *Zwischen Thorsberg und Bornstein*, see http://www.kaiserzeitimnorden.de/ (including detailed publication list).
80 Lønstrup unpublished, quoted by Komnick 1994.

81 Hagberg 1967-1977; on the coins see Lind 1981, 102-103.
82 Ørsnes 1988.
83 Andersen 2003.
84 Von Carnap-Bornheim 2003; for the date RIC III, 17.

ferings. It is therefore evident that the coin must have been closely connected to the other objects. It may have been used as a pendent decoration of the belt.

Two bronze coins were also found during the new excavations. They were heavily corroded, but most probably struck during the 4th century.[85] They are among the rare examples of Roman bronze coins found *in situ* in Iron Age contexts in Denmark.

5.2.1.6 Vimose
The Vimose weapon sacrifice was discovered in 1848, and since then a large number of artefacts have been recovered, first as the result of private finds, and later as the results of both archaeological investigations and local farmers' peat digging.[86] The first find from the Vimose, however, was a Roman sestertius struck in 165-166 AD. It was found during peat digging, probably in the 1780's, and given to King Christian VIII in 1831.[87] In 1862 also a denarius struck for Faustina Minor was found during peat cutting in the moor.[88] It was found together with other artefacts, but the nature of these is not described.[89] It cannot be excluded that one or both the coins may have belonged to the large sacrifice, normally dated in the first half of the 3rd century (period C1b).[90]

5.2.1.7 Summary
The weapon sacrifices constitute a continuous series of special events that can hardly be interpreted as anything but celebrations of military victories. The continuous use of the same sacrificial moors seems to imply that these places had a special significance that was known to the "locals" that must have performed the rituals. This does not imply that the "locals" were living on the brink of the particular moor or lake in question. The large weapon sacrifices may have been performed at special places that were sacred on a regional rather than a restricted local level, more so as the sheer amount of weaponry included in the sacrifices tells us that the warriors taking part in the decisive battle must have been gathered on at least a regional level. The sacrificed objects cannot be regarded as "local"; on the contrary most scholars agree that they reflect the usage of the loosers. The loosers may come from afar to attack the region of the moor, or the battle had been delivered somewhere else and the booty subsequently brought back home for sacrifice. No matter which possibility is right, there can be no doubt that both sides of the war were Germanic peoples, as only a minor group of material is made up of Roman imports (e.g. sword blades), while spears, lances and shields, as well as the personal equipment, were produced in Barbaricum.

The finds underline the impression already provided by the graves with coins: Roman coins were luxury items, found in small numbers in particular contexts. In the weapon sacrifices the coins were deposited as part of a larger entity – the army's equipment as a whole. They were not sorted out, on the contrary the evidence from Illerup clearly shows that they were thrown into the moor while still hidden in the purses.

The sacrifices with coins can be dated from the early 3rd century (i.e. from the beginning of period C1b) and into the 4th century, perhaps until the end of the 4th century.

Except for the extremely badly preserved bronze coins from Ejsbøl that might belong in the 4th century, all the coins from weapon sacrifices belong to what may be termed the denarius horizon: the majority are denarii, and the few other coins are an aureus (Ejsbøl) or sestertii (Illerup and perhaps Vimose). The coins must reflect the pool of coins that were available in the area where the loosing party came from, whether this was their home or an area were they had previously fought – and perhaps won booty! Thus it is very difficult to use the coins from the large sacrifices as evidence of any kind of geographical distribution.

If – in some cases – only part of the booty from a battle was sacrificed, we may speculate whether some of the Roman denarii that have been found in other Danish contexts arrived as part of booty and were redistributed among the winning warriors, as amulets, tokens, souvenirs.

---

85 200302 sb 73: HAM 3434x226 and x214. Horsnæs 2006a, 92 nos. 103-104.
86 080406 sb 1. Xenia P. Jensen is preparing a publication on the Vimose find. For a summary of the finds see Pauli Jensen 2003.
87 NM I C 4756; Breitenstein 1943, 4 no. VII.2; Horsnæs 2006a, cat.no. 27. Struck by Marcus Aurelius in 164-165 AD.
88 NM I 20271; Breitenstein 1943, 4 no. VII.1. Struck by Antoninus Pius for Faustina Minor.
89 Engelhardt 1869, 31.
90 Pauli Jensen 2003 and 2008.

5.2.2 Denarius hoards from moors and wetland areas

The weapon sacrifices have been discussed at some length because the coins from the large offerings are rare examples of dated depositions of Roman coins. As is well known moors (or wetlands) had been used for religious purposes long before the first weapon sacrifices,[91] and while there is a number of weapon sacrifices that do not contain coins, there is also a considerable number of coin finds that are best interpreted as religious depositions in wetland areas (in or at moors, lakes, or streams, and at the coastline).

5.2.2.1 Råmosen

The numerically largest find is the Råmose Hoard that was discovered in 1782 close to Høng in western Sealand. The number of denarii from the hoard cannot be exactly given today, but a summary list of finds made by Christian Ramus in 1800 is commonly employed for the composition of the hoard (see intro etc.).[92] This list numbers 428 denarii, and thus the Råmose Hoard makes up for more than half the number of coins found on Sealand.

The hoard was found while digging for peat in the Råmose. The right to the peat from the moor was then divided between the peasants from the three villages of Solbjerg, Kragerup and Tjørnelunde (modern spelling of names). A peasant from Solbjerg found the first coins "a small *Fjerdingvey*", i.e. less than 2 km, from Solbjerg.[93] The coins were found within an area of 3 to 4 by 1½ *alen* (*c.* 1.90-2.50 by 0.95 m)[94] and the coins were encountered in *c.* 1½ quarter[95] (*c.* 20-25 cm) depth. The local authorities were sent to interrogate the finder and in a second instance to make an excavation around the find spot. It was noted that in spite of both official search undertaken by the *amtmand* (chief administrative officer of the area), Cederfeld, and the treasure hunting by the other peasants, no coins were found outside the original find spot. At this point only some unidentified pieces of wood were found, and Cederfeld excluded that they could derive from a chest or a coffin. It was explicitly noted that no iron objects were found, nor were there any traces of a bag or the like that may have held the coins. It was furthermore noted, how the peat cutting had taken place for many years before the find, but then only in dry periods and on small islands, as the major part of the moor had then been below water most of the year. The moor had only been partly drained *c.* 20 years before the find.

The investigations of course did not live up to modern archaeological standards, and although it has not been possible to pinpoint the exact find spot, the accurate descriptions provide us with valuable information about the nature of the find. There can be little doubt the denarius hoard had been deposited as one act, and that it was not mixed with other objects.

Denmark was mapped on the initiative of the Royal Danish Society of Sciences in 1762-1820. On this map the Råmose (here spelled Rov Mose) is indicated as a wetland area with a lake stretching from west to east almost halfway between the villages of Solbjerg (spelled Soelbierg) and Tjørnelunde (spelled Tiörnlund). A road carries north from Solbjerg passing east of the wetlands towards "Kragerup Gaard og M:" (Kragerup farm and mill). The wetlands still exist, as does the road from Solbjerg to Kragerup. The Råmose is situated in a landscape typical of western Sealand: heavily undulating hills formed by glacial deposits. The water from the Råmose area runs towards east, where it joins the Tude Å (Tude Stream) that meanders southwest to its outlet in Storebælt (Great Belt) south of Korsør. Tude Å is one of the major streams in the area, and it may be no coincidence that it passes right by the large Viking Age site of Trelleborg shortly before its outlet. The areas immediately south and west of the Råmose are relatively flat, and it is possible that this is the area that had been drained "20 years before" the Råmose Hoard was found. This topographical indication as well as the information that the hoard was found less than 2 km from Solbjerg and in an area divided between the three villages, suggest that the most likely find spot for the hoard must have been in the northernmost part of the Solbjerg *ejerlav* south of the present lake. North of the Råmose the landscape rises more

---

91 Kaul 2003.
92 030205 sb 59. The find has been discussed in a number of articles: Galster 1938, 63-69; Breitenstein 1946, 2 no. 1; Kromann 1995, 348-351. Copies of the acts regarding the find in The Royal Collection of Coins and Medals.
93 A *Fjerdingvey* or *Fjerding Vej* is *c.* 1883 m.
94 One *Alen* is *c.* 62.8 cm.
95 One *Quarter* is ¼ of an *Alen*, i.e. *c.* 15.69 cm.

abruptly. No other Iron Age finds are noted in the area.

In spite of the great efforts undertaken by in particular the then leading statesman – and coin collector – Ove Høegh-Guldberg to gather as much information as possible about the hoard, the find circumstances did not facilitate the work of the local officials. As soon as rumours about the find of ancient coins had spread, a treasure hunt was initiated. The finds were sold off to local collectors and to a gold smith, from whom they were bought back little by little. When retrieved the coins were forwarded to Copenhagen, where Professor Abraham Kall was handed over the coins for identification. He gave a lecture about the find in the Royal Academy of Science in April 1783 and finished his manuscript for publication in 1784. Unfortunately, his study was never published and today only 8 pages of the manuscript exist. In this he gives the total number of coins as 388 denarii of 260 different types (the word used is "*sorter*") beginning with Tiberius (14-37 AD) and ending with a coin struck in AD 188. The coins remained in his custody until 1800 when they were returned to the Royal Coin Cabinet. Christian Ramus at that instance registered the coins as 428 denarii, and he provided the shortlist of the chronological distribution of the coins used for the present study. He agreed with Kall that the oldest coin in the find was struck by Tiberius, but the latest coins mentioned in this list are the 26 coins struck by Marcus Aurelius. Thus the information gathered from Ramus and Kall differ on two important points: the total number of coins and the latest coin in the finds. The archival material on the find is quite extensive, still it is quite hard to follow the numbers of coins that were handed in little by little, and this complicated find history must indeed explain the difference between the figures indicated by Kall in his manuscript and the figures given by Ramus 16 years later.[96]

We must, however, also take into consideration that even the list provided by Ramus is not comprehensive. Some coins undoubtedly escaped notice. In fact a few years ago, Christian Adamsen found a reference to a coin from Råmosen in a manuscript in Nasjonalbibliotekets Håndskriftavdeling in Oslo, Norway. The author, official in the customs (*toldembedsmand*) in Norway, Machesen, tells how he had seen a Roman silver coin belonging to the vicar Mr. Bang, previously vicar in Korsør. According to Machesen, Mr. Bang had told him that the coin came from a hoard found by a gold smith in his moor at Slagelse. As mentioned above a number of the coins from the Råmosen Hoard had been sold to a gold smith in Slagelse, and it is very likely that in the story told to Machesen by Bang the gold smith had already become the finder of the hoard, or that Machesen had misunderstood Bang, and believed that the gold smith was identical with the finder.[97]

Not only the number of the coins, but also the composition of the hoard, is uncertain. As previously noted, Kall mentioned a coin from AD 188, i.e. struck during the reign of Commodus, as the latest one from the hoard, while Ramus closed his list with Marcus Aurelius. But already Høegh-Guldberg made preliminary studies of the coins during the period while they were still being collected, and he reported about them in his letters. He noted coins with the portrait of Commodus, and in fact we can almost follow how he worked his way through the material. In a letter to Jon Erichsen dated August 9, 1782 he mentioned two coins of Commodus,[98] while in a letter to his protégé and designated head of the Royal Coin Cabinet, Georg Zoëga, dated August 13, the number had already risen to three Commodus coins.[99] It is of course likely that the Commodus coins mentioned by Høegh-Guldberg were struck as Commodus Caesar during the reign of Marcus Aurelius – the lack of Crispina coins in the lists may indeed point in that direction (cf. below on denarii) – but

---

96 Galster 1938, 67 mention 518 as a possible total figure.
97 I owe this information to Christian Adamsen, to whom my warmest thanks.
98 Quoted in Galster 1938, 67.
99 Andreasen 1967, 292, letter no.184: "… über 300 Römische Denarien, von welchen der älteste ein Tiberius war, dann einige von Nero, 3 Galba, 3 Otto, etliche Vitellius, 72 Vespasiani, etwa 30 Titi, einige Domitiani, wenige von Nerva, viele von Traian, Adrian, 6 Sabinae, 20 Ant. Pii, eben so viele von der ältern Faustina, ein Paar Aulii Veri, einige Marc Aurel, mehrere von der jüngeren Faustina, 3 Commodi, 2 Lucilla, un hiemit hörten sie auf."

Fig. 29. Råmosen seen from northeast. Photo HWH.

all in all it raises some doubt as to using the Marcus Aurelius reign as a *t.p.q.* for the hoard.[100]

In the letter to Erichsen Høegh-Guldberg also mentions that "Es sind viele Dubletten darunter. Von Vespasian sind 5 oder 6 *Iudaea capta*". Likewise Kall mentions duplicates among the Vespasian coins, up to 22 examples of the same type. While it seems that Høegh-Guldberg by the word duplicate (Dubletten) intended that there were several coins with the Iudaea capta inscription, but not necessarily of the same obverse type or issue, it is more difficult to know exactly what Kall intended by his wording. We may infer that the 22 Vespasian coins had the same reverse motive (i.e. type identity), but this does not necessarily imply that they were from the same issue. Die studies as a common numismatic method was only introduced after the middle of the 19th century,[101] and it is highly unlikely that Kall should have thought of noting die identities in the late 18th century.

In his letters Høegh-Guldberg also provides the important information that the Antonine coins were slightly circulated, while the earlier coins were considerably worn. He suggested that the coins had been deposited in the moor "nicht lange nach Commodus' Zeit".

Ramus unfortunately did not note the provenances of the coins in his catalogue of the Ancient coins in the Royal Collection of Coins and Medals.[102] Therefore the denarii from Råmosen, some of which undoubtedly still in the collection, no longer can be identified. Today, the questions discussed above must remain unsolved. For the present work it has been decided to use the figures indicated by Ramus for statistics and diagrams, but keeping in mind the quite firm indications given by Høegh-Guldberg and Kall that the latest coins of the find must have been struck during the reign of Commodus rather than by Marcus Aurelius.

---

100 Lind 1988, 58-59 and n. 5 described how coin identifications from the 19th century and early 20th century tend to assign too many coins to Marcus Aurelius and too few to Commodus. Is it possible to imagine that Christian Ramus, a specialist of Ancient coins and later author of the catalogue of Ancient coins in the Royal Collection (Ramus 1816) made the same mistake, while Høegh-Guldberg and Kall may have had better eyes for Commodus – or more time to study the individual coins? Note that the coins carrying the images of Faustina Minor and Lucilla have likewise disappeared in the Ramus' list.

101 As described by e.g. Mørkholm 1982, 15.
102 Ramus 1816.

Fig. 30. Excavating the Orup Hoard. Photo HWH.

5.2.2.2 Other denarius hoards

At Orup, north of Næstved, a denarius hoard was excavated in 2004. The first two coins from this hoard were in fact discovered during agricultural works in the 1950's, but it was only in 2002, when the original finder joined arms with an amateur detectorist, that more coins were discovered and the true nature of the find was revealed. During the excavation campaign more coins were found, and subsequent detector surveys are still today yielding more material. It was obvious that all the coins, denarii ranging in time from Nero to Septimius Severus (64/65-202/210 AD), originally must have been deposited together, but the hoard was totally ploughed up at the time of excavation. From an area of *c.* 180 sqm all plough soil was removed and searched by detector and/or by sieve. No other archaeological finds were made in this area. The find spot is close to a former wetland area, and we must conclude that the denarius hoard, consisting of at least 109 denarii, had been deposited in a marginal area with no other contemporary finds.[103] The composition of the Orup Hoard with

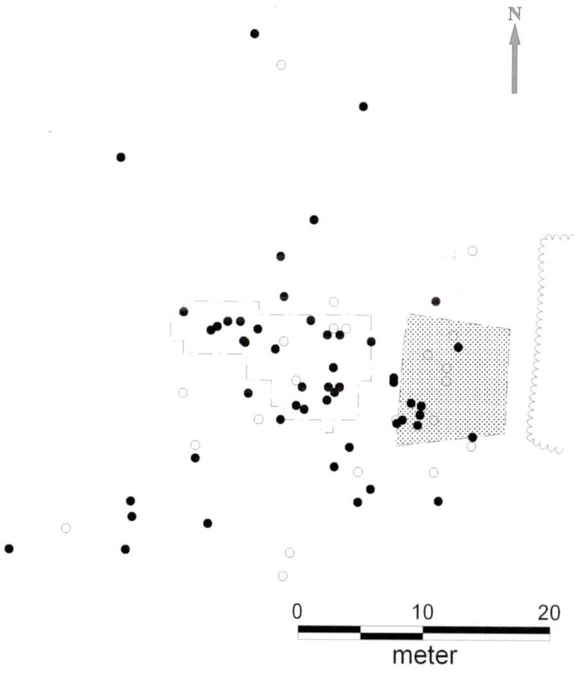

Fig. 31. Orup Hoard, the distribution of denarii (status 2004). After Roland & Horsnæs 2004, fig. 7.

---

103 050711 sb 26. FP 6831, 6982, 7017, 7095, 7343-7344 and 7419-7420. Roland & Horsnæs 2004. Three coins were found in 2008, bringing the total number of coins from the Orup Hoard up to 109 denarii, and we can expect more denarii to be found in future detector surveys.

Fig. 32. Denarii from the Orup Hoard. Photo Jens Olsen/ Næstved Museum.

Fig. 33. Denarii from Hellerne/Ledøje. Scale 1:1. Photo MLSS.

a relatively large number of Flavian coins is closely comparable to the Råmosen Hoard.

It is likely that seven denarii from Ledøje west of Copenhagen derive from another ploughed up hoard from a similar deposition in a marginal area (*Fig. 33*). The coins have been found with detector on a field south of the medieval village of Ledøje, sloping down towards the Tysmose Å (Stream).[104] The coins are ranging in time from Vespasian to Commodus (69/70-183/184 AD). Another denarius, struck by Antoninus Pius, has been found at Gersager in the village of Ledøje itself,[105] but otherwise the area has yielded no finds from the Late Roman or Early Germanic Iron Age.

In 1850 a denarius hoard, consisting of 45 coins, was found in Bagsværd north of Copenhagen on a field belonging to the peasant Peder Madsen (*Fig. 34*). This time we have good information on the find circumstances: the coins were found bundled together beneath a big stone, and it is specifically noted that no other finds were noticed. Unfortunately it has not been possible to locate the exact find spot. The registration number of Peder Madsen's farm is known, but it is today parcelled out, and there are two areas that may have yielded the find. One possibility is a gently sloping area west of the ancient village Bagsværd, the other is a low-lying area north of the village turning towards Bagsværd Sø (Lake). Both areas are today built-up, and there is little chance of finding additional evidence, but in particular the possible setting towards Bagsværd Sø is intriguing seen in relation to the topographical position of the hoards from Råmosen, Orup and Ledøje. The Bagsværd hoard consisted of 45 denarii ranging in time from Vespasian to Macrinus (69/79-217/218 AD).[106]

A denarius hoard was found at Præstemosen in the outskirts of the central place Gudme (see below). The site is situated on the border of area sb 140 (with two denarii), c. 400 m north of the Halls. The hoard was totally ploughed up. 160 denarii were found scattered in an area close to a small pond that lent

---

104 020209 sb 28: FP 6298 and 6490.
105 020209 sb 34: FP 7019; *RIC* 313, 160/161 AD.

106 020303 without sb no; Breitenstein 1946, 2-8 no. 2. Only seven of the denarii from the Bagsværd Hoard are still preserved, see Kroman 1995, Taf. 13:V nos. 40.1-40.7.

Fig. 34. The seven preserved denarii from the Bagsværd Hoard. Scale 1:1. Photo MLSS.

hoard, and the fact that both denarii were struck during the reign of Trajan (98-117 AD), are intriguing hints that they were part of the same hoard and that it is related to a wetland area.

Two denarius hoards from Jutland have been found in isolated wetland areas. One is the denarius hoard from Hvornum Kær consisting of 23 coins from Vespasian to Commodus (69/79-192 AD). The hoard had been deposited in the wetland area *c.* 1 m below surface in a low-lying area sloping towards Skals Å, only 8-10 m from the old course of the

its name to the hoard (Præstemosen = Vicar's Moor). As had by then become usual the first coins were found during a detector survey in 1991. Excavations in 1993 revealed the presence of what has been interpreted as a line of postholes, but the excavation area was too restricted to allow for further interpretation as to the age and nature of the construction (*Figs. 35-36*). Only few other finds were noted in the excavation area. The area has been used for grazing until recently, and it is likely that the hoard had been ploughed up only few years before the find was made. In several places two to five coins were found close together, and the excavators noted a blackish-brown greasy substance adhering to some of the coins, possibly the remains of a container of perishable material as for example a leather purse.[107]

Two denarii from Fangel Mose, also in Funen, can with good reason be ascribed to a now lost hoard. Already in 1819 a denarius found in a moor in Fangel was handed in to the National Museum,[108] but in the 1890's a hoard was found. The hoard was stolen, and only one denarius survived in the possession of the finder. This find passed unnoticed until 2001 when a grandchild of the finder told the story and showed the coin to archaeologists from Odense Bys Museer (*Fig. 19*). Unfortunately the exact find spot cannot be pinpointed for either of the denarii, but the information that the second coin was part of a

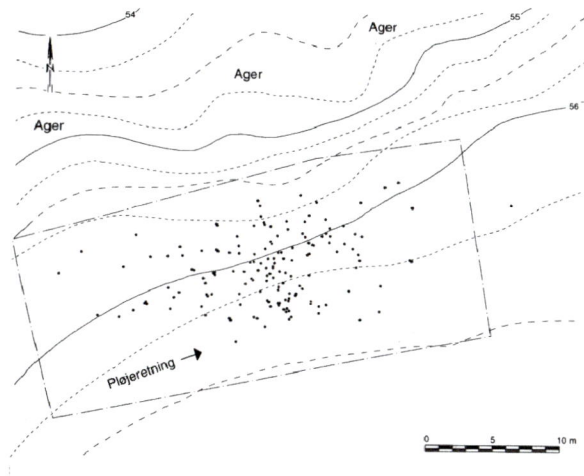

Fig. 35. Præstemosen, distribution map. After Madsen & Michaelsen 1998, 67 fig. 3.

stream.[109] The coins were found during peat cutting in 1936. A peat broke and a small blackish roll came out. As also the roll broke some coins came forward, but no other finds were made. The blackish substance was analysed and it was concluded that it was formed by oxidation of the coins and their stay in the peat. The coins are quite worn and some of them may have been intentionally cut (*Fig. 37*).

A hoard consisting of eight denarii, ranging in time from Hadrian to Commodus (118-191 AD),

---

107 Madsen & Michaelsen 1998; Horsnæs 2000.
108 NM I inv. CXIX. The coin was reported lost in Breitenstein 1943.

109 140704 without sb no.: FP 1894, Breitenstein 1936, 89-94; Balling 1962, 34-35 no. 16.

Fig. 36. Denarii from Præstemosen. Scale c. 1:1. Photo Odense Bys Museer/Claus Madsen.

in a ceramic pot was found in 1906 while digging for clay at Testrup Teglværk (tileworks). Two years later the same workman found an Antoninus Pius denarius in another pit at the tileworks, also accompanied with pottery (*Fig. 38*).[110] The site yielded several other finds of pits with pottery, both in 1906 and in 1908, and the workmen related that similar finds had been made earlier. The pots were deposited along the brink of the former bog where the tileworks was situated.[111] Some of the fragmented pots are dated in the Pre-Roman Iron Age, and the description seems to indicate that the finds represent a series of sacrifices characteristic of the Pre-Roman Iron Age, but also in some cases documented through the Roman Iron Age into the Early Germanic Iron Age.[112] This type

110 150406 sb 36; C 13326 (vessel) and Dnf. 11/06 (coins from hoard) found 1906; Balling 1962, 42-44 no. 33 and C 14079 (single find from 1908), Balling 1962, 48 no. 47.

111 Thanks to Jens Jeppesen, Moesgård Museum, for information on the site.

112 Becker 1972; for a recent summary see Kaul 2003, in particular 32-37. All preserved pottery fragments from Testrup belong to the Pre-Roman Iron Age. I thank Flemming Kaul, who has examined the pottery, for this information.

Context types

Fig. 37. The denarii from Hvornum Kær, now in Sydhimmerlands Museum. Note the unusual wear and degree of fragmentation not parallelled in other finds. Scale c. 1:1. Museum photo.

of offerings would normally include animal bones, which are not recorded in the case of Testrup. The presence of Roman coins is, however, unique.

The abovementioned denarius hoards have all been recovered near wetlands, and the coins are normally the only find from the site. The only real exception is the Præstemosen Hoard, found in the outskirts of Gudme (see below) in an area with possible traces of postholes. The exact find spot of the Bagsværd Hoard is not identified, but one of the two possible find spots is a wetland area towards Bagsværd Lake. The remaining denarius hoards are from topographical situations that allow them to be interpreted as sacrificial deposits from a wetland area.

5.2.3 Other denarius finds from wetland areas

To the denarius hoards should be added a number of minor (single or "double") finds of denarii that may be interpreted similarly. Two single finds derive from Sperrestrup in northern Sealand. In 1909 an Antoninus Pius denarius was found by peat cutting in Sperrestrup Mose (Moor). The exact find spot must be located somewhere in the hollow created by Sperrestrup Å (Stream). Another Antoninus Pius denarius was found by detector immediately west of the stream in 1992 (*Fig. 39*). Sperrestrup is situated only about 2 km south of the Lærkefryd site (see below section 5.3.2.3), and the denarius finds must obviously be seen in relation to the rich Iron Age finds in this area.

Fig. 38. Denarii from Testrup Teglværk. Note the difference in wear between the single find to the left (NM I C 14079) and the small hoard to the right (NM I C 13326). Scale 1:1. Photo MLSS.

Fig. 39. The two denarii from Sperrestrup. Left FP 1168 found 1909 (RIC 136, 145-161 AD); right FP 5162 found 1992 (RIC 59 or 80, 139-143 AD). Scale 1:1. Photo MLSS.

A Republican denarius was said to be found in Birkede Mose (Moor) in eastern Sealand before 1907, but the information derives from a coin dealer and cannot be verified. In light of the rarity of Republican denarius finds in Denmark, it would indeed be interesting if the find could be verified. There are no other finds noted in the immediate vicinities of Birkede Mose, but the site has an intriguing geographical position midways between the sites Østervang and Øm (see below on settlements).

In 1887 a denarius found in a moor in Mørkøv parish in western Sealand was handed in to the National Museum. The exact find spot is not recorded, but I believe that it was probably somewhere near Mørkøv Kirkeby, situated south of the Kobbelå (Kobbel Stream) and its surrounding wetlands, rather than at modern town Mørkøv that grew up as a rail station.

Two worn denarii were found at Erikstrup on the island Lolland south of Sealand in 1880 together with "a stone with a human face incised" on a field that had previously yielded gold objects (*Fig. 40*). Some of the finds had been made while constructing the railroad through a formerly wooded area. The gold objects are a neckring,[113] a broad finger ring and

List of denarius hoards from wetland areas

Hoards				
Site	Sb	Name	Period	Total coins
020209	28	Hellerne, Brydegård	Vespasian to Commodus	7
020303		Bagsværd	Vespasian to Macrinus	45
030205	59	Råmosen	Tiberius (sic) to Marcus Aurelius (or Commodus?)	(?) 428
050711	26	Orup	Vitellius to Septimius Severus	109
080405	35	Fangel	Trajan	?
090104	162	Præstemosen	Otho to Macrinus	160
140704		Hvornum Kær	Vespasian to Commodus	23
150406	36	Testrup Teglværk	Hadrian to Commodus	8

List of single finds of denarii from isolated wetland areas

Site	Sb	Name	Find	Total coins
010306	106	Sperrestrup	Denarius	1
010306	34	Sperrestrup Mose	Denarius	1
020102	18	Birkede Mose	Republican denarius	1
030708	0	Mørkøv parish	Denarius	1
070321	19	Erikstrup	Two denarii + gold	2
090510	117	Øster Åby	Denarius	1
100203	383	Hjallerup Mose, Dronninglund	Two denarii	2

---

113 Jørgensen & Petersen 1998, 122 date the neckring *c.* AD 200.

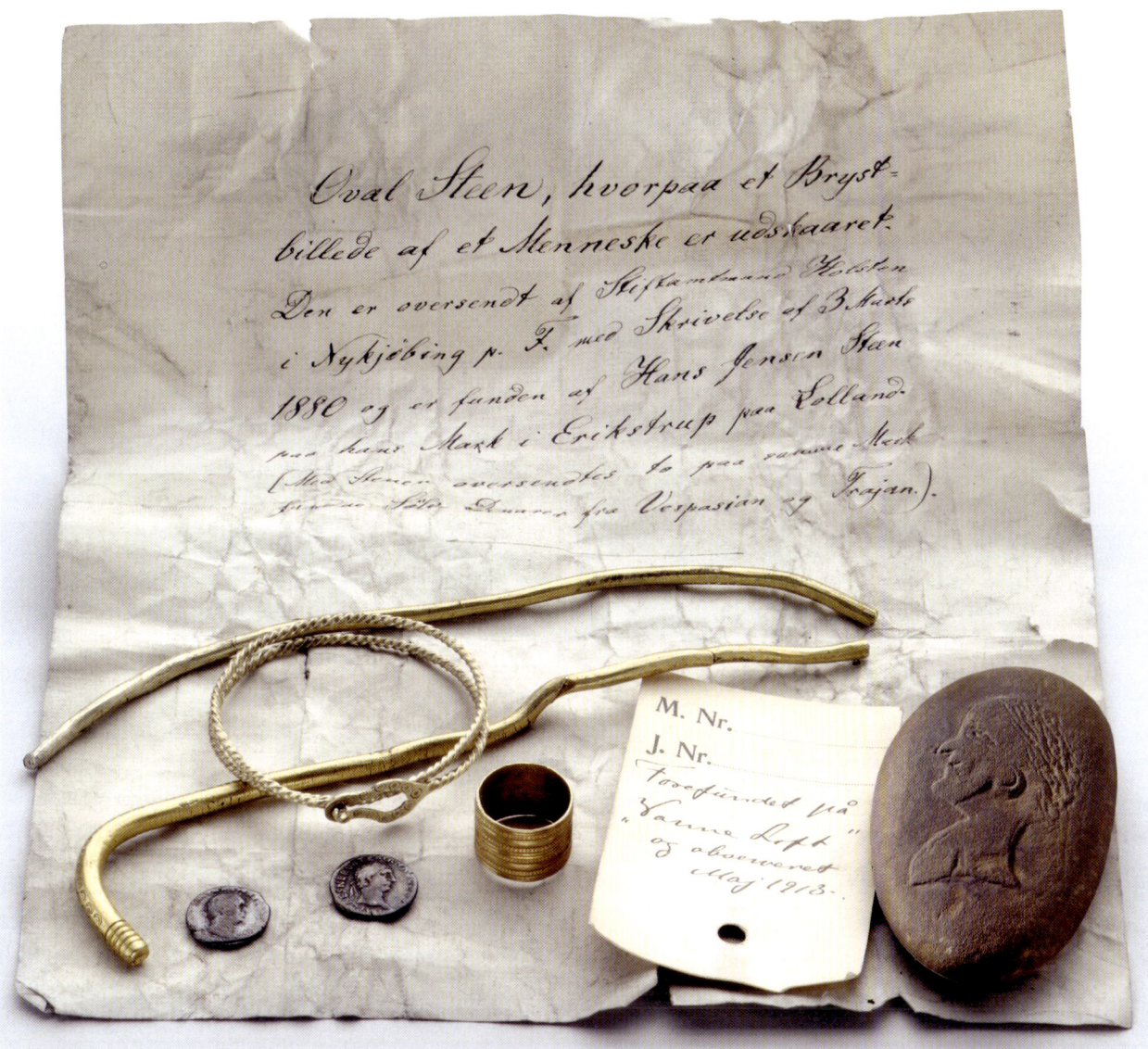

Fig. 40. Finds from the same field? Erikstrup. Gold jewellery and gold rod from the Early Germanic Iron Age, two Roman denarii, and a stone with a portrait. The latter is clearly a modern hoax, but it was sent to the museum together with the two denarii "found on the same field". Made by the finder – or made to fool him? Erikstrup, Lolland. Denarii NM I C 3660-3661, gold NM I 19250, C 1610 and C 1763a-b. Stone in The Royal Coll. of Coins and Medals (not inventorized). Photo John Lee/National Museum of Denmark.

three pieces of gold bars, all probably from the Late Roman Iron Age. The stone with the human face, however, is clearly produced quite recently – perhaps the finder was inspired to draw this portrait by the portraits on the coins?

A single find of a denarius was made in 1979 at Øster Åby on the slopes of Vejstrup Å (Vejstrup Stream), Funen, in a topographical situation not dissimilar from the denarii from Sperrestrup. The stream runs from Brudager, where several finds of material from Roman Iron Age to Viking Period have been noted, and eastwards to the Great Belt. Subsequent detector surveying on the field where the coin was located, however, yielded no other finds, and reports from 1918 of urns found on the field could not be verified. It is therefore unlikely that the coin pertained to a settlement or a cemetery.

Hjallerup Mose in northern Jutland (c. 20 km northeast of Aalborg) has yielded two denarii. They were found in 1921 above ground, but it was assumed that they derived from a ditch dug at the site.

Fig. 41. The Simmersted Hoard, some of the siliquae are visible at the centre of the photo.
Photo Lennart Larsen/National Museum of Denmark.

The exact find spot cannot be identified. Hjallerup is situated at Klavsholm Å, and it has long been an important crossing of the stream. Already on late 18th century maps a mill is indicated, and Hjallerup was (and still is) an important market site.

This review of denarii from probable wetland area does not claim to be comprehensive. Other single finds of denarii may derive from similar circumstances, but in cases where there is no indication that the find derive from a wetland area, it has been decided to list it among the settlement material. This means that future research may suggest that some of the single finds listed among the settlement material, should indeed be transferred to the group of wetland finds or *vice versa*.

It is suggested that the wetland finds as a group should be interpreted as deliberate and most probably religious depositions following an already then age-old tradition of moor sacrifices. The date of the depositions can in reality only be given as a *post quem* date provided by the production date of the coin. The earliest independently dated depositions of the Flavian-Antonine group of denarii are from the early 3rd century (Illerup), but as we have seen, also the later weapon sacrifices and burials have yielded denarii as well. We may infer from the lack of later material, and in particular the lack of later coins in the denarius hoard from Præstemosen at Gudme that it might have been deposited before the influx of Constantinian gold coins into Gudme/Funen had started, suggesting a deposition date between *c.* 200 and 350 AD. Extending this deposition date to the other "pure" denarius hoards (or single depositions) is possible, but it is highly speculative: The Gudme IV hoard with denarii and siliquae clearly points to a later deposition date, and there are numerous examples outside the area of the present investigation of denarius finds from contexts with Late Roman solidi. Moreover, as we shall see below, the settlement material suggests that denarii may have been as common in the Early Germanic Iron Age, i.e. after *c.* 375 AD, as in the preceding Late Roman Iron Age.

5.2.4 Mixed hoards

It is possible to make a rough distinction between on the one hand Hacksilber hoards containing one or more coins, and on the other hand gold hoards containing one or more coins. The Hacksilber hoards in question are the Høsten Torp Hoard and the hoard from Simmersted Mose in Jutland, both containing siliquae (on a similar hoard from settlement context see below).[114]

The hoard from Høsten Torp consisted of 4453 kg of silver including eight siliquae struck by Constantius II (337-361) and during the Valetinian dynasti, i.e. from the last third of the 4th century or perhaps even a bit later. Three of the coins were struck in Trier. Two of the coins were pierced, one was cut and no less than three were clipped (on clipping see below).[115] The hacked silver included a large variety of types: ingots, rods and wire, fragments of Scandinavian silverwork as well as a large number of

---

114 In January 2009 an amateur detectorist located a new Hacksilber hoard with siliquae in southern Jutland.
115 040205 sb 5: FP 1830.1-8; Breitenstein 1946, no.36.

Fig. 42. The Boltinggård Hoard. Scale c. 1:1. Photo John Lee/ National Museum of Denmark.

fragments of Late Roman silver plate. The hoard was dated *c.* 500 AD.

The Simmersted Hoard (*Fig. 41*) is closely comparable to the find from Høsten Torp. The hoard was found in 1945 during excavations in a river bank.[116] The 968 g of hacked silver found along with the coins consists of a mixture of local and imported Late Roman objects, all cut into minute pieces. The hoard probably contained eight siliquae. They are slightly later than the ones from the Høsten Torp Hoard, struck in the period from Julian to Honorius (360-423 AD). Two of them are from the Trier mint, while a third comes from Lugdunum, the mint of the remaining coins cannot be identified. Three of the coins are clipped.

The presence of coins in these contexts is probably accidental in the sense that they appear as pieces of silver rather than as coins/objects.

5.2.5 Gold hoards

The majority of the Roman gold coins from Denmark have been found as parts of hoards, most often in combination with other types of objects. The hoards have normally been found outside defined

---

116 200205 sb 38: FP 2158; Voss 1954; Munksgaard 1955, 34-35 listed five coins, while Balling 1962, 62-63 no. 84 listed six coins and two unidentified fragments. Only the five coins listed by Munksgaard have been identified.

Fig. 43. A selection of material from the Brangstrup Hoard. Photo Anne Vibeke Leth/National Museum of Denmark.

settlement areas, the most important exception being the gold hoards from Gudme (see below). The greatest concentration of gold coins has been found on Funen. Apart from the Gudme finds there is an important hoard from Elsehoved (south of Gudme), a hoard from Slipshavn on Storebælt close to Nyborg, and three hoards from Central Funen: the Boltinggård Hoard, the Brangstrup Hoard and the Rynkebygård Hoard.

The Boltinggård Hoard (*Fig. 42*) and the Brangstrup Hoard (*Fig. 43*) were found only 700 m apart, and they are closely related. There are 67 coins from the two hoards in all. Both hoards cover the period from 251 to 335/6 AD, and the centre of gravity are in both cases the Constantinian period. In both hoards the coins are combined with gold jewellery, and many of the coins are reworked into jewellery, either by piercing a hole or by an added loop. There are, however, also a number of minor differences between the two hoards. The 15 coins from the Boltinggård Hoard are three aurei and 12 solidi. Among the latter six were struck in Trier, and six solidi were struck in the same year: 335/6 AD. The number of coins in the Brangstrup hoard is far greater, a total of 52 coins. The distribution of aurei and solidi is more balanced, and the eastern mints are better represented in the Brangstrup Hoard. While the solidi from the Boltinggård Hoard are in almost mint condition, the coins from the Brangstrup Hoard are more worn, and some of them seem to have been deliberately bent before they were deposited.[117] In both cases the coins provide the best evidence for the date of the depositions in the middle or second half of the 4th century, the differences in wear of the coins perhaps suggesting that the Brangstrup Hoard is deposited a bit later than the Boltinggård Hoard. Both hoards have been found in topographical settings that suggest they may have been deposited in marginal areas, perhaps in a liminal area between two centres.[118] There is archival evidence of a third gold hoard from this area, but neither the exact location of this find, nor the composition of the hoard is known.

---

117 At Vestergård, *c.* 200 from Boltinggård and 500 m from Brangstrup, a third gold hoard has been found, but the gold was melted down, and no details as to the size and contents of the hoard have been preserved, nor is there any indication whether this hoard also contained coins.

118 Henriksen & Horsnæs 2004; 2006.

Fig. 44. The Rynkebygård Hoard. Scale c. 1:1. Photo John Lee/ National Museum of Denmark.

A pierced Constantinian solidus from Trier dated 312-317 AD was found in a garden in Ringe parish in Central Funen and sent to the Royal Coll. of Coins and Medals in 1863.[119] Whether this coin is to be regarded as (part of) yet another gold hoard or it may in some way be related to one of the two known gold hoards with Constantinian solidi cannot be ascertained, yet the fact that this coin fits in so well with the finds from Boltinggård and Brangstrup must be underlined.

At Rynkebygård north of Ringe town a hoard consisting of five Late Roman solidi was found during peat-cutting in 1848. The coins were struck during the reigns of Valentinian III, Marcianus and Leo I (425-474 AD) in Ravenna and Constantinople.[120] The hoard also contained a spiraliform finger-ring, a bracteate with a Runic inscription and an electrum ingot (*Fig. 44*). This hoard thus represents a period of production a century later than the two hoards from the area south of Ringe, and it was deposited in the late 5th or early 6th century.

The Rynkebygård Hoard is related to the Elsehoved Hoard (*Fig. 45*). Elsehoved is a small promontory in Storebælt south of Lundeborg and southeast of Gudme. The first finds of gold coins were made around 1826 when the previously forested area was taken in for agriculture. In the following years more finds were made when ploughing the soil. Unfortunately the finder was not aware of the nature and importance of the find, and the objects were sold to a local man, who in 1833 resold the coins and jewellery to the Oldnordisk Museum, although with a false provenance "Scania", probably invented to cover the fact that the objects undoubtedly were *danefæ*. More finds were made during the 19th century, and an interview with the original finder in 1876 clarified the provenance, although the exact find spot cannot be pinpointed today. It also revealed that the hoard as known today is not complete. The preserved hoard consists of a large fibula, a spiral finger ring, nine spiral beads, an ingot (210 g), and eight Late Roman solidi, but at least 10 to 12 coins seem to have existed. The Elsehoved Hoard was deposited 530-550 AD.[121]

The large Broholm Hoard also contained two Late Roman solidi. The hoard was found in 1833 and weighing more than 4 kg it is still one of the largest gold hoards from Denmark. The hoard contains a number of heavy neck rings and arm rings, sword

---

119 090108 sb 125: FP 242. The coin was of the same type as a coin from the Brangstrup Hoard and was therefore exchanged. Its present whereabouts is unknown. Breitenstein 1942, 86, VI.

120 090108 sb 7 and sb 8: FP 72 and NM I 10038; Breitenstein 1942, 89, X.

121 Jørgensen *et al.* 2003, 432.

Crossing boundaries

Fig. 45. Coins and beads from the Elsehoved Hoard. Scale c. 1:1. Photos Lennart Larsen/National Museum of Denmark.

fittings, ingot fibulas and other jewellery, bracteates and two Late Roman solidi.[122] The bracteates from the hoard indicate that it was deposited in the early 6th century, roughly contemporary with the Elsehoved Hoard.[123]

The last gold hoard with Roman coins from Funen is the Slipshavn Hoard found by detector surveying on a promontory north of Nyborg on eastern Funen, close to an excellent natural landing place. The topographical setting can thus be compared to the probable find place of the Elsehoved Hoard. The hoard includes a large variety of gold types, many of which had been cut into small pieces.[124] The locally made objects clearly indicate that the hoard must have been depostited in the Early Germanic Iron Age, probably not before c. AD 500, but the two Roman coins from the hoard are both struck in the 3rd century, by Valerian and Diocletian, and their nearest parallels can thus be found in the Boltinggård and Brangstrup Hoards.

There is only one, very insecure, report on multiple finds of gold coins from Sealand. Unidentified (and undated!) gold coins were said to be found twice in molehills on the eastern side of Gettehøj, a disturbed prehistoric dolmen in Broby parish between Næstved and Fakse in southern Sealand.[125]

Jutland has yielded three examples of hoards including gold coins. In all cases the coins are Late Roman solidi, while the Constantinian phase so prominent in Funen is totally absent. In Apholm, a low-lying area north of Frederikshavn, a now lost coin was found as part of a hoard also containing a bracteate,[126] and gold and silver ingots.[127] Two solidi were part of a larger hoard found in the years 1902-1914 in Års in northern Jutland. The hoard also consisted of

---

122 Michaelsen & Thomsen 1991.
123 It must be stressed that the Gudme area has yielded a considerable number of other gold hoards from the same period. They have, however, not been considered in the present work, unless they also include Roman coins. See also below on Gudme.
124 Jørgensen & Petersen 1998, 195-196.

125 040223 sb 2; Breitenstein 1946 28.
126 NM I inv.no. MDCLXVI (bracteate) and MDCCLVI (silver ingot).
127 100303 sb 85; Balling 1962, 70.

three pieces of spiraliform gold wire and three bracteates.[128] No other Iron Age finds are registered in the immediate vicinity. In both cases the presences of bracteates in the hoards date the depositions in the early 6th century.

Two coins, both fitted with a rim and a somewhat unusual loop, were found in 1899 and 1909 respectively on the same field (matr. no. 7d) in Jordrup (southern Jutland) and earlier finds of coins of unknown type from the same field were reported.[129] The find was made in an area north of Jordrup traversed by a small stream on old maps of the area. A third solidus mounted with a rim and a loop of exactly the same type as the rim and loop used for the two coins from Jordrup was found already in 1861 by the farmer Ferdinand Schwincke on Ejstrup Mark. The find spot was described as close to the former ford crossing Kolding Å (Stream).[130] The two sites are situated *c.* 8 km apart as the crow flies. There is no objective reason to doubt the provenance of the find from Ejstrup Mark. Yet the similarities with the Jordrup coins are intriguing, as is the information that coins were probably found in Jordrup prior to 1899. I am convinced that these three coins originally were parts of the same ensemble, although it is not possible to say anything about how, why and when they were split.

5.2.6 Single finds of Ancient gold coins

Although a considerable number of the gold coins are parts of hoards, there are many finds of a single gold coin in an isolated area, without any indication of other Iron Age finds in the vicinity. In practically all the cases the find was made before the 1st World War, and farmers working in their fields were responsible for most of the finds.

These single finds have been overlooked hitherto, probably because they are hard to handle. Most of the coins in question have been found when marginal soils were first taken in for agriculture in the late 19th century or during peat cutting in moors.

Other finds have been made in coastal areas. Practically all of them were accidental finds, and information on find spot and find circumstances is rarely detailed. These landscape types have no appeal for the modern detectorist. The soil in the wetland areas is not turned by the plough which means that no new finds surface, and the knowing detectorist would not survey areas that were unlikely to have been settled in prehistoric times. I believe that it is possible to interpret some of, if not all, these finds as the result of deliberate depositions in line with the coins from the gold hoards described above: depositions of a religious nature made in marginal areas not settled by man.

Fig. 46. The solidus from Ejstrup (NM I 19695) and the two solidi from Jordrup (NM I C 9536 and Dnf. 19/09). Scale 1:1. Photos HWH.

---

128 120814 sb 152: FP 853 and NM I C 11369; Balling 1962, 64-65 no. 89; Axboe 2004, 321.

129 190105: NM I C 9536 and 19/09; Balling 1962, 65-66 no. 91.

130 170203 sb 5: NM I 19695; Balling 1962, 66 no. 92 and fig. 9.

List of isolated single finds of Roman gold coins from Denmark

site	SB	provenance	Year of find	emperor	denomination	mint	Type RIC	Coin date	w.	Comment	Inv.no.
020302		Hvidøre[131]	1869	Leo I	solidus	-	-	457-474	-	-	FP 309, lost
020306	410	Slotsfruens Vænge[132]	1919	Theodosius II	solidus	Constantinople	257	430-440	4.42		FP 1446
040112	445	Assentorp[133]	1868	Leo I	solidus	-	-	457-474	-	Loop	FP 304, lost
040210		Kværkeby[134]	1851	Constantin II Cæsar	solidus	Thessalonica	132	324-326	4.45	Loop	FP 99, lost
040506	4	Haldagerlille[135]	1874	Crispus Cæsar	solidus	Sirmium	6	317-326	5.01	Loop	FP 355
040509	71	Klinteby[136]	1939	Titus	aureus	Rome	90 (2nd ed.)	?79-80	7.08		FP 1993
050104		Herfølge[137]	1859	Theodosius II	solidus	Constantinople	324	441-450	5.76	Double beaded rim, probably broken off loop	NM I C18617
050302		Fakse[138]	1768	Valentinian I	medallion	Antiochia	13	367-375	18.44	Loop	NM I 8511
050503	17	Store-Lind[139]	1893	Vespasian	aureus	Rome	10	69-71	7.28	Nick and cut	FP 652
050505	163	Færgegården[140]	1937	imitation/"Valentinian 3"	solidus	Gallic	3711/3	425-475	5.47	Beaded rim, loop	FP 2072
050604	51	Gjorslev[141]	<1886	Constantin II Cæsar	solidus	Constantinople	94	335-336	3.89	Pierced twice & loop	NM I C 5510
070110	65	Strangegården[142]	1929	Imitation	solidus	-	-	4th cent.	6.01		FP 1733
080108	80	Midskov Skov[143]	c. 1899	Imitation/"Julius Nepos"/ Eurich(?)	solidus	-	-	474-484	4.23	Pierced	FP 1166
080301	3	Allese[144]	<1908	Constantius II	medallion	Antiochia	69	347-355	20.55	Trace of loop and granulation	NM I Dnf. 3/08
080406	18	Næsby[145]	<1993	Imitation/"Valentinian III"	solidus	Gallic	3713(?)	425-500	5.27	Looped and mounted	NM I 7610/93
080604	49	Gamby[146]	1942	Constans	solidus	Siscia	22C	337-340	4.44	Loop	FP 2067
080703	63	Broskov/Åbanken[147]	1855	imitation/"Diocletian"	"aureus"	-	-	284-?	8.33	Pierced	FP 141
080717	19	Rørup[148]	1875	Constantius II	solidus	-	-	337-361	-		(lost)

---

131 Breitenstein 1946, 26 no. 40; Fagerlie 1967, find 196, cat. 440; Kromann 1995, 350 no. 72. Found in garden, close to beach.
132 Breitenstein 1946, 26 no. 39, fig. 22; Fagerlie 1967, find 197, cat. 265; Kromann 1995, 350 no. 70.
133 Breitenstein 1946, 26-27 no. 41; Fagerlie 1967, find 200, cat. 520; Kromann 1995, 350 no. 73.
134 Breitenstein 1946, 20 no. 31, fig. 7; Kromann 1995, 350 no. 55.
135 Breitenstein 1946, 19 no. 29, fig. 6; Kromann 1995, 350 no. 53.
136 Breitenstein 1946, 9 no. 5, fig. 2; Kromann 1995, 349 no. 5.
137 Breitenstein 1946, 25-26 no. 38, fig. 21; Fagerlie 1967, find 198, cat. 274; Kromann 1995, 350 no. 69.
138 Breitenstein 1946, 21-22 no. 35, fig. 10; Kromann 1995, 350 no. 65.
139 Breitenstein 1946, 9 no. 4, fig. 1; Kromann 1995, 349 no. 4. Found while digging, c. ½ alen below surface.
140 Breitenstein 1946, 24-25 no. 37, fig. 20; Fagerlie 1967, find 199, cat. 85; Kromann 1995, 350 no. 71. Found while ploughing.
141 Breitenstein 1946, 20 no. 32, fig. 8; Kromann 1995, 350 no. 56.
142 Breitenstein 1946, 21 no. 34, fig. 9; Kromann 1995, 350 no. 63. Found while digging clamp.
143 Breitenstein 1943, 16-18 no. XXVII, fig. 20; Fagerlie 1967, find 192, cat. 183.
144 Breitenstein 1943, 14-15 no. XXII, fig. 17.
145 *AUD* 1993, 229 and fig.; Henriksen 1994, 15. Found in garden.
146 Breitenstein 1943, 11-12 no. XX, fig. 15.
147 Breitenstein 1943, 10-11 no. XVII, fig. 13; Horsnæs 2001.

site	SB	provenance	Year of find	emperor	denomination	mint	Type RIC	Coin date	w.	Comment	Inv.no.
080806	18	Nørre Søby[149]	1898	Valentinian I	solidus	Arles	1	364-367	4.13	Loop (broken off)	FP 745
090108	125	Ringe[150]	1863	Constantin I	solidus	Trier	-	312-317	-	Pierced	FP 242, lost
090411	1	Sallinge[151]	1863	Theodosius II	solidus	Constantinople	225 (X, 257)	423-424	4.90	Looped, mounted in beaded rim	NM I C 21307
090416	36	Tange[152]	1935	Imitation	"aureus"	-	-	238-?	6.80	Loop	FP 1977
090506	7	Kværndrup[153]	1861	Imitation/"Maximinus Hercules"	"aureus"	-	-	286-?	3.68	Loop	FP 229
090506	32	Trunderup[154]	1893	Constantius II Cæsar	medallion	Trier	570	335	19.99	Traces of loop	FP 639
090507	78	Vornæs Skov[155]	1851	Imitation/"Probus"	"aureus"	-	-	276-?	6.24	Pierced, hole filled in, loop	FP 110
090511	22	Hundtofte[156]	1774	Constantin I	solidus	Nicomedia	-	335-336	-		(lost)
090618	39	Ørbæk[157]	1777	Trajanus Decius	aureus	Rome	16a	249-251	4.37	Pierced from obverse	BP 217
140313		Kinbjerg[158]	1670	Imitation/"Julius Nepos"/Eurik(?)	Uniface "solidus"	-	- RIC [D N IVI NE-POS AVG]	466-484	1.62	Beaded rim, trace of loop eye	R barb
140509		Eeg[159]	<1853	Leo I	solidus	Constantinople off. S	605 or 630	457-474	5.65	Beaded rim, trace of loop	NM I 13623
140706		Hou[160]	1820	Carinus	aureus	Siscia	193	282-283	4.99		R 19aa
141103		Hjortshøj[161]	1943	Valens	medallion	Constantinople	Not in RIC	364-378	94.06	Loop and elaborate rim	FP 2084
170202	61	Eltang[162]	<1920	Imitation/"Justinian"	solidus	Ostrogothic?	BMC ostrogoths p. 60ssq.	522-534	4.30		FP 1590
170504	0	Bet. Fredericia/Pjedsted[163]	<1970	Imitation/"Anastasius"/Theoderic	solidus	Rome	Metlich 8, cf. BMC p. 55,61ff	491-518	4.32		FP 3064
170704	0	Seljumshave[164]	1841	Valentinian I	solidus	Antiochia	2b (272)	364-367	4.39	Loop	R 31a
170704	153	Sønder Stenderup[165]	<1993	Gallienus	aureus		58	253-268	3.44	Pierced	FP 5265

---

148 Hauberg 1875, nr. 134; Breitenstein 1943, 15 no. XXIII.
149 Breitenstein 1943, 15-16 no. XXV, fig. 18.
150 Breitenstein 1942, 86 no. VI. Found in a garden. The coin was exchanged from the Royal Coll. of Coins and Medals between 1865 and 1942.
151 Breitenstein 1943, 16 no. XXVI, fig. 19; Fagerlie 1967, find 195, cat. 210. Found while ploughing close to fence.
152 Breitenstein 1943, 9 no. XIV, fig. 10.
153 Breitenstein 1943, 10 no. XVI, fig. 12; Hertz 1987, 228 no. 647a.
154 Breitenstein 1943, 12-14 no. XXI, fig. 16 with references.
155 Breitenstein 1943, 9-10 no. XV, fig. 11.
156 Breitenstein 1943, 11 no. XIX.
157 Breitenstein 1943, 6 no. XII, fig. 8.
158 Balling 1962, 66-68 no. 93, fig. 9; Fagerlie 1967, find 186, cat. 184.
159 Balling 1962, 65 no. 90, fig. 9; Fagerlie 1967, find 187, cat. 460.
160 Balling 1962, 58 no. 75, fig. 8.
161 Breitenstein 1943b; Balling 1962, 64 no. 87; Horsnæs 2002.
162 Balling 1962, 69 no. 97, fig. 9; Fagerlie 1967, find 191 cat. 746. Found not far from the Gudsø Vig sea barricade.
163 Kromann 1983-84, 71 no. 10; Westermark 1983, 37 no. 21.
164 Balling 1962, 63 no. 85, fig. 8.

site	SB	provenance	Year of find	emperor	denomination	mint	Type RIC	Coin date	w.	Comment	Inv.no.
170908	0	Frederikshåb[166]	<1846	Constantin I	medallion	Trier	-	307-312	3.61	Loop and rim made in one pjece with the "coin"	NM I 9409
190502	0	NE of Gjesting[167]	<1832	Imitation/"Marcianus"?/"Justinian I"?	solidus	Rome?	-	450-527	4.00	Loop	R barb
190706	0	Lunde[168]	1850	Valentinian I	solidus	Antiochia	2a (272)	364-367	4.42		FP 92 / R 30a
200507	60	Stepping[169]	<1923	Anastasius	solidus	Constantinople	MIB 4	493-	4.36		FP 1559

5.3 Settlements

Until recently Roman coin finds from settlements were quite few, and most often they were found as the result of planned archaeological activity. The vast majority of finds were accidental, and the overwhelming majority of the coins came from hoards.[170] Detector archaeology has changed this pattern significantly. As has been shown denarii have dominated the finds since the early 1980's, and the majority of these have been found in sites which yielded other finds as well, and which have been interpreted as settlement areas.[171] Furthermore it has been pointed out that denarii are probably under-represented from settlements in which the metal detector and/or sieving of topsoil have not been used systematically during investigation. It is therefore of interest to review old single finds of denarii and compare them with settlements with denarius finds retrieved during controlled archaeological fieldwork and specialized metal detecting. A list of denarius finds from settlement areas forms the basis for this inquiry (see list of denarius finds, pp. 117-120). The list should be considered a snapshot of the find situation as it was in 2008/09. Changes happen all the time. Note for example that two new sites were identified within the first months of 2008 (Kvosted and Tranbjerg).

One settlement area, however, demands special consideration. It is the large site at Gudme and its surroundings, including its cemetery at Møllegårdsmarken, the port-of-trade at Lundeborg and the gold hoard recovered in the surroundings of Gudme. This area has yielded almost half the Roman coins found in Western Denmark, and it is in all respects atypical. In this survey of sites with Roman coin finds it will therefore be treated as a separate entity.

5.3.1 Gudme, Lundeborg and the surrounding area

5.3.1.1 *Gudme*

Modern Gudme is situated *c.* 4 km from Storebælt on the eastern side of Gudme Sø (Lake). The name, Gudme, means "Home of [the] gods" and three other toponyms are of major importance for the interpretation of the site: Galdbjerg ("Hill of sacrifice"), Gudbjerg ("Hill of gods") and Albjerg ("Hill of sanctuary[?]"), 2 km to the north, west and south-southeast of Gudme respectively, give evidence of ritual centres involving sacrifices. They show that Gudme was closely connected to an important cult centre.[172]

The area has long been known for rich archaeological finds. The Hesselagergård medallion(s) mentioned above (*Fig. 1*) was struck from ancient gold

---

165 *AUD* 1993, 255; Kromann 2003.
166 Alföldi 1958; Balling 1962, 59 no. 79, fig. 8.
167 Balling 1962, 68 no. 94 fig. 9; Fagerlie 1967, find 189, cat. 747.
168 Balling 1962, 63 no. 86, fig. 8.
169 Balling 1962, 68-69 no. 95, fig. 9; Fagerlie 1967, find 185, cat. 700.
170 Lind 1988, 38-41. It is quite striking that the observation made by Majvor Östergren that the majority of the single finds of denarii were made on settlements in Gotland is mentioned in note 8, but not further discussed in Lind's study.
171 On denarii from settllements in Jutland see also Bjerg 2007.

172 Kousgård Sørensen 1985.

found in this area in the 16th century, and in 1833 one of the heaviest gold treasures from Denmark, now known as the Broholm Hoard, was found on the field Enemærket belonging to the Broholm Manor. The owner of the manor, the widow Edel Sehested, accompanied by her young son Frederik, brought the Broholm Hoard to the National Museum. This trip evidently left an imprint on Frederik Sehested who later in life took a keen interest in archaeology and among many other things excavated and published a large number of graves in the cemetery at Møllegårdsmarken.[173]

Also early finds of Roman coins were noted, and in 1942 Breitenstein published the coins from the Gudme district as the first of his series of articles compiling Roman coin finds from Denmark.[174] He described 11 finds of Roman coins in details, and of these finds nos. I-III, VII-IX and XI are from Gudme and Oure parishes, while finds IV-VI and X are from Ringe parish. Finds nos. I and II are single finds of denarii, find no. III covers a sequence of finds consisting of two denarii and six solidi that Breitenstein interpreted as the remains of a mixed hoard of solidi and denarii.[175] Finds nos. VII-IX are single finds of solidi, and finally find no. XI is the Elsehoved Hoard, the provenance of which is discussed and fully established. Breitenstein furthermore referred to three finds of gold coins from Gudme then only known from Sehested's publication.

In 1980 amateur archaeologists initiated detector surveys in Gudme guided by the old maps from Sehested's publications and other known archaeological finds.[176] They started out in the area, now known as Gudme I,[177] where the two denarii and six solidi had been found in the period 1885 to 1941, and already in 1980 the amateur archaeologists found new gold coins from the area with their detectors.[178] Since then the total number of Roman coins from Gudme I has risen to 56: 37 denarii, 8 siliquae and 11 solidi of which one is a multiplum. An excavation in 1984 revealed post-holes of seven houses dated from the 4th to the 7th centuries, but no coins were found below the plough soil. The solidi were found within a relatively restricted area above Houses IV and V, two houses partly overlying each other and both with preserved wall-posts. Houses IV and V were the two oldest houses in the area, typologically dated in the 4th-5th centuries.[179] The solidi are all dated within the reign of the family of Constantine the Great, and they were found within a restricted part of the Gudme I area (*Fig. 48*). They can therefore be interpreted as a disturbed hoard (the Gudme I Hoard). The denarii and siliquae were, however, spread over a far greater part of the field, and are best interpreted as single finds. The area has furthermore yielded a hacksilver hoard from the Early Germanic Iron Age (sb 76: Stenhøjgård Hoard).

The area of Gudme II,[180] immediately to the northeast of Gudme I, has yielded the majority of detector finds from Gudme. Also the number of Roman coins from this area is impressive. A total of 250 Roman coins distributed as 226 denarii, 19 siliquae, 3 solidi and 2 bronze coins. Fibulas found in the same area indicate that the 4th-5th centuries may have been the most prolific periods in Gudme II, but finds range from the 3rd to the 12th centuries. Two of the denarii (struck by Domitian in 90 and Commodus in 190/1 AD) were found in a pit with pottery dated in period C1, around or shortly after AD 200.[181] Traces of seven houses have been found in the area.

One of the denarii from Gudme II was part of a hoard consisting of nine bracteates, two gold pendants, a spiraliform fingerring, and a gold button inlaid with almadine garnet.[182] The hoard had been deposited in a small pit interpreted as the hole of one of the roof-bearing posts of a small house. The denarius is looped, and it is extremely worn. This coin is clear

---

173 Sehested 1878 and 1884. On Sehested see for example Thrane 1994.
174 Breitenstein 1942.
175 Breitenstein 1942, 70-73 no. III.
176 The first detector finds from Gudme were discussed in Kromann 1987.
177 090104 sb 144.
178 The first of these coin finds were listed in Kromann 1983-84, 74-100 as "find" nos. 21 (Gudme area I) and 22 (Gudme area II).

179 Sb 144. Petersen 1987, 51-57; Petersen 1994, 30-31 and Fig. 2.
180 Sb 143. Petersen 1994, 34-35 and Figs. 11-13; Jørgensen 1994; Jørgensen 1998.
181 Excavation report OBM 7542. FP 6544.1-2.
182 Poulsen 1987; Axboe 1987; Petersen 1988.

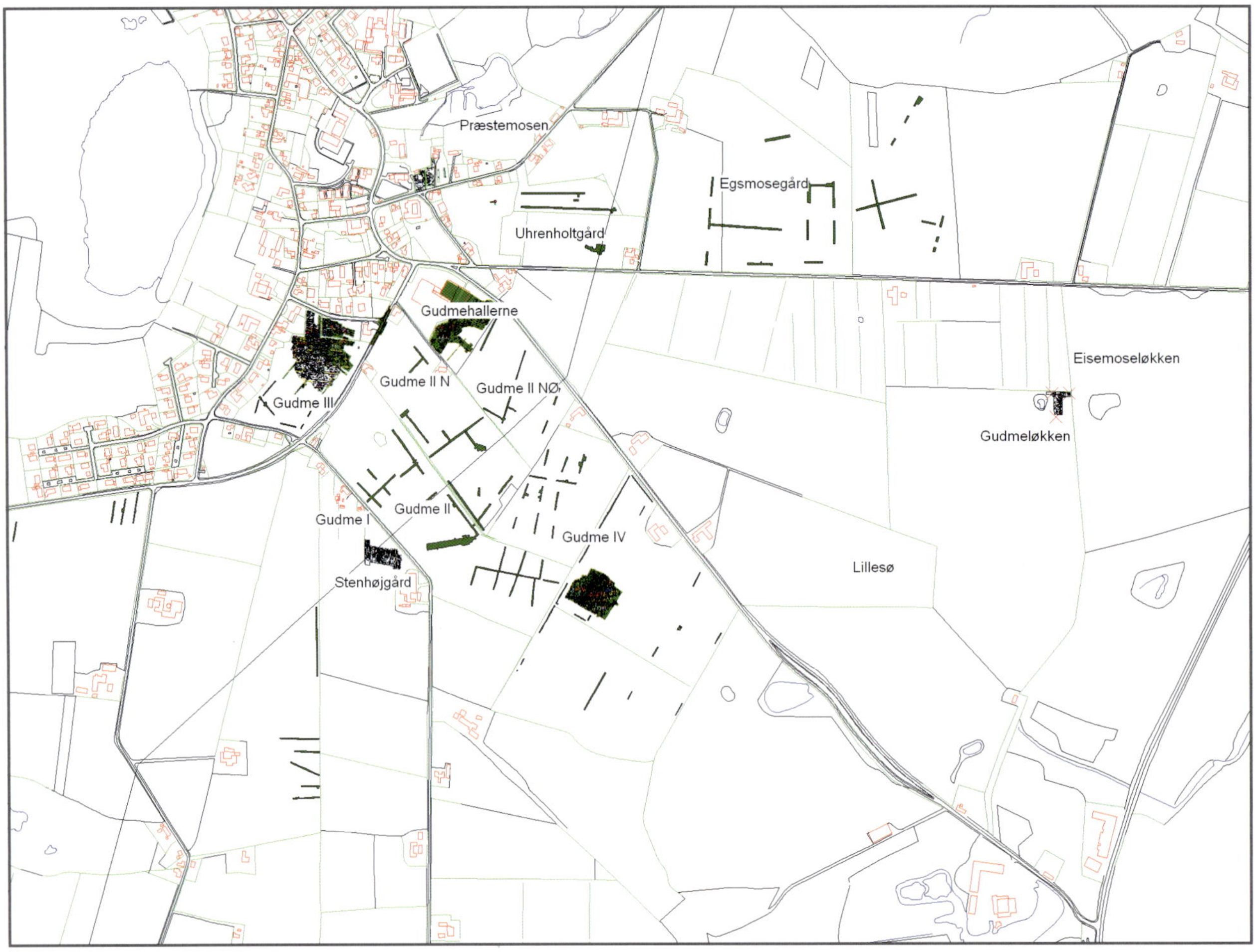

Crossing boundaries

Fig. 47a. Map of the Gudme site indicating the excavation and survey areas. Map generously provided by Lars Jørgensen/The Gudme Project.

Fig. 48. Solidi from Gudme I. Scale 1:1.
Photo Lennart Larsen/
National Museum of Denmark.

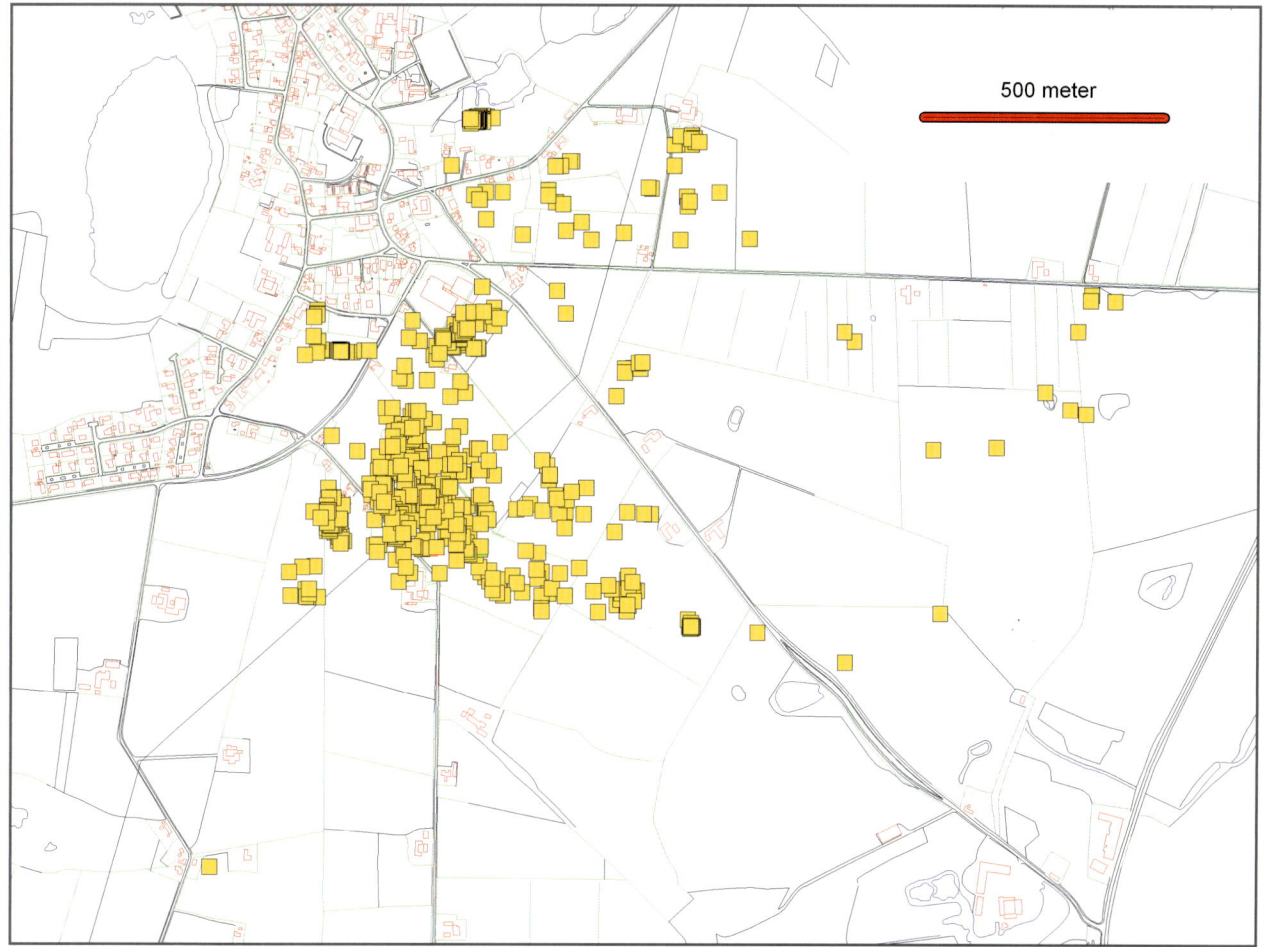

Fig. 47b. Gudme. Coins found during detector surveys. Note that finds made during excavations were not included in the map. The majority of the coins found during detector surveys were Roman, to this should be added a small number of dirhams and Medieval European coins. Distribution map by Palle Østergaard Sørensen/The Gudme project.

evidence that at least some 2nd century denarii were available into at least the late 5th or early 6th century, as the bracteate hoard could not possibly have been deposited before that date.

The area north of Gudme II has yielded some of the most impressive finds from Gudme, namely the Great Halls. The halls, two long buildings situated next two each other and both with several phases of reconstructions, were clearly the administrative and/or ritual centre of Gudme.[183] Spread over the area 116 denarii and one siliqua were found. The chronological distribution of the denarii from the Halls area is consistent with the finds from other areas of Gudme, and with the Danish finds as a whole. The Halls area is significant as no less than 15 denarii were found in archaeologically dated contexts. The fill of the posts that carried the roofs of Houses I, II, V and VI yielded 11 denarii, while three were found in pits and one came from the layer above House I.

The dated contexts stress that Roman denarii from the late 1st and 2nd centuries AD were in use and deposited in Gudme at least from the late 3rd to the early 6th century. The denarii from the Halls area have been found within a relatively restricted area, but they present great variation in state of preservation. A considerable number of coins are fragmented, and in all cases it seems to be unintentional, post-depositional fragmentation. Also the degree of corrosion varies from coin to coin. This must be due to a combination of the micro-environment surrounding the individual coin and the coin's inherent proper

---

183 Sb 142. Sørensen 1994a and b.

Gudme, the Halls area.[184] List of denarii from dated contexts.

Exc. no.	Serial no.	Emperor	Type RIC	Coin date	Context no.	Context type	Phase	Context date
1174	3	Trajan	101	103-111	556	Pit	End 2	c. 275
402	92	Commodus	251	191-192	556	Pit	End 2	c. 275
120	116	Antoninus	-	138-161	95	House I	3-4	275-420
144	82	Commodus	162	187-188	105	House I	3-4	275-420
121	54	Aurelius	263, 282, 296 or 307	171-174	99	House I	3-4	275-420
147	45	Aurelius	22	161	99	House I	3-4	275-420
123	1	Vespasian	-	69-79	110	Above House I	-	4th cent. or later
208	47	Aurelius	40	161-162	170a	House V	4	300-350
207	101	-	-	-	177	House VI	5	400-450
145	30	Antoninus (Diva Faustina)	351a	141-161	186	House VI	5	400-450
132	110	-	-	-	247/322	House II	7	500-550
209	112	-	-	-	247/322	House II	7	500-550
138	34	Antoninus (Aurelius Caesar)	447(?)	148-149	247/322	House II	7	500-550
148	37	Antoninus	-	138-161	247/322	House II	7	500-550
135	40	Antoninus	-	138-161	295	Pit	7	500-550

ties (chemical composition of the silver). There is, however, no progressive wear of the coins (*Fig. 49* and List of denarii): in fact the fragment of an Antonine denarius struck in 138-161 AD, but found in a pit with material from the early 6th century (context no. 295), is not significantly more worn than the two denarii struck by Trajan (103-111 AD) and Commodus (191-192 AD) from the so-called ritual deposit/pit with material dated in period C1b and considered to be deposited *c.* 275 AD (context no. 556).[185]

Gudme III is the area northwest of Gudme II. Large continuous areas were excavated in 1985-1988 and 1999.[186] The area presents evidence of human activity from both the Late Bronze Age and the Pre-Roman Iron Age, but settlement remains do not appear until the development of Gudme into a central place started *c.* 200 AD. Postholes representing nine subsequent phases of three farmsteads existing in the period *c.* 200-650 AD were examined. A hoard of siliquae had been deposited close to a fence delimiting the largest farm in its latest phases (phases 6 to 8 dated in the mid-5th to 6th century). The plough had destroyed the upper part of the hoard, and a number of coins were found scattered in the plough soil, but the majority were still *in situ*. The coins had been deposited in a pit that was hardly visible, without any traces of a container. The siliquae are dated within the period 337-375 AD. Eastern mints are dominant, and only a relatively low number of types are represented. The majority of the reverse types are VOTIS types (*Fig. 72*).[187] Apart from the many siliquae, six denarii were found scattered in plough soil.

Gudme IV[188] is situated southeast of Gudme II. The area was noted for a find of a hoard of dirhams,[189] deposited in the 10th century. West of the Dirham Hoard excavations in 1995 have revealed a series of continuously used houses dated from the 3rd to the

---

184 Royal Coll. of Coins and Medals, inv.no. FP 6202.
185 I thank Palle Ø. Sørensen for all information on the contexts of the denarii from the Halls area. On pit 556 see P.Ø. Sørensen in Jørgensen *et al.* 2003, 431 section 7.10b.
186 Sb 139. Petersen 1994, 32-33 and Fig. 5; Sørensen 1994b, 41-44 and Figs. 1-5, Sørensen 2000.
187 The Siliqua Hoard was published by Kromann 1988. Since then more siliquae have been found in the same area, and there can be little doubt that they originate from the same hoard.
188 090104 sb 154.
189 Sb 107.

Fig. 49. The Halls area. Denarii from dated contexts. Top row *c.* 275 AD; second row 275-240; third row 4th cent. or later; fourth row 300-350; fifth row 400-450, bottom rows 500-550. Scale 1:1. Photo MLSS.

9th century. Apart from a number of detector finds of Roman coins, a hoard consisting of both siliquae and denarii was found in a pit within a building (*Fig. 73*). It seems that the digging of the pit disturbed the hoard, and that the coins afterwards had been (partly) reinterred.[190] In the area between Gudme III and Gudme IV a solidus was found around 1940.[191]

The area northeast of Gudme IV, Ejsemoseløkken, has yielded 16 denarii, one siliqua and a Barbarian imitation in gold of a Roman coin.[192]

Bjørnebanken is situated in an area east of Gudme II and northwest of Ejsemoseløkken. A hoard consisting of three solidi and 360 fragments of a Late Roman silver platter has been excavated.[193] However, already in 1875 a solidus struck by Constantius II in 337-361 AD was found in a molehill on the same field. Although it cannot be proved, it is not impossible that this solidus also belongs to the hoard.[194] The same area has yielded five denarii that probably had nothing to do with the hoard.[195]

The Roman coins are clearly clustering around

---

190 Information kindly provided by P.Ø. Sørensen.
191 Sb 149. Kromann 1983-84, 102 no. 25.
192 Sb 155.

193 Sb 109. Jørgensen *et al.* 2003.
194 FP 383. Breitenstein 1942, 88 no. VIII and fig. 61.
195 FP 7128.

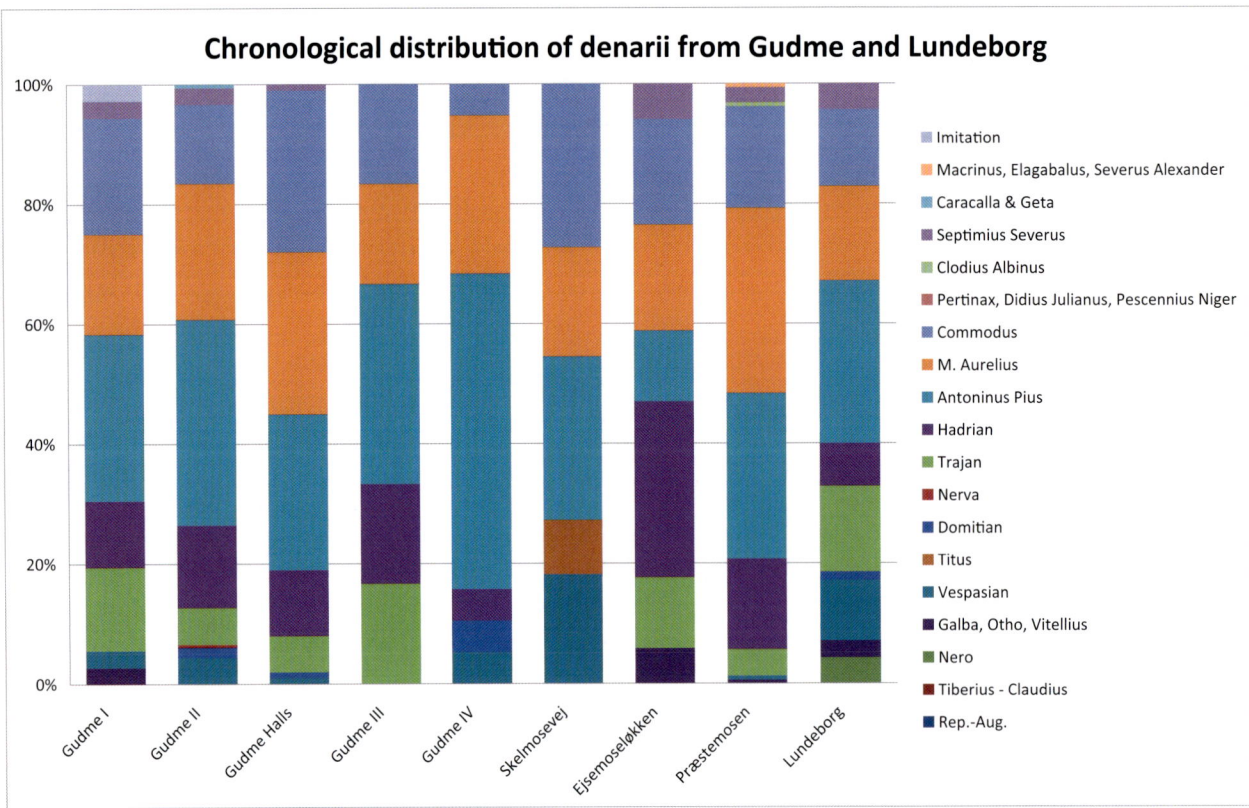

Fig. 50. Chronological distribution of the denarii from Gudme and Lundeborg. The diagram shows that there are only minor variations in the chronological distribution of denarii from one area to another within Gudme. The variations are more likely to be due to statistical insecurities in areas with few finds than to chronological differences in the material.

List of sites within the Gudme complex

Sb	Site	Roman coins total	Roman coins, denominations				
			denarii	siliquae	aurei	solidi	Æ
55	East of Broholm Manor	1	1				
138	Modern town	1	1				
139	Gudme III	299	6	293			
140	Skelmosevej (north)	2	2				
141	Skelmosevej (south)	21	19			2	
142	Halls	117	116	1			
143	Gudme II	250	226	19		3	2
144	Gudme I	66	47	8		11	
145	Gudme south	2	1	1			
149	Broholmvej	1				1	
150 (109)	Bjørnebanke	9	5			4	
151	Egsmose	7	7				
154 (107)	Gudme IV	92	62	29			1
155	Gudme V-VI, Ejsemoseløkken	18	16 (1 barb)	1			
156	Møllegårdsmarken	8	6		1	1 (+?)	
162	Præstemosen	160	160				
219	Broholm, Svineengen	1				1	

the Halls, and in the Gudme II area in general. The longer the distance from these areas the less finds of Roman coins. Among the areas with a less dense scatter of finds are the areas on both sides of Skelmosevej north of the two Great Halls. The closest area, south of Skelmosevej, has yielded 19 denarii and probably two late Roman solidi, while the relatively large Egsmose area east of this has yielded 7 denarii, and the area north of Skelmosevej has produced only two single finds of denarii.

Although the number of single finds decreases considerably outside the central areas of Gudme, a denarius hoard has been found at Præstemosen (see above).

Gudme South[196] constitutes the western periphery of the settlement of Gudme I. The area has yielded material from the Late Roman and Early Germanic Iron Ages, but it is clearly less densely occupied than Gudme I, and the number of coin finds is much lower. So far only two Roman coins have been noted, a denarius and a siliqua.

C. 2 km east of the Halls is the largest Iron Age cemetery on Funen, Møllegårdsmarken, where a number of Roman coins have been discovered (cf. above on graves). The *Videnskabernes Selskabs* map from the late 18th century shows a road leading from the church of Gudme almost directly east through the cemetery at Møllegårdsmarken to cross the Tange Å (Stream) at the Tange Mill.[197] It is therefore not impossible that the cemetery originally grew up along the road leading from Gudme to Tange Å and thence to Lundeborg at the shore, and that the Iron Age track, including the crossing at the mill, may be the forerunner to the one preserved in the map from the pre-industrial period. Remains of two Iron Age roads have in fact been found at the eastern outskirts of the cemetery. One leads SW-NE from the cemetery towards the Tange Å, the other, with two preserved tracks, is roughly N-S towards a crossing of the stream of which remains were found.[198]

Furthermore, a single find of a denarius was made already in the 19th century in the fields east of Broholm Manor,[199] and a solidus was found at Svineengen north of Broholm Manor.[200]

Gudme is a brilliant example of how much detector archaeology has changed the find combinations and our opportunities for interpretation. Although Gudme had long been known as a very rich site, the number of Roman coins has exploded since detector archaeology was initiated in 1980. Most of the coins have in fact been found in plough layers, and thus strictly speaking already drawn out of their archaeological contexts, and the few coins from excavated archaeological layers have only been found due to the indications already provided by detector surveys. Most of the coins known are denarii, but as shown above they were a minority until *c.* 1980.

5.3.1.2 Lundeborg

The archaeological site of Lundeborg is situated directly on the shore on the south-eastern coast of Funen. The site is extending on both sides of the small Tange Å.[201]

A total of 174 Roman coins have to date been found during the detector surveys and excavation of the Lundeborg sites.[202] The overwhelming majority of these coins are denarii (a total of 167 denarii), but there are also one aureus, three siliquae, two sestertii and one Late Roman bronze coin. The coins were found scattered throughout the excavations areas, both on the south and on the north of the Tange Å (areas formerly designated as Lundeborg I and II, respectively), and the two areas have yielded material that are closely comparable, both in regards to the number of coins and their chronological distribution.

At Lundeborg I the total number of coins is 85: 80 denarii struck between 65 and 228 AD, two sili-

---

196 Sb 145.
197 Christoffersen 1987, 87, presented a map with the 20th century excavation area inserted on the Sehested's 1878 map.
198 Madsen & Thrane 1995.
199 Sb 55: OBM 2443; Sehested 1878, 195-196, pl. XL, 11-12; Breitenstein 1942, 70 no. I.
200 Sb 219: FP 787; Breitenstein 1942, 86, VII.1 fig. 60.
201 Formerly finds were divided into sb 132 south of Tange Å, also known as Lundeborg I, and sb 133, north of Tange Å known as Lundeborg II.
202 The 72 coins found during the excavation campaigns in 1986-89 were published by Anne Kromann (1990), who has also discussed the coins from Lundeborg in relation to the finds from Gudme (Kromann 1994). The most recent finds were registered in 2008 (inv. FP 7269).

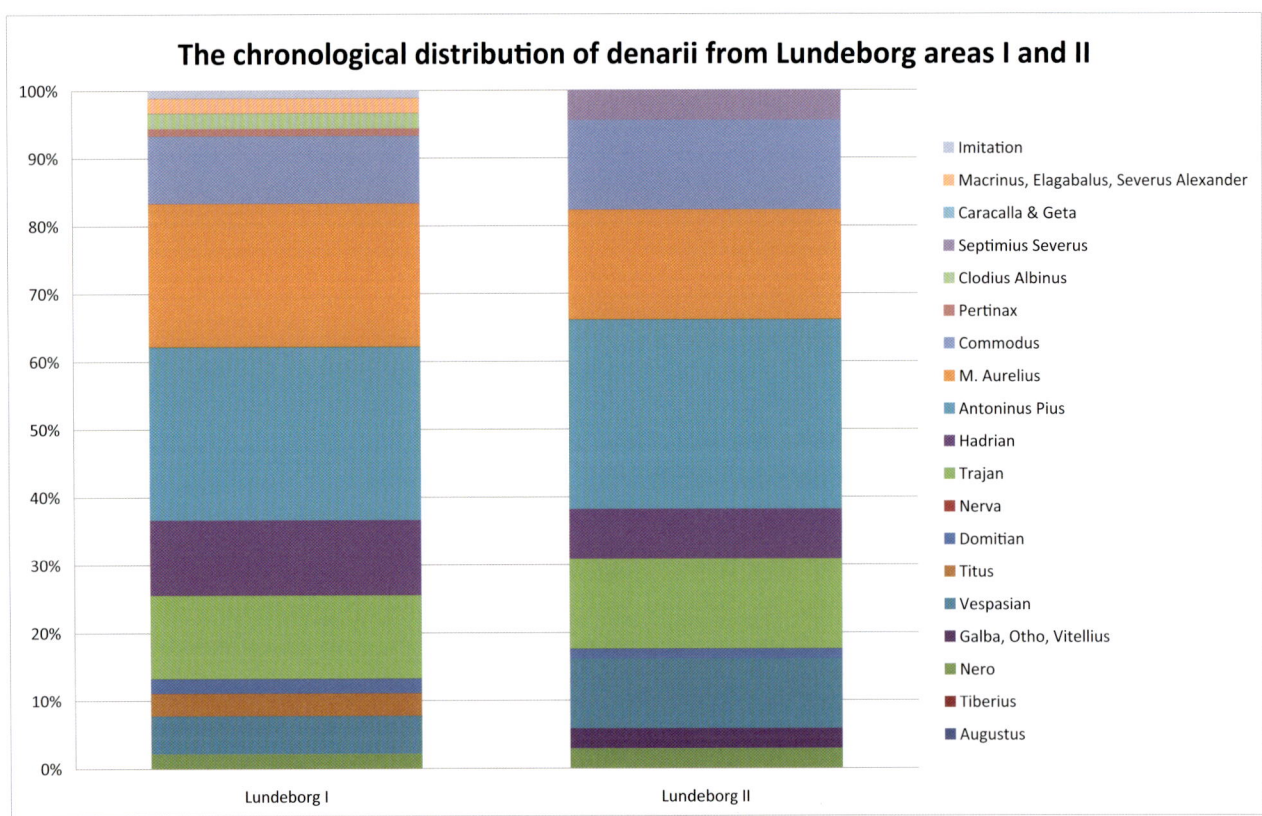

Fig. 51. Chronological distribution of denarii of Lundeborg I and II. The chronological distribution of the denarii from the two areas of Lundeborg is almost identical and underlines that there was no differences in the coins nor in their use on either side of the stream dividing the two areas. In both areas the issues of Antoninus Pius dominate, followed by the issues of the other Antonine emperors and the issues of Trajan and Hadrian.

quae from 336 to 340 AD, and a sestertius. Furthermore two renaissance coins were found within the Lundeborg I area.[203] The 91 coins from Lundeborg II are: one aureus struck by Nero, 87 denarii from 64 to 211 AD, one sestertius struck by Trajan (103-111 AD), one siliqua and one bronze coin, both struck by Constantius II.[204]

All coins from Lundeborg present traces of wear, but the degree of wear varies greatly, from almost fresh to very worn with a smooth surface. However, there seems to be no differences in the degree of wear of the coins from the two areas, Lundeborg I and II. The patina and colour of the coins vary. Some denarii have a bright silvery surface, that can be either very fresh or present a dull and opaque surface, while other coins are dark brown. There is a number of very corroded coins, as well as a minor number of coins of which a fragment has been broken off, yet none of these seem to be intentionally reworked. Only one of the sestertii, of which little more than a quarter of the coin is preserved, may have been cut to fractions. A few coins seem to be burnt. The state of preservation is likely to be ascribed to the differences in the chemical composition of the soil in the areas where the coins were found. Yet the soil composition may not be responsible for all differences or likenesses in the state of preservation. A comparison of the coins from stacks with the remaining finds, as well as comparisons between coins from the same layer, has shown that the differences within the same strata are not smaller than within the group as a whole.

Among the denarii all major emperors from Nero to Commodus are represented, the exceptions being only some of the emperors who reigned for less than a year during the civil wars in AD 69, and the emperor Nerva, who also ruled for a relatively short pe-

---

203 The area now named sb 132.
204 The areas now sb 133, 166 and 168. Sb 166 however covering both material north and south of the stream.

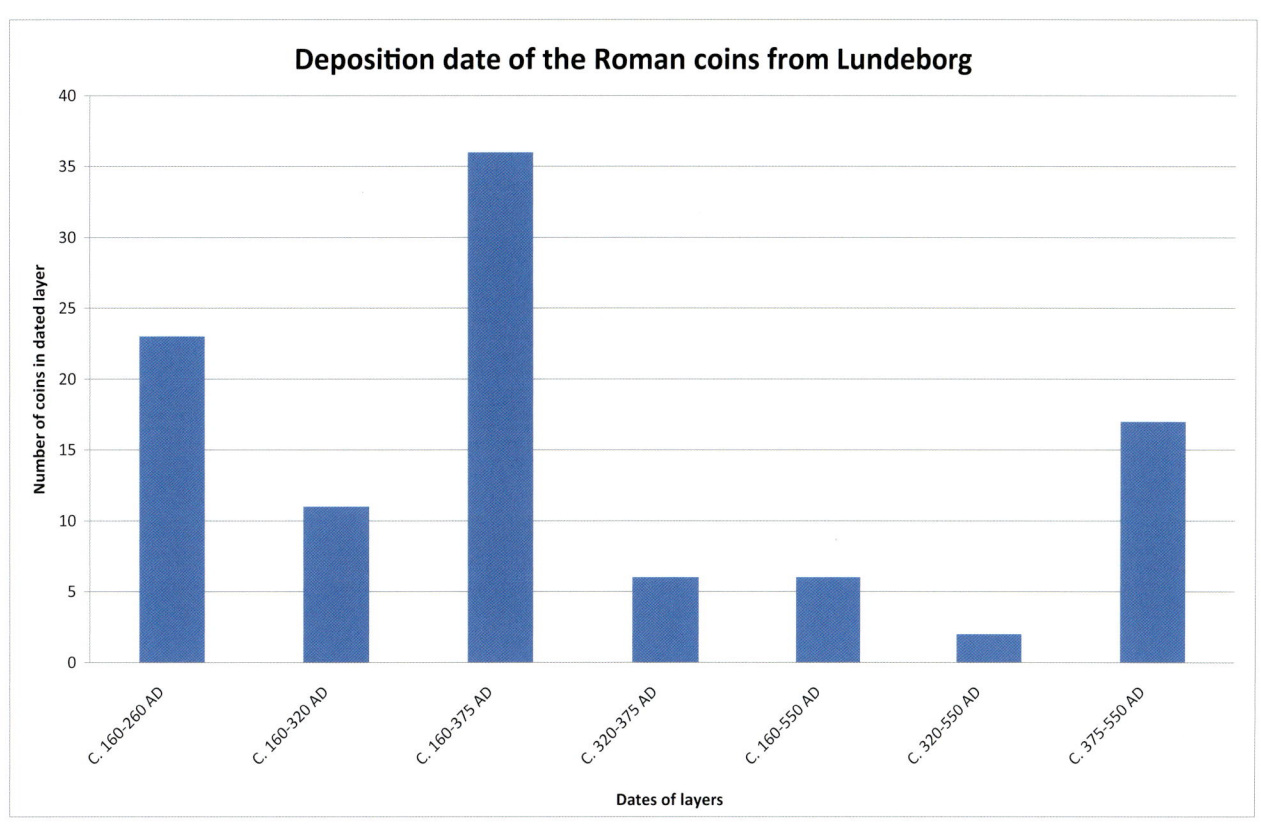

Fig. 52. Diagram: Deposition dates of the Roman coins from Lundeborg.
A part of the coins from Lundeborg were found with metal detectors, and they derive from the topsoil, but contrary to most single finds of Roman coins from Denmark, no less than 70 coins were found in archaeological layers. The majority of the coins from Lundeborg were deposited within the Late Roman Iron Age (i.e. before c. 375 AD), and a considerable number of these (24 of 69, i.e. 35 %) were deposited within period C1, i.e. the earliest of the three phases of Late Roman Iron Age. A smaller number, however, were deposited after c. 375 AD and may have been above ground into the early 6th century. No Roman coins were found in layers dated after c. 550 AD.

riod in 96-98 AD. Furthermore, Septimius Severus, Clodius Albinus, Elagabalus and Severus Alexander are represented. Thus the majority of the denarii fall within the period 69 to 192 AD, and particularly the Antonine emperors were well represented.

The excavations at Lundeborg have for the first time provided us with a large number of single finds of Roman coins in archaeologically dated contexts. The material underlines that the coins were normally deposited (or lost) in the 3rd or 4th centuries AD. At least 50 % of the coins were deposited in layers datable within the Late Roman Iron Age (periods C1-C3), and thus before AD 375. Another 21 denarii have been found in layers dated in the later part of the Roman Iron Age or in Early Germanic Iron Age.[205] Yet, the same issues appear no matter which period the context belongs to, for example the chronological range among denarii found in contexts dated in period C1 (c. 150/160-250/260 AD) goes from Vespasian (69-79 AD) to Elagabalus (218-222 AD).

The majority of the coins were single finds, yet in some cases more than one coin was retrieved from the individual layer: In a number of cases two or more coins were found closely packed. This applies to find numbers x606 (four coins from trench G, Late Roman Iron Age, period C), x615 (four coins from trench F, Late Roman Iron Age, period C), x617 (two coins from trench K, Late Roman Iron Age, period

---

205 Denarii: 23 in C1 context, 11 in C2 context, 6 in C3 context, 36 in period C context.

C), and x648 (two coins from trench N, Late Roman Iron Age, period C). In other cases two or more coins derive from the same stratigraphic entity.[206]

When coins are found in stacks or closely packed it is commonly regarded as indicative of coins originally deriving from a hoard. Yet, as the small stacks from Lundeborg derive from different trenches it seems that they cannot be part of the same hoard, although they may have been lost or deposited as small individual hoards.

There is a great variety of types represented in the material from Lundeborg, but in some cases the same type has appeared in two or three examples. There is, however, no example where two coins of the same type have been found together, nor are there any examples of die links among the coins found in Lundeborg.

The latest silver coins from Lundeborg are the three siliquae from the reigns of Constantine I (minted in Constantinople) and Constantius II (minted in Thessalonica), found in the Lundeborg I area, and the tiny fragment from Lundeborg II identified as another Constantius II. The siliquae are thus closely comparable to the ones found in Gudme both as regards the period of issue and as regards the mints.

It is possible that the siliquae were not deposited until the Early Germanic Iron Age, and they thus belong to the latest depositions of Roman coins in Lundeborg.

Only one aureus, struck by the emperor Nero in 64-65 AD, has been found in Lundeborg.[207] The coin unfortunately was not found in a dated context. It is not only one of the oldest coins from Lundeborg, but also one of the oldest coins found on Funen. There is only one older coin, namely the aureus struck under Tiberius that was found at Rørbæk in 1859 (cf. above on grave finds).[208] It may seem strange that no other gold coins were found in Lundeborg, in particular in comparison with the rich finds of solidi from Gudme, but one should keep in mind that the very rich gold finds from the area, and from Funen in general, are mainly found outside settlement areas – the gold hoards from Gudme I and Gudme II are exceptions to this rule.

Roman bronze coins are rarely found in well-dated Iron Age contexts in Denmark.[209] Therefore the three bronze coins from Lundeborg are of enormous importance, as they are the proof that bronze coins were indeed brought to Denmark during the Iron Age, albeit in very small numbers. The two sestertii were both found in areas with remains of bronze working activities, one of them – struck by Trajan – in a layer dated in the Late Roman Iron Age, period C. The third bronze coin, struck by Constantius II, was found in a layer with material from the 4th and 5th centuries AD.[210]

The fact that two of the bronze coins, both large sestertii, were found in areas with bronze working activities should not be overlooked. It is very possible that bronze coins may have been brought to Denmark as bullion, and these few coins could indeed be the ones that were *not* melted down in the metal production of Lundeborg. However, in light of the very low number of finds of bronze coins from Denmark in general it is also possible to interpret them, as well as other Iron Age finds of Roman bronze coins in Denmark, as relatively rare exotica from the Roman Empire.

The Roman coins from Lundeborg are closely connected to the finds from Gudme. In both areas 2nd century denarii make up the overwhelming majority of the Roman coin finds, while bronze coins are rare. The single aureus from Lundeborg has no parallel in the Gudme material, and Lundeborg lacks the gold

---

206 In the Lundeborg I area, south of the Tange Å: two coins in XIII:7 layer b, dated in period C3; two coins in XIII:5 layer a, dated in Early Germanic Iron Age (D1); two coins in XIII:1 layer e, dated in period C1; three coins in XIII:21 layer c, dated in period C2; three coins in XIII:19 layer d, dated in period C1; two coins in IX layer a, dated in Early Germanic Iron Age (D1). In the Lundeborg II area, north of Tange Å: three coins in XXIV:3 layer b.

207 FP 4859.1; excavation no. x1221.

208 Breitenstein 1943, 2 no. II. Two Greek coins found on Funen are probably imported by modern collectors.

209 Horsnæs 2006a.

210 Information from Per O. Thomsen, Svendborg og Omegns Museum.

finds from the Gudme settlement. More important are the siliquae which may be interpreted as part of a single batch of siliquae arriving to the Gudme/Lundeborg centre as one event and subsequently being split up in the area.

One of the most important results of the Lundeborg excavations is the fact that Roman coins have been found spread over the whole site in various stratigraphical entities that prove that the coins have been deposited in the area in all periods from the beginning of the Late Roman Iron Age (period C1-3) to the Early Germanic Iron Age (period D1).

5.3.1.3 The territory of Gudme and Lundeborg

A number of hoards have been found in the area around Gudme, Møllegårdsmarken and Lundeborg, and the hoards must clearly be interpreted as belonging to the same entity. The hoards including coins, Elsehoved and Broholm Hoards, have already been discussed (see above). Furthermore there is a small number of stray finds of coins, mainly gold coins, for example a solidus struck by Constantine I in Thessalonica found in 1900 while digging a clamp in the "Svineengen" outside the garden of Broholm,[211] and some now lost finds.[212]

A denarius struck by Trajan found at Skråhøjsløkke close to Broholm was first mentioned by Sehested,[213] and another denarius, also struck by Trajan, was found before 1967 at the coast *c*. 4 km from the cemetery at Møllegårdsmarken.[214]

It must be stressed that the Gudme-Lundeborg area is unique in all aspects: the monumental halls, the landing place at Lundeborg, the many gold hoards, the enormous number of finds in general and the high number of Roman coins in particular. The area assumes a particular role as a central place with secular as well as religious significance, and it was probably an important station in an over-regional elite network. The only comparable site from Denmark is Sorte Muld on Bornholm, whereas sites as Uppåkra in southern Sweden or Tissø on Sealand, as well as the landing places in Sealand, are peaking in later periods.

5.3.2 Three sites with denarius hoards

5.3.2.1 *Ginderup*

Ginderup is a settlement site in Thy Herred in northwestern Jutland.[215] The site is often described as a "tell", because the combination of continuous settlement activities and the characteristic use of thick walls of turf in the area has accumulated up to 2 m thick occupation/culture layers, somewhat more than is common in Denmark. The site was excavated in various campaigns in the period 1916-1934.

During the excavations at Ginderup in 1934 a stack of Roman coins was discovered below a floor level of House III. Originally 24 denarii and an aureus were found, but many years later seven more denarii were recovered from a lump of soil from the excavation. The 31 denarii are struck in the period 125/120 BC-74 AD. The exceptional early composition of the hoard is underlined by the presence of no less than 18 Republican and eight Julio-Claudian coins. Also the single aureus from this hoard, struck by Nero, falls within this period. Only the two latest coins were struck during the reign of Vespasian.[216]

List of coins from Ginderup

	Number of specimens	%
Republic	13	40.6
Mark Antony	5	15.6
Augustus	6	18.8
Tiberius	1	3.1
Caligula or Claudius	1	3.1
Nero	2	6.2
Vespasian	2	6.2
Unidentified	2	6.2
TOTAL	32	100.0

---

211 090104 sb 207: FP 787; Breitenstein 1942, 86, VII.1 fig. 60.
212 Breitenstein 1942, 96.
213 Sb 55. Sehested 1878, 195-196, pl. XL.11-12; Breitenstein 1942, 70 no. I. The coin was then in Odense City Museum.
214 090107 sb 170: FP 2963; Kromann 1983-84, 71 no. 11. The exact find spot cannot be located, and it is not impossible that the coin might be ascribed to the more recently discovered site of Lundeborg.

215 110605 sb 88. Hatt 1935; Lund 1973; Bjerg 2007, 41-55.
216 Two coins cannot be dated.

The composition of the hoard is closely comparable to other hoards with end coin in the Flavian period, found both within and outside the Empire.[217] The percentage of Julio-Claudian coins is in this connection important. The figures in the Ginderup Hoard are somewhat higher than in the Flavian hoards mentioned by Bolin and considerably higher than in the Trajanic hoards. Coins of Vespasian are, on the contrary, less well represented than in the comparative material. It is thus most likely that the hoard was composed during or only shortly after the reign of Vespasian, and it is quite possible that the coins were assembled within the Empire.

A recent study of the Ginderup Hoard and its contexts has revealed that both the pottery found in House III and some of the characteristics of the house itself indicate that House III must belong to Early Roman Iron Age. The house is overlaid with clay from the fallen-in walls of the house. Above this is a layer of mud that indicates that the site must have been open for some time before the erection of House II that partly overlies House III. Also House II can – although with some caution – be dated in the Early Roman Iron Age. This means that the deposition of the coin hoard must have taken place between AD 74 (the closing date of the hoard) and c. AD 150/160, i.e. the commonly accepted end date for period B2. If House II should be dated within period B2 as well, the most likely deposition date for the hoard is probably closer to AD 100 than to AD 150.[218]

No other coins were found during the Ginderup excavations, and the composition of the Ginderup Hoard is unique in Denmark. It is therefore most likely to see the Ginderup Hoard as the result of a single batch of Roman coins accumulated within the Empire and arriving at Ginderup very soon after.

5.3.2.2 Hoards and single finds from Dankirke

A cluster of denarius finds has been found in sites around Ribe in south-western Jutland. The most important find is the Dankirke site, probably extending over c. 40.000 sqm of which 3.000 sqm have been excavated. The site is situated between the marshland and the North Sea. It has been known since 1882, but only in 1964 excavations were initiated by a group of amateurs. The rich finds imposed them to contact the local museum, and in 1965-1970 the National Museum undertook excavations at Dankirke.

A total of 51 coins were found during the excavations. Among these were 38 Roman coins and 13 coins from the 7th and 8th centuries AD.[219] Furthermore two Roman denarii have been found in 1904 and in the 1990's.[220] The Roman coins have often been referred to as single finds, and they have been used to argue for a secondary coin economy in Dankirke. A recent re-evaluation of the coins and their find circumstances has questioned this view.[221]

The Dankirke excavations took place in two areas: Dankirke Øst (East) and Dankirke Vest (West). The two areas are situated c. 50 m apart, and both areas have yielded Roman coin finds. Dankirke Øst, excavated 1965-67, yielded nine Roman denarii, seven of which were found in the low area north of House I in layers J, H and Z.[222] Layers J and H are dated early in the Late Roman Iron Age (per. C), while Z is mixed. The last two coins cannot be fixed exactly to a layer, but the latter must belong within 1 sqm. The scatter of these coins indicate that they may have been moved into the low area while cleaning up after a fire in House I, or they may have been a small hoard scattered by the plough.

Some of the coins found in Dankirke Øst seem to have a common characteristic (FP 3224.33 and .34 found within the same square), namely the much abraded surfaces (some of the coins have been restored from fragments), while the remaining five coins from this area (FP 3224.7, .9, .13, .28 and .35) are relatively well preserved and easily legible. A coin, found in the easternmost part of the excavated area, has been published as a denarius,[223] but it looks

---

217 Diagrams in Bolin 1958, 338-341.
218 Bjerg 2007, 41-55.
219 All coins from the excavations have inv. no. FP 3224. The most recent study of the 13 coins from the 7th and 8th centuries, Feveile 2006, suggests that the sceattas and Merovinginan coins represent two distinct hoards, deposited as sacrifices.
220 FP 928 and FP 6994.
221 Bjerg 2007, 57-75.
222 FP 3224 nos. 7, 9, 13, 28, 32, 33, 34, 35, 36. Distribution map in Bjerg 2007, 67 fig. 14.
223 FP 3224.32 (excavation no. 1449); Kromann 1983-83, 70, no. 9.35.

much more like a copper coin. The coin has been cut in half in modern times, perhaps during conservation of the coins.

During the excavations of Dankirke Vest in 1968-1969 29 Roman coins were found.[224] The earliest coin is a Republican denarius.[225] This is also the only coin from Dankirke found *in situ* in the north-western corner of House VII, layer VR which is dated in the 1st century AD by the pottery found in the layer.

The majority of the coins from Dankirke Vest were found concentrated in the area of Houses V and Vb, and Bjerg has suggested that they represent a scattered hoard that was originally deposited in or near one of these houses. It is however not possible to date the deposition with any certainty. It should be noted that among these coins is a single antoninianus struck during the reign of Probus. Antoniniani are extremely rare among the Roman coin finds from Denmark, and it is the only case in which they may be connected to a possible denarius hoard.

Bendixen noted that some of the coins presented imprints left by woven cloth.[226] The coin FP 3224.37 from the area south of House V in Dankirke Vest still presents a layer of copper(?) that may carry an imprint of a piece of cloth, but this is not visible on any other of the coins from Dankirke (Vest or Øst). Nor was it noted during restoration of the coins.

One coin fragment was found in a layer consisting of a number of pottery fragments just below the plough soil in the southernmost part of Dankirke Vest. This coin presents a surface structure that differs from the other finds, as it may be partly melted.[227] The distance to the other coins, as well as the different state of preservation, indicate that at least this coin must be seen as a single find. Also a coin fragment found above House V seems to be secondarily burned.[228]

Finally there is a coin from Dankirke Vest that has so generic information on the find spot that it cannot be decided whether it belonged to the presumed hoard or was a single find.[229]

In general, the majority of the Dankirke denarii present the same degree of wear and corrosion, and only in the few cases noted above a combination of the state of conservation of the coin and its find spot may indicate that some of them must be regarded as single finds, comparable with the coin finds from for example Østervang in Sealand. The coins from the area south of House V in Dankirke Vest are found no further apart than what has seen to be the case for several ploughed up denarius hoards, and it is most likely that they should be interpreted as a hoard.

5.3.2.3 Lærkefryd

The Lærkefryd site in northern Sealand is situated on a natural plateau. The area is surrounded by wetlands, and in this respect the topographical situation is similar to the denarius hoards in wetland areas (see above), but the site characteristics are clearly different from them. Up to now 51 denarii have been found ploughed up in secondary position, but unlike the hoards previously mentioned from Sealand, the Lærkefryd Hoard was found in a site that additionally yielded a large number of luxury objects. The nature of the finds, mostly made with detector in the plough soil, of course inhibits any definite conclusions as to the nature of the coin hoard. The denarii, ranging in time from Vespasian to Commodus (69/79-180/192 AD), were found in a relatively restricted area of the larger Lærkefryd site. It therefore seems most likely that the coins were deposited together as a single act, but it cannot of course be excluded that this deposition also contained some of the other objects from the same field. The denarii are among the earliest datable finds from the area. The coins are extremely corroded, but the corrosion although clearly a post-depositional change of the coins cannot be the effect of the soil composition alone, as other silver objects have suffered considerably less. Apart from the coins, the oldest finds from Lærkefryd are a fibula from period C1b and a serpent's head ring from period C2 indicating that the earliest depositions of locally made objects took place in the Late Roman Iron Age. The find density seems to be highest in the latest Roman and the Early Germanic Iron Ages. The Late

---

224 Distribution map in Bjerg 2007, 68 fig. 15.
225 FP 3224.1.
226 Bendixen 1972, 62.
227 FP 3224.30 (excavation no. 2280); Kromann 1983-84, 70 no. 9.33.
228 FP 3224.31.

229 FP 3224.24.

Germanic Iron Age is hardly represented, but the site seems to have revived during the Viking Age.[230] The area has been interpreted as a sacred area, where the denarius hoard was only one of a number of depositions, and recently Jørgensen has taken the interpretation a step further by suggesting that the Lærkefryd site is the "hørg" mentioned in texts of the Viking Age.[231] However, a trial excavation in 2008 revealed a large number of "cooking" pits as well as traces of what may be interpreted as the western end of an Iron Age long house. The nature of this site is thus hard to interpret and opinions vary, so we must await future excavations to have more definite answers as to its function. Presently is seems that it was not a stable settlement site, although it must have been in use for many centuries.[232]

5.3.3 Other settlements with denarius finds

Most other sites with finds of more than one denarius have appeared during the last decades, and they have often been subject to archaeological investigations (See: List of denarius finds from settlements). The Iron Age settlement at Hørup in northern Sealand, only few kilometres from Lærkefryd, has well-documented workshop activities from the early Roman Iron Age onwards. There is evidence of metal production, as well as bone and horn workers. Only a minor part of the site has been excavated, much information from this site in fact derives from the detector finds.[233] Among the detector finds are 14 Roman coins: 12 of them are denarii, ranging in time from Vespasian to Septimius Severus (77/78-193/200 AD). There is furthermore a sestertius and a siliqua. The latter is struck in Arles during the reign of Valentinian I (364-367 AD) and it is looped. Also a Vespasian denarius may have been reworked: there are traces of bronze along the rim that may pertain to a mounting or a loop (*Figs. 53 and 90*).[234]

Fig. 53. Recent finds of denarii from Hørup (FP 6686, FP 7564.1-3, FP 7649). Scale 1:1. Photo MLSS.

Østervang is a relatively small site near Køge on eastern Sealand, but it was settled continuously from *c.* 50-600 AD. Excavations in 1999-2003 have uncovered remains of *c.* 50 houses, among which several phases of longhouses, minor houses and dugouts. Furthermore there is an extraordinary large number of pits, containing large amounts of pottery and animal bones. One of the houses had been destroyed by fire, and the clearing level contained among other things fragments of Roman glass indicating the relatively high status of the site.

There is evidence for working in bone and antler, as well as evidence for bronze working. Iron slags may indicate that iron was also worked at the site. One of the pits contained a small gold hoard, and there are a number of finds of silver: ingots, fibulae and hacked silver. Detector finds from top-soil include 11 denarii, dated from Nero to Geta Caesar (72/73-200/202 AD), and numerous other metal finds (*Fig. 54*). Østervang probably was a specialized workshop site inhabited by one or two families during the first six centuries of our era, and in many respects Østervang can be compared to Hørup.[235]

Four other sites in the Køge area have yielded denarii. At Ellebækgård a considerable number of detector finds have been found. They range in date from *c.* 250 BC to the Medieval Period, but with the majority from the Late Germanic Iron Age and Viking Age. The finds include five denarii (72/73-190/919 AD and an unidentified fragment), as well as Viking Age and Early medieval coins. Excavations have un-

---

230 010306 sb 1: FP 5148, 5305, 5373, 5535, 5994 and 5995. Sørensen 1993 (with map of find distribution), Sørensen 2000 (with selection of finds on fig. 118) and Sørensen 2000b.
231 Jørgensen 2006.
232 Trial excavation by P.Ø. Sørensen and S.A. Sørensen, to whom I owe all information on the results.
233 Sørensen, S.A. 2000; 2006a and 2006b.
234 010312 sb 36: FP 5163, 5525, 5534, 5959, 5986 and 6686. Sørensen, S.A. 2000.

235 020103 sb 16: Tornbjerg 2002. Horsnæs *et al.* 2005 on analysis of silver objects from Østervang.

Context types

Fig. 54. Eleven denarii from Østervang and, second row left, a Danish penning (1340-1375). FP 6159,1-3, 6188.1-2, 6189.1-3, 6538, 6770, 6771, 6832. Scale 1:1. Photo MLSS.

Fig. 55. Kirsebærhaven, four denarii. The site is situated on a stream opposite Ejrebækgård. FP 5123.1-2 (Kromann 1995, Taf. 13:IV 39,1 and Taf. 13:V 39,6), 5166.1 (Kromann 1995, Taf. 13:IV 39,2) and 5557. Scale 1:1. Photo MLSS.

Fig. 56. Ejrebækgård, eight denarii. The site is situated on a stream opposite Kirsebærhaven. FP 5161.1-5 (Kromann 1995, Taf 13:V 39,4; 39,3; 39,5; 39,7; 39,5), 5555 and 5792. Scale 1:1. Photo MLSS.

covered three houses dated in Early Roman Iron Age, Late Roman/Early Germanic Iron Age and Viking Age respectively.[236] Kirsebærhaven and Ejrebækgård have been registered as two sites, but they are situated on either side of a small stream, and it is very possible that they might be interpreted as two parts of the same site. A total of 12 denarii (96-161/180 AD) have been found during repeated detector investigations of the areas (*Fig. 55-56*). Other detector finds from these sites are considerably later than the coins, but Iron Age settlements have been identified in two different sites both situated less than 2 km from Kirsebærhaven/Ejrebækgård.[237]

Toftegård is of major importance as a possible central place in the Late Germanic Iron Age and Viking period. The site has yielded extraordinary finds of among other things seven gold foil figurines and shards of Frankish glass, as well as buildings.[238] The Late Roman and Early Germanic Iron Ages seem less well represented, still, a single denarius has been recovered.

The single find of a denarius from Gl. Kærup on central Sealand was made in 2004 and it is probably too early to give a good evaluation of its context. The general area of Kærup is rich in Iron Age finds, and in 2006 excavations less than 2 km to the northeast of the denarius find revealed more than 50 longhouses and 11 burials from the Roman and Germanic Iron Ages.[239]

Neble on western Sealand has been subject to intensive investigations. The area has yielded a considerable number of sites dating from the Early Roman Iron Age until the Medieval Period. The main period, however, is the Late Germanic Iron Age to Viking Age.[240] The two denarii deriving from Neble have been found in two different areas, both dominated by considerably later material.

It is often difficult to interpret the early single finds, but in some cases other finds nearby – although not always on the exact same spot – reveal indications that future investigations may turn out fruitful. This may be the case with the denarius found on the fields

Fig. 57. Denarius Early Germanic Iron Age from dated context. Farvergade, Næstved. Scale 2:1. Photo MLSS.

of Idagård at Slagelse before 1873. No other finds were noted then, but today both settlement material from various periods including Roman Iron Age[241] and an Iron Age burial[242] are recorded quite close to Idagård.

Tyrstrup in southern Sealand has yielded extensive remains of a Roman/Germanic Iron Age settlement, including finds of iron working activities. The detector find of a denarius on the Tyrstrup III area must therefore be interpreted in light of the other finds of Roman coins from workshop areas.[243] The denarius found during the excavations in Farvergade in Næstved assumes a special importance (*Fig. 57*). It came from a layer dated in the Early Germanic Iron Age, and it is therefore one of the very few finds of Roman coins from independently dated archaeological layers.[244]

The many Roman coins from Gudme and Lundeborg have had surprisingly little influence of the availability of denarii in other sites on Funen. Except from Gudme and Lundeborg (see above), the most important sites in Funen are clustering around Odense where urban development has necessitated large trial and rescue excavations (cf. above on Funen). Seden,[245] Lundsgård/Toruplund (*Fig. 58*),[246]

---

236 020105 sb 36: Tornbjerg 2003.
237 020510 sb 23 and 25.
238 050111 sb 36: Tornbjerg 1997.
239 040213 sb 47.
240 Nielsen, H. 1997.

241 040313 sb 46.
242 040312 sb 25.
243 Møller Hansen & Staal 1996; Staal 1997.
244 050707 sb 29: NÆM 81/100 + 86/200; Petersen 1987, 180 and fig. 10.
245 080809 sb 7.
246 080811 sb 98.

Context types

Fig. 58. Denarius from Toruplund. Struck by Antoniuus Pius in the name of Faustina Major. The reverse is completely illegible. Scale 2:1. Museum photo.

Troelsegård[247] and most recently Horsemosegård[248] have all yielded extensive remains of settlements from the Roman and Early Iron Ages. The two adjacent sites Seden and Lundsgård have yielded a total of six denarii, all found with detector in plough soil within the settlement areas, while tree denarii were found at Troelsegård, and one derives from Horsemosegård.

Fyns Hoved is strategically situated controlling access to Odense Fjord, and – on a clear day – with a view to both Samsø in Kattegat and the north-western tip of Sealand. Here, a port of trade dated in the Viking Age has been investigated. Below the Viking Age layer, also a layer with some Iron Age pottery has been found, and a stray find of a denarius may belong to this phase.[249]

Recent finds of a denarius at each of the sites

Fig. 59. Denarius from Ringe Golf Course. Scale 2:1. Museum photo.

247 080409 sb 51.
248 080810 sb 73.
249 080112 sb 137: FP 5387; Henriksen 1994a.

Ringe and Falle Mølle (Mill), both on central Funen, can be related to Iron Age settlements. The Falle Mølle site is situated not far from a workhop area excavated at Kværndrup,[250] and it is also close to the area where a gold medallion was found (see section 6.3.3). In 2008 a Hadrianic denarius was found in Herringe, a new site in central Funen, not far from Ringe.[251]

A single denarius was found by detector surveys at Nøddekroggård south of Gudme. During the subsequent excavations (1991-1992) the finds of among other things glass shards and beads and fragments of clipped gold gave the impression of a site of extraordinary status level, comparable with for example the workshop sites in Sealand.[252]

In Jutland settlements with denarius finds are becoming increasingly numerous, and again most of the new finds are the result of detector investigations.[253] The northernmost part of the peninsula has been particularly rewarding. Detector surveys at Vester Mellerup have yielded three denarii.[254] The survey were undertaken in an area were jewellery from the Roman Iron Age, as well as "settlement finds", were made in the 1940's. The jewellery is comparable to material from the Juellinge grave (Lolland) dated in period B2.[255] Two denarii from Stentinget are detector finds from an area covering *c.* 500 x 500 m. The site is rich in metal finds, dating in particular from the Early Germanic Iron Age to the Viking Age, and trial excavations in two areas have uncovered remains of *Grubenhäuser* and graves from the Viking Age.[256] Excavations in Ejstrup uncovered remains of a large settlement with at least five longhouses and numerous *Grubenhäuser*. The building remains are dated in

250 Thomsen 1998.
251 090410 sb 36. FP 7969.1.
252 *AUD* 1993, 251.
253 A list of finds, enumerating also other finds from each site and an evaluation of the character of the site, was published by Bjerg 2007, 107-109. To this list should be added both new sites and more coins from previously known sites.
254 100106 sb 183.
255 Norling-Christensen 1942.
256 100205 sb 64: Nilsson 1990 and 1992.

Fig. 60. Seven denarii from Lille Norge. Scale 1:1. Photo MLSS.

the Late Germanic Iron Age and Viking Age. Detector finds include material from the Viking Age and Early Medieval Period, as well as eight coins, six of which dating from the Viking Age (one Carolingian coin) to the 16th century. The last two coins are Roman denarii, but there seems to be few (no?) other objects datable before *c.* 750 AD.[257]

Detector surveys on two different sites in Saltum parish, Torpet[258] and Lille Norge,[259] have given denarius finds. In particular the seven denarii from Lille Norge deserve attention (*Fig. 60*). Few other sites have produced so many denarii, and while six of the coins are dated within the period of the commonly found denarii (69-183 AD), the last is an unusually early, Augustan, denarius, struck during the reign of Tiberius.[260] The coins have been found with numerous other objects dating from the Roman Iron Age to the Early Medieval period. The coins were found on a field that is gently sloping towards a wetland area to the northeast. The topographical situation seems comparable to the find from Hellerne in Sealand that has been interpreted as possible remains of a hoard deposited in a wetland zone, but the presence of many other finds suggests a settlement area rather than a sacrificial deposition. However, the area will need to be investigated systematically to decide the nature of the finds.

In the Thy region, the Vestervig Kirke site has yielded a considerable number of detector finds from the Late Germanic Iron Age to the Viking Age, and to date two denarii, a 4th century Roman bronze coin and an aureus have been recovered. Intensive surveying of the site Øster Vandet took place during the yearly gathering of detector enthusiasts in 2007 and 2008. The results are amazing. Apart from the many other finds no less than nine Roman denarii (134/138-201 AD), including one Barbarian imitation, and a sestertius were located (*Fig. 20*), and the discovery of these new sites are indeed changing the picture of our understanding of the Roman coin finds from northern Jutland.[261]

A very large number of detector sites are located at and around Aalborg. The main occupation period of the many sites on the banks of Limfjorden west of Aalborg belong to the Viking Age and Early Medieval Periods, but a small number of Roman coins have been found: There are two relatively recent finds of denarii, one from Sønderholm[262] and one from Kærgård/Mellemholm.[263] To these should be added several finds of Roman bronze coins.[264] Bejsebakken at Aalborg is on the contrary an important settlement from the Germanic Iron Age to Viking Age. The site has yielded few detector finds from the Late Roman Iron Age (among which are two denarii) and some houses from the Early Germanic Iron Age, but it only assumes its full flowering during the Late Germanic Iron Age.[265] Within the larger area that covers both the extensive Lindholm Høje cemetery (burials from the 5th to 10th centuries) and settlements from the 5th to 11th centuries four denarii have been found with detector.[266] Oddershøjgård just south of Aalborg is another site with a considerable number of detector

---

257 100214 sb 150: Michaelsen 1989-90. Coins FP 5849.1-8.
258 100406 sb 77.
259 100406 sb 78.
260 *AUD* 1999, 277, *RIC* (I, 2nd ed.) type 28 or 30.

261 110612 sb 419 (Vestervig Kirke) and 110213 sb 56 (Øster Vandet). Special thanks to Jens Henrik Bech, Thisted Museum, who informed me on these two sites before formal registration. See also Horsnæs & Ingvardson 2010.
262 120511 sb 144.
263 120508 sb 51.
264 From both Sønderholm and Bækgård, and from Mellemholm (120508 sb 54).
265 Nielsen 2002.
266 120607 sb 20, covering sb 14 as well as 120608 sb 8 and 11.

finds with a wide chronological span, including five denarii (134/138-170/171 AD). Again only future investigation will provide a better understanding of this site.[267]

In the part of northern Jutland situated south of Limfjorden a number of sites have produced finds of denarii in settlement contexts. The two denarii from Malle Langhøj Syd were found in plough soil, but an excavation below the area of the finds revealed traces of a house from the Late Roman Iron Age. Other finds indicated smithing activity in the house.[268] At Toftum two denarii were found by detector together with objects dated in the Germanic Iron Age, and later excavations on the site have revealed houses dated in the Early Roman Iron Age.

The detector site at Kvosted was identified in 2008 and it is hard to give an evaluation of the finds. Three denarii and a sestertius were found within a very short period.[269] Two denarii were found in almost the same period in connection with excavations at Tranbjerg. The excavations have revealed evidence of an Iron Age settlement, but the denarii were found in an adjoining field outside the excavation area proper.[270]

Six denarii were found in plough soil at Katrinelund and led to the excavations of the site, during which the seventh denarius was found. All coins were found above a farm, dated in the Early Germanic Iron Age, in the western part of the settlement. There were no traces of earlier buildings in this part of the settlement.[271] The coins were found within the same general area of the excavation, yet the distances between them are considerable, and the ploughsoil had been moved around prior to some of the coins being found. It is therefore not possible to determine whether the coins originally had been deposited together.

Ryde Mølle (Mill) is a particularly interesting site. Numerous artefacts from all periods have been found on the site, but no excavations have been conducted

Fig. 61. Coins from Katrinelund. Scale 1:1. Photo Knud Bjerring Jensen/Silkeborg Museum.

here. In the surrounding area there are settlements from Early Roman and Early Germanic Iron Ages as well as parts of a cemetery. The finds from Ryde Mølle are wholly unusual.[272] The area is very rich in archaeological finds compared to other sites from western Jutland, and there are in particular many detector finds from the Late Iron Age to the Early Medieval periods. The rich finds are probably due to the possibility of crossing the Hellegård Å (Stream). There is an undated ford, and the water mill referred to in the name of the site, Ryde Mølle, was founded here in the Medieval period. Roman coins have been found over most of the field. There is therefore no reason to consider it a scattered coin hoard. It must rather represent a number of single losses. The coins are unusual as they include not only two denarii, but also at least four, perhaps five, Roman bronze coins, dating from Vespasian to the Constantinian period (69/79- early 4th century AD).[273] The many later coins from the area are evidence of a continuous use of the area well into the Medieval period or even later. Indeed the Roman bronze coins in particular may be interpreted in light of other finds of Roman bronze coins from Medieval contexts as losses from these later periods, rather than a consequence of occupation in the Iron Age.

---

267 120504 sb 16.
268 120707 sb 67: Bjerg 2007, 81-83.
269 130114 sb 147 and 148.
270 150409 (no sb no.). I thank the staffs at Viborg Stiftmuseum and Moesgaard Museum who readily shared information on these exciting new sites with me.
271 160115 sb 198: Bjerg 2007, 77-80.

272 180206 sb 143, a part of the area 180502 sb 666.
273 Horsnæs 2006a, nos. 8, 28, 57 and 72. A bronze disc may be a fifth Roman bronze coin. The site has furthermore yielded a considerable number of Medieval and later coins.

A few kilometres north of the main site in south-western Jutland, Dankirke, two other sites have yielded denarii: Skanet Bro and Ulhøj. The Skanet Bro coins may derive from soil brought in from another area, and should therefore be treated with care.[274] The exceptionally early, Republican, denarius from Ulhøj had already been found in 1933.[275] It may be related to material from the Late Roman and Early Germanic period from the site. Only 4 km to the south of Dankirke, Gl. Hviding is an extensive site with remains from the Iron Age until the Medieval Period visible on air photos.[276] Detector surveys have yielded important material, among other things three denarii found at some distance from each other. Minor areas have been excavated. One of the denarii was found in an area where pottery from the Early Roman Iron Age was also recovered.[277] A report from 1925 mentions the find of a fourth Roman coin; the denomination and the date of the coin, however, remain unknown.

A striking feature on the list of coins in possible settlement contexts is the relatively late date given for the contextual material (in pratice: other metal detector finds) from the sites with denarii. More often than not the denarii are found on sites that have yielded material from the Germanic Iron Age onwards (i.e. from *c.* 350/400 AD and later, depending on the chronology used by the archaeologist registering the finds), and when the Germanic period is subdivided into an Early and a Late phase, we see that material is sometimes dated in the Late Germanic Iron Age and Viking Age, rather than in the earlier part of the period. This observation poses a number of questions that cannot be answered with the material available, but which must be kept in mind during future investigations.

The discrepancy between the date of the coins and the date of other artefact types might be explained by the method of retrieval. We could suggest that denarii of good silver should be easier to find than other, perhaps more rare metal objects from the Roman Iron Age, while pottery, glass or other datable material from the Roman Iron Age is not noticed during detector surveys. But we cannot overlook the possibility that a considerable part of the denarii, although struck in the period *c.* 69-193 AD, were not deposited (or lost) on settlements until well after AD 350. The sites with denarius finds that do go back to the Roman Iron Age are often the sites that have been excavated. Still, a close look at the find circumstances of the individual coins reveals that even on excavated sites the coins are almost invariably found in plough soil, rather than in undisturbed layers. This means that even when a site has a period of activity during the Roman Iron Age the denarii may in fact have appeared on the site only during the Germanic Iron Age, this being the reason why they surface among detector finds dated in the Germanic Iron Age or even later. The few sites with denarius finds in dated layers seem to support this possibility: In Lundeborg the Roman coins were found in layers dated up to the end of the Early Germanic Iron Age, the denarius from Farvergade in Næstved derived from a layer from the Early Germanic period, while the deposition of the denarius hoard from Dankirke was dated between AD 276 and the 5th century.[278]

In some cases the context is even considerably later: during excavations in 2007 at Rødvigsvej, southern Sealand, a single denarius was found in a layer with Medieval material,[279] and in Poland there is a considerable number of Roman denarii from Early Medieval contexts.[280]

Only a specialized study of *all* detector finds from a number of sites with occupation from the Roman Iron Age onwards will reveal, whether the denarii are the only objects produced during the Roman Iron Age that appear on the sites as detector finds.

A restricted number of sites have yielded two or more denarii, but it is important to note that even sites with only one or two denarii may stand out in respect to many other sites, and that they are often clustering in particular areas. Moreover, in spite of the many sites here listed, one should keep in mind that the overwhelming majority of the many Danish Iron Age

---

274 190407 sb 8.
275 190411 sb 26.
276 210103 sb 107 and 109.
277 FP 7136, struck by Domitian.

278 Bjerg 2007, 73.
279 Information from Jonas Christiansen and Mads Dyhrfeld.
280 Zapolska 2007.

sites that have been investigated have yielded no finds of Roman coins. The fact that most coins have been found by detectorists is important. We must expect coins to be under-represented in sites investigated without the use of the detector.

The western suburbs of Copenhagen have been investigated intensively since the 1990's due to modern building activity.[281] This is one of the areas, where a cluster of sites with single finds of Roman coins are found. But considering that millions of square meters have been excavated revealing traces of hundreds of Iron Age buildings, the number of Roman coins is surprisingly low.

The many denarius finds from settlements is the most important novelty in the find spectrum from Denmark. It is caused solely by the use of the metal detector. Even the largest sites, known literally for centuries for their rich finds, have yielded surprisingly few denarii until the 1980's. This is clearly demonstrated by the finds from Gudme. Until 1980 only five denarii were known from Gudme, and three of these came from the burials at Møllegårdsmarken. However, no less than 11 gold coins were known, among them the aureus from Møllegårdsmarken. A similar example is provided by the central place Sorte Muld and the sites clustering around it in Ibsker parish on Bornholm. Again, a considerable number of gold coins were known from the area, including gold hoards, but only four denarii had been found until detector surveying started. Today this cluster of sites has yielded more than 700 denarii of the little more than 900 coins from the area.

Metal detectors are not regularly used on archaeological excavations outside Denmark, and amateur use of metal detectors is prohibited for fear of plundering in some countries. Therefore the material from the settlements in Denmark cannot be readily compared to similar sites in other countries. There are, however, a still growing number of sites that have been investigated in ways that render them comparable to the Danish settlements.

5.3.4 Hacksilber hoards from settlements

The Engelsborg Hoard from Sealand, the Bjørnebanken Hoard from Gudme and the hoard recently discovered at Faugde in Central Funen can be compared with the hacksilver hoards from Høsten Torp (Sealand) and Simmersted Moor (southern Jutland), but contrary to these they have been found within settlement areas and they are all somewhat smaller in weight.

The hoard from Engelsborg west of Ringsted was found with detector and excavated in 1994. The hoard consisted of 725 g silver including two siliquae from the mid-4th century, silver ingots and fragments of Roman silverware cut to pieces. The excavations revealed several pits and postholes, probably deriving from two buildings. Finds of pottery dated the buildings to the Early Germanic Iron Age, and they must thus be considered contemporary to or only slightly later than the hoard.[282] The two siliquae were slightly older than the ones from the Hacksilber hoards Høsten Torp and Simmersted. Both were slightly fragmented and one was clipped, but none of them was intentionally cut (*Fig. 76*).[283] The silver mostly consisted of chopped up silver plate, but there were also some ingots and fragments of local silverware, for example a piece of a large gilded fibula. The material as a whole is dated in the Early Germanic Iron Age.

Hacksilber hoards have been found in other settlements, for example at Stenhøjgård in Gudme, without the inclusion of coins. In one case a Hacksilber hoard has been combined with gold coins. The Bjørnebanke Hoard from Gudme consists of 360 cut up fragments of a large Late Roman silver platter, adorned with incised and gilded portraits in medallions along the rim.[284] Along with the silver fragments three Constantinian solidi were found,[285] and it is possible that an earlier find of a Constantinian solidus from the same area may have been part of the hoard as well.[286]

---

281 Boye 2008.

282 040101 sb 44: FP 6518; *AUD* 1994, 124-125.
283 040101 sb 44: FP 6518; *AUD* 1994, 124-125.
284 Sørensen, P. 2003.
285 090104 sb 109: FP 6391.1-3:
 Constans, Trier, *RIC* 135 (347-348), w. 5.56, looped
 Magnentius, Rome, *RIC* 162 (350 AD), w. 4.36
 Constantius Gallus, Constantinople, *RIC* 97 (351-354), w. 4.4.
286 090104 sb 109: FP 383; Breitenstein 1942, 88, no. IX.

At Fraugde east of Odense a smaller hoard was found below the floor of the main building of a settlement. The hoard consisted of pieces of hacksilver, ingots and jewellery, as well as a solidus struck in Milan during the reign of Theodosius I.[287] The closest parallel to this hoard consisting of a mix of hacked silver and gold coin(s) is the Bjørnebanke Hoard from Gudme, but contrary to the latter, the relationship between the Fraugde Hoard and the building is very close.

5.3.5 Settlements with other Roman denominations

Denarii dominate the finds from settlements. Yet, a few coins of other denominations have been found. Apart from the finds from Gudme and Lundeborg, there are finds of a Roman bronze coin from Hørup for example – a site that also yielded a siliqua, Vårkærgård, and Kvosted, while Ryde Mølle produced four or five bronze coins.

A number of other sites have yielded bronze coins only. In these cases is seems that the coins have been deposited considerably later than the period of issue. Bronze coins in securely dated Viking Age contexts have been found in Ribe, below the Art Museum[288] and at the "Post Office" excavations.[289] In both cases the coins are found in contexts from the first half of the 8th century. Another coin was found during the excavation of a *Grubenhaus* in Okholm in a layer dated in 700-750 AD.[290] Some detector finds can also be related to Viking Age contexts – or broader: to the period from the Late Germanic Iron Age to the Early Medieval Period. At Stavnsager a Constantinian bronze coin was found in a field yielding detector finds dating in the period 400-1200 AD. The field is situated not far from an excavation area that produced building remains dated in the 6th-7th century.[291] On Meløse/Gammeltofter two Roman bronze coins have appeared. The remaining finds from the sites are from the Late Germanic Iron Age and from the Viking Age, while a smaller number of finds can be dated in the Medieval period.[292] Detector surveys at Kirke Hyllinge have yielded finds from *c.* 600-1300 AD, and subsequent excavations have revealed settlement remains from the same periods.[293] The large concentration of detector sites at Nørholm (northern Jutland) has yielded two Roman bronze coins (from two sites), as well as many other finds dating from the Iron Age to the Medieval period. The finds are, however, concentrated in the periods from the Late Germanic Iron Age onwards.[294]

Antoniniani are extremely rare in Denmark as a whole (cf. below), and few can be related to settlements: One antoninianus was among the Roman coins from Dankirke, and another was found at Fugledegård/Tissø, where the majority of the finds are somewhat later than the coin.

---

287 080803 sb 153: NM I C 37066; Runge 2007.

288 190409 sb 50: FP 3727.33 a 4th century coin struck in Nicomedeia; Bendixen 1981, 97 no. 33; Horsnæs 2006a, cat. 99.

289 190409 sb 50: FP 5607 dupondius portraying Faustina Minor; Jensen 1991, 19.

290 190411: FP 7134.1 Urbs Roma struck in Siscia; Feveile 2001, 24 and fig. 23.1.

---

291 141006 sb 57: FP 6502; Horsnæs 2006a no. 79, on the Stavnsager site see Høilund Nielsen & Loveluck 2006. The coin was found close to Høilund Nielsen & Loveluck 2006, fig. 1 area B. I thank Karen Høilund Nielsen for information on the find spot of the coin.

292 010504 sb 88: FP 6071 Constantius II struck in Trier; *AUD* 1999, 263 and FP 7018.1 Crispus Caesar struck in Rome.

293 020605 sb 55: FP 5922.17 Constantin II Caesar struck in Lyons; *AUD* 1998, 284 and. fig. 1; Ulriksen 1998 (on the excavations).

294 120508 sb 54: From the Mellemholm site FP 5576.1 an unidentified sestertius; *AUD* 1995, 270 and from the Bækgård site 120508 sb 51: FP 6700.3 an Urbs Roma (mint not legible). The Nørholm sites have yielded numerous other coin finds from later periods, and a single siliqua, also from the Mellemholm site FP 5576.2 (Valentinian I struck in Rome) – but so far not a single denarius has been found.

List of denarius finds from settlements (excl. Gudme and Lundeborg)

Legend:

FP	The Royal Collection of Coins and Medals inventory no.
Alternative inv.no.	Inventory no. for coins not in the The Royal Collection of Coins and Medals – indicates that the coin is not preserved.
Found	Normally the year of finding of the first denarius found on the site, but in some cases the registration year differ from the year of finding. < indicates that the coin was found before the year indicated.
Context date	Date of other finds from site: Early Roman (Period B); Late Roman (period C); Roman; Early Germanic (period D1-2); Germanic (Period D2); Viking; Medieval. Finds from Bronze Age or earlier are not considered.
Context type	Settlement; Settlement/Workshop; ? (undertermined); 0 (no other finds recorded); – (no exact location); added (soil added from unknown site)

Site	Sb	Name	FP	Alternative inv.	Found	Until Nero	Galba, Otho Vitellius	Vespasian	Titus	Domitian	Nerva	Trajan	Hadrian	Antoninus Pius	M. Aurelius	Commodus	Civil war	Septimus and later	Unidentified	Other denomi-nations	Total no. of Roman coins	Context date	Context type
010105	90	Græsted	2437		<1880	1																	–
010304	41	Egholm-Nord	6488		2002									1							1		?
010312	36	Hørup	5525 5534 5959 5986 6686 7564 7649					1				1		4	3	2		1		2	15	R G	SW
020103	16	Østervang	6159 6188 6189 6538 6770 6771 6832					1		1		2	2	2	1	1		1			11	RG	SW
020105	36	Ellebækgård	5721 6158 6187 6539 6560					1						2	1			1			5	RGV	S
020202	0	Vridsløselille Fængsel	2962		1969							1									1		0
020204	10	Vissinge Vest 2		SØL 1061	2001			1													1	G	S
020205	19	Hyldager Kongsholm-sparken	5124		1992									1							1	RG	S
020208	29	Ishøj		SØL 1042	2000													1			1	RG?	S
020209	34	Gersager	7019		2002									1							1		?
020215	25	Vallensbæk Nordmark	6358		2001							1									1	RG	S
020306	412	Brønshøj	1405		<1918						1										1		–
020402	22	Glim, south	7824		2008																1		–
020402	24	Glim	4642		1989										1						1	?	S
020402	41	Glim, east	5287 5991		1993									2							2	GVM	?
020402	43	Øm-Gammel-toft	6636		2003							1									1	GVM	?
020409	18	Højbjerggård	4708		1988							1									1		0

Crossing boundaries

Site	Sb	Name	FP	Alternative inv.	Found	Until Nero	Galba, Otho Vitellius	Vespasian	Titus	Domitian	Nerva	Trajan	Hadrian	Antoninus Pius	M. Aurelius	Commodus	Civil war	Septimus and later	Unidentified	Other denominations	Total no. of Roman coins	Context date	Context type
020510	28	Kirsebærhaven	5123 5166 5557		1992									3	1						4	VM	?
	37	Ejrebækgård.	5161 5555 5792		1993									3	3	1					8	M	?
020510	31	Lisagergård	6687		2003								1								1	VM	?
020601	0	Lejre		NM I C 4815	<1882									1							1		-
020601	106	Ledreborg	3573		1979							1			1						2		O
020601	115	Lejre	4681		1989	1															1	G V	?
020603	87	Lindholm 2	5196											1							1	V?M	?
020611	174	Vårkærgård E	6919		2003															1	2		O
030202	0	Selchausdal		NM I C 295	1869													1			1		O
030211	0	Laurvig	3572		1952									1							1		-
040203	2	Bringstrup	5985		1999							1									1	RGM	?
040206	0	Skee-Tåstrup	-	-	<1890									1							2		-
040213	64	Cirkelhusene	5860		1998									1							1		
040213	69	Gl. Kærup	6990		2004									2							1		?
040301	101 105	Neble	4475 4586											1 1							1 1	RGVM	S
040302	0	Asbjerggård	3718		1980									1							1		added
040313	0	Idagård		NM I C 1612	<1873								1								1		O
050103	16	Slimminge Mark	2098		1942								1								1		O
050110	16	St. Tårnby	1746		1930									1							1		-
050111	36	Toftegård	5556		1995											1					1	GV	S
050302	36	Tyrstrup III	5992		1995									1							1	LR	S
050407	32	Søndergård			1959														1		1		O
050600	0	Stevns	592		1885														1		1		-
050610	0	Bjælkerup		NM I C 4412	1959							1									1		-
050606	16	Rødvigsvej		SMV 8034x1311	2007									1							1	M	?
050701	7	Assenhøj	5531		1995									1							1		O
050707	29	Farvergade Næstved		NÆM 86/200-ACR-01	1981									1							1	EG	S
070000	0	Falster	468		<1882	1								1							2		-
070403	37	Kohave	6480		2002	1															1		O
070512	0	Søllested	3052		1969									1							1		
080112	137	Baes Banke/ Fyns Hoved	5387		1993									1							1	R?GV	SP
080409	51	Troelsegård Syd	6791		2003								1			2					3	RG	S
080506	19	Rorslev	3331		1975									1							1		?
080609	55	Moderup		NM I C 7775	1895									1							1		-
080710	37	Wedellsborg			<1940														1		1		-
080712	62	Skrillinge Mark		NM I C 5846	1887									1							1		-

Context types

Site	Sb	Name	FP	Alternative inv.	Found	Until Nero	Galba, Otho Vitellius	Vespasian	Titus	Domitian	Nerva	Trajan	Hadrian	Antoninus Pius	M. Aurelius	Commodus	Civil war	Septimus and later	Unidentified	Other denominations	Total no. of Roman coins	Context date	Context type
080809	7	Seden Syd	5983		1999														1		1	RG	S
080810	73	Horsemosegaard	7472		2006									1							1	LRG	S
080811	98	Lundsgård (sb 25) Toruplund (sb 99)	5805 6843		1998			1	1	1	1								1		5	LRG	SW
090101	16	Nøddekroggård	5160		1992							1									1	RGV	S
090107	170	Broholm	2963		<1967					1											1		-
090108	160	Ringe Golfbane	7565		2006					1											1	RG	S?
090411	74	Skelbo Lykkenssæde	3968		1982								1								1		0
090506	51	Falle Mølle		SOM 01.307x6	2005											1					1		S
090513	169	Kobberbæksvej	6772		2003									1							1		added
090601	78	Rabenslyst NE	6149		1999									1							1		?
090605	55	Flødstrup parish	1968		<1938											1					1		-
100106	183	Vester Mellerup	5375 5984		1993		1			1									1		3	R?	S
100111	20	Stenum	2301		?1941		1														1		0
100205	164	Stentinget Klokkerholm	5012		1990									1	1						2	RGVM	S
100214	150	Ejstrup	5849		1998				1			1									2	LGV	S
100215	50	Ørum parish	5046		1992																1		0
100406	77	Torpet	4457 7008		1985																2		0
100406	78	Lille Norge	5009 6231			1		1	1			1			2	1					7	GVM	?
100605	0	Hjørring	2855		1964									1							1		-
100612	77	Gaarestrup, Sct. Olai	5276		1992													1			1	LG	S
100618	92	Ugilt	1508		1921									1							1		0
100705	99	Lerup Kirke, S of	7542													1					1	V	?
100707	96	Overgård	2751		1962					1		1									2		0
110612	419	Vestervig Kirke	6282 7751		2000							1	1								3	LGVM	?
120108	67	Kirkebakken Nørre Tranders	576		1890					1											1		0
120201	54	"Illerknoppen" Kaldalgård	6294		2000							1									1		0
120312	0	Ejstrup St.	3014		?1950	1															1		-
120504	16	Oddershøjgård	5709 5710 6126 6226 6237		1997							1	2	2							5	RGM	
120506	57	Bejsebakken sb 57 Bejsebakken sb 64	4679 4257		1989 1985							1				1					1 1	GV	S

Crossing boundaries

Site	Sb	Name	FP	Alternative inv.	Found	Until Nero	Galba, Otho Vitellius	Vespasian	Titus	Domitian	Nerva	Trajan	Hadrian	Antoninus Pius	M. Aurelius	Commodus	Civil war	Septimus and later	Unidentified	Other denominations	Total no. of Roman coins	Context date	Context type
120508	51	Kærgård	7167												1						1		
120511	144	Sønderholm NE	7722											1					1		2		
120607	20	Hvorup Nymark sb 14 Lindholm Høje + 120608 sb 8 + Same, sb 11	4628 4376 4165 5420		1988 1986 1982			1								1		1 1			1 1 2	GV	S?
120707	67	Malle Langhøj sb 64	6295		2001			1						1							2	LR	SW
130110	106	Toftum	6236		1999										2						2		
130114	147	Kvosted		VSM 08964	2008								1		1	1			1		4		S
130702	0	Gudenåen Bjerringbro	4630		1988	1															1		-
130816	157	Hjarbæk Strand	2451		1955								1								1		0
140108	67	Grenå	2061		1942								1								1		
141011	70	Ryomgård Skov	6637		2002										1						1		
150210	0	Rathlousdal		NM I C 6657	1850								1								1		
150409	0	Tranbjerg		FHM 4845A	2008						1	1									2		S
160115	198/199	Katrinelund	4333 4639 4678 4788 5145		1984		1						1		3	2					7	EG	S
160203	0	Klostervej	3841		1982										1						1		0
160203	216	Simgårdsmark	2269		1949			1													1	ER	S
160411	104	Hem Mark	2627		1959										1						1		0
160507	0	Fredens Hjem	1727		1930								1								1		0
170203	28	Ejstrup Harte	7405										1								1	LR	?
170205	0	Kolding Nørremark	1875		1935			1													1		0
170904		Jelling			2007									1							1	RGVM	?
180206	143	Ryde Mølle	4560 5075		1987			1					1						5		7	GVM	?
180404	18	Holmslands Klit, S of Nr. Haurvig	4051		1984								1								1	VM	?
190407	8	Skanet Bro	3046		1968								1			1					2		0
190411	19	Dankirke	928 3224 6994		1904	1							5	10	10	7		2	4	1	40	ER-EG	S
190411	26	Ulhøj	1819		1933	1															1	LREG	?
200205	0	Magstrup	-	-	<1775									1							1		-
210103	109	Gl. Hviding	6283 7136						1						1						2	ERL-RGVM	S
220102	0	Volmerstoft / Oldemorstoft	-	-	<1860								1								1		-
		TOTAL																			241		

120

CHAPTER 6

Coins
Denominations and striking periods

6.1 Denarii

By far the overwhelming majority of the Roman coins found in Denmark are denarii that make up for 74 % of the total number of coins. Denarii have been found over most of the country, only the central/western part of Jutland has yielded very few finds. The finds from the central place at Gudme and its surroundings by far outnumber all other sites. Gudme has yielded 676 denarii (single finds and hoards) and another 150 denarii come from its port of trade Lundeborg. The largest hoard is Råmosen with *c.* 500 coins. Among the denarii, coins struck during the period from the Flavian to Antonine dynasties (69-192 AD) are the most common ones. Within this general pattern, which is comparable to the situation in other areas outside the Limes, there are significant differences from one site to another.

6.1.1 Finds of Republican and Julio-Claudian denarii (until AD 68)

Republican[1] denarii are rarely found in Denmark, and of the 25 examples known no less than 18 were part of a hoard found in the Ginderup settlement in north-western Jutland (cf. 5.3.2). The remaining seven denarii struck during the Republican period have been found as single finds on Sealand and in Jutland, and most of them are deprived of an archaeological context. An exception from this rule is a denarius found during the Dankirke excavations (south-western Jutland) in a layer that according to Bjerg should be dated in period B2.[2] At Uldhøj not far from Dankirke, another Republican denarius was found during agricultural works. Excavations in the 1980's have revealed finds from Late Roman and Early Germanic Iron Ages on the same fields, and there is thus a possibility that the Republican coin may be related to these finds.[3]

Among the remaining Republican denarii, three have very generic information on the find circumstances. One was found near Græsted in northern Sealand around 1888, but only handed in to the National Museum in 1955,[4] another was acquired in 1888 with the very broad find provenance of the island "Falster" south of Sealand,[5] and a third was

---

1 The division between Late Republican and Augustan coinage is hard to draw. In the first volume of RIC issued in 1923, H. Mattingly argued for a division in 27 BC, but noted: *"it is impossible to draw a hard and fast line between the Republic and the Empire…"* (p. 41). It has been decided here to follow the division in 31 BC used by Sutherland and Carson in RIC I, 2nd ed., 1984.

2 190411-19: FP 3224.1; Bjerg 2007, 57-75, in particular 68-70.
3 190411-26: FP 1819.
4 010105 sb 90: FP 2437.
5 FP 468.

Crossing boundaries

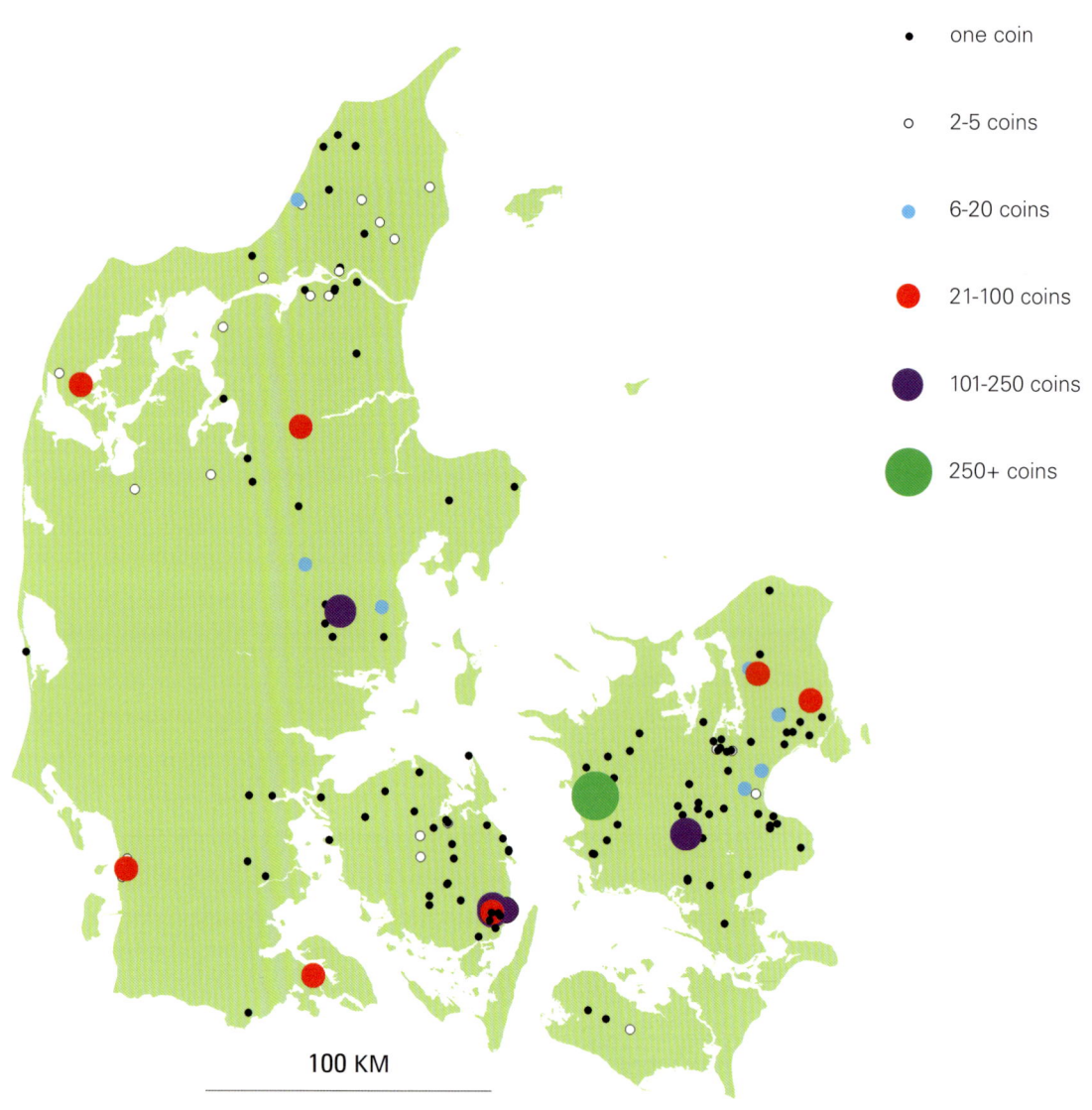

Fig. 62. Denarius finds from Denmark (excl. Bornholm). Distribution map Josefine Franck Bican.

found in Birkede Moor in Dåstrup parish, Sealand.[6] The moor provenance in itself is of course suggestive. There is, however, no other archaeological evidence from the moor, or for that matter any evidence from the Iron Age in the parish of Dåstrup. Likewise, a recent detector find from Kohave on Lolland south of Sealand cannot be related to other finds,[7] but one should keep in mind the extremely rich 1st century Hoby burials with imported Campanian silver ware found few kilometres from Kohave.[8] The last known find is from Lejre in central Sealand.[9] The denarius was found with detector on a site that also yielded a Dorestad coin, but no finds except from the coin from the Roman Iron Age.

Tacitus' mention of the Barbarians' preference for the good old *serrati* and *bigati* with high silver content is often quoted,[10] but the phrase has certainly no bear-

---

6   020102 sb 18: FP 1095.
7   070403 sb 37: FP 6480; Horsnæs & Schilling 2002.

8   070504 sb 1 (area sb 21); Friis Johansen 1923.
9   020601-115: FP 4681.
10 *Germania* I.5: "Pecuniam probant veterem et diu no-

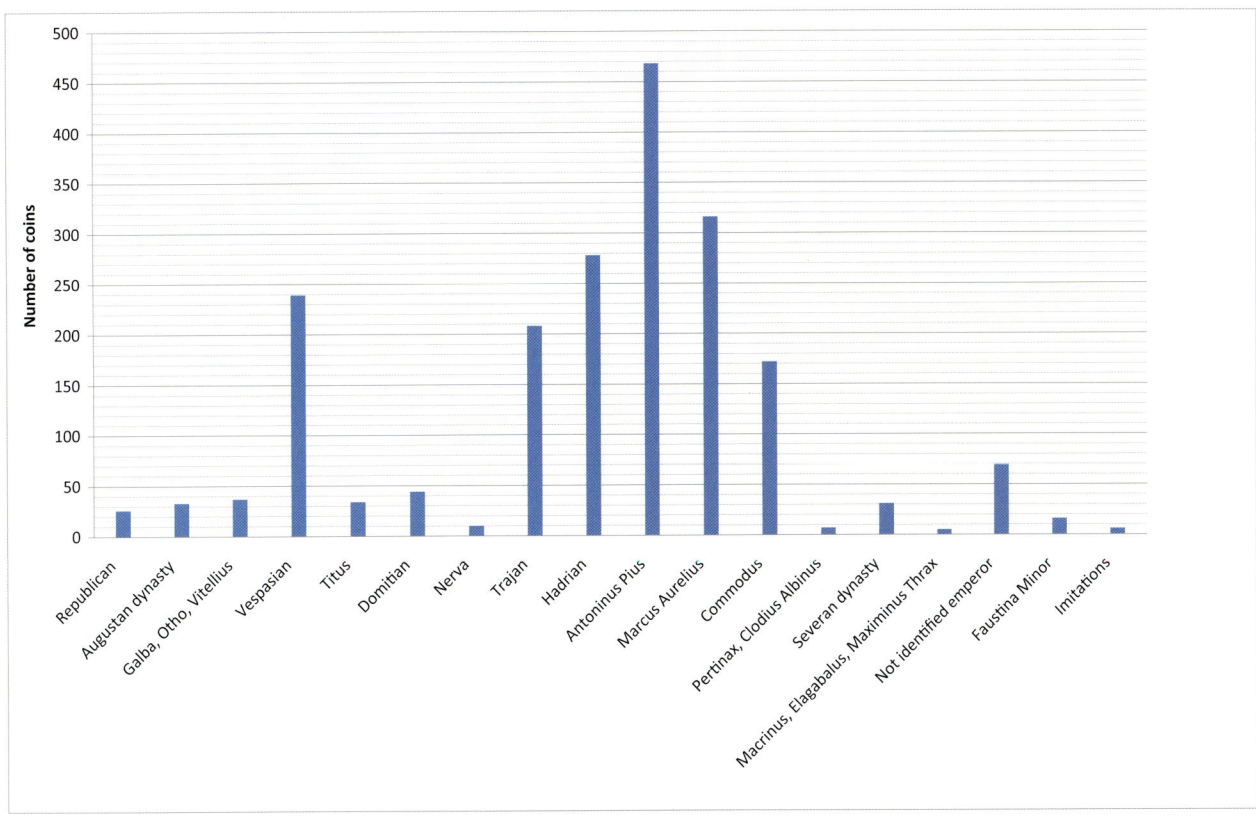

Fig. 63. Denarius finds from Denmark (excl. Bornholm), chronological distribution.

ing on Southern Scandinavia, where no examples of these types have been found.

Also the number of Julio-Claudian denarii (31 BC-68 AD) is low, only 30 recorded examples, among which 21 are Neronian (54-68 AD). Again the Ginderup Hoard takes a special position with seven of the Pre-Neronian coins. Furthermore, two Tiberian denarii have been found. One is the earliest coin from the Råmose Hoard (see above). The other was found in Lille Norge in northern Jutland.[11] This is a detector site that has so far yielded finds with continuity from the Roman Iron Age to the Medieval Period, among which a total of seven denarii (Tiberius, Vespasian or

Fig. 64. Republican denarius from Kohave. Scale 2:1. Photo HWH.

tam, serratos bigatosque", discussed by among others Wolters & Stoess 1985, 4-7.

11 100406-78: FP 5990.1.

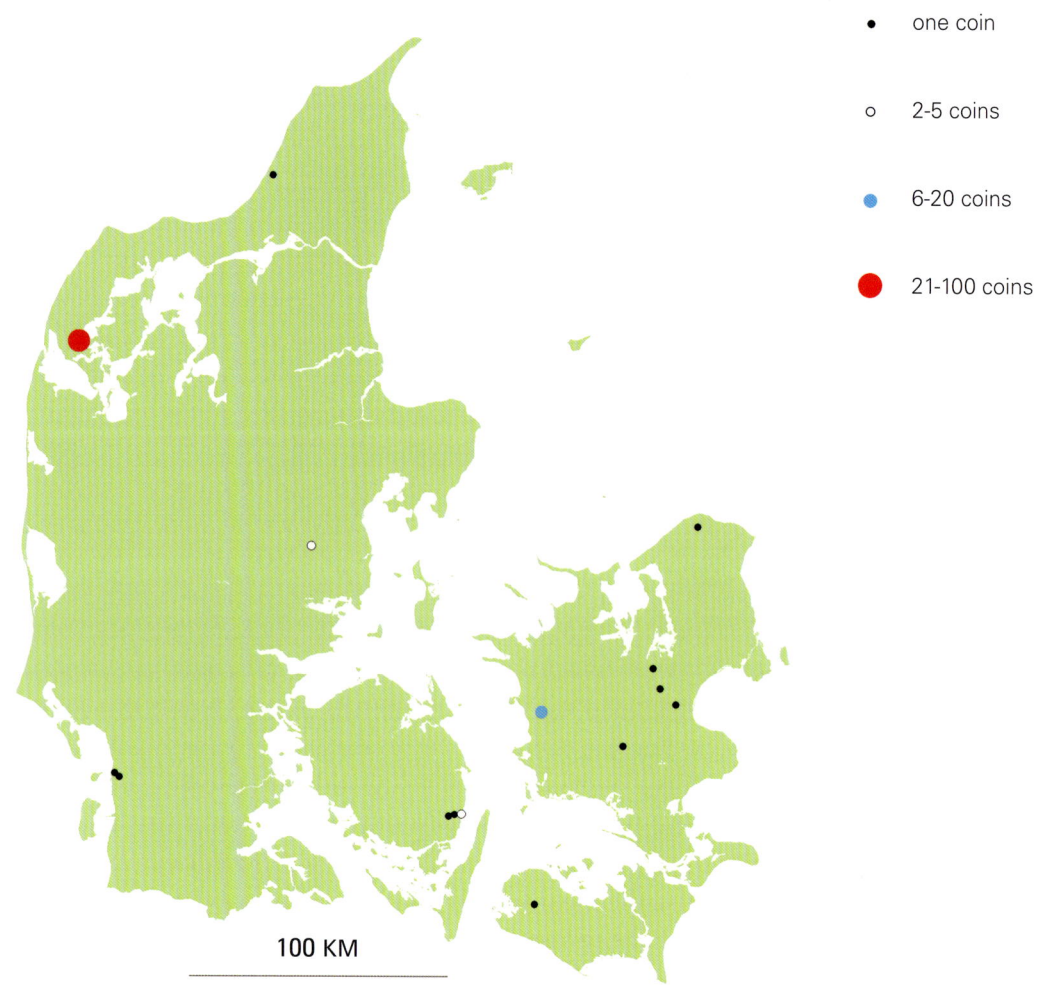

Fig. 65. Finds of Republican and Julio-Claudian denarii (until AD 68). Distribution map Josefine Franck Bican.

Domitian, Titus, Hadrian, two Marcus Aurelius and one Commodus). Thus there seems to be no reason to believe that the Tiberius coin should be seen as anything but an extraordinarily early denarius among the more common ones.

As mentioned the remaining Julio-Claudian denarii were all struck during the reign of Nero. No less than 11 of the 21 specimens were found in the Råmose Hoard; the production and trade site Lundeborg yielded four denarii (and a Neronian aureus) and three Neronian denarii came from the weapon sacrifice from Illerup Ådal. Furthermore the production site Østervang and the Orup Hoard both yielded a Neronian denarius, as did the Ginderup Hoard. The Neronian denarii have been counted among the Julio-Claudian coins, but all the nine type identified specimens (RIC vol. I, 2nd ed., types 53, 60, 62 and 68) from Denmark belong to the post-reform period stressing the lack of the early full weight denarii of the Julio-Claudian period among the Roman coin finds in Barbaricum.[12]

It is generally acknowledged that Republican denarii were circulating in the Empire until the Trajanic monetary reform took place, probably in 107-108 AD.[13] Republican denarii still appear in some numbers (c. 20 %) in hoards ending with coins of Trajan, while the number of Republican denarii drops to 10 % in Hadrianic hoards, and practically disappear in later hoards. The Julio-Claudian denar-

---

12 Three Neronian aurei have been found in Denmark, similarly they are all post-reform (RIC 2nd ed., type 52). Thanks to Richard Reece for asking me to clarify this point.
13 Duncan-Jones 2005, 481.

ii seem to have disappeared from circulation before the Republican denarii. It is therefore conceiveable that the Republican denarii found in Denmark must have left the Empire before the end of Trajan's reign, but not necessarily long before that, and the find circumstances of the Ginderup and Dankirke coins support this view. They need not have left the empire much before the late 1st century AD, indeed the extreme rarity of Julio-Claudian coins in the Danish material seems to indicate that the Republican coins should be regarded as Flavian, rather than earlier, exports from the Empire. Their presence in Denmark therefore tells little about Roman-Germanic contacts in the period before the reign of Vespasian.

6.1.2 Post-Neronian denarii

None of the emperors Galba, Otho and Vitellius reigned for much more than a couple of months. One would therefore expect that denarii from the three emperors following the reign of Nero should be relatively few. Yet with a total of 36 denarii, the year 68-69 AD has yielded more denarii than both the Republican and the Julio-Claudian periods, and in fact the coinages of the emperors following Nero not only herald the period of major influx of Roman denarii, but they are even over-represented in the material in comparison with the Flavian coins. This picture is consistent with the find pattern in northwestern Germany.[14]

The majority of the denarii from 68-69 AD have been found in hoards and/or in the large and well-known sites. Galba is known in six examples, of which three are from the Råmose Hoard and one from the Orup Hoard. The remaining two Galba coins are from Gudme and Lundeborg. Otho is known from five examples: two from the Råmose Hoard, one from the Orup Hoard, one from the Præstemosen Hoard and one from the Katrinelund site. Katrinelund is a settlement with other finds from the Late Roman and Early Germanic Iron Age (see above).[15] Vitellius is more common with a total of 25 denarii. 12 came from the Råmose Hoard, two from the Orup Hoard, three from Gudme and Lundeborg, six from Illerup and one from Nydam, and finally one with only a generic provenance from Ejstrup.[16]

The Flavian emperors are generally well represented. A total of 311 coins fall within the reign of Vespasian and his sons. The majority derive from the hoards already mentioned above: 161 from the Råmose Hoard and 25 from the Orup Hoard, while the Ginderup Hoard is represented only by the two latest coins from this hoard. The settlements at Gudme and Lundeborg have yielded 23 and 18 Flavian denarii, respectively, and the Illerup finds comprise 47 Flavian denarii.

Flavian denarii are the oldest coins in a number of denarius hoards with so-called "late" composition (see below), for example in the Lærkefryd,[17] Hellerne,[18] Bagsværd,[19] and Hvornum Kær hoards,[20] and from the weapon sacrifice at Nydam.[21] Also a number of settlement sites have yielded a single Flavian coin as the oldest of a number of Roman coins (see list: Denarius finds from settlements, above).

Denarii of Nerva, Trajan and Hadrian are common, but less well represented when compared to the relatively long reigns of both Trajan and Hadrian. A total of 480 denarii have been recovered. Naturally, very large proportions derived from the hoards of Råmosen (147 denarii) and Orup (43 denarii), and denarii from this period are prolific in sites as Illerup (71 denarii), Gudme (80 denarii, + 31 from the Præstemosen Hoard) and Lundeborg (38 denarii).

Antonine denarii often make up for 60-80 % of the denarii from a Danish find. Almost half the denarii found in Denmark were struck during the 55 years from 138 to 192 AD, and the Antonine denarii have been found all over the country. Trajan and Hadrian were represented by *c.* 10 coins pr. year in office, but the figure rises to more than 20 coins pr. year during the reign of Antoninus Pius. Already during the reign of Marcus Aurelius the figure has dropped considerably again, to *c.* 15 coins pr. year,

---

14   Berger 1992, 129 Abb. 45 (single finds only).
15   160115 sb 198: FP 4639.1. *AUD* 1988, 201. Bjerg 2007, 77-80.
16   120312: FP 3014. Kromann 1983-84, 62 no. 3.
17   010306 sb 1: four Flavians.
18   020209 sb 28: one Flavian.
19   020303, without sb no.: three Flavians.
20   140704, without sb no.: five Flavians.
21   230304 sb 30: three Flavians.

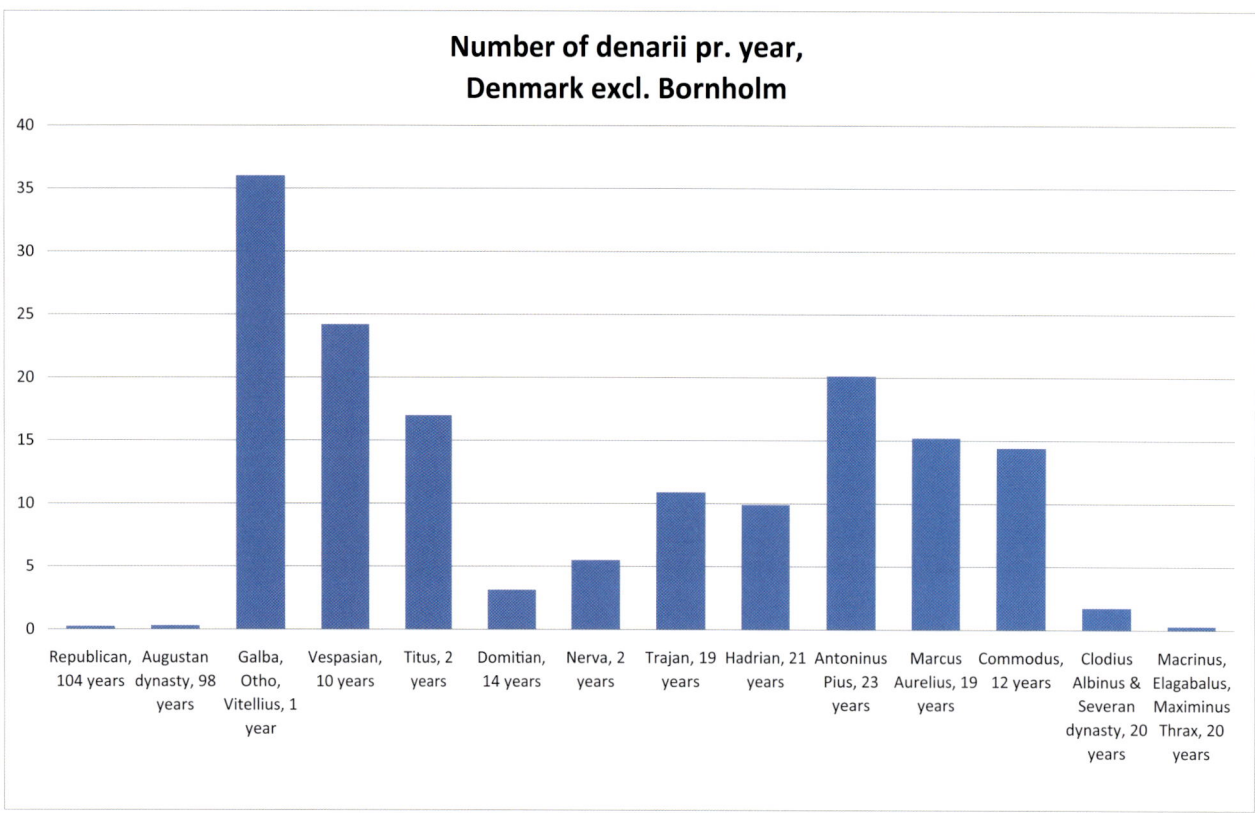

Fig. 66. Number of denarii pr. year. n=1803, all denarii have been counted by emperor. 202 coins were excluded, as the emperor could not be identified. Among these are a number of Faustina Minor coins that may have been struck during the reign of either Antoninus Pius or Marcus Aurelius.

and the level drops gradually during the reign of Commodus.

It is therefore interesting to see if it is possible to get closer to the peaking years. Luckily, many of the issues of the Antonine emperors can be dated within a year, but there are nevertheless a great number of undated coins, and therefore the following figures should be used with caution.

6.1.3 The chronological distribution of Antonine coinages

Most of Antoninus Pius' coinage (171 coins) can be dated within a year. The exceptions are the COS III and IIII issues. In the diagram (*Fig. 67*) the COS III coinage *(RIC 61-106)* has been divided equally between the years AD 140/141, 141/142, and 142/143. Likewise the COS IIII coinage *(RIC 124-161)* has been used to fill in the years AD 145/146 and 146/147 before the dating by TR P begins. The differences from one year to another, for example the very low figure for the year AD 149/150, should probably be ascribed to differences in mint output (only five issues in AD 149/150 according to *RIC* III) rather than differences caused by local preferences in Barbaricum.

The coinage of Marcus Aurelius Caesar *(RIC* Antoninus 411-491, 43 coins) follows that of Antoninus Pius, and from AD 146/147 *(RIC 435 ff.)* it can be dated within a year.[22] The earlier issues have been divided equally between the six years from AD 140/141 onwards.

The coinages struck in the names of the empresses are normally harder to date. The coinage of Faustina Major comprises 72 coins, among them *RIC* 327-334 are not represented, and the two coins in the series *RIC 335-342* have been divided equally between AD 139/140 and 140/141. The coinage

---

22 From AD 149/150 only two issues, not represented in the Danish material; from AD 150/151 no coins recorded in *RIC*; from AD 152/153 only two issues, not represented in the Danish material.

struck for Diva Faustina Major (*RIC* 343-407) is represented by 70 coins. The only means of dating them is the *t.p.q.* at the death of Faustina in AD 141. Theoretically they may have been struck until the death of Antoninus Pius himself. Mattingly and Sydenham regarded the Aeternitas and Augusta issues to have been struck soon after Faustina's death, while the Vota Publica should refer to the marriage between Faustina Minor and Marcus Aurelius in AD 145. They also regarded the later issues (i.e. of *c.* AD 145) to be characterized by the DIVA AVG(VSTA) FAVSTINA legend, which, however, is also used on a number of the Aeternitas and Augusta issues.[23]

The fact that such a large part of the Danish finds of denarii of Antoninus Pius were struck for Faustina Major makes it difficult to evaluate the number of coin finds pr. year within this period. The date assigned to the Faustina coins assumes enormous importance. In case the Diva Faustina coinage was struck until AD 160/161, we should add 3.5 coins pr. year during these years. Instead, if the Diva Faustina coinage mainly belongs to the years immediately following her death we should for example add 10 coins pr. year in seven years from AD 141 onwards or even more coins pr. year in a shorter period. In the diagram it has been decided to add 10 coins pr. year in the years AD 141/142-144/145 and 5 coins pr. year in the years AD 145/146-150/151, but it must be stressed that this division is purely hypothetical.

The coinage struck by and in the name of Marcus Aurelius is represented by 117 coins. The coins of Marcus Aurelius are normally closely datable, and for the use of the diagram coins dated within two years are given 0.5 value to each of the years etc.

The coinage for Faustina Minor (103 denarii found in Denmark) falls into three distinct periods. The first period consists of the coins struck while her father Antoninus Pius was still in office. The issues probably started in connection with her marriage to Marcus Aurelius in AD 145, and the issues *RIC* Antoninus 493-517 (represented by 28 coins) should thus be dated AD 145-161 (16 years). The next two periods consist of the coins struck for her during the reign of Marcus Aurelius, first the coins struck during her lifetime until AD 175 (RIC Aurelius 667-737, 57 coins in 14 years), secondly her *consecratio* issues, dated in AD 176-180 (*RIC* Aurelius 738-754, 13 coins in 4 years). As a closer dating of the Faustina Minor issues is not possible, the coins have been divided equally within the three striking periods.

Lucius Verus was Marcus Aurelius' co-emperor from AD 161 until his death in early AD 169. The issues in his name can be dated within a year. The coinage struck in the name of his consort Lucilla must be dated AD 164-169, and the 17 coins in her name have been distributed equally in this period in the diagram.

The coins struck for Commodus Caesar in AD 172-180 (10 coins) and for Commodus as *augustus* (132 coins) have been inserted in the diagram according to the principles described above. Crispina (*RIC* 276-290) fell from grace in *c.* AD 183. It is therefore normally believed that coins were struck for Crispina only during the first third of the 12 years reign of Commodus, so all issues in her name, represented by 27 coins, have been placed in the three years AD180/181-182/183.[24]

The relatively high number of coins struck in the name of the empresses of the Antonine family is a striking feature. Among the 783 coins struck during the reigns of Antoninus Pius and Marcus Aurelius there are 249 struck in the names of Faustina Major, Faustina Minor and Lucilla – 31 % of the total number of coins from the period! The 27 Crispina denarii from Denmark constitute 15 % of the whole material from his reign. These figures are, however, consistent with the figures from a number of selected hoards, and must therefore be seen as a norm rather than as something unusual.[25]

The diagram presents figures based on 325 denarii of 496 denarii from the reign of Antoninus Pius (65 %), 214 of 310 denarii from the reign of Marcus Aure-

---

23 *RIC* III (1930), 3.

24 It has, however, recently been argued that the coinage of Crispina as empress continued uninterrupted until the death of Commodus in spite of Crispina's falling from grace in *c.* 183 AD, cf. Duncan-Jones 2006. This has quite important implications for the diagram: in stead of dividing 27 coins in three years (9 coins pr. year), they should be divided equally in 12 years (*c.* 2 coins pr. year).

25 Duncan-Jones 2006.

Crossing boundaries

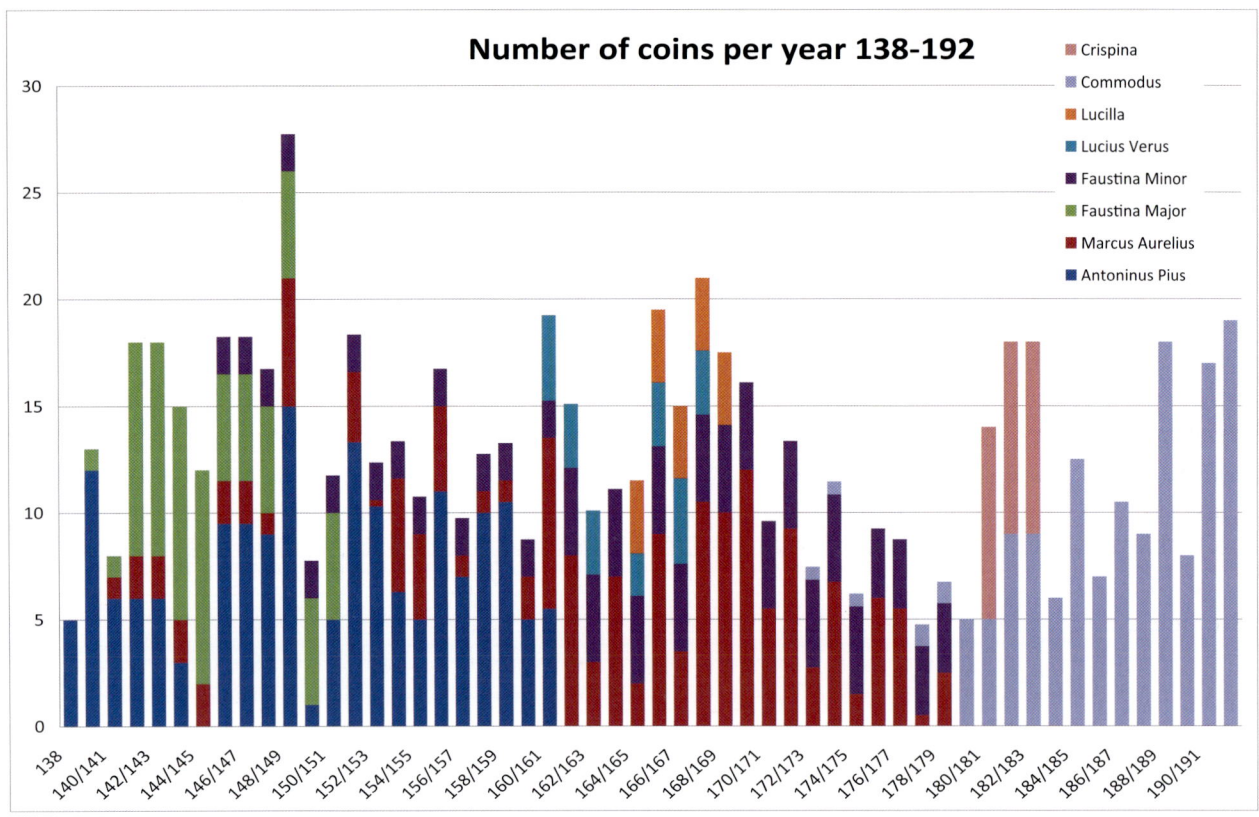

Fig. 67. Chronological distribution of the denarii struck by Antonine emperors from Denmark.

lius (69 %), and 162 of 180 coins from the reign of Commodus (90 %). A relatively large number of coins struck during the reigns of Antoninus and Marcus Aurelius cannot be dated more precisely than within the reign. One of the main reasons for this is the loss of the Råmosen Hoard, but also the bad preservation of many recent detector finds inhibits precise identification of reverse type and issue. The undated coins have not been inserted in the diagram, which therefore tends to overemphasize the coinage of Commodus, whose coinage is better represented.

The reading of the diagram is by no means easy. Within the reign of Antoninus there is great oscillation in the figures that are clearly due to the annual mint output rather than political events. Years with a low number of issues, for example AD 149/150 with three denarius issues for Antoninus Pius and two only for Marcus Aurelius Caesar, are of course badly represented, and the problems with exact dating of the Antoninus coins around AD 144-145 are also visible in the diagram. This underlines that the Roman denarii that came to Southern Scandinavia were not chosen from a particular lot. If indeed the denarii came to Barbaricum in batches as payment for peace or mercenaries, as has been maintained by some scholars, they were clearly not drawn directly from the mint, but rather from the stock of used coins from the treasury. This has the implication that it is quite difficult to use the date of issue of the coins as anything but a rough *terminus post quem* in discussions of known historical events as explanatory models for the export of coins into Barbaricum.

There is a great variety in the issues represented in the Danish finds. As an example let us take a closer look at the denarii struck during the reign of Commodus. It should be underlined that the picture emerging by studying his coinage is closely comparable to the one seen presented by other coinages. Among the 182 Commodus denarii from Denmark 124 denarii can be identified to a specific issue recorded in the *RIC*.[26] A total of 228 denarius issues are described and recorded in *RIC*, and among the 124 identified

---

26 Some coins have been lost or they are too badly preserved to be identified to a specific issue.

coins from Denmark no less than 72 different issues are represented. Most of the issues are represented by one coin only, and there is no single issue that is better represented than any other. It is among the coins struck for the empresses that we find the most often repeated issues, Commodus *RIC* 279 and 286a (both found in six examples). It should be noted that coins of the same issues have been found widely apart, and that no die identities have been found among the Crispina coins. A study of the coin types (reverse motives) reveals that there seems to be no particular prevalence for one or a group of types.

Severan and post-Severan (struck 192-230's AD) coins are only rarely found. There are only 41 examples from Denmark, and they are most often found on the same sites as the Antonine denarii and in contexts dominated by Antonine denarii.

6.1.4 Chronological composition of closed finds with several denarii

The general characteristic of the denarius hoards from Denmark is that they are normally single type hoards. Exceptions are the unique Ginderup Hoard treated above, the Gudme IV Hoard and the probable hoard from Dankirke south of House Vb. The siliquae from the Gudme IV Hoard indicate that the deposition of these denarii must have taken place no earlier than the *t.p.q.* provided by the three Procopius coins struck 365/366 AD. The deposition of the second Dankirke Vest Hoard must post-date the Probus antoninianus (276-282 AD) from the coin concentration found south of House Vb.

The largest hoard is the Råmosen Hoard that originally contained *c.* 500 coins, a number that is considerably lower than the largest denarius hoards of for example Sweden or Poland. The remaining hoards are all relatively small. The chronological distribution of the coins in the denarius hoards all fall within the common pattern for denarius hoards in Barbaricum.

List of closed finds with several denarii

Site	No. coins	Date range[27]	Site no.	Year(s) of finding
Lærkefryd	51	72-191	010306 sb 1	1990-2008
Hellerne	7	69-184	020209 sb 28	2000-2002
Bagsværd	45	69-218	020303	1850
Råmosen[28]	c. 500	54-180/192	030205 sb 59	1782
Orup	106	64-210	050711 sb 26	1950s & 2004-
Gudme IV[29]	14	69-193	090104 sb 107	1991-2003
Gudme Præstemosen	161	81-186	090104 sb 162	1993
Hvornum Kær	23	69-192	140704	1936
Testrup Teglværk	9	118-191	150406 sb 36	1906
Dankirke Øst	7-9	138-201	190411 sb 19	1965-1967
Dankirke Vest (house V)	6	117-192	190411 sb 19	1968
Dankirke Vest (south of house Vb)	16	119-190	190411 sb 19	1968

---

27 Earliest possible date-latest possible date of issue.
28 The find list indicates that the latest coin was a Marcus Aurelius, but letters by Ove Høegh-Guldberg clearly state that also Commodus was represented, perhaps as Caesar? See above section 5.2.2.1.

29 The Gudme IV area has yielded a total of 108 coins among which 62 denarii, 28 siliquae and a sestertius. Only the denarii from the probable mixed hoard of 14 denarii and 24 siliquae (excavation no. SOM A 94.315 = FP 6007) are included in the list.

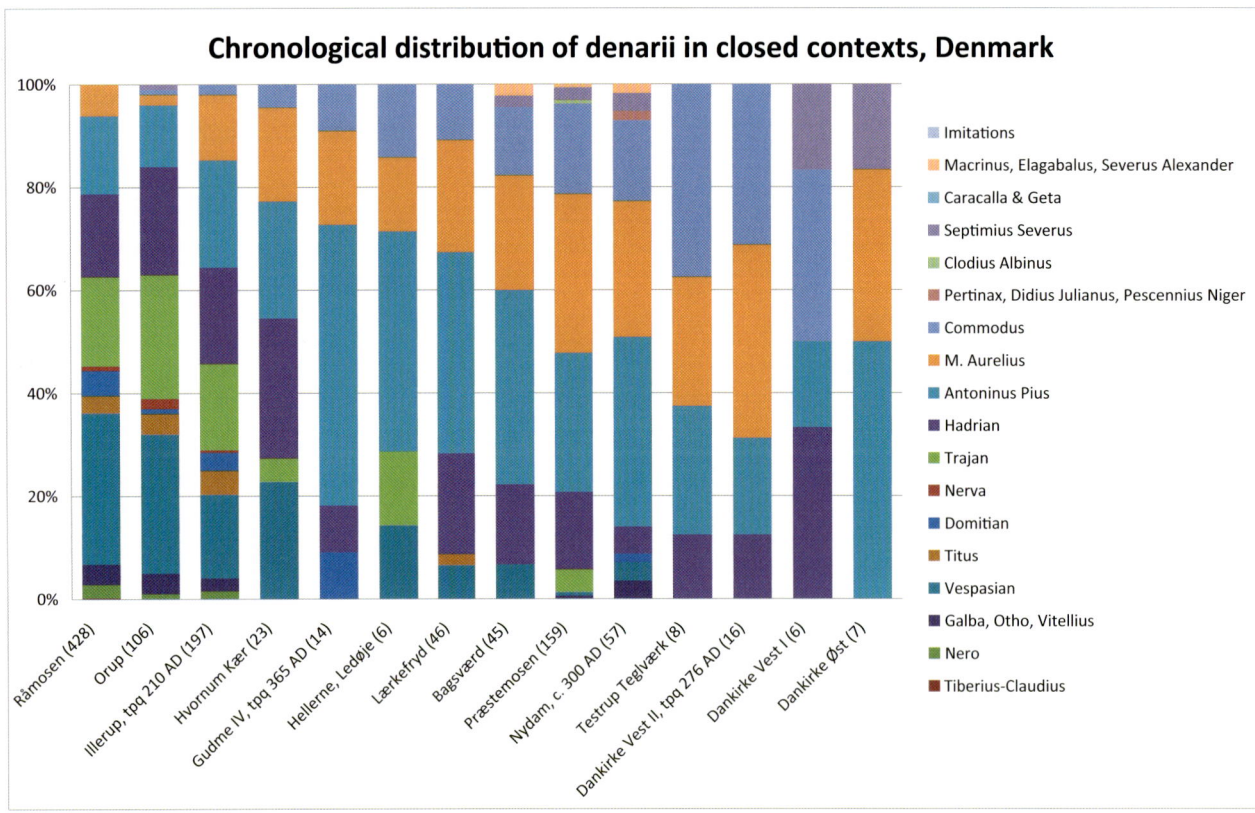

Fig. 68. The chronological distribution of the denarii within closed contexts in Western Denmark.

A considerable number of denarii have been found in four of the weapon sacrifices, two in Denmark (Illerup and Nydam), one in Germany (Thorsberg) and one in Sweden (Skedemosse). It is suggested that the word "assemblage" should be used about these finds that may contain series of single finds and/or smaller hoards. In each of these cases we have a number of coins that were deposited at one time. Therefore these assemblages can – with due caution – be treated as the hoards. The Illerup sacrifice is dated by dendrochronological analysis of some of the weaponry, whereby the sacrifice must have taken place after c. 210 AD. The coins from the Nydam moor belong to the sacrifice that is archaeologically dated c. 300 AD/ early 4th century.

Fig. 68 is an attempt to present an overview of the chronological distribution of the denarii within the closed contexts in Denmark. The hoards and assemblages have been ordered with the "earliest" composition from the left. Caution should be taken, as some of the hoards contain a very low number of coins (Hellerne, Testrup Teglværk, Dankirke Øst and Dankirke Vest I), but leaving aside these finds would not change the picture considerably.

The Ginderup Hoard clearly is a unique composition in a Danish context, and therefore not included in fig. 68. Regarding the denarius finds with material from the Flavian to Antonine dynasties mainly ("Flavian/Antonine hoards"), the lack of a clear division line between "early" and "late" compositions of the assemblages is one of the most striking features. Secondly, it is important to notice that some of the assemblages with relatively "early" composition have a relatively late end coin (the Orup Hoard) or a late deposition date (the Gudme IV Hoard, where the denarii were mixed with siliquae). Studying the Danish material only it is therefore difficult to conclude that significant and sudden changes took place in the chronological composition of the denarius assemblages according to the deposition date.

Scholars have discussed differences between denarius hoards with an "early" composition and a "late" composition, a distinction that ultimately derived from

Coins. Denominations and striking periods

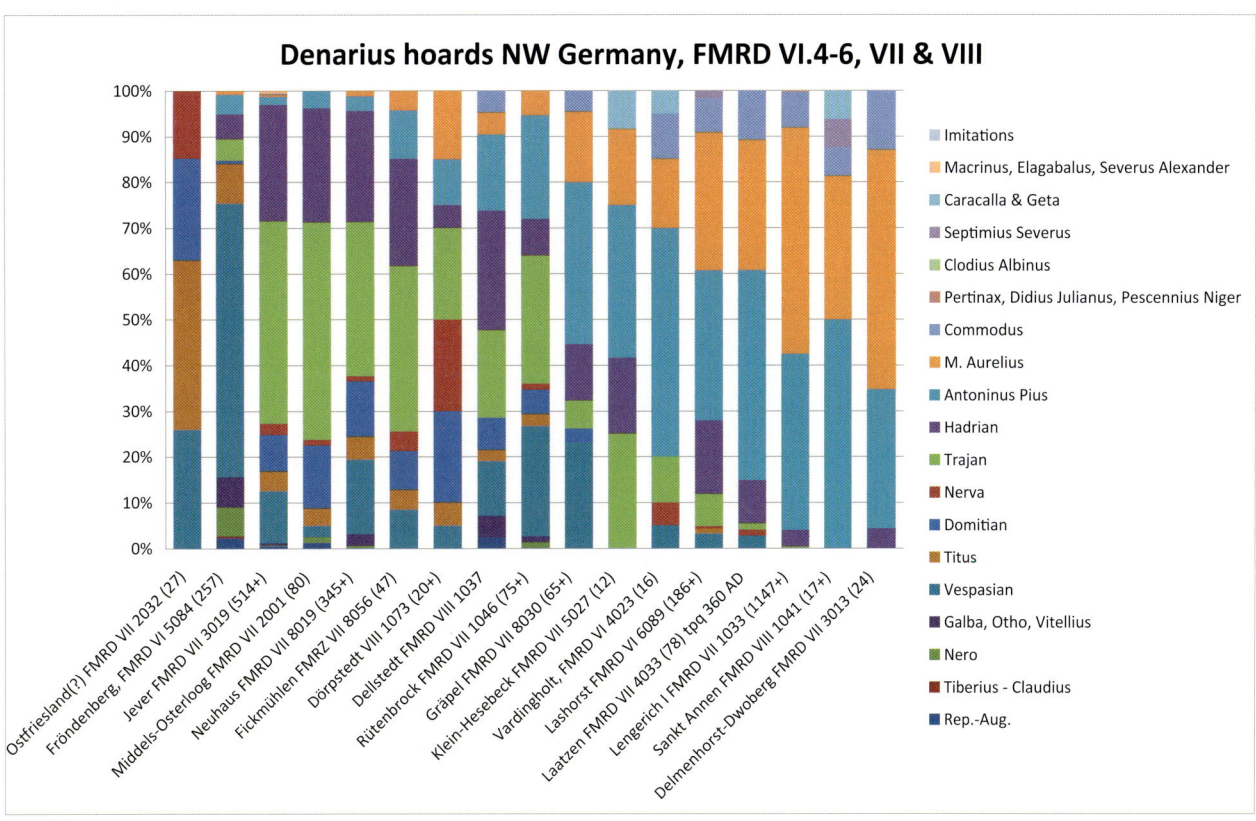

Fig. 69 a. The chronological distribution of the denarii in hoards: North-western Germany.

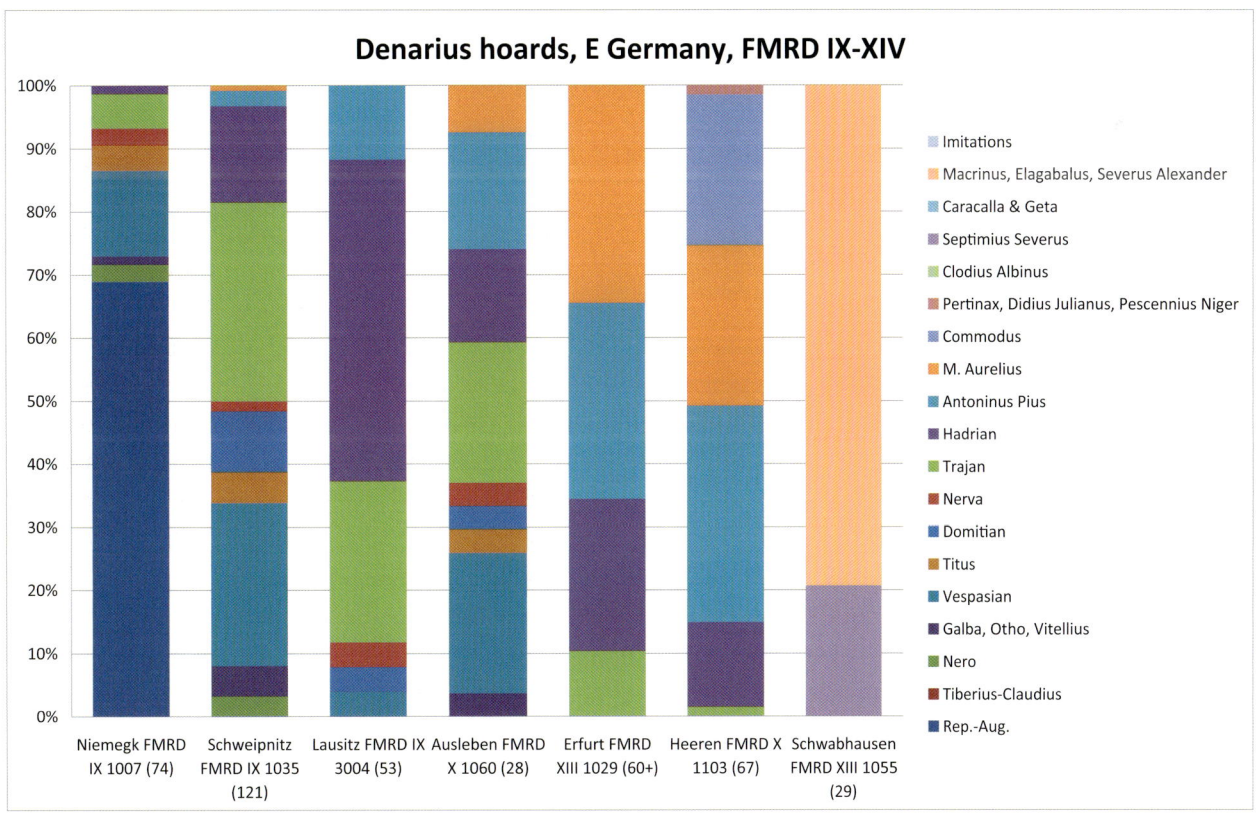

Fig. 69 b. The chronological distribution of the denarii in hoards: Eastern Germany.

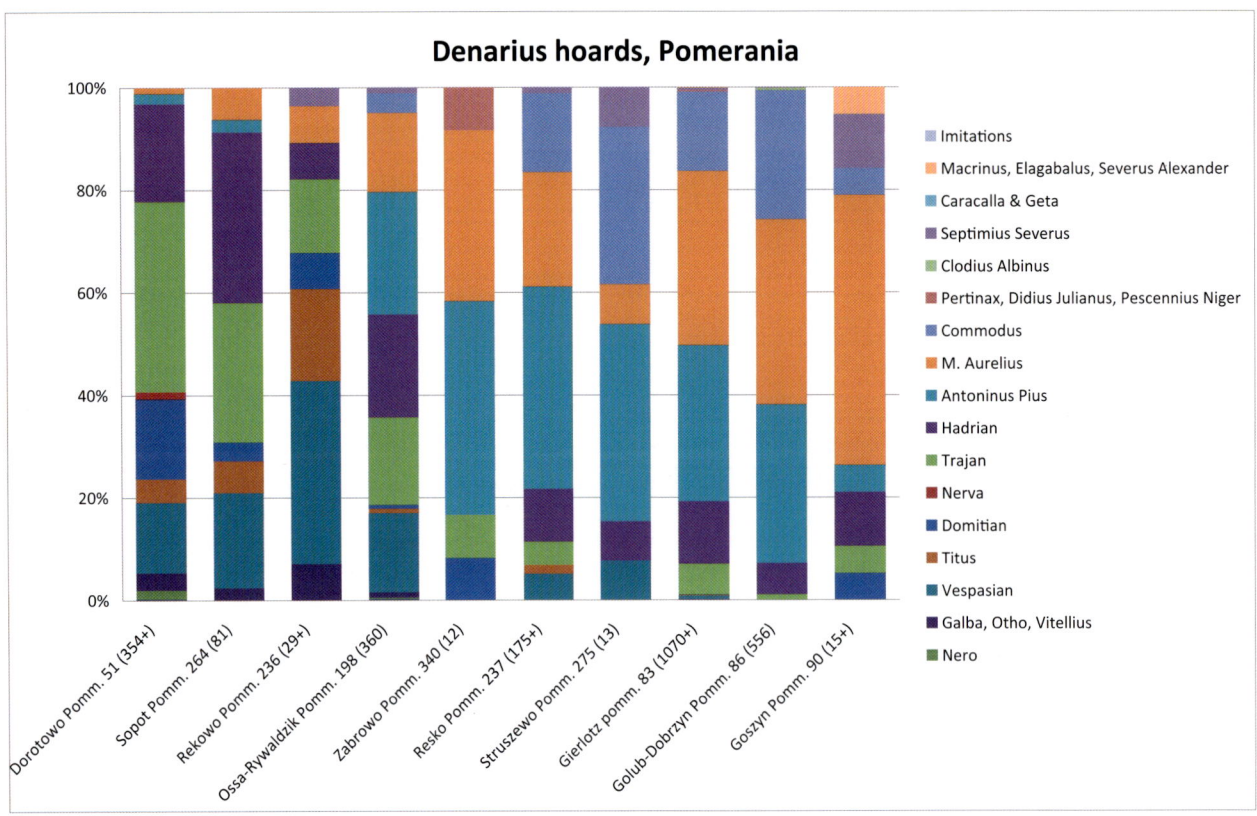

Fig. 69 c. The chronological distribution of the denarii in hoards: Northern Poland.

the studies of Sture Bolin.[30] Kromann divided the denarius hoards into three groups:[31]

1. (The Ginderup Hoard) with majority of Republican/Augustan coins and latest coin struck during the reign of Vespasian.
2. Hoards where the majority of the coins were pre-Antonine and the latest coin was struck during the reign of Marcus Aurelius; the hoard from Råmosen was the only Danish example of a hoard with a "group II" composition, and Kromann compared it to the incomplete Dörpstedt find from Schleswig. As noted the letters from Høegh-Guldberg indicated the presence of coins struck by (or for) Commodus in the Råmosen Hoard. If the coins were struck by Commodus this hoard would fall outside Kromann's definition. The Orup Hoard with a general composition similar to the Råmosen Hoard has an end coin struck by Septimius Severus, and thus falls outside her category as well.
3. Hoards with a majority of Antonine coins and the latest coins struck during or after the reign of Commodus. All hoards from Denmark, except Ginderup and Råmosen, would according to Kromann fall within this category.

The hoards from northern Germany and Pomerania have been inserted into diagrams similar to the Danish material (*Figs. 69 a-c*). Also here the distinction between "early" and "late" composition of Flavian/Antonine denarius hoards may be hard to see, although there seems to be a greater variation in the composition of finds. It is interesting to note the variation in find density of denarius hoards in these areas. No denarius hoards are noted from Mecklenburg-Vorpommern at all, and the eastern part of Germany as a whole have few finds compared to northwestern Germany and Denmark. Also Pomerania has relatively few finds.

This distinction between "early" and "late" denarius hoards was used by Fonnesbech-Sandberg in her dis-

---

30 Fonnesbech-Sandberg 1989, 53.
31 Kromann & Watt 1984, 35.

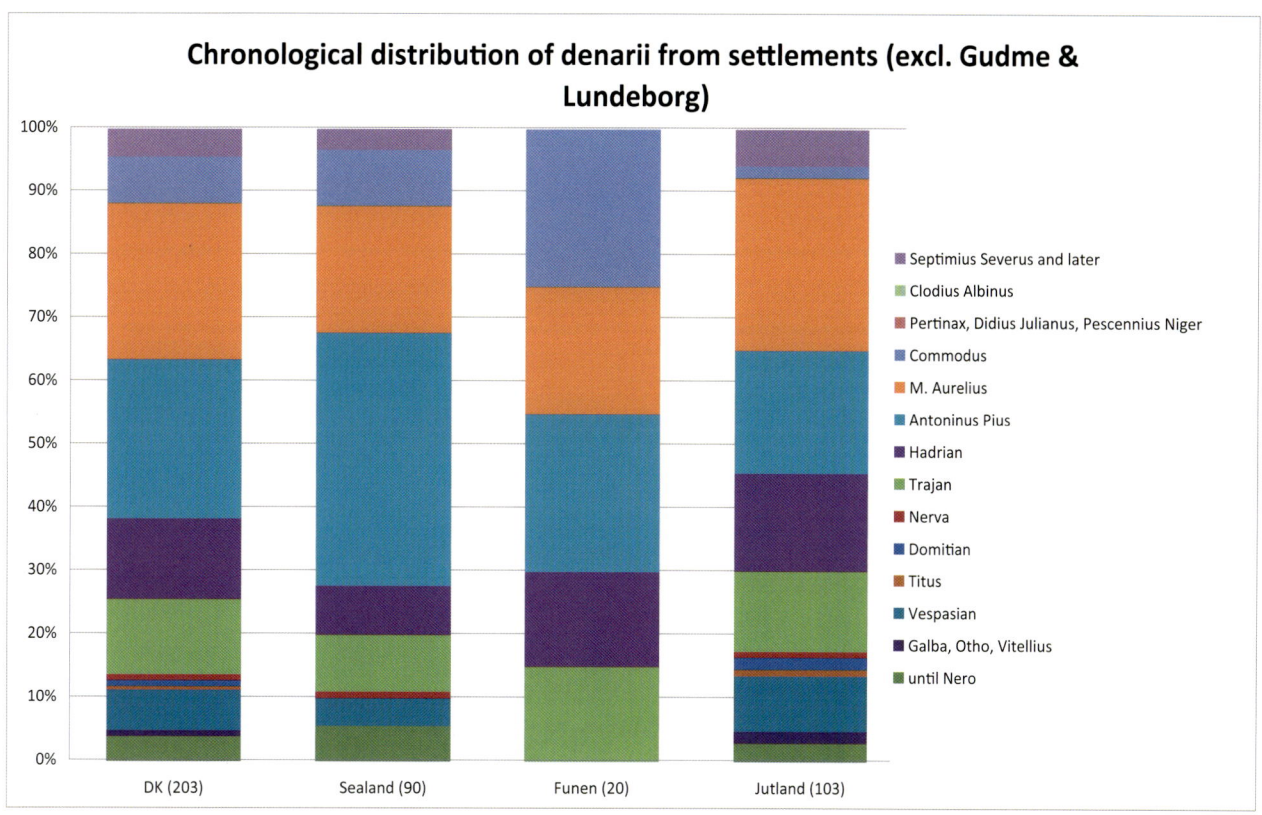

Fig. 70. Diagram. The chronological distribution of denarii from settlements in Western Denmark.

cussion of the date of deposition: "early" hoards were deposited in the Late Roman Iron Age and the "late" hoards in the Early Germanic Iron Age.[32] Unfortunately the deposition of denarius hoards – or for that matter finds containing a number of denarii from the same site – cannot be dated with such accuracy. The diagrams reveal that there is a gradual transition from one find to another. Although it is possible to distinguish between "early" and "late" composition of denarius finds, there is no clear-cut distinction, and finds with "early" composition may indeed have an end coin struck in the late 2nd or even the early 3rd centuries. To enlarge the material as much as possible Danish detector sites (settlements) with series of single finds have been analysed in the same manner, and although it is a numerically restricted material it confirms the large chronological span seen in the hoards. The same applies to the picture emerging from an analysis of the denarii from Gudme and Lundeborg (see above *Fig. 50*).

There is, however, an interesting "early" composition in the settlement material from Jutland with 45 % pre-Antonine coins. This may – with some caution due to the relatively low number of coins inserted into the diagram – be related to the chronological distribution in the hoard material in Barbaricum, where hoards with "early" composition are slightly more common in north-western Germany than in eastern Germany and Poland. The chronological composition of denarii from Funen apart from Gudme/Lundeborg seems comparable to the material from Sealand, but as the material comprises only 20 coins this may be misleading.

There can be little doubt that the chronological distribution of striking periods within a find assemblage (hoards as well as series of single finds from the same site) has a chronological significance. Assemblages containing coins from the Julio-Claudian dynasty (in practise mostly Neronian coins), also have a relatively high number of coins from AD 68-69 and from the Flavian dynasty, and although the closing date of these assemblages may be late-Antonine or even Severan the proportion of Antonine coins is relatively low.

---

32 Fonnesbech-Sandberg 1989 and 1990b.

Two finds (the hoards from Råmosen and Orup) have almost 80 % pre-Antonine coins. Both hoards were found on the western part of Sealand, in areas with little evidence for contemporary finds and few other finds of Roman imports. In both cases the hoards must have been deposited in marginal soil, in a wetland area, with no indication of settlement in the vicinity.[33]

A small number of finds has 55-65 % pre-Antonine coins. This group includes two finds that strictly speaking were found outside Denmark, namely the large Flintarp Hoard from Mainland Sweden and the Thorsberg weapon sacrifice, as well as a relatively small find, namely the 11 denarii from the workshop site at Østervang – clearly such a small number of coins has restricted statistical significance. Yet, this group also includes a context dated assemblage, namely the 200 coins from the weapon sacrifice at Illerup deposited as one single act shortly after AD 210. The coins from the Thorsberg sacrifice present a similar composition, but the find circumstances are not as eloquent as the Illerup find.

The remaining assemblages may be divided into three groups: one with 30-40 % pre-Antonine coins, containing the coins from Lundeborg (cf. above on contexts); one with around 20 % pre-Antonine coins and one with 15-20 % pre-Antonine coins, containing the Nydam weapon sacrifice that were deposited *c.* 300 AD. It should be noted that the number of coins from several of the finds is so low that only a few new finds from the sites in question may alter the picture significantly.

This refined diagram warns us that it is not straightforward to use the chronological composition of the find to date its deposition. The composition of the weapon sacrifices may argue for the not surprising indication that the later the composition, the later the deposition, but the material is so small that it is by no means safe enough to use this parameter to date the deposition of hoards without external dating evidence.[34] This rather pessimistic view upon the validity of the chronological composition of the (mainly) 2nd century denarius hoards from Denmark may be extended to other non-Roman areas, and the old theory of two main sources for denarii in Southern Scandinavia – an earlier western one and a later eastern one – must give way to a more complicated picture of many denarius "hoards" that must have left the Empire as un-coordinated and unrelated "export events" over a period.

While Lind suggested that the denarii did not leave the Roman Empire until the second half of the 3rd century, Berger and Bursche agree that they must have left the Empire before *c.* 240 AD, when the denarii from the Flavian to Severan periods have disappeared from circulation within the Empire, as indicated by the fact that denarii from this period do not appear in Roman hoards of the second half of the 3rd century.[35] Berger and Bursche seem to agree that the outflow of the denarii happened considerably before that date, and Berger claimed that the formation of the hoards started already during the reign of Marcus Aurelius.[36] Apart from the Ginderup hoard and a few other examples of Early Imperial coins, we must conclude that the great outflow of denarii happened throughout the half-century following the latter part of the reign of Marcus Aurelius.

The date of the denarii's arrival in Southern Scandinavia is hard to pinpoint. There is no archaeological evidence for Flavian-Severan denarii in Denmark before *c.* AD 200, but from that time and well into the 6th century (and sometimes even later) denarii have been deposited at various instances. This means that the denarii may have arrived at any time from *c.* AD 200 onwards, and the differences in the chronological composition from find to find indicates that they did not arrive as one single batch, but rather as a (large?) number of smaller ensembles.

The commonly mentioned reason for the stop of import of Roman silver coins (seen from a Barbarian point of view) namely that the silver content dropped considerably after the reign of Marcus Aurelius, is rejected by Berger and Bursche alike, both arguing that the lower silver content of the coins would not be easily recognizable. Bursche furthermore stresses the importance of the use of subaerati that seems to have

---

33 A related, but not identical, composition can be seen in the coins from the in-complete hoard from Dörpstedt in Schleswig; FMRD VIII, 1073.
34 I therefore find it hard to follow the discourse developed by Fonnesbech-Sandberg 1989.

---

35 Lind 1988; Berger 1992; Bursche 1996.
36 Berger 1992, 157-158.

been accepted by the Germanic peoples. He claims that the number of subaerati in finds from Barbaricum in general is underestimated as there has been a tendency to base studies on coin lists – often repeating old coin attributions and descriptions – rather than on a study of the coins themselves.[37]

Rejecting the theory that the Germanic peoples deliberately chose not to receive payment in other denomination than pre-3rd century denarii forces us to consider that it was not a stop of import into Barbaricum, but a stop of coin export decided by the Roman side.

It is even more difficult to establish the route of the denarii to Denmark – or other areas of Barbaricum – let alone whether they travelled as closed assemblages from the Roman Empire all the way to the final destination. Yet I believe that the denarii normally left the Empire as "hoards"; but once outside the Empire any denarius hoard may have been split up into smaller entities, or topped up with extra coins – or both.

6.1.5 Single finds in dated contexts

Coins deposited in burials are often used to date the burials, but in the case of the Roman coins in the north, the burial took place at some time after the striking of the coin: The Danish burials containing a denarius have all been dated in period C1b (210/20-250/60 AD).

In one case a denarius has been found in a mixed hoard of a considerably later date. It is the Gudme II bracteate hoard dated in the early 6th century that also contained a denarius.

A small number of denarii has been found during excavation of archaeologically dated layers. The denarii from Lundeborg make up the most important group among these coins, but also Gudme have yielded examples of denarii in archaeologically dated layers (section 5.3.1).

6.1.6 Single finds of denarii from detector sites

Many of the coins from Gudme and – it seems – all the coins from Lundeborg must be considered accumulations of single finds. The same applies to the denarii that have been found on the various types of settlement sites all over the country, most importantly Hørup and Østervang on Sealand, Lundsgård, Seden and Troensegård on Funen, and Malle Langhøj, Kvosted, and the recently discovered site at Øster Vandet in Jutland.

We are left with a considerable number of single finds of denarii that are very hard to interpret, because of lack of archaeological activity in the find area. Many are old single finds and it might prove useful to test the areas in question with a modern and archaeologically planned settlement survey.

6.1.7 Barbarian denarii

Among the denarii at least eight are examples of Barbarian imitations.[38] Four of the imitations were found in the Illerup sacrifice, one came from Ejsbøl moor, and three are detector finds from Gudme, Lundeborg, and Øster Vandet.

- The four Barbarian imitations of denarii from the Illerup A sacrifice were found within find group no. RLF. They were all struck from the same set of dies in what is described as "a style of its own": the portrait is much barbarised (Kromann believed it to imitate the portrait of Commodus), and the legend is blurred.[39]

---

37 The present study is no exception to this unfortunate rule. Peter 1990, 66-73 suggested that the workshop producing subaerati based on prototypes from Hadrian to Commodus was active in the period c. 195-210 AD, i.e. after the reform of Severus in 194/5 that lowered the silver content of the denarii considerably.

38 It has not been considered possible to go through all the denarii from Denmark in order to identify more Barbarian imitations within the scope of the present work. Thus more Barbarian imitations from western Denmark may exist. Furthermore Bornholm has yielded at least six Barbarian imitations: FP 636.180 (= NM I C 7776) from the Robbedale Hoard; FP 6201.18 and 6688.10 from Sorte Muld and FP 6546.3 from Sønderhøj Syd, two sites that are both part of the largest Migration Period site on Bornholm, namely the chieftain site in Ibsker parish (060403 sb 93 and sb 169); FP 5965 from Smørenge that is the second large site of Migration Period Bornholm (060305 sb70); and FP 5446.2 from Sandegård Øst (060205 sb 33) which is similarly counted among the central places of Bornholm. Except for the coin from the Robbedale Hoard all these imitations have been found during detector surveys.

39 Stribrny 2003, 13; photo in Kromann 1991, 47 fig. 2.

- The imitation from Ejsbøl was found during the excavations undertaken in 1957. The portrait and obverse legend refer to Faustina Minor as Diva, while the reverse is a Junoni Regina type. The coin is pierced in front of the portrait.[40]
- The coin from Gudme is a relatively worn fragment. The obverse imitates the portrait of Antoninus Pius, the reverse has a standing female figure *en face*.[41]
- The coin from Lundeborg seems to imitate the portrait of Marcus Aurelius. It was found during excavation in a layer dated in period C2 (250/60-310/20 AD).[42]
- The coin from Øster Vandet imitates the portrait of Antoninus Pius. The coin was found during a detector "rally" in 2008.[43]

The recent finds from Gudme and Øster Vandet, as well as five new finds from Bornholm, have all appeared on detector sites. This growth of material, also when it comes to Barbarian imitations, is not surprising, rather it underlines that settlement material has been underrepresented in the finds until detector archaeology became common.[44]

Republican and Early Imperial denarii were already imitated in Barbaricum, but only the more common imitations of 2nd century denarii reached Denmark. This group has been the subject of a number of studies.[45] The Barbarian imitations of Roman 2nd century denarii have been found spread over a large area of Barbaricum: from the Black Sea to the Baltic area and the North Sea. A certain concentration has been noted in modern Hungary just outside Limes, and several scholars have suggested that the imitations of 2nd century denarii were produced in the Sarmatian area.

In several cases imitations found widely apart can be interconnected through die links. Die links were established on the one hand between the four hoards from Laatzen, Lashorst, Gierloz and Kecel II,[46] and on the other between finds from the Baltic islands.[47]

Zedelius[48] and later Lind noted that the imitations could be divided into three groups depending on the degree of barbarisation. In Lind's definition the "degree of barbarisation" varied from:

1. with a portrait of a recognizable emperor
2. with a portrait that cannot be identified
3. with a motif that derives from the portrait of an emperor, but has no human features left

The die links established by Lind, all came from within the first group, consisting of 17 examples. He divided his group into three "types", produced in two "officinae" (I producing "type A" and II producing "types B and C"). These coins were all much worn, and all examples were found in Gotland:

A. recognizable portrait of Trajan, type postdating 103 AD. Three coins, two pair of dies
B. recognizable portrait of Trajan, type postdating 103 AD, but of another type than "type A". Five coins, one pair of dies
C. recognizable portrait of Hadrian. Two coins, one pair of dies

The coins ascribed by Lind to his "Officina III" were found on both Öland and Gotland. All the coins were unique in the sense that three obverse and three reverse dies were used in various combinations.[49] Furthermore there were a number of coins with a

---

40 200302 sb 19: FP 2550. Balling 1962, 51 no. 53; Ørsnæs 1988, 107-8, Taf. 7, 11:2 & 210:7-8. Legend: DIVAF AVST[IN]A / IVNONI REGINAE – combination not in *RIC*.
41 090104 sb 144: FP 3840.3. Kromann 1983-84, 74-84 no. 21.26.
42 090105 sb 132: FP 5279.38.
43 110213 sb 56: FP 7923.1.
44 Stribrny 2003, 15 mentioned that hoard finds may have played a too prominent role in his study. This view seems supported by the recent detector finds from Denmark.
45 Zedelius 1974 and 1980; Lind 1988, 112-126; Stribrny 2003; Lind 2007 and 2008.

46 Zedelius 1974 and 1980.
47 Lind 1988, 112-126.
48 Zedelius 1980, 58.
49 Other coins have been added to this group by Stribrny 2003 and Lind 2007. The group consists of two die chains, as the obverses of the coins Lind 1988, B14 and B42 (Stribrny 2003, Al 1 and Hu 2; Lind 2007, figs. 4 and 5) are not die linked, note the position of the legend in relation to the portrait.

"good" portrait that could not be ascribed to any of these types.

Among the coins with more barbarised portraits two were considered produced in the same workshop, "Officina IV". Lind suggested that many of the Barbarian imitations were produced only shortly later than their prototype, the majority before *c.* AD 200, while the coins from "Officina III" imitating reverse types from the reigns of Pescennius Niger and Alexander Severus should belong in the 220's. He wondered whether the coins from his "officinae" might have been produced in Balticum, but seemed more inclined to locate the production area in Hungary.

Stribrny discussed 88 Barbarian imitations of Roman denarii from the 2nd cent. AD.[50] He followed up on the research initiated by Volker Zedelius on the Barbarian denarii of the Laatzen and Lashorst Hoards,[51] and he developed the die chain that connects the four hoards from Laatzen, Lashorst, Gierloz and Kecel II, the so-called SALVS AVGVSTI Group (SAG). He suggested that the SAG was produced within a relatively short period in the second quarter of the 3rd century and that many dies were in use contemporaneously to give the impression of a common mixture of coins. The *terminus post quem* for the group is provided by the latest coin imitated, namely a reverse type in use during the reign of Elagabal. Among the portraits of the obverse, however, the latest original is Marcus Aurelius. It was suggested that the workshop producing the imitations of the SAG deliberately avoided portraits postdating Marcus Aurelius.[52] The very large Réka Devnia Hoard (Marcianopolis), found in 1920 inside the Empire, also contained Barbarian imitations that are stylistically similar to coins from Kecel II (but not linked to the SAG), and the suggested deposition date of this hoard is in fact used as an argument for dating the production of the imitations before *c.* AD 250.[53]

Stribrny also noted the varying degrees of barbarisation. The coins of the SAG are stylistically closely connected to the imperial coinage. This is due to the production technique: the die is hubbed directly from a Roman coin and can thereafter be re-engraved, which leads to more or less confused legends, as well as some cases where the motif has been slightly changed. The more barbarised imitations are produced by another technique. They are struck from dies that are engraved in Barbaricum, and therefore tend to be stylistically more "barbarous", and their legends far more confused than the SAG. A number of these are found in the Kecel II Hoard, while some others without provenance can be found in the Hungarian National Museum, Budapest.

Among the *c.* 2250 coins from the large Kecel II Hoard there are 44 Barbarian imitations. Two of them belong to the SAG, and among the remaining imitations two sets of die-linked coins can be linked stylistically to the SAG, although no dielink can prove the connection. Stribrny suggested that the imitations indeed must have originated in Hungary on the basis of the distribution of dielinked coins from the Kecel II Hoard. At first sight this seems convincing, but there is a danger of a circular argument. The coins considered forms only part of the material. Stribrny took as a starting point for his investigation the Kecel II Hoard and the coins linked to it, instead of considering the many other Barbarian imitations – a total number of *c.* 200 – that he himself referred to.[54] Stribrny mentioned the few finds from Denmark, but as none of them were related to the SAG, they were not discussed in detail.[55]

The coins from Illerup sacrifice would belong to Lind's group 2, with a portrait that cannot be iden-

---

50 Stribrny 2003. The contexts were chosen because of the die identical coins, with the explicit wish to analyse the distribution of finds and the possible workshop area.
51 Zedelius 1974 and 1980.
52 Other workshops did use later portraits for imitations, Lind 1988, 114 and n. 21 refers to finds from Gotland, and from the large Reka Devnia Hoard, found inside Roman territory.
53 Stribrny 2003, 61. For the hoard see Mouchmov 1934. On the distribution of Barbarian imitations see also Peter 2008.
54 As this book went to press a new specimen of the SALVS AVGVSTI group was published. It was a single find from Lichtenau, a bit south of Lashorst and Laatzen, and it is die linked to coins from Lashorst and Gierloz in Poland. I thank Peter Ilisch for sending me his publication of the coin: Aeternitas und Mark Aurel auf einem imitative Denar, NNB 4, 2010, 144.
55 Stribrny mentioned 11 coins, which in reality should be 10: Four of them, from the Nydam weapon sacrifice, are however not imitations.

Crossing boundaries

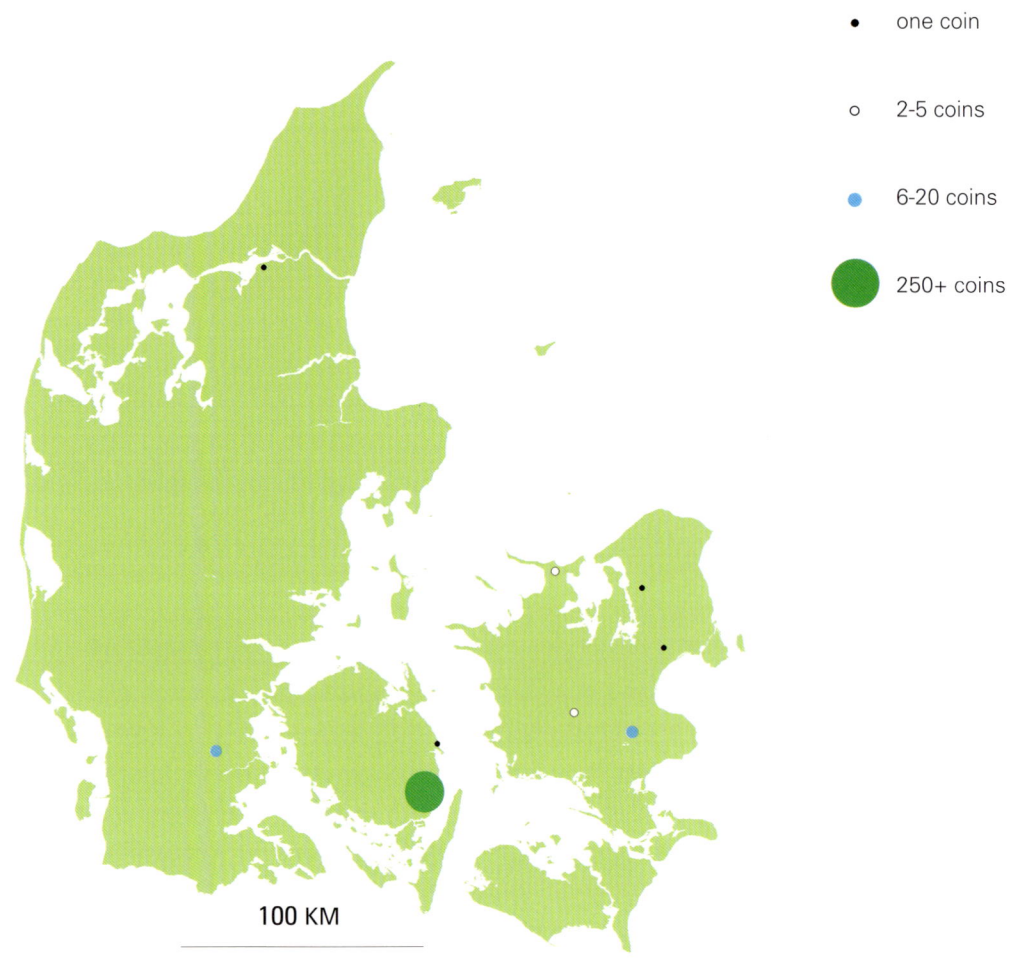

Fig. 71. Distribution of siliqua finds. Map Josefine Franck Bican.

tified, there seems however to be no die link to the coins published by Lind. The deposition date of the Illerup sacrifice in the early 3rd century has been established with good precision by the use of dendrochronology. This indicates that the imitations from Illerup are slightly older than the date suggested for the SAG, and it shows that even quite barbarised coins may have been produced before *c.* AD 200. Thus the style is of no use for a chronological evaluation of the imitations.

The other coins from Denmark have recognizeable portraits. The one from Ejsbøl imitating the portrait of Diva Faustina Minor must consequently be dated after her death.[56] The JVNONI REGINA reverse is used for issues struck for Faustina before her death (*RIC* 694-696), and thus it cannot narrow down the date. The coins from Gudme and Lundeborg similarly should be dated by the *t.p.q.* inherent in the portrait, but the context-dated Lundeborg imitation narrows the date of production of this coin down to no later than *c.* AD 310/20.

6.2 Siliquae

Siliquae are not common in Danish finds. Although a total of almost four hundred coins are known today, the overwhelming majority of the finds, 351 coins, have been made at Gudme, thus biasing the material severely.

The largest find was made in the area Gudme III in 1985 (*Fig. 72*). Around 20 coins had been ploughed up, and subsequent excavations revealed that they derived from a hoard of 4th century siliquae that had

---

56 Note that all the coins listed by Lind have a male portrait.

Coins. Denominations and striking periods

Fig. 72. Siliquae from the Gudme III Hoard. Scale c. 1:1. Photo Kit Weiss/National Museum of Denmark.

been deposited at a fence that delimited the largest farm in that part of Gudme. Apart from the large siliquae hoard from the Gudme III area, now consisting of 293 coins,[57] a smaller hoard found in the Gudme IV area consisted of both denarii and 28 siliquae (*Fig. 73*).[58] Furthermore 30 siliquae have been recorded as single finds from various areas in Gudme,[59] and three

---

57 FP 4486 published in Kromann 1988. The article includes lists of comparable siliqua hoards from central and south-eastern Europe. Also from 090104 sb 139: FP 4041, 4136 and 4448, these coins not necessarily originated from the hoard.

58 090104 sb 107: FP 6007. Also FP 4563 and 6199 (3 siliquae) were found in sb 107.

59 Sb 142: FP 6202; sb 143: FP 3950.16-17, 3967.3, 4041.29, 4216.3, 4358.30, 4366, 4436.8-9, 5385.4-5, 6198.12, 6710.11-13; sb 144: FP 3874.17-18, 4042.2, 4214.7-10, 5181.2; sb 145: 1 siliqua without inventory no.; sb 155: FP 6489.9; without sb: FP 6792.10.

Fig. 73. Siliquae and denarii from the Gudme IV Hoard. Scale c. 1:1. Photo Cille Krause.

139

Crossing boundaries

Fig. 74. The five preserved siliquae from the Simmersted Hoard Scale 1:1. Photo MLSS.

75. The eight siliquae from the Høsten Torp Hoard. Scale 1:1. Photo MLSS.

76. Two siliquae from the Engelsborg Hoard. Scale 1:1. Photo MLSS.

siliquae were found in Lundeborg.[60] Almost all the siliquae from Gudme and Lundeborg were issued in eastern mints between 340 and 367 AD (*Fig. 73*).

Outside the Gudme-Lundeborg area three smaller hoards have been found at Simmersted in southern Jutland (originally eight coins *Fig. 74*),[61] and at Høsten Torp (eight coins *Fig. 75*)[62] and Engelsborg[63] (two coins *Fig. 76*) on Sealand. In these cases coins and coin fragments were found as part of hack-silver hoards probably deposited in the late 5th or early 6th century AD.[64]

Three siliquae have been found in tombs.[65] Two were found together with a solidus in the Nyrup tomb dated in period C3,[66] while a third was part of the long necklace of amber and glass beads worn by the lady buried in a tomb likewise from period C3 found at Torstorp Vesterby, west of Copenhagen.[67]

Only two sites from Western Denmark have yielded single finds of siliquae – one from each: Hørup on Sealand[68] and Mellemholm close to Aalborg in Jutland.[69] Furthermore two coins have recently been found on the large detector sites of Brændesgård[70] and Agerbygård[71] at Bornholm. All these sites are well known from other finds of Iron Age material, notably Hørup, where a workshop area with traces of metal working activities has been excavated.[72]

---

60 090105 sb 132: FP 5279.54-55; 090105 sb 133: FP 4859.22.
61 FP 2158; Balling 1962, 62-63 no. 84.
62 040205 sb 5: FP 1830; Breitenstein 1946, 22-24 no. 36.
63 040101 sb 44: FP 6518.
64 Munksgård 1955.
65 On coins in tombs cf. also below.
66 030405 sb 100: C 1975-76; Breitenstein 1946, no. 28; Norling-Christensen 1956, 125.
67 020213 sb 20: FP 5164, struck in Nicomedeia; Fonnesbech-Sandberg 1990.
68 010312 sb 36: FP 5959.3, struck in Arles; S.A. Sørensen 2000, 33.
69 120508 sb 54: FP 5576.2, struck in Rome.
70 060403 sb 107: FP 5236.3, mint not identified.
71 060405 sb 201.
72 A recent find of a siliqua near Nyborg (Funen) seems to be a secondary deposition. 090610 sb 152: FP 7726.2. It is a Constantius II coin struck in Sirmium, RIC 17, as are 28 coins from the Gudme III hoard.

The coins from Gudme and Lundeborg constitute a relatively closed group. Although one of the Lundeborg coins is a Constantine I, not otherwise present in the area, the two other coins are struck during the reign of Contantius II, the most prolific emperor among the issues found in Gudme (282 coins struck during his reign). There is more diversity in the remaining finds. The two coins from the Nyrup grave are among the earliest siliquae found in Denmark, and both are struck during the reign of Constantine I (in Thessaloniki and Antiochia). Constantius II, prominent in the Gudme/Lundeborg material, also struck the coin from the Torstorp Vesterby grave, at least one of the two Engelsborg coins (the other was an almost contemporary clipped and cut siliqua, *Fig. 76*, struck in Sirmium), and the earliest coin from the Høsten Torp Hoard. The remaining coins from the Høsten Torp Hoard were later, four were struck by Valens (three in Trier, one unidentified mint), one in the period from Gratian to Honorius, and two are unidentified.

The single finds from Hørup and Mellemholm are relatively late. They were both struck during the reign of Valentinian I in western mints: the Hørup siliqua in Arles and the Mellemholm one in Rome.

The latest assemblage is made up by the eight siliquae from the Simmersted Hoard. The identified coins range in time from Julian (360-363 AD) to Honorius (393-423 AD). The mint could only be identified for three of the coins, one from Lugdunum and two from Trier.

Thus the two hoards from Høsten Torp and Simmersted both contain siliquae that have a composition that differs from the Gudme material. The Høsten Torp coins are dominated by issues of the emperor Valens, who is relatively rare in Gudme-Lundeborg, while the Simmersted coins are dominated by issues struck during the reigns of later emperors (until Honorius) that are even rarer in Gudme. Both are dominated by coins struck in western mints, notably Trier that is totally unknown among the finds from the Gudme-Lundeborg area. Both hoards furthermore contain examples of clipped siliquae (cf. section 6.8.6).[73]

The Danish siliquae can be divided into two groups, an earlier group containing mainly coins from the reigns of the sons of Constantine I, where eastern mints dominate, and a later group with coins struck from the reign of Valentinian I onwards, dominated by western mints and with several examples of clipping.

Siliquae are not only rare in Denmark. No siliqua was ever found in Sweden,[74] while three are known from Norway, two from western Norway and one from southern Norway.[75] The siliqua from Holvik was struck in Siscia by Constantine I in 326-327 AD, it was pierced in front of the emperor's portrait.[76] The siliqua was found in a grave dated *c.* 350 AD. The two other siliquae belong to the relatively late ones. The coin from Kolle in western Norway was struck in Trier during the reign of Valentinian II (375-383/392 AD),[77] and it is described as burnt. It was found in a grave dated *c.* 400 AD,[78] but is seems that the date of the burial is most likely based on the coin date. The coin from Frestad in southern Norway was struck in Trier during the reign of Magnus Maximus 383-388 AD, *RIC* 84b1.[79] The coin is pierced above the head of the emperor. Its provenance seems less well established as it was described as found "near a burial mound".

The three finds from Norway can be compared to the richer Danish material, in as such as it contain one example of the earlier group and two of the later group. The fact that two of the coins were pierced points to their secondary use.

---

73 The two single finds of siliquae from Bornholm are both clipped. They can be identified as late 4th century coins from western mint.

74 I thank Lennart Lind for assuring me this.

75 Skaare 1976, 35 and finds 74 (Frestad), 105 (Kolle) and 121 (Holvik).

76 Skaare 1976, plate I.3. http://www.dokpro.uio.no/perl/arkeologi/visetekst.cgi?DATABASE=B&KRYSS1354@=on on context with Late Roman fibula, Vedel type F I. RIC 210, assignment based on photo in Skaare 1976.

77 http://www.dokpro.uio.no/perl/arkeologi/visetekst.cgi?DATABASE=B&KRYSS5312@=on reference for type to Ramus 1816 no. 15.

78 Skaare 1976, 155.

79 Assignment to RIC type based on photo and description in Holst 1929, 115-116.

List of 4th century siliquae found in the Netherlands

Prov.	Emperor	Date	Mint		RIC	Weight	NUMIS No.
Doetinchem	Constantius II	(337-361)	Siscia?		-	2,33	1032783
Houten	Constantius II	(340-350)	Aquileia	pierced	66	2,78	1015360
Olst-Wijhe	Constans	(342-347)	Trier	fragment of multiplum	145/148	- (20mm)	1032816
Tiel	Constantius II	(353-355)	Arles	pierced	207	-	1032601
Cuijk	Valens	(364-378)	Imit.		-	-	1041040
Houten	Eugenius	(392-394)	Trier		106d	-	1012783

In the non-Roman areas of the Netherlands only a single siliqua was listed in FMRN. It is a looped siliqua of Arcadius (383-408 AD), from Friesland without more precise find spot. The authenticity of the find has been questioned.[80] Since then two sites in Friesland have yielded detector finds of Ostrogothic quarter siliquae, one from Leeuwarderadeel and one or perhaps two coins from Franekeradeel,[81] while a third Ostrogothic quarter siliqua has been found near Nijmegen.[82] These issues are not seen in the Danish material. The only six specimens of 4th century siliquae from the Netherlands have been found closer to the Limes. Four are from the Constantinian dynasty, and two belong to the late 4th century. Western mints dominate.

Northern Germany has yielded more siliqua finds, but still they are unusual. In Berger's study of northwestern Germany (Nordrhein-Westfalen and Niedersachsen), there are eight finds: the two well-known hoards from Lengerich and Laatzen, four finds in connection with Migration period graves, and two single finds.[83]

The Lengerich find from 1847 consisted of three separate hoards: one with +1147 denarii struck in 100-222/235 AD, one with c. 10 Constantinian solidi (313/315-361(?) AD), and one with +70 siliquae. The siliquae, of which only one is preserved to our days, were described as mainly struck by Magnentius in Trier in the 350's AD and in mint condition. Also a silver medallion struck by Constantius II is mentioned, as are up to four siliquae struck by Constantine I (unknown mint).[84] The Laatzen hoard was found in 1967. It consisted of 78 coins deposited in a ceramic jar. Denarii prevailed (74 coins dated 73-192 AD), but there were also two miliarense, a siliqua and a Barbarian imitation of a siliqua. The Roman siliquae were dated 351-361 AD, and were struck in Constantinople, Arles and Lyons respectively.[85]

Three siliquae were found in 1886 in the urn cemetery at Altenwalde. The excavations are described as badly recorded, and unfortunately there seems to be no information of possible connections between the coins and the burials. The siliquae were struck by Theodosius I (383-388 AD in Trier, and 378-395 AD unidentified mint) and Arcadius (392-294 AD in Milan). The weights of the coins (0.73-0.88 g) are extremely low, and indicate that they must be either fragmented (indeed the unassigned Theodosius I coin is described as having a modern break) or clipped.[86]

A clipped and pierced siliqua struck during the reign of Gratian (378-383 AD), probably in Trier, was found in an urn burial at Issendorf. Osteological analysis revealed that the deceased was an adult woman (aged 20-39 years).[87] Another siliqua struck

---

80 FMRN I, no. 249.34 and note.
81 The NUMIS database on www.geldmuseum.nl: NUMIS nos. 1011908 (Leeuwarderadeel), 1008808 and 1008734 (Franekeradeel).
82 NUMIS no. 1020989.
83 Berger 1992, 199.
84 FMRZ VII.1-3, no. 1035.
85 Zedelius 1974 (primary publication); FMRZ VII.4-9, no. 4033.
86 FMRZ VII.4-9, no. 8009; Bemmann 2006, 41 no. 60. Frank Berger kindly informed me that the graves are probably somewhat younger than the coins.
87 Bemmann 2006, 41 no. 69 urnengrab 3773; Hässler 2001, 160 and Taf. 33. The coin was identified by Frank Berger who also suggested that the burial

Coins. Denominations and striking periods

by Gratian was found during excavations in an urn cemetery at Perlberg in 1860. The coin is described as "beschnittene und stark mitgenommene Silbermünze", i.e. it was most probably clipped. Mint and type are unknown.[88] In the last example of a siliqua in connection with a burial, the coin was found as part of the grave goods ("als beigabe") in the Saxon urn cemetery at Wulsdorf. The siliqua was struck in Aquilea by Theodosius I in 378-383 AD.[89]

The two single finds are a lost Constantin I coin from Lüneburg[90] and a fragmented Constans siliqua struck in Trier.[91]

Siliquae are very rare in the area east of the Elbe. Two coins were found as grave gifts in two urn burials in Schmalstede,[92] and a siliqua struck by Constantius II was found before 1753 in "Brandenburg und Prignitz" together with two Antonine denarii. The provenance is obscure.[93] No other siliquae are recorded from the *Länder* in the eastern parts of Germany.[94]

Similarly, there are few finds of siliquae from Poland. The famous Zamość Hoard was found in south-eastern Poland within the area of the Wielbark Culture in 1839. The hoard consists of gold-plated silver ornaments and 16 siliquae struck by Constantius II in eastern mints. The deposition of the hoard of Zamość is dated early in the 5th century.[95]

Two siliquae finds have been made in West Balt Circle cemeteries in Mazuria, one is a Constantius II coin struck in Cyzicus from a cemetery in Boćwinka and the other is the find of two siliquae from a grave in Grunajki. The coins, Constantius II from Sirmium and Constantinople, were described as "identical to the hoard from Zamość".[96]

This short survey serves to demonstrate the rarity of siliquae finds in general in northern Europe. The situation is markedly different from Britain, where late 4th century siliquae struck in western mints have been found in large numbers.[97] Also the hoards deposited during the reigns of the sons of Constantine reveal marked differences between Britain and in particular south-eastern Europe,[98] where the Gudme III Hoard clearly is part of the south-eastern European group.[99] It therefore seems reasonable to suggest that not only the Gudme III Hoard, but also the remaining siliquae from Gudme and Lundeborg might have arrived in Funen as one larger parcel to be split up in the area. The geographically closest finds of similar coins are the Zamość and the Lengerich Hoards, and the general impression is that siliquae of the Constantinian dynasty only occasionally arrived in northern Europe. It is therefore most likely that the Gudme III Hoard must have been formed in south-eastern Europe. The Gudme group is made up of coins in almost mint condition. It does not necessarily imply that they were deposited shortly after they left the mint, but they were certainly not handled very much.

While the Gudme group points towards southeast, the later group of siliquae points west. Not only are the late 4th century siliquae very common in Britain, but also the use of clipping of the edges seen on some of the Danish siliqua finds is a British feature. The siliquae from the Netherlands and north-western Germany range in time during most of the 4th century, but with a marked prevalence for western mints. There are furthermore examples of clipped siliquae. Thus the later, western issues of siliquae found in Denmark most likely arrived through the Frisian area. Apart from the clipped coins this group contains examples of cut and/or fragmented coins. The deposition of the Simmersted and Høsten Torp Hoards is normally dated *c.* AD 500, and the coins need not have arrived in Denmark much before that.

---

should be dated c. 450 AD, based on the coin that according to him would not have arrived in the area until 380/410 AD.
88 FMRZ VII.4-9, no. 8034; Bemmann 2006, 42 no. 80.
89 FMRZ VII.4-9, no. 9022. The coin is lost.
90 FMRZ VII.4-9, no. 5022.
91 FMRZ VI.5, no. 5077.5. Type C 152.
92 FMRZ VIII, no. 1071.
93 FMRZ XI no. 1084.
94 FMRZ IX-XIV. Also closer to the Limes siliquae are rare, cf. lists of coin hoards in Kent 1994. A very important find, though, is the Wiesbaden-Kastel Hoard consisting of 16 solidi and *c.* 650 badly preserved siliquae, the majority of which were struck in western mints, cf. Alföldi 1968.
95 Bursche 1996, 160 no. 100.

96 Bursche 1996, 89, 172 no. 4 and 173 no. 15.
97 Guest 2005.
98 RIC VIII, 76-77 (Sutherland & Carson 1981).
99 Kromann 1988.

Crossing boundaries

The late 4th century siliquae, often clipped, may therefore be indications of connections towards Britain, perhaps via Frisia. Connections between southern Britain (in casu East Anglia) and the Elbe area have been suggested by Weber studying the similarities in ceramics used for burials.[100] We may with some caution see these finds as a preamble to the contacts across the North Sea that developed during the Germanic Iron Ages to peak in the Viking Age. The greater focus on north-western Barbaricum in Late Antiquity may be reflected in the shifting distribution patterns of a series of other artefacts types, *in casu* Roman provincial types. Types found in Central Europe in period C1-C2 move towards the northwest in the 4th-5th centuries, as do the use of depositing coins in connection with burials.[101]

Curiously, two late 4th century siliquae from western mints, both heavily worn and clipped, and one of them furthermore pierced, have recently been discovered on two of the major detector sites in Bornholm, Agerbygård and Sorte Muld. Both sites were occupied continuously throughout the Iron Ages and into the Early Medieval periods, and it is therefore extremely difficult to date the deposition of the coins.

6.3 Roman gold coins

6.3.1 Aurei and solidi until AD 395

The Roman period gold coins found in Denmark have been divided into 126 gold coins and medallions that were struck before the division of the Ro-

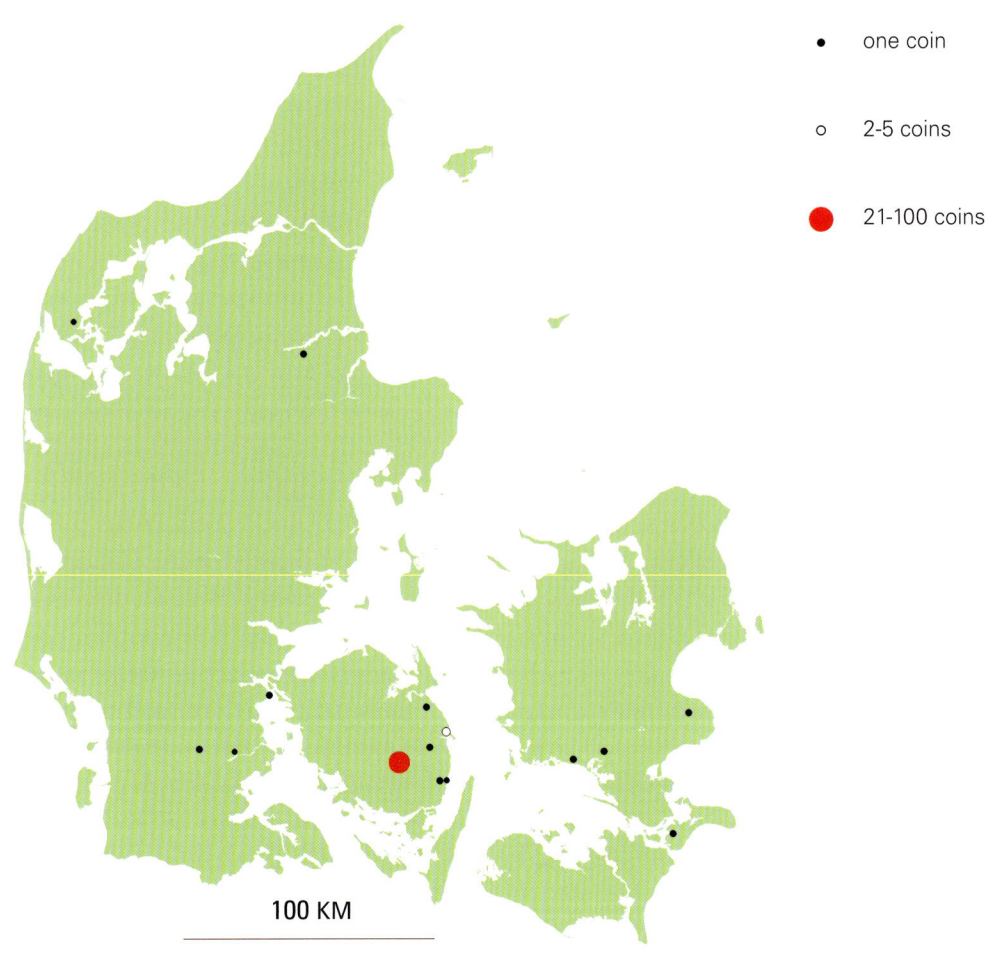

Fig. 77. Distribution of aurei. Map by Josefine Franck Bican.

---

100 Weber 1998.
101 Bemmann 2003.

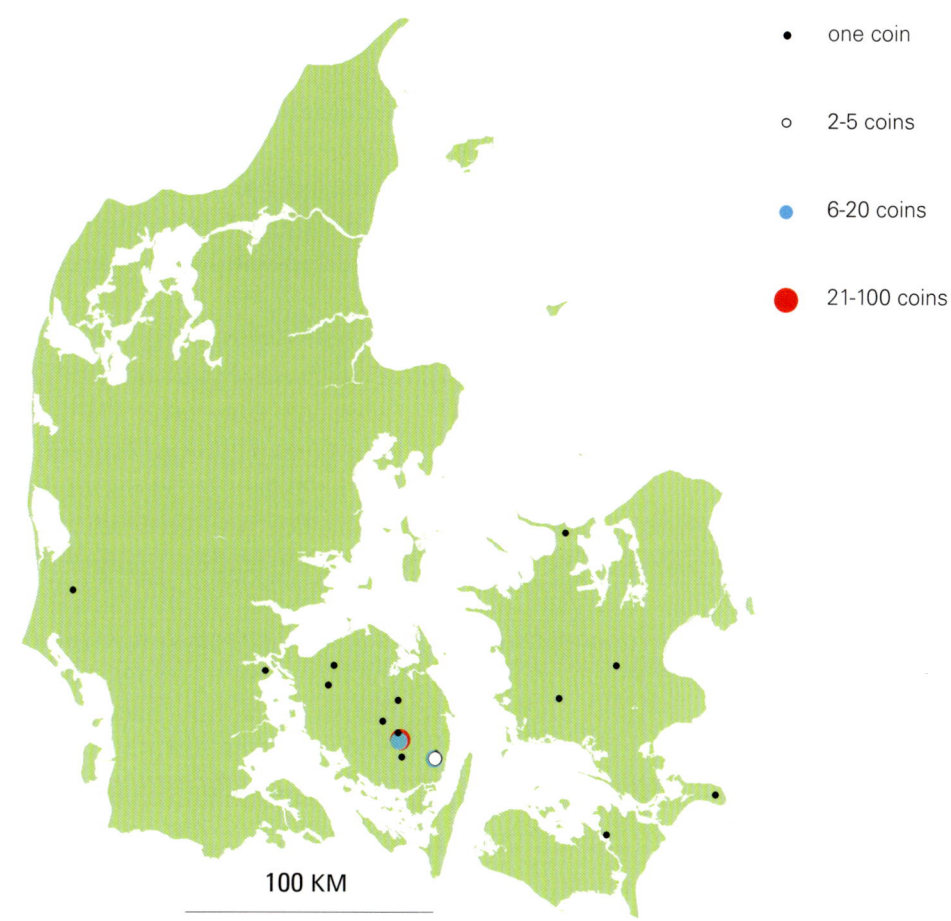

Fig. 78. Distribution of solidi struck before 395. Map by Josefine Franck Bican.

man Empire in 395 AD, and 42 Late Roman solidi (see below).[102] The overwhelming majority of the pre-division gold coins have been found on Funen, in particular in a number of hoards, but there is a number of significant single finds from both Sealand and Jutland. A very large part of the gold coins – both coins from hoards and single finds – are pierced and/or looped, clearly indicating a secondary use as amulet/jewellery. The gold coins mainly belong to the issues of Constantine and his sons, while issues from the 1st to 3rd centuries and the latter part of the 4th century are rare.

No less than 52 of the aurei and early solidi were part of the Brangstrup Hoard[103] and another 15 gold coins derive from the Boltinggård Hoard,[104] found c. 700 m from Brangstrup in central Funen. Both hoards contain both aurei from the 2nd half of the 3rd century and Constantinian solidi as well as various jewellery, and both have a t.p.q. in 336 AD provided by the coins.

Two hoards with solidi were found in Gudme. One is the Gudme I Hoard consisting of 11 solidi, among which one is a multiple (*Fig. 48*). The other is the Bjørnebanke Hoard[105] consisting of hacked sil-

---

102 On the Late Roman solidi see also Horsnæs 2009. Bornholm has yielded one gold coin only from the early period: NM I C 1547, a mounted solidus struck during the reign of Theodosius the Great (379-395 AD); Breitenstein 1944, 45-46.

103 090108 sb 19; Breitenstein 1942 find no. IV; Henriksen 1992; Storgaard 1997; Horsnæs 2004.

104 090108 sb 13; Breitenstein 1942, 85-86; Henriksen & Horsnæs 2004 and 2006.

105 Sørensen, in Jørgensen et al. 2003, 435.

ver deriving from Late Roman silverware comparable to the Kaiseraugst material, and three solidi. An old find of a solidus from the same field may or may not be related to the hoard.[106] Both these hoards contain coins struck during the reigns of the sons of Constantine (337-355 AD). A scattered gold hoard found at Slipshavn in eastern Funen included two 3rd century aurei. The other material from the hoard was: ingots, jewellery, fragments of bracteates and a statuette. The bracteates date the deposition of the hoard in the late 5th-early 6th century AD.

The Ginderup Hoard consisted of 31 denarii and a single Neronian aureus. This is the only example of an Early Imperial aureus from a Danish hoard.

The weapon sacrifice at Ejsbøl has yielded an aureus struck for Diva Faustina Major, as well as a denarius (Barbarian imitation of Marcus Aurelius), and two bronze coins. The aureus was somewhat worn and pierced twice.

The remaining 42 gold coins were single finds. Many of them are old finds, where the find circumstances are only superficially known, a fact that of course makes interpretation of the finds difficult. Yet, a survey of even the more general characteristics of the finds proves useful.

In six or seven cases a gold coin has been found in connection with a burial (cf. also above on coins in funerary contexts). At least four of them were looped. The striking periods of the coins from burials ranges from a Tiberian aureus found in connection with a grave at Bæk (Jutland) dated in period B1/B2a and another from Rørbæk (Funen) – in the latter case the association with a burial is highly questionable. An aureus struck during the reign of Caracalla was found in the urn burial at Møllegårdsmarken grave 1796a from period C2, and another struck during the reign of Probus was found in an inhumation burial at Varpelev normally dated in period C2. A period C3 grave from Nyrup held three coins, one solidus struck by Constans and two siliquae both struck by Constantine. The Brøndsager grave and the Årslev grave were both dated late in period C, and they both held a Barbarian imitation of a 3rd century aureus.

Apart from the hoards mentioned above Gudme parish has yielded five single finds: two Constantinian solidi from Gudme II and one from Broholm, one Barbarian imitation of a 3rd century aureus, and the previously mentioned aureus from Møllegårdsmarken grave 1796a. A Neronian aureus was found in Lundeborg. These coins may safely be attributed to the Gudme centre, and must be interpreted in light of the other finds from the area.

In addition to the two Tiberian aurei mentioned above, three aurei from the 1st century AD have been found, two from Sealand and one from Jutland. One is a Vespasian that was found in 1893 while digging on the property of Lars Peter Lind in Store-Lind c. ½ alen (c. 30 cm) below the surface.[107] Store-Lind in southern Sealand is situated to the south of a large area that has been reclaimed in modern times.[108] Thus during the Iron Age the find spot was only c. 1 km from the sea. Iron Age finds are, however, rare in the area; there is only mention of a couple of jars set in the moor northeast of Store-Lind. The other first century aureus is of Titus. It was found in 1939 on the property of Hans Petersen, "Friheden" in Klinteby, in an area less than 1 km from the sea.[109] The most recent find is an aureus struck by Nero from Vestervig Kirke in northern Jutland. This site has previously yielded two denarii, struck by Trajan and Hadrian. The site is situated close to the outlet of Limfjorden into the North Sea and not far from Ginderup, where a Neronian aureus was found as part of the Ginderup Hoard.

The 2nd century, so well represented among the denarii, has yielded only two aurei: the above-mentioned Diva Faustina Major aureus from the weapon sacrifice in Ejsbøl Moor, and a pierced Marcus Aurelius aureus that was found during archaeological excavations in Næstved in a layer dated in the 14th century.[110]

There are three single finds of 3rd century aurei. A pierced Trajan Decius was found in 1777 in Ør-

---

106   090104 sb 150: FP 383; Breitenstein 1942, 88 no. IX.

107   050503 sb 157: FP 652; Breitenstein 1946, 9 no. 4 and fig. 1.
108   050503 sb 151.
109   040509 sb 71: FP 1993; Breitenstein 1946, 9-10, no. 5 and fig. 2.
110   050707 sb 53: FP 6060; Larsen 1996, 18-23 in particular p. 22.

bæk on Funen by a smallholder, Jens Madsen, who is known to have had farm no. 3 in Ørbæk in tenancy in that period,[111] and in 1991 a pierced Gallienus was found on a beach at Sønder Stenderup close to Kolding in eastern Jutland.[112] Finally a Carinus aureus was found in 1820 at Hou less than 1 km south of Mariager Fjord in eastern Jutland. When the find had been reported an excavation was undertaken at the find spot, however, without any further finds.[113]

The single finds from the 4th century are represented with 12 solidi, 1 solidus imitation and 5 medallions. A solidus struck by Constantine II Caesar, was found in 1851 while working a field in Kværkeby on Sealand, but a subsequent search in the area revealed no other finds.[114] The exact find spot is not known today, but it should be noted that Kværkeby is situated close to extensive wetland areas and forests. Another solidus struck by Crispus Caesar was found in 1874 while ploughing the property of Peder Hansen in Haldagerlille,[115] little less than 2 km west of a small cemetery from Late Roman Iron Age.[116] Both these coins were looped. Finally a solidus by Constantine II Caesar was discovered while gardening c. 2-300 alen (125-200 m) from Gjorslev Manor in Magleby parish (on Stevns) in 1886. The much worn coin was pierced twice and mounted with a small loop (*Fig. 79*).[117]

Three single finds of 4th century solidi from Gudme have already been mentioned. From Funen there are furthermore five solidi. A solidus struck by Constans was found in 1942 on a field in Gamby,[118] and a Constantius II was found in 1875 in Rørup. No details are preserved about this find, and the coin no

Fig. 79. Constantine II Caesar from Magleby. Scale 2:1. Photo MLSS.

longer exists.[119] In 1898 a Valentinian I solidus was found in a field in Nørre Søby. A loop may have been broken off with a fragment of the rim.[120] A solidus struck by Constantine I in Trier was found in 1863 in a garden in the parish of Ringe. The coin is pierced. The similarity with coins from the two large hoards in Brangstrup and Boltinggård, also in Ringe parish, is striking, but there seems to be no reason to believe that it originally pertained to any of these hoards. The Brangstrup Hoard was found in 1865 and the first find from the Boltinggård Hoard appeared in 1867 (the first coin, however, was not found until 1888), and we may expect the locals to have remembered about the coin find from 1863 if it had been from the same area.[121] A 4th century solidus was found already in 1774 while working a field north of Hundtofte. The coin was struck by Constantine. It is now lost.[122] In 2007 a Theodosius I solidus struck in Milan was found as part of a small hoard deposited below the floor of the main building of an agrarian complex at Fraugde near Odense. The coin had been looped (loop broken off), and it is mounted in a beaded rim. The hoard consists of hacked silver, gold bars and parts of a large fibula with ornaments dated c. 500 AD.[123] The last 4th century solidus, found "on Funen" in 1863, is a Constantine I that is both pierced and

---

111 090618: BP 217; Breitenstein 1943 6, no. XII and fig. 8.
112 170704 sb 153: FP 5265; Kromann 2003.
113 140706: Ramus 19aa; Balling 1962, 58, no. 75 and fig. 8.
114 040210: FP 99; Breitenstein 1946, 20 no. 31 and fig. 7.
115 040506 sb 4: FP 355; Breitenstein 1946, 19 no. 29 and fig. 6.
116 040506 sb 2.
117 050604 sb 51: NM I C 5510; Breitenstein 1946, 20 no. 32 and fig. 8.
118 080604 sb 49: FP 2067; Breitenstein 1943, 11-12 no. XX and fig. 15.

---

119 080717; Breitenstein 1943, 15 no. XXIII.
120 080806 sb 18: FP 745; Breitenstein 1943, 15-16 no. XXV and fig. 18.
121 090108 sb 125: FP 242; Breitenstein 1942, 86 no. VI.
122 090511 sb 22; Breitenstein 1943, 11 no. XIX.
123 080803 sb 153: OBM 2823. Runge 2007.

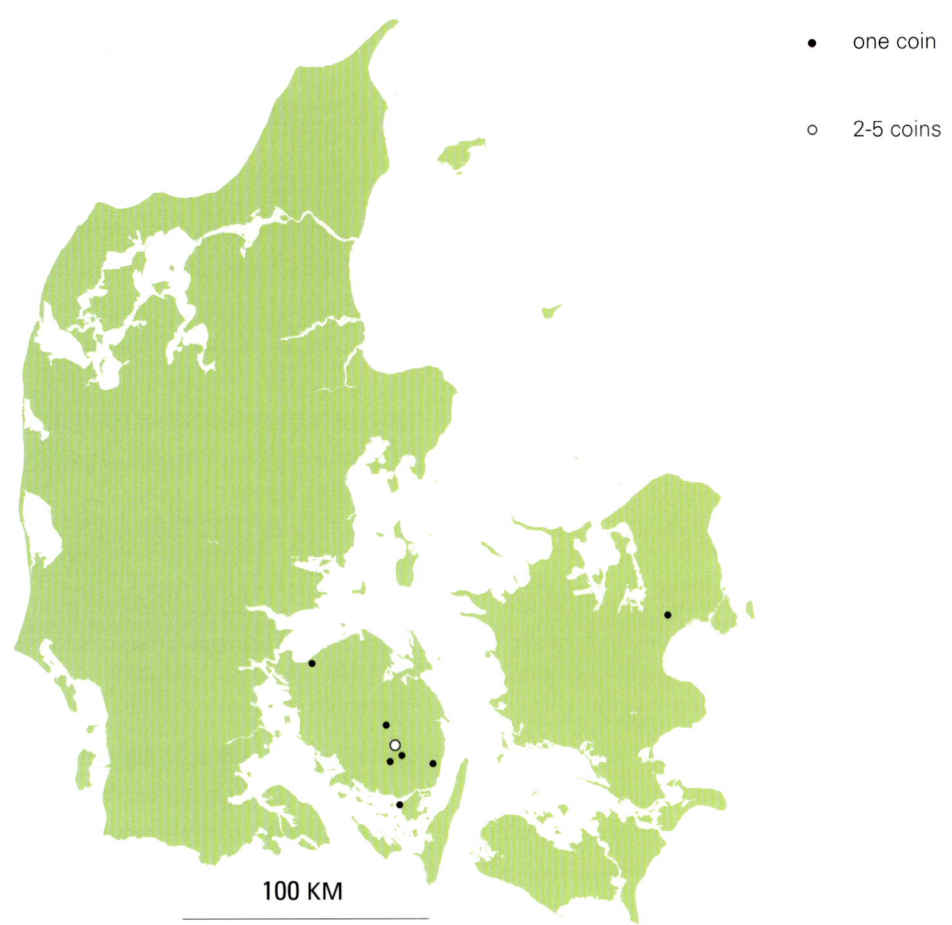

Fig. 80. Distribution of Barbarian imitations from Denmark. Map by Josefine Franck Bican.

looped. No details about the find circumstances have been recorded.[124]

From Jutland come two solidi, both struck during the reign of Valentinian I. One was a looped coin found while building the ranger's house in Seljumshave (Sønder Stenderup),[125] only 1.5 km from the find spot of the above-mentioned Gallienus aureus. The other one was found in 1850 on the priest's field in Lunde. There is evidence of Iron Age settlement in the area around Lunde.[126]

A solidus that is mounted with a frame, pierced and probably later looped was handed in to the Museum of Nordiske Oldsager in 1818. The solidus is struck by Constantius II, and it was said to be found in Denmark, but no details are preserved as to its provenance.[127]

6.3.2 The Barbarian imitations of aurei and early solidi

A special group consists of 10 imitations of Roman gold coins.[128] Two were found in burials, in the Brøndsager and Årslev graves (cf. below), one is a detector find from Gudme, and four Barbarian imitations of 3rd century aurei have been found as isolated single finds. All the imitations are pierced and/

---

124 FP 257; Breitenstein 1943, 11 no. XVIII and fig. 14.
125 170704: Ramus 31a; Balling 1962, 63 no. 85 and fig. 8.
126 190706: FP 92; Balling 1962, 63 no. 86 and fig. 8. Iron Age settlement in sb 122 and traces of ancient ploughing identified by air photo reconnaissance in sb 57A and 123.

127 NM I CXVI; Balling 1962, 70 and fig. 8a-b.
128 Horsnæs 2002b. A more detailed study of this group of finds was undertaken in 2009, see Horsnæs 2010 (with illustrations) and *forthcoming B and C*.

or looped. Except for the coin from the Brøndsager grave, all have been found on Funen. One coin was found in 1855 in Broskov on north-western Funen. It was found above ground, and it is believed that it was dug up with marl somewhere in the vicinity.[129] A coin was found in 1935 in Tange in an area that may have been un-cultivated until *c*. 1919,[130] another in 1861 in Kværndrup close to a stream.[131] Excavations in the 1980's in the area of the latter find spot have revealed no Iron Age material that could be related to the coin. The last example was found in 1851 on a field close to Vornæs Skov on Tåsinge,[132] and not far from the find spot in the sea (in 4 m depth) of a gold neck ring dated to the Early Germanic Iron Age.[133]

The Brangstrup Hoard has yielded a total of three imitations: one is an imitation of a Diocletian aureus, the other two coins imitate Constantinian solidi. All the coins are pierced.

The Barbarian imitations of Roman gold coins from the 3rd and early 4th century were first studied by Alföldi,[134] who discussed 89 examples of Barbarian imitations. Most of his examples were probably found in Hungary, but also some examples known from auction catalogues were included in his study. The majority of his samples were solidus imitations, while the remaining 32 "coins" (36 %) were imitations of aurei. Alföldi noted that the majority of the imitations in his catalogue came from areas close to the Danubian Limes, but the majority had a very generic provenance only. He argued that around 300 AD a major production of imitations took place in modern Hungary, and he believed this production to have been undertaken by Romans for trade in the Limes area.

Kropotkin described 58 imitations from museums in USSR and Poland, among which only 6 had a known provenance. These were all from the area between the Dnepr and the Dnestr. Based on die links and close relations between dies he suggested that the 58 coins should be divided into 7 groups. 53 of these coins were imitations of pre-Constantinian aurei or quinarii (91 %). Contrary to Alföldi, Kropotkin argued that the imitations were produced outside areas of Roman influence, namely within the Cernachov culture, in the second half of the 4th cent. AD and he believed that they never had a monetary function.[135]

There are some overlaps between the material presented by Alföldi and Kropotkin, but when adding more material to their catalogues it becomes obvious that Barbarian imitations of aurei and early solidi may be divided into two production areas. It seems that the tetrarchan and Constantinian imitations are more common in a relatively restricted area outside the Danubian Limes, while the imitations of earlier aurei (and the so-called quinarius imitations) can be described as part of a group produced in "Outer Barbaricum" and found spread over a large area from the Cherniachov Culture in the Kiev area to Denmark. The finds from the Brangstrup Hoard are clearly related to the Danubian group, while the remaining specimens from Denmark belong to the eastern/northern group.[136]

6.3.3 The Roman 4th century medallions

The remaining single finds from the 4th century are five Roman gold medallions. They are almost evenly distributed throughout the country, and four of the medallions are large multipla that are looped. The first is an extremely worn medallion struck by Valentinian I in Antiochia in 373 AD(?). It was found in 1768 in Fakse Mark (Sealand) on property belonging to the University (of Copenhagen, then the only university in Denmark).[137] Two medallions were found in Funen. A Constantius II medallion struck in Antiochia was found in 1908 in a garden in Allese. The loop has fallen off, but below its position is still a triangle in granulation technique.[138] A medallion struck by Constantius II as Caesar in Trier was found

---

129 080703 sb 63: FP 141; Breitenstein 1943, 10-11 no. XVII and fig. 13; Horsnæs 2002.
130 090416 sb 36: FP 1977; Breitenstein 1943, 9 no. XIV and fig. 10; Horsnæs 2002.
131 090506 sb 7: FP 229; Breitenstein 1943, 10 no. XVI and fig. 12; Horsnæs 2002.
132 090507 sb 78: FP 110; Breitenstein 1943, 9-10 no. XV and fig. 11; Horsnæs 2002.
133 401561 sb 5.
134 Alföldi 1928-29.
135 Kropotkin 1976.
136 Horsnæs *forthcoming B and C*.
137 050302 without sb no.: NM I 8511; Breitenstein 1946, 21-22 no. 35 and fig. 10. Weight 18.44 g.
138 080301 sb 3: NM I 3/08; Breitenstein 1943, 14-15 no. XXII, fig. 17. Weight 20.55 g.

Crossing boundaries

Fig. 81. Distribution of gold medallions. Map by Josefine Franck Bican.

in 1893 in a small forest north of Trunderup. This piece has also been looped.[139]

The largest medallion comes from Jutland (*Fig. 82*). It is a very large, unique medallion (diameter *c.* 5 cm) struck by Valens in Constantinople. It is mounted in a broad rim consisting of a zigzag pattern between two beaded rims. The loop is quite broad and elaborate. The total weight of the medallion and its setting is 94.06 g. It was found in 1942 in Hjortshøj near Århus, on a field that had previously been used for drying peat. It is likely that the medallion had originally been deposited in the nearby peat bog.[140] The Hjortshøj medallion is the most elaborately dec-

orated medallion from Denmark. The rim and the loop carry a characteristic zigzag pattern that is reminiscent of the rims applied to the Valens medallions from the Szilágy Somlyó Hoard,[141] a pattern also seen on medallions in Berlin (Valens TROBNS/Trier?)[142] and Vienna (Valens, Rome).[143] Also some bracteates, notably the bracteate from Senoren in Blekinge, Sweden, has a very broad rim with three concentric lines of zigzag decoration in the same manner.[144] A solidus from Denmark, but without more precise provenance, has a less elaborately executed rim with a similar zigzag pattern. The solidus, struck by Constantius

---

139 090506 sb 32: FP 639; Breitenstein 1943, 12-14 no. XXI, fig. 16. Weight 19.99 g.
140 141103 without sb no.: FP 2084; Balling 1962, 64 no. 87; Horsnæs 2002. Weight 94.06 g.
141 Seipel 1999, cat.nos. 8 and 10, cf. also cat.no 7 with two concentric bands of zigzag pattern (enlarged photo on p. 38).
142 Gnecchi 1912, tav. 15.2; Bursche 1999, 44 fig. 10.
143 Gnecchi 1912, tav. 16.2.
144 Mackeprang 1952, no. 222, pl. 3.3.

Coins. Denominations and striking periods

Fig. 82. The Hjortshøj medallion. Scale 2:1. Photo Lennart Larsen/ National Museum of Denmark.

II in Nicomedeia, seems to have been looped, and there is a triangular decoration in granulation technique below the position of the loop.[145]

The Roman medallions are commonly regarded to be issued in order to be presented as imperial gifts. It is believed that the reverse motif and inscription designate the occasion in which the medallion was issued.[146] The Roman gold medallions have been found in a broad band from the Black Sea area and Hungary towards Denmark, with a clear preponderance of finds from eastern Europe, in particular in modern Hungary with the important finds of the Szilágy Somlyó Hoard and from modern Poland. Most of these medallions have been looped and many have been mounted in elaborate rims, clearly the work of non-Roman craftsmen.[147] The close correspondence in the rims mounted on the medallions from Szilágy Somlyó and Hjortshøj may indicate that the Hjortshøj medaljon travelled from Constantinople via eastern Europe to Jutland.

The gold coins from Denmark are dominated by the issues of Constantine I and his sons, while the multipla are slightly later, with two examples struck by Constantius II, one by Valens and one by Valeninian I.

The last medallion belongs to a group of small uniface gold medallions struck during the reign of Constantine. The medallion was found before 1946 on a field belonging to Frederikshåb, close to the heath area of central Jutland.[148] Among the 46 examples of the uniface medallions listed by Depeyrot only four are provenanced: a single find from Clisson in Loire-Atlantique, France, two medallions of the same die

Fig. 83. Uniface medallion from Frederikshåb. Scale 2:1. Photo HWH.

from the Ormod Hoard in Hungary, and finally the medallion from Jutland.[149] Many of these medallions are looped, as is also the case with the example from Denmark. It was noted by Depeyrot that the uniface medallions must have been intended for non-monetary use, because of the loops, but as noted later by Holmes, the loops (and occasional piercings) of the uniface medallions are of many different types, and it is therefore unlikely that the medallions were originally intended to be looped.[150] Indeed the Danish example carries a loop of the most common type (ridged band loop) among the pendants from Scandinavia.

6.3.4 Imitations of Constantinian medallions and other 4th century coins

A small group of 18 imitations of the Roman 4th century medallions are known. They are normally two-sided and struck in the same manner as the original

---

145 NM I CXVI. Balling 1962, 70 and fig. 8a-b.
146 E.g. Bursche 2003.
147 Bursche 1998, summarized in Bursche 2001. Unfortunately a similar mapping of finds of Roman medallions from within the Empire has not been made. The corpus published by Gnecchi (1912) does not consider the issue of provenance at all.
148 170908 without sb no.: NM I 9409. Balling 1962, 59 no. 79; for the type Depeyrot 1996, cat.no. 3. See also Holmes 2004 for an un-provenanced example of the type in the National Museums of Scotland. I owe these references to Ted Buttrey. Frederikshåb was a colony of German immigrants founded in 1804.

---

149 Depeyrot 1996.
150 Holmes 2004.

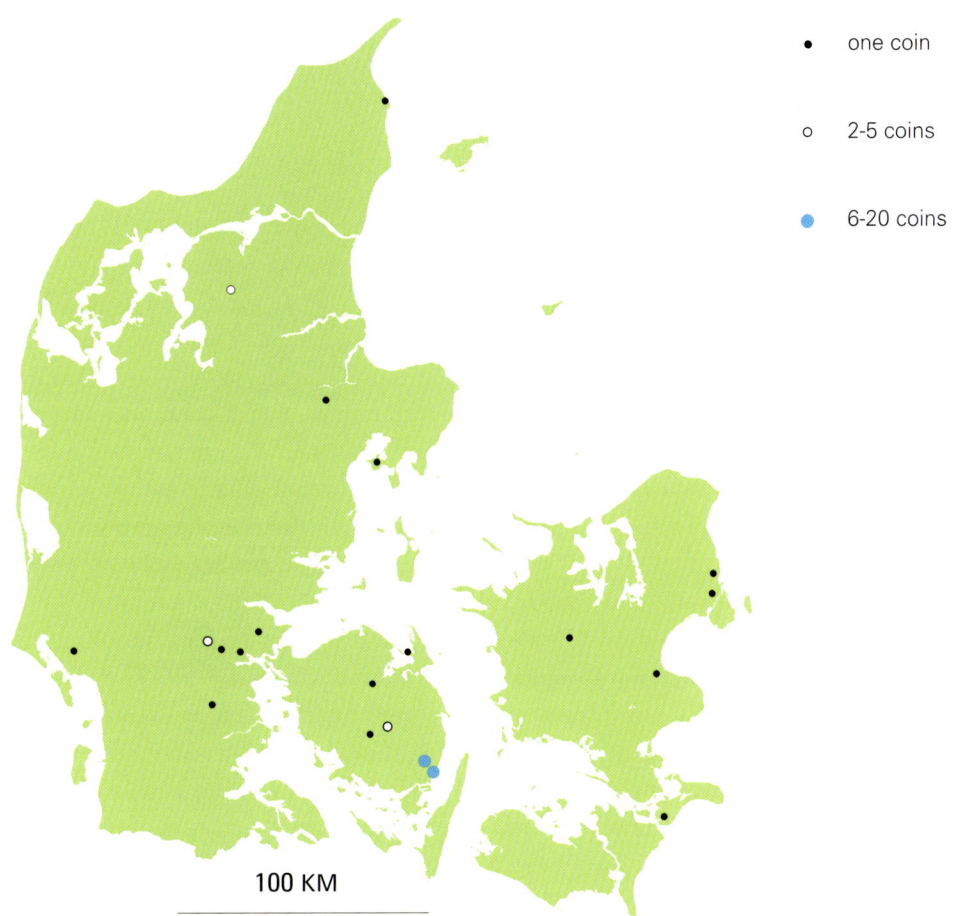

Fig. 84. Distribution of Late Roman solidi. Map by Josefine Franck Bican.

medallions. Only two come from Denmark. One was found in 1925 while ploughing in Gundsømagle-Holme in Sealand, in a moor that had not been cultivated until then,[151] the other – that may technically be a double bracteate rather than a struck medallion – was found during work in Frejlev on Lolland south of Sealand.[152]

The remaining examples of these relatively rare imitations of Constantinian medallions are found widely apart in Sweden and Norway.[153] They are often rather crude, but the way the rim and loop are fitted is clearly comparable to both the reworked Roman coins and the later Nordic bracteates (cf. below). Datable contexts are from period C3, which means that the medallions must have been produced and deposited within a relatively short period.[154] The fact that all known examples of the medallion imitations are found in Scandinavia, and often in areas where finds of Roman coins and medallions are rare, might indicate a local production. The motives, however, are related to the motives of the contemporary coin imitations.[155]

A unique one-sided imitation of a solidus from

---

151 020403 sb 122: NM I DNF 11/25; Mackeprang 1952, 107 no. 7 and pl. 1; Skaare 1993, 475.
152 070608 sb 220: NM I C 9473; Mackeprang 1952, 117 no. 48. Not mentioned by Skaare 1993; cf. Axboe 2004, 280.
153 Skaare 1993, 486.

154 Axboe 2004, 218-223.
155 Skaare 1993, 479 considered the mountings of the medallion imitation from Hove in Norway to be similar to the mountings of the medallions from Hjortshøj and from the Szilágy Somlyó Hoard, and he therefore suggested that the medallion imitations may have been produced in Hungary.

the 4th century was found in 1929 while digging a clamp in the Strangegård property in Sundby on Falster south of Sealand.[156] Close parallels are lacking for this piece (*Fig. 17*).

6.3.5 Late Roman solidi

The solidi that were struck in the period after the division of the Empire in 395 AD are here termed "Late Roman solidi". The group includes both truly Roman pieces that were struck within the Eastern and Western Empires, the so-called Non-Imperial coinages struck in the names of Roman emperors, but attributed to the Visigoths, Burgundians and Suevi, and finally the seemingly more "Barbarian" pieces that have not been attributed to any of these known issues.[157]

41 Late Roman solidi have been recorded from Western Denmark. Two hoards from Funen have yielded 13 of the solidi: eight coins came from the Elsehoved Hoard also containing nine beads, a fibula, a spiraliform fingerring and an ingot all made of gold. All the coins were looped, and together with the beads they have been interpreted as an exquisite necklace.[158] Five coins came from the Rynkebygård Hoard.[159] Furthermore two Late-Roman solidi probably belonged to the large Broholm Hoard.[160]

The centre of Gudme has yielded at least six Late Roman solidi. Two have been found in the Eisemosegård area, but details as to the finds circumstances are not known.[161] Another solidus was found in Broholmvej 16 around 1940 and only acquired by the National Museum in 1975.[162] The last solidi from Gudme are deliberately fragmented: one is a halved solidus,[163] while the other is a very small fragment weighing only 0.68 g. Both were found during detector surveys of the Gudme area (on cut coins see below).[164] Finally some fragments of one or more solidi have been found in the area of the Møllegårdsmarken cemetery (see above).

Jutland has yielded three gold hoards with one or more Late Roman solidi (section 5.2.5).

The remaining 13 Late Roman solidi are all single finds. As was the case with the single finds of the earlier Roman gold coins the majority are old finds, and their provenances are often less than satisfactory recorded. Yet, a review of the topographical situation will be made.

Sealand has yielded five finds. A now lost Leo I solidus was found in 1869 close to the beach between Emilies Kilde and Bellevue Beach north of Copenhagen.[165] A Theodosius II was found in 1919 in Slotsfruens Vænge in Husum, in a suburban area of Copenhagen that was then being taken in for building constructions. The site is close to Harrestrup Å (Stream), which interconnects with one of the main water-systems in the Copenhagen area.[166] From the western part of Sealand is another lost Leo I found in 1868 on Assentorp Mark.[167] The exact find spot is not known, but Assentorp is situated in an area that on a 18th century map was almost enclosed by wetlands. South of Køge is Herfølge Mark, where a Theodosius II was found in 1859.[168] Again this find spot cannot be pinpointed exactly, but the finder had the Holmegård in tenancy since 1858, and it is most likely that the coin was found in his fields that were situated at the Tessebølle Å (Stream) close to Vallø

---

156 70110: FP 1733; Breitenstein 1946, 21 no. 34 and fig. 9; Mackeprang 1952, 117 no. 45 – here described as an A-bracteate; Axboe 2004, 208.

157 The classification proposed by Kent 1994 has been followed.

158 090107 sb 85: NM I 2700-01, 10575, 22375 and C 1532; Breitenstein 1942, 90-96 no. XI with a full account of the history of the find. Note that the original number of coins in the hoard seems to have been higher.

159 090108 sb 7: FP 72 (one coin) and NM I 10038 (four coins); Breitenstein 1942, 89 no. X.

160 090107 sb 40: FP 3949 and 6197; Kromann 1983-4, 102 no. 24; *AUD* 2000, 296.

161 Present whereabouts unknown.

162 090104 sb 149: FP 3330; Kromann 1983-4, 102 no. 25.

163 FP 6792.11.

164 090104 sb 143: FP 4224.5. Unpubl.

165 020302 sb 120: FP 309; Breitenstein 1946, 26 no. 40. Now lost.

166 020306 sb 410: FP 1446; Breitenstein 1946, 26 no. 39 and fig. 22.

167 040112 sb 445: FP 304; Breitenstein 1946, 26-27 no. 41.

168 050104: NM I C 18617; Breitenstein 1946, 25-26 no. 38 and fig. 21.

Fig. 85. Imitation of a Late Roman solidus from Næsby. Scale 1:1. Photo Kit Weiss/National Museum of Denmark.

Storskov which is still forested today. No other Iron Age finds are noted from the area.[169] The last find from the Sealand area is a Gallic I/Visigothic solidus found at the Færgegård (ferryman's farm) on Møn at Grønsund dividing Møn from Falster.[170]

Considering the large number of solidi from south-eastern and central Funen, the only three finds from the remaining part of the island are not impressive. One solidus was found on the small peninsula of Midskov that controls the narrow entrance to Odense Fjord,[171] another was found in 1863 north of Sallinge on central Funen while ploughing close to a fence that constituted the border between arable land and the Køllenbjerg moor.[172] A systematic detector survey undertaken in the area around the find spot in 2004 proved that there were no other traces of human activity in the area. A Barbarian imitation of a Late Roman solidus was found in a garden in Næsby close to Stavis Å (Stream) in the north-western outskirts of Odense.[173]

Jutland has yielded five single finds of coins and an imitation. As was the case with the earlier gold coins the majority come from the eastern areas of Jutland. A coin was handed over to the national Museum in 1853. It had allegedly been found in Eeg on the southern tip of Mols "many years before".[174] The area around Kolding has yielded two finds. One solidus was handed over to the museum in 1924 with second-hand information that it was found in Eltang.[175] Another solidus was found in 1970 in a potato field between Pjedsted and Fredericia, but it was sold by the finder and was only somewhat later handed over to the National Museum without exact provenance.[176] At Stepping between Kolding and Haderslev a solidus was found in 1923 in a field where – as it was said – several pots previously had been found while digging for gravel.[177] Only one Late Roman solidus has been found in western Jutland. A solidus was found in 1832 half a "fjerdingvej" (i.e. c. 900 m) northeast of Gjes[t]ing in Bryndum parish. The finder is described as Hans Jørgensen of Tarpgård, and it is very likely that the exact find spot should be located in/below the modern settlement Tarp, between Gjesing and Bryndum.[178] Finally a unique one-sided imitation of a Julius Nepos solidus was found on a hillock in Kinbjerg south of Randers (Jutland). The "coin" is made of a piece of gold sheet so thin that the motif can be seen in negative on the reverse (*Fig. 2*).[179]

A striking feature is the fact that no less than seven of the ten 5th century coins from Jutland are Non-Imperial issues. The remaining three coins were struck in Constantinople (two) and Rome. Another point is the geographical distribution: Almost half the gold coins are found concentrated along the Lille Bælt coast, while the remaining finds are scattered throughout Jutland. This distribution may be related to the many gold coins found on Funen.

A recent reassessment of the Late Roman solidi from Denmark has revealed interesting differences in the material from on the one hand Bornholm and on the

---

169 Thanks to Svend Åge Tornbjerg, Køge Museum, for the identification of the find spot.
170 050505 sb 163: FP 2072; Breitenstein 1946, 24-25 no. 37.
171 080108 sb 80: FP 1166; Breitenstein 1943, 16-18 no. XXVII and fig. 20.
172 090411 sb 1: NM I C 21307; Breitenstein 1943, 16 no. XXVI and fig. 19.
173 080406 sb 18: NM I 7610/93; *AUD* 1993, 229; Henriksen 1994b, 15 (find circumstances).

174 140509: NM I 13623; Balling 1962, 65 no. 90 and fig. 9.
175 170202 sb 61: FP 1590; Balling 1962, 69 no. 97 and fig. 9.
176 170504: FP 3064; Kromann 1983-84, 71 no. 10.
177 200507 sb 60: FP 1559; Balling 1962, 68-69 no. 95 and fig. 9.
178 190502: without inv.no; Balling 1962, 68 no. 94 and fig. 9.
179 140313 sb 21.

other the remaining parts of the country.¹⁸⁰ The work was based on a new classification of the Late Roman solidi (for the period 395-491 AD based on Kent 1994) and an analysis of the mints have revealed that apart from the coins that cannot be classified, either because they no longer exist or because of bad preservation, a very large proportion (25 %) of the Late Roman solidi from Western Denmark belong to the so-called non-imperial coinages or un-attributed imitations. Only 25 of 41 Late Roman solidi are ascribed to types mentioned in Kent 1994/RIC X. Among the coins 15 were struck in Constantinople, one in Rome, one in Ravenna, and one is described as Pseudo-Ravennate. There are no die links in the material, but six coins struck in Constantinople during the reign of Leo I are all of types *RIC* 605 or 630. Similarly the two coins from the joint reign of Leo II and Zeno are of type *RIC* 803, but they are not die linked. Contrary to this the majority of the coins from Bornholm proved to be of regular issues minted in Constantinople.

No less than 19 of 36 Late Roman solidi available for study are reworked into jewellery – again a proportion that contrasts enormously from the finds from Bornholm, where pierced coins form the exception to the rule.¹⁸¹

The number of Late Roman and Early Byzantine solidi from Western Denmark is – as we have seen – relatively low, and there are few and small hoards: 13 coins are from two hoards, 13 coins are single finds while 15 coins have come from very small hoards and/or from hoards with mixed material. Thus also the find density is very different from both Bornholm and the two Swedish islands Öland and Gotland.

6.3.6 A 6th century triens

Around 1880 a Burgundian triens imitation was found at Rollerup in Sealand. The coin imitates the coinage of Justinian I (527-565), and must consequently be dated after 527 AD. Tomasini ascribed the coin to his style group JAN 11.¹⁸² The find spot is a Late Medieval castle mound, today destroyed by ploughing, close to a spring (Valdemarskilde) and the large forested area between Slagelse and Sorø. The triens is so far unique among the Danish finds, although there are two solidi that may be dated during the 6th century. A relatively restricted number of single finds of Byzantine gold coins struck during the reigns of Justin and Justinian have been made over a large area from Hungary, the Czech Republic, southern Poland and Germany.¹⁸³

6.3.7 Bracteates and Roman coins

The almost 1000 gold bracteates known today were produced in Southern Scandinavia and perhaps northern Germany in the period *c.* 450-550 AD. The bracteates are one-sided amulets, produced by pressing a thin (0.2-0.4 mm) gold sheet into a matrix where the motif is cut in negative, comparable to the obverse die of a coin. The bracteate itself is afterwards mounted with a rim and a loop. Based on the motif, the bracteates are divided into five groups A-D and F. The head on the A-bracteates is clearly inspired by the emperor's portrait on the Roman gold coins from the Constantinian period. During the relatively short period of production there is a stylistic development from bracteates with a "naturalistic" motif towards an almost non-figurative abstraction in the motifs of the D- and F-bracteates.¹⁸⁴

The bracteates are often found in the same circumstances as the contemporary Late Roman solidi.¹⁸⁵ There are several instances of coins and bracteates in the same context, and both coins and bracteates appear in hoards with other gold objects as rods or jewellery. The closed contexts are of course of great importance for the absolute chronology of the bracteates, but they also hint that bracteates and Roman coins may have played parallel roles in the Nordic Iron Age societies.

There are examples of bracteates found within

---

180 Horsnæs 2009.
181 Less than 10 % of the solidi from Bornholm are reworked, 10 coins are pierced (which is not seen among Late Roman solidi from the remaining parts of Denmark), and only the coins from the Fuglesangsager Hoard are looped (cf. Horsnæs 2009).

182 040312 sb 36 and 58: FP 1484; Breitenstein 1946, 27 no. 42; Tomasini 1964, 229 no. 400 (where the coin is erroneously described as part of a hoard.
183 Berger 1992, 207; Wołoszyn 2008; Militký 2004.
184 There is a vast literature on the Nordic gold bracteates, see most recently Axboe 2007.
185 List in Axboe 2004, 321-327.

settlements, and even in close connection with a building, as e.g. the Gudme II Hoard (containing also a denarius(!), see above) and the Fuglesangsager Hoard from Bornholm, but there are many cases where bracteates have been found in the outskirts of the settlements (around Gudme) or even in places where they can best be interpreted as ritual deposition in a liminal area.[186]

The bracteates clearly show that Roman coins of the first half of the 4th century must have been visible above ground into at least the mid-5th century.[187] Bracteates are found in most parts of Southern Scandinavia: all Denmark, southern Norway, western and southern Sweden and the Baltic Islands, and less frequently in Britain and in northern Germany and western Poland.[188] Gudme is one of the areas where the typologically earliest bracteates (A, B and C bracteates of Group H1) occur, and therefore one of the places where the first bracteates may have been produced.[189] In fact it seems possible to take the argumentation one step further.

Gudme is unique in many aspects: apart from the many detector finds that provide evidence of an area that was densely settled throughout centuries, the large halls have also commanded respect, and the rich finds of gold from Southeast Funen are justly famous. Furthermore, Gudme and the surrounding area (including the Ringe area with the Brangstrup and Boltinggård Hoards) are the only places in Scandinavia, where a considerable number of 4th century coins have been found – coins of exactly the types that must have been the source of inspiration for the local gold smiths who created the bracteates. I would therefore not hesitate to consider Gudme the home of the first bracteates.

This of course again has implications on our view of the coins. First of all, this view presupposes that solidi struck during the reigns of the house of Constantine and shortly thereafter were still easily accessible and visible – perhaps in connection with religious festivals or rituals – in the mid-5th century. This is not to say that the coins recovered today are the exact forerunners for the bracteate production and that the deposition of e.g. the Gudme I Hoard must have taken place only in the second half of the 5th century, but it is certain that a number of 4th century solidi had not been drawn out of reach by deposition until at least the second half of the 5th century.

6.3.8 Gold – Summary

As can be seen, many of the gold coins were single finds in a numismatic sense. This, however, need not have any significance for the interpretation of the deposition circumstances. Unfortunately, the find circumstances are often ambiguous or not recorded at all, but I am quite convinced that most of the single finds should be considered as small treasure deposits. Gold as material was valuable, and the symbolic value of the Roman coins in Scandinavian contexts should not be under-estimated. In this connection it is important to take a close look at both the Roman gold medallions, that may be interpreted as special purpose coins, and on the Barbarian imitations of Roman coins. Furthermore, there are traditions about some of the early finds indicating the other coins had already been found in the same area before the one recorded today. This may implicate the possibility that some of the alleged single finds are in reality the only preserved evidence of a hoard.

The numismatic division between on the one hand aurei and early solidi and on that other hand Late Roman solidi prove to have little significance for the finds. The division line should rather be drawn at the mid-3rd century, between on one hand the very rare aurei from the denarius period and on the other later aurei and solidi.

It is clear that the early aurei were deposited in very restricted numbers; only 11 aurei struck before 213 can be counted, and of these no less than five antedate the great denarius period starting with the reign of Vespasian. The find circumstances of the early aurei are special: three were related to funerary contexts, one came from a weapon sacrifice, one came from the Iron Age settlement and port of trade at Lundeborg and another from the seemingly rich settlement site at Vestervig Kirke, and one came from the 14th century town contexts. Only one is related to a hoard, namely the Nero aureus from the Ginderup Hoard. In fact only three of the early aurei are single finds *without* a context, an astonishingly low number

---

186 Wiker 1999 and 2001.
187 As noted by Axboe 2004, 265.
188 Schematic distribution map in Axboe 2007, fig. 1.
189 Axboe 2001, 45.

in comparison with the later aurei and solidi. It is interesting to note the extremely rare occurrences of aurei and contemporary denarii together. It clearly indicates that the aurei from the 1st and 2nd centuries did not come to Denmark together with the large numbers of denarii from the late 1st and 2nd century AD.

The gold coins struck within the period c. 250-350 AD mainly derive from hoards, but there are also a couple of finds from burials. None of the depositions of these coins can be safely dated before 336 AD. This date is the *t.p.q.* of the two large hoards from Funen (Boltinggård and Brangstrup) provided by the coins themselves. In some cases we can be confident that coins have been above ground for some time before they were deposited. The two gold coins from the Slipshavn Hoard are both struck in the second half of the 3rd century AD, but the other material from the hoard provides a *t.p.q.* of the deposition around 500 AD.

It is possible to argue that at least some of the coin ensembles within the hoards were composed outside Denmark. The Brangstrup and Boltinggård Hoards both contain coins struck in the period 250-336 AD with Constantinian coins as the main group, whereas the Gudme material, notably the Gudme I Hoard, contains coins struck during the reigns of the sons of Constantine. Two hoards from Funen, the Rynkebygård Hoard and the Elsehoved Hoard, contain Late Roman solidi. Thus all the larger groups of coins within the hoards came from defined chronological strata.

It is also suggested that hoards that arrived assembled in Denmark may have been partly redistributed here. It is noticeable that among the single finds from Gudme there are several coins struck during the reigns of the sons of Constantine. Where they originally part of the same batch as the Gudme II Hoard? The same phenomenon applies to the siliqua finds from Gudme: the majority of the single finds as well as the siliquae from the Gudme IV Hoard are of the same period and mint distribution as the much larger number of siliquae from the Gudme III Hoard.

Even though the coins may have arrived to Denmark in small batches, the coin ensembles did not remain isolated. They entered new contexts. Local elements were added to the coin hoards – or the Roman gold coins were mixed with other exotic and prestigious imports. In the case of the Brangstrup Hoard the coins may have been mixed with the jewellery *en route* to Denmark, but in the cases of the hoards containing both coins and bracteates, the mixing must certainly have taken place in Southern Scandinavia.

The deposition date of the gold coins can normally be established only as a *terminus post quem*, based on the coins themselves. The most precisely dated contexts are as usual the graves. In four cases one or more gold coins from the 3rd and 4th century have been found in a grave. In all cases the coin was reworked into a pendent and the burial clearly belonged to the *elite* sphere. The Varpelev grave contained a Probus coin, and the burial is traditionally dated in period C2. It should, however, be remembered that the contemporary female grave next to the Varpelev burial among other things contained a hairpin. The pin is of a type similar to the one in the Årslev grave, and its pendants are similar to the ones from the Brangstrup Hoard. Thus the Varpelev burials can be related to the famous period C3 finds from Funen. The Brøndsager, Nyrup and Årslev graves are all dated in period C3.

In some cases other types of objects from a hoard – bracteates or other jewellery – prove that the deposition date must be considerably later than the mint date. The hoard from Slipshavn is a very good example. We must keep in mind that coins struck in the second half of the 3rd century may easily be found in a context dated around or even after 500 AD. We have no safe evidence (in spite of the Varpelev grave) that any of the gold coins were deposited before c. 300 AD, and the mint dates themselves prove that the majority of the depositions – also of the single finds – must have taken place in the period from 350 to 500 AD.

The gold finds from Western Denmark peak during the Constantinian period. Before then, there are a number of isolated finds of aurei from the 1st and 2nd century, but it seems possible to argue that the 3rd century aurei in reality belong to a 4th century find pattern in Denmark. After the period of Constantine and his sons the number of finds drops dramatically. The many hoards of 4th and 5th century coins from Funen dominate the picture, but even eliminating the larger hoards (Boltinggård, Brangstrup, Rynkebygård, Gudme I, Elsehoved) there are still more gold finds in and around the pivotal centre at Gudme than in other areas of Denmark. Other finds are distributed throughout Sealand and eastern Jutland.

The single finds of gold coins struck from *c.* 250 AD onwards have a number of characteristics in common when it comes to the find circumstances. First of all, most of them were found accidentally, and the vast majority are old finds, made when somebody was working his fields or for some other reason digging the soil manually. Many of these activities have come to an almost complete stop with the introduction of modern farming with heavy machinery, and since the 2nd World War single finds of gold coins have rarely been made. There is a relatively low number of single finds of gold coins from the large detector sites. In fact the volume of gold finds has been much less affected by the introduction of detector archaeology than the finds of silver or base metal coins. A comparison between find patterns in Denmark and in other parts of Barbaricum is therefore much easier to make when dealing with gold coins than with other types of numismatic material.

There are also striking similarities when it comes to the topographical context of the coin find. A few exceptions can of course be noted, the most obvious one being the aureus found within the town of Næstved in the 14th century context. But the single finds of gold coins are most often made in marginal soils and in areas close to natural water (a stream, a wetland area, the coast), where there is no other evidence for Iron Age activity at all. This coincidence may indicate that the single finds of gold coins should be seen as individual depositions of a ritual character, comparable to the larger gold hoards.[190] In Norway, an analysis of the find circumstances of old single finds of bracteates has provided similar results.[191]

Seen in a broader geographical perspective there are clear regional differences in the distribution of finds of gold coins. Norway has yielded very few finds of Roman coins, but of the 13 gold coins struck in the period 250-500 only one is from the 5th century. The coins are often from very old finds without precise information on the find circumstances, but it seems that several of them can be connected with burials, among which at least some can be dated in period C3.

From Sweden (excluding Öland and Gotland) there are on the contrary only three coins from the period 250-400 AD, but more than 30 from the 5th century. The Baltic Islands – Öland and Gotland in Sweden and Bornholm in Denmark – have all yielded a considerable number of Roman gold coins, almost all of which were struck in the 5th century.

Berger's study of the Roman coin finds in northwestern Germany covered the area of Niedersachsen and Bremen, and parts of Sachsen-Anhalt, Thüringen, Hessen and Nordrhein-Westfalen north and east of the Limes. He noted 19 sites with finds of Roman aurei from the 1st to early 3rd centuries and 16 aurei from the 3rd century. Finds of solidi from the 4th and 5th centuries are more prominent with 76 single finds and 12 hoards, but the division of this material into solidi struck before and after the division of the Empire reveals a marked drop in numbers in the 5th century.[192] In Schleswig and Holstein 17 sites have yielded one or more Roman gold coins. The majority are aurei, and the remaining ones are solidi from the 4th century. 5th century gold coins are completely lacking. In Mecklenburg-Vorpommern and in the northernmost part of Brandenburg there seems to be a slight predominance of solidi, while aureus finds dominate the majority of Brandenburg (with Berlin) and Sachsen. In Sachsen-Anhalt and Thüringen both aurei and solidi have been found, but still aurei and pre-395 AD solidi dominate.[193]

The recent inventory of Roman coin finds from Pomerania reveals a pattern that is closely comparable to the find composition of the Baltic Islands. The number of finds of aurei and early solidi is relatively low, while there are 12-14 hoards of 5th century solidi containing a total of 650-800 coins, as well as 51 single finds of solidi of the 5th century.[194] It is noted that this is a particular situation, and that no solidus hoards are known east or south of Pomerania.

Bohemia and Moravia have yielded a relatively low number of gold coins struck in the period from

---

190 Henriksen & Horsnæs 2004 and 2006.
191 Wiker 1999.

192 Berger 1992, in particular pp. 150-151, 161-162, 171, 175, and 185.
193 Counts based on the relevant volumes of FRZD.
194 Ciołek 2001 and 2003.

the 1st to the first half of the 4th centuries AD. An increase in the number of finds is visible from the last decades of the 4th century and it lasts into the 6th century with a marked peak in the 5th century. It is noted that the gold finds are often related to finds of other types of gold objects and that a considerable number of the coins themselves are reworked into jewellery.[195]

Thus there is a very clear distinction between a "western" or "early" distribution of gold coins beginning in the mid-3rd century AD (Germany, Western Denmark and Norway), and an "eastern" or "late" distribution of coins taking over in the 5th and early 6th centuries (Pomerania, Bohemia, Moravia and the Baltic Islands). The division is not only visible in the quantities of coins found in the various areas. There is also a marked difference in the mints represented in the finds of Late Roman solidi, with a considerable number of Non-Imperial and Barbarian mints in the "western" areas, and a clear domination of coins struck in Constantinople in the "eastern" areas. Furthermore Late Roman solidi (and imitations) are often reworked when found in the "western" areas.

6.4 Base metal coins

Roman bronze coins and antoniniani are found in relatively low numbers. There is a great chronological variation within this group. It has been argued that many of these coins have been deposited a long time after they were struck, and in this they present a particular methodological problem.

The expression bronze coins here includes more than 130 Roman coins from Western Denmark from the senatorial mint or later the imperial mints, struck in non-valuable metals and intended as fiduciary coins.[196] The vast majority of the bronze coins are single finds. The chronological distribution differs from both the silver coinage, where the 2nd century coins are dominant, and to a certain degree from the gold coinage in that the 5th century coinage is hardly attested among the bronze coins. A marked concentration of finds can be seen in the suburban areas of Copenhagen, but also a number of other towns and cities have yielded finds. This must be due to the fact that Roman bronze coins for many centuries have been easily accessible and cheap to acquire for collectors and tourists alike. A considerable number of the Roman bronze coins found in Denmark have probably arrived long after the end of the Iron Age. It is hard to draw a line between finds of coins that were deposited in modern times and finds that were deposited in the Iron Age or in the Medieval period, as many of the coins are single finds without any context at all. It has, however, been suggested that the find circumstances often may be a hint as to the deposition circumstances: for example finds on modern surfaces in densely populated areas are more likely to be modern losses than finds from fields. A classification of the find circumstances proved revealing.[197]

Coins from the 4th century followed by coins from the 6th century dominated among finds from areas where a Prehistoric deposition was unlikely and among finds with no information on the find circumstances. Contrary to this coins from the 2nd and 4th centuries were equally well represented among finds from archaeological investigations and detector surveys, and these find circumstances have also yielded a considerable number of 3rd century coins, while 6th century coins were totally absent. This seems to indicate that a considerable number of the coins from the 4th and 6th centuries that are very common on the modern coin market indeed were deposited in modern times. This is supported by the find circumstances of a group of 6th century coins: they were found during the construction of the Great Belt bridge together with a Turkish coin of the late 19th century and a modern copy of an Athenian tetradrachm. Both Republican-1st century AD and 5th century AD coins are hardly ever found. The evidence suggests that a restricted number of bronze coins struck in the 2nd-4th centuries AD arrived in Denmark not long af-

---

195 Militký 2004.
196 There are 12 base metal coins from Bornholm. They will not be further discussed, only should it be noted that the 12 coins from Bornholm make up an astonishingly low figure in comparison with the fact that the number of Roman coins as a whole from Bornholm is almost as large as the number of finds from Western Denmark.

197 Horsnæs 2006a with further discussions, also including an illustrated catalogue of Roman bronze coins from Denmark.

Coins. Denominations and striking periods

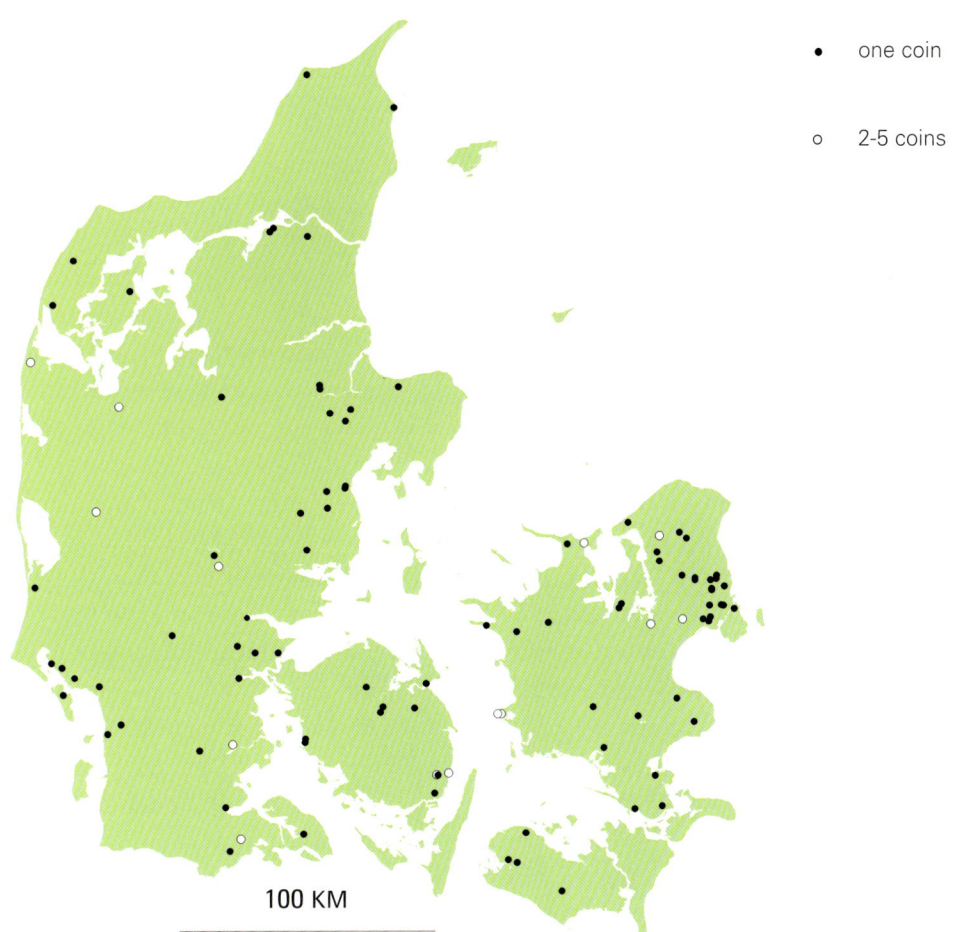

Fig. 86. Distribution of Roman bronze coins. Map by Josefine Franck Bican.

ter the time of issue, but compared with the number of silver and gold coins from the same periods the number is extremely low, and the bronze coins must have played a very restricted role.

The absolute figures are low, and the above-mentioned tendencies can only be used with caution as guidelines for an interpretation of the likely deposition date of a given single find of a Roman bronze coin outside the Empire. Yet in a number of cases we do have information on the contexts that allow a more specific date of the deposition. Four groups stand out:

1. Roman bronze coins deposited during the Iron Age. The coins mostly derive from contexts dated in the Late Roman and Early Germanic Iron Age. These coins should be considered as part of the Roman coin import in general. These coins include finds from workshop areas,[198] from weapon sacrifices,[199] and from the Gudme centre.

2. Roman bronze coins found in layers from the Viking Age. It is significant that on the Viking Age sites with Roman bronze coins no denarii have appeared, although they normally by far outnumber the Roman bronze coins and therefore should be expected to turn up. The bronze coins may have come to Denmark along with other Roman objects – gems and jewellery – perhaps as part of looted Roman burials in the Limes area. Bronze coins are known from sev-

---

198 Lundeborg (3 coins) and Hørup (1 coin). In 2008 a sestertius was discovered at Kvosted in northern Jutland on an Iron Age site that also yielded denarii. The nature of this settlement is not clarified yet.
199 Illerup (1 coin), Ejsbøl (2 coins) and possibly Vimose (1 coin).

eral Viking Age contexts: not only from Scandinavian trade centres as Hedeby, Kaupang and Birka, but also even from Iceland.[200]

3. Roman bronze coins found in Medieval contexts. These coins are in some cases from ecclesiastical areas, and may be interpreted in a Christian context. One of these coins was found below the floor level of Sct. Villads Church in Viborg. It was struck by Constantine, who is regarded the first Christian emperor, and it carries traces of a bronze loop. The coin may have had a special significance as a religious souvenir.[201] A sestertius of Marcus Aurelius (161-180 AD) was allegedly found near Holeby Church on Lolland. The church, originally dedicated to St. Chrysostomos, goes back to the Early Medieval Period (choir in romanesque style).[202] An Alexander Severus (222-234 AD) coin was found "at the ruin" of the Dalum convent. The convent originally was situated in Odense, whence it was moved to Dalum around 1200.[203] The coin could have been lost at any time from the 13th century to our days. An ancient coin that cannot be identified any closer was found at Sønder Tranders Kirke.[204]

4. Surface finds of Roman bronze coins from modern gardens, parks, on streets etc. The majority of these coins are – as mentioned above – interpreted as collectors' or tourists' modern losses.

6.5 Antoniniani

Only 16 antoniniani have been found in Denmark, and only in one case was the coin most likely deposited in the Late Roman or Early Germanic Iron Ages. It is the Probus antoninianus struck in Rome and found in the Dankirke West area, south of House Vb (southern Jutland). It came from plough soil between areas D and G and was found during sieving of the soil. The find spot is therefore not precise, and the coin may have been moved a bit around by ploughing. Yet the fact that it was found close to a cluster of 16 Roman denarii made Bjerg suggest that it may have been deposited together with these. The latest finds from House Vb have been dated in the 5th century AD, and it is therefore possible that a coin hoard consisting of denarii and the Probus antoninianus may have been deposited in or at House Vb some time between the late 3rd and the 5th century AD.[205]

The excavations of Viking Age Ribe have yielded one antoninianus, probably struck by Postumus. It was excavated from an 8th century layer in a house that yielded evidence of metal-working.[206] This coin, therefore, should be interpreted in line with the Roman bronze coins from Ribe as an example of the sporadic influx of Roman coins in the Viking Age.

Four antoniniani have been found in connection with archaeological fieldwork, but not in layers that can be dated with precision. A cut antoninianus was found at Kirke Hyllinge, a site that has also yielded a Constantinian bronze coin. None of the Roman coins were found in dated contexts. A single waste pit containing material from the Late Roman Iron Age was found at Kirke Hyllinge, but the site was only permanently occupied from c. AD 500. It cannot be excluded that the antoninianus as well as the Constantinian bronze coin were deposited in the latest part of the Roman or the Early Germanic Iron Ages, but it seems more likely that they were deposited in the Late Germanic Iron Age or the Viking Age.[207]

The Fugledegård site at the Late Germanic/Viking Age chieftain's manor at Tissø has yielded an antoninianus struck by Allectus in London. This is the only example of a Roman coin struck in Brit-

---

200 Gullbekk 2009 with references.
201 130815 sb 348: FP 2782; Horsnæs 2006a, 72-73 and cat.no. 69. Reverse motive is two Victories holding a shield.
202 070309. Horsnæs 2006a, cat.no. 26.
203 080404 sb 30: FP 2657; Kromann 1983-84, 73 no. 17; Horsnæs 2006a, cat.no. 44.
204 120113: FP 6702.19.
205 Bjerg 2007, 66-75, in particular 73-75. See also Feveile 2006 for a discussion of eight sceattas from the 8th century from Dankirke West.
206 190409 sb 77: ASR 1085x38.
207 020605 sb 55: FP 6587.1. Information on find circumstances of the coins from Jens Ulriksen. See also Ulriksen 1998; on the Viking Age coins from Kirke Hyllinge see Aarsleff 2006.

Coins. Denominations and striking periods

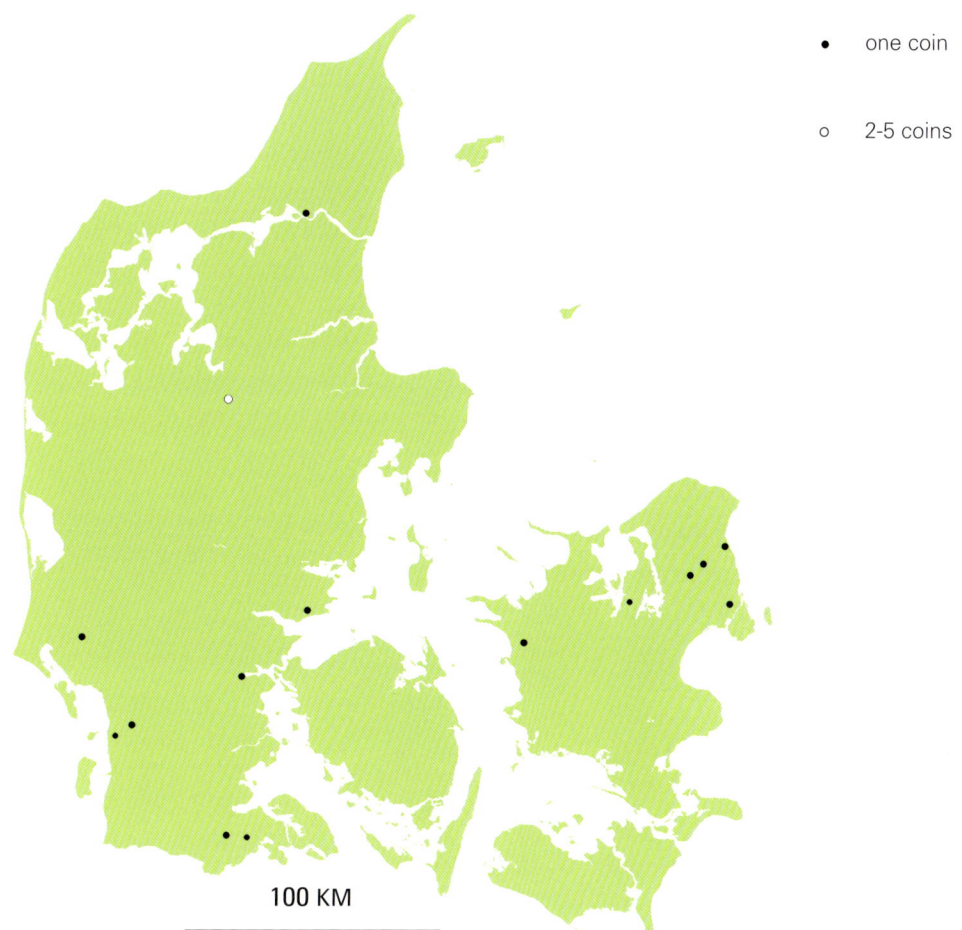

Fig. 87. Distribution of antoniniani. Map by Josefine Franck Bican.

ain found in Denmark. The coin was found by metal detecting the ploughsoil in an area that has mainly yielded finds from the period 550-1050 AD, and it thus seems likely that this coin may have been deposited during the Late Germanic/Viking Age. The general Tissø area has, however, also yielded some Roman Iron Age burials, as well as Medieval and later detector finds, so another deposition date cannot be wholly excluded.[208]

During excavations at Åvænget in Søndervarde (Jutland) an antoninianus struck by Gordian III in 238-239 AD was found in the fill of a ditch that cuts both a dug-out house and a long house. The buildings are dated in the Late Roman or – however less likely – in the Early Germanic Iron Age. The ditch is not dated, but it is possible that the fill contains material from the disturbed house layers. In that case the deposition of the coin may be dated in the Roman Iron Age.[209]

The find circumstances of the remaining antoniniani are of little help to establish the deposition date of the coins. Two almost contemporary antoniniani struck by Tetricus (270-273) and Divus Claudius Gothicus (AD 270) were found in a garden in Viborg (northern Jutland) together with a coin struck by the Danish king Christopher II (1276-1332).[210] Another Divus Claudius Gothicus comes from a garden in Hørsholm north of Copenhagen on a site less than 200 meters from the Usserød Stream and two wa-

---

208   03010: FP 6886.1.

209   190712 sb 90: FP 7575. Information on the find circumstances kindly provided by Jens G. Lauridsen of Varde Museum.

210   130815 sb 349: FP 1612.1-2; Balling 1962, 57 no. 71.

termills.²¹¹ The owner of the Søtoftegård in Ganløse, also north of Copenhagen, had found an antoninianus struck by Diocletian in his field in 1933. Today the area east of Ganløse has yielded material that indicates continuous occupation of the area from the Bronze Age to the Germanic Iron Age with among other things traces of workshop activities, and the old single find of an antoninianus may belong in this assemblage.²¹²

A Probus antoninianus was found during gardening in the outskirts of Aalborg in 1946. Today numerous archaeological sites are known both in and around Aalborg, but it is not possible to connect the coin with any of them.²¹³ Nor is it possible to tell where an antoninianus struck by Claudius Gothicus and found in the courtyard of the Mosegård north of Vejle in eastern Jutland was originally deposited, as the coin was found in sand brought in from Rosenholm to the southwest of the farm.²¹⁴ Also in eastern Jutland, a Valerian antoninianus was found close to Kolding. No other finds were made.²¹⁵ A Postumus antoninianus was struck in Lugdunum in 259-267 AD and found in a garden in Kliplev (southern Jutland) "opposite the railway station".²¹⁶ Traces of a destroyed barrow have been noted close to the station,²¹⁷ but no finds indicate Roman or Germanic Iron Age activity. Finally the 19th century find of an antoninianus together with two Roman bronze coins in Kværs in southern Jutland unfortunately cannot be further investigated.²¹⁸

In two recent cases a Roman antoninianus has clearly been above ground in modern times. A pierced antoninianus was found on a street (Amaliegade) in central Copenhagen,²¹⁹ and a silverplated antoninianus fitted with a now broken-off loop was found in a sand box in a children's playground in Farum, a suburban area north of Copenhagen.²²⁰

The antoninianus was originally intended to be a double denarius, but its debasement came so quickly that it obviously never gained any confidence outside the Empire. The find circumstances of the few finds from Denmark are closely comparable to the ones noted above for the bronze coinage: Some coins clearly were "deposited" recently, others were found in circumstances that suggest a possible deposition date during the Viking Age, and a few may have been deposited during the Late Roman or Early Germanic Iron Age. Several coins are single finds from areas where no other finds have been noted. It is therefore obvious that in an area as far outside the Limes as Denmark the antoniniani should be treated with other base metal coinages in spite of the nominal value as a silver coin.

6.6 Roman Provincial coins and Alexandrian coins

Roman provincial coinage is a common denominator for Roman period coins struck in the former Hellenized areas until the coinage reform of Diocletian in AD 293. The coins were for example struck by Greek city-states, *poleis*, or leagues, *koina*, and in some cases as provincial issues, as for example the Roman period coinages of Alexandria. The provincial coinages were mainly intended for local circulation in the areas where they were issued, and this is particularly the case with the closed currency of Roman Egypt.

Roman provincial issues are therefore not to be expected among the finds from Western Europe. The finds from Denmark are six provincials of various issues and nine Alexandrians. The most recent find of a provincial coin is a hardly legible small bronze that was part of a "hoard" containing also some Roman bronze coins and a modern medallion combining a portrait of Lucius Verus with the reverse of the famous Syracusan decadrachm of the late 4th century BC.²²¹ There can thus be little doubt that it was deposited recently, probably as a hoax. Two coins have

---

211 010410 sb 142: FP 3719; Kromann 1983-84, 107 no. 38.
212 010602 sb 115 in area sb 103: FP 1825.1; Breitenstein 1946, 18 no. 25. The coin was returned to the finder after inspection in the National Museum. On other Iron Age finds from Søtoftegård: Stenalt 2000.
213 120108: FP 2155; Balling 1962, 57 no. 73.
214 170102: FP 2702; Balling 1962, 56 no. 69.
215 170205: FP 3037; Kromann 1983-84, 63 no. 8.
216 220107. FP 2298; Balling 1962, 55-56 no. 68.
217 220107 sb 6.
218 220108; Balling 1962, 55 no. 66.
219 020306: FP 3641; Kromann 1983-84, 107 no. 39.

220 010601 sb 87: FP 6493.
221 Horsnæs 2008a.

Coins. Denominations and striking periods

Fig. 88. Distribution of Roman Provincial coins. Map by Josefine Franck Bican.

been found in urban areas in circumstances that are most readily interpreted as modern losses,[222] and two other coins have been found by gardening.[223] The last provincial coin, from Sagalassos in Pisidia (on the southern coast of modern Turkey), was found in north-eastern Sealand "c. 500 m from Fredensborg in direction Helsingør". It was found in the same field as a Roman bronze coin, c. 10 m apart.[224] There are no certain Iron Age finds from the area northeast of Fredensborg.

Nine Alexandrian coins have been found in seven different sites, and as could be expected from this coin type, none of them are from areas with other archaeological finds. Two Alexandrians were in clearly secondary positions, as they were found *on* streets of central Copenhagen.[225] One was found while raking the courtyard in front of the Esrum Kro (Pub) in northern Sealand,[226] two were found while digging in a garden in the north-western outskirts of Svendborg,[227] one coin, handed in to the National Museum in 2004, was allegedly found c. 1920 during the construction of the Tangeværk (power station)

---

222 070207: FP 4042 from Laodicea in Phrygia and 190503: FP 6382 from Antiochia ad Orontem (Horsnæs 2006a, no. 54).
223 080710: FP 7687 from Nicaea and 150309 sb 55 (unidentified).
224 010301 sb 122: FP 4044.1; Horsnæs 2006a, no. 31.

225 020306 without sb no., a Hadrianic tetradrachm that was returned to the finder, and 020306 sb 411: FP 946, a drachm struck during the reign of Antoninus Pius.
226 010103 sb 156: FP 2116.
227 090513: FP 3869.1-2.

165

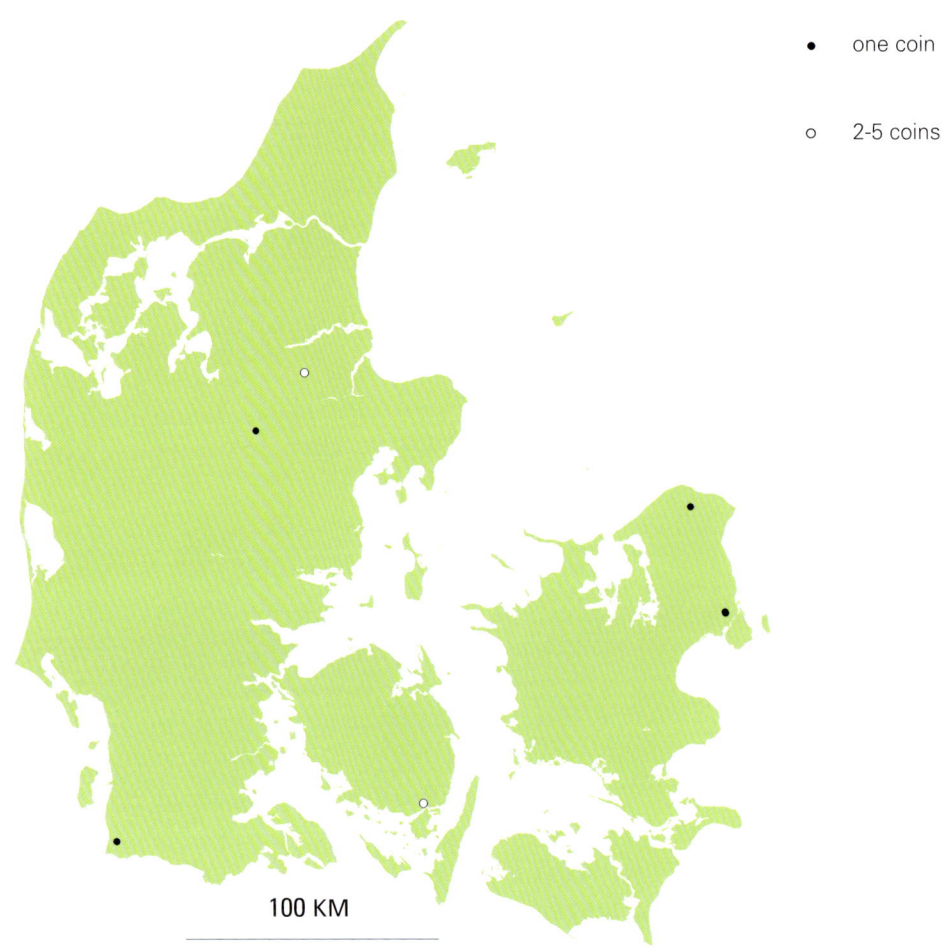

Fig. 89. Distribution of Alexandrian coins. Map by Josefine Franck Bican.

at Gudenåen in central Jutland.[228] During the 2nd World War two Alexandrian coins were handed in to the National Museum together with a *hvid* struck during the reign of Christian I (1448-1481), and the owner believed her father had told her that they had been found in the fields of the farm Jørgensminde in Jutland already around 1900.[229] Finally a coin has been found in an unspecified field in the Højer area in south-western Jutland.[230] Thus there is no reason to believe that these types should be treated as anything but recent imports.

6.7 Geographical distribution of mints

Rome was the most important mint during the first two centuries of the empire. Therefore the majority of the Roman coins from this period were struck in Rome. This applies of course to almost all the denarii from Denmark, where only a very small number of coins from the minor mints have been identified.

From the mid-3rd century more mints were active, but in reality the majority of coins with identified mints from the second half of the 3rd century derive from the gold hoards from Funen, and as these form a closely knit group of coins that may have been formed far from Denmark, it is hard to base any conclusions as to routes from mint to soil on these finds. The shortlived Gallic Empire 260-273 AD, created by Postumus after having defeated invading Germanic tribes, had a very active mint. Coins from the Gallic Empire are, however, rarely found outside

---

228   130606 sb 39: FP 7048.
229   140601: FP 2082.1-2.
230   210204: FP 2653.

the realm. Some Postumus aurei have been found in Türingen, but only one Postumus aureus has been found in Denmark, in the above-mentioned Brangstrup Hoard. Furthermore, three antoniniani can be ascribed to the Gallic Empire, but these coins were probably deposited recently.

The short reign (193-196 AD) of the usurper Allectus in Britain is represented by a single antoninianus found at Tissø. This coin is likely to have been deposited in the Late Germanic Iron Age or the Viking Age, and therefore may have come to Denmark with other British objects of that time.

The establishment of additional mints throughout the Empire after the reform of Diocletian provides new possibilities for the study of the Roman coins in Barbaricum. In Denmark the coins from the first part of the 4th century mainly derive from eastern mints, while the relatively few coins from the later part of the same century are often from western mints. Again the material is not balanced, as most of the gold coins from the early 4th century derive from the same hoards as mentioned above, while the overwhelming majority of the silver coins come from the Gudme III Hoard that I suggest was formed in south-eastern Europe and imported to Funen as a closed entity (see above). The 5th century solidi derive from either Constantinople (i.e. the main eastern mint) or from western – and sometimes unidentified – mints. The dominance of Constantinople seen among the 5th-early 6th century coins from the Baltic area is however, not reflected in the material from Western Denmark, and seems to indicate that Southern Scandinavia was part of routes other than those of the Baltic area.[231]

6.8 Reworked coins

Coins may be secondarily reworked. When this is done, the original function of the coin as a monetary unit is normally lost, even if the reworking has taken place within the monetary systems in which is was produced. Thus the meaning of the coin changes dramatically. In the present case the coins have been reworked in two basically different ways: Some coins have been cut or clipped, probably to reduce the

Fig. 90. Denarius from Hørup with traces of mounted rim. Double struck obverse. Scale 2:1. Photo HWH.

original weight of the coin, while the majority of the reworked coins have been changed in order to function as a piece of ornament or jewellery and/or as an amulet. The coins are reworked in a number of different ways that can be summarized as piercing, mounting with a loop or mounting in a frame, and different techniques have been used.

6.8.1 Denarii

Denarii are rarely reworked. Only eight examples of reworked denarii have been verified in the Danish material, and there is great variation in the methods employed. It is notable that the majority of them have been found in datable contexts.

Four reworked denarii have been found in burials. The oldest context is the C1b female burial from Skovgårde tomb 209.[232] The denarius was part of the elaborate necklaces of the deceased woman. It was struck by Hadrian and is fitted into a bronze mounting in one piece with the loop eye.[233] In this case the loop is placed in front of the emperor's face. A denarius struck by Vespasian and found at the workshop site Hørup presents bronze/copper traces around the rim that might derive from a similar mounting (*Fig. 90*).[234] A denarius struck by Titus was part of the jewellery of the lady buried in Himlingøje tomb 1949-2, dated in period C2. The coin was pierced, seemingly

---

231 Horsnæs 2009.

232 Ethelberg 2000, illustration.

233 A similar, although not identical, type of mounting was used on a denarius found on Bornholm in 2002: Horsnæs 2002a.

234 FP 6686.

Fig. 91. Denarius with drilled hole from Bregentved. Scale c. 2:1. Photo HWH.

from the obverse, below the neck of the emperor.[235] Two reworked denarii have been found in burials from period C3. One, a denarius struck by Commodus (or Marcus Aurelius for Commodus Caesar), was part of the jewellery of a lady buried in the Stålmosegård cemetery. It was mounted with a bronze loop (*Fig. 22*).[236] The other, a subaeratus struck for Marcus Aurelius Caesar, was part of a necklace consisting of amber beads found in tomb LØ in the Bregentved cemetery (*Fig. 91*).[237] This denarius presents a drilled hole placed below the neck of the emperor. While the coin is heavily worn, the edges of the hole are still quite sharp, but with trace of wear from the string from which it hung.

A Barbarian imitation of a denarius (Marcus Aurelius for Diva Faustina Minor) was found together with the military equipment deposited in Ejsbøl Mose (Moor) in the 4th century. It seems to have been pierced in front of the face of the empress.[238]

An extremely worn denarius was included in the bracteate hoard found in Gudme area II in 1982 (*Fig. 92*).[239] The hoard consisted of nine bracteates, two gold pendents, a gold spiral fingerring, and a gold button inlaid with almadine. The deposition must be dated in the early 6th century at the earliest. The denarius is fitted with a ridged band loop, closely reminiscent of the loops employed for the bracteates of the same hoard. However, it seems that it must have been necessary to hammer the loop onto the coin, perhaps with the use of some glue or welding material, in order to fasten the loop on the denarius that is considerably thicker than the ordinary bracteates or Late Roman gold coins in general. The loop is placed at the neck of the obverse portrait of Faustina Minor.

The last coin to be mentioned is a denarius found with detector on the Iron Age workshop site Lundsgård (*Fig. 93*).[240] It has been pierced from the obverse in front of the eyes of the portrait, but the hole has been filled in with a copper alloy. On the reverse of the coin a similar in-fill can be seen, but the hole is not visible on the obverse. Another hole has been drilled closer to the rim in front of the nose. This hole, comparable to the one on the Bregentved coin, has been torn open.

Fig. 92. Looped denarius from the Gudme II Hoard. Scale 2:1. Photo HWH.

The lack of uniformity among the reworked denarii is the most striking feature. Among the coins deposited within period C we find that holes may have been pierced or drilled, in one case the coin is mounted in a quite elegant bronze frame. The denarius deposited in the somewhat later bracteate hoard, on the other hand, has been fitted with a loop not dissimilar to the ones employed for the then contemporary bracteates

---

235 Lund Hansen 1995, fig. 4:27 (obverse).
236 Birkebæk 1997, 30-31 (photo).
237 Henriksen 1992b.
238 Balling 1962, no. 53 and fig. 7; Ørsnæs 1988, 107-8 Taf. 7, 11:2 & 210:7-8.

239 Axboe 1987, photo on Taf. XIII = Abb. 25.
240 FP 5805.3.

Coins. Denominations and striking periods

Fig. 93. Denarius with torn hole from Lundsgård. Photo HWH.

and coins, and it is suggested that the reworking of this particular coin took place considerably later than the other ones. No matter how the reworking was done, little attention was paid to the coin motives.

6.8.2 Siliquae

Among the siliquae from Denmark there are five (perhaps six) cases of reworking into jewellery. Two of the siliquae from the Høsten Torp hack-silver hoard have been pierced. In both cases the hole is situated above the head of the emperor, and the hole has been torn. One of the coins has furthermore been clipped, as is the case with at least two of the other coins from the hoard, and a second hole has been made next to the first one, close to the temple of the emperor, thus ruining the view of the image. The siliqua that was part of the jewellery of the lady buried in Torstorp Vesterby in period C3 was mounted with a simple loop, consisting of a thin band of silver riveted onto the siliqua above the head of the portrait, and the same technique was used on the siliqua from the workshop site at Hørup. Three coins were found in the period C3 burial at Nyrup, a solidus mounted with a beaded rim and a loop (below), and two siliquae, of which one show clear traces above the head of the portrait of a fallen-off loop of the same type. The other siliqua is quite worn, but there might be slight traces of a similar and similarly placed loop.

As noted above, the distribution of siliquae throughout Denmark is not even. No less than 356 of the 377 siliquae registered from Denmark have been found on Funen. None of these have been pierced or looped. In fact all siliquae that have been reworked into jewellery are among the 14 coins found on only five sites in Sealand.

6.8.3 Gold coins

None of the six aurei struck in the 1st century AD have been reworked. But reworking is the rule rather than the exception for 2nd and 3rd century aurei, solidi, imitations of aurei and early solidi, and in particular the Roman gold medallions and imitations of these. The large gold hoards from Funen naturally have yielded the numerically largest assemblage of reworked gold coins, but considering the general distribution of gold coins the reworked coins follow suit.

Among the 39 Roman 2nd and in particular 3rd century aurei found in Denmark no less than 37 have been reworked. 32 have been pierced, and in many cases the hole is placed above the head of the emperor. There are, however, a considerable number of cases where the hole is situated either in front of the face or behind the neck. Five of the coins (four from the Brangstrup Hoard and one from Ejsbøl Moor) have been pierced twice, and in three cases the second hole must be intended to replace a torn out hole.

Looped aurei are less common, only five examples have been found. Three of these were initially pierced and only in a second instance the loop was added, in two cases the hole had been filled in before the addition of the loop. The reason for the refilling of the coin must be purely aesthetical. When a coin was pierced it did not loose weight, so the in-fill would add weight to the coin rather than restore the original weight.

Also the majority of the solidi struck before AD 395 are reworked: of a total of 67 coins, 40 were reworked. Here the relative numbers of pierced and looped coins are reversed: 16 coins are pierced and 24 are looped, a single coin was both pierced and

Fig. 94. Pierced solidus. Detector find from Gudme area II. The coin is quite worn and bent, it is pierced from the obverse above the head of the emperor. Constantine the Great, struck in Sirmium 320-326 AD, *RIC* type 9. FP 6710.10. Scale 2:1. Photo John Lee/The National Museum.

looped. A large number of coins belonging to this period derive from the hoards at Brangstrup, Boltinggård and Gudme I, and among the single finds and smaller hoards Funen is also very well represented.

The five Roman gold medallions and the seven Barbarian imitations of aurei and quinarii are all reworked. Two Barbarian imitations have been pierced, in one case the hole was filled in and the coin was subsequently looped. The remaining imitations and the medaillons were looped.

The majority of the 5th century coins are not only looped, but they have also been fitted in a rim similar to the rims employed for the medallions and the Nordic bracteates. Two larger hoards from Funen belong to this period: the Elsehoved Hoard, where all the coins are looped and two of them furthermore mounted in a rim, and the Rynkebygård Hoard, where only one coin of five is looped. The remaining finds are spread evenly across the country. They are regular (Roman/Byzantine) as well as irregular issues and Barbarian imitations of the Late Roman solidi, and there are no clear differences in the reworking (or lack of reworking) among these relatively few coins. Three coins from two finds at Jordrup and Ejstrup in Jutland should be mentioned. They are all fitted with the same elaborate type of loop, and it is plausible to see them as originally belonging to the same ensemble (*Fig. 46*).

The aurei struck in the 2nd and 3rd centuries are most often pierced, as are the earliest Constantinian solidi, but a transition seems to take place in the early 4th century. Coins struck from around AD 325 onwards are more likely to have been fitted with a loop (and in some cases mounted with a rim) than to be pierced. In particular the evidence from the Brangstrup Hoard, and to a lesser degree the smaller Boltinggård Hoard, are important. In both cases the hoard must have been deposited as a single act that took place sometime after AD 336, thus even the pierced 3rd century coins from the hoard have been handled until that date. The evidence from the single finds supports this date.

There are occasional examples of the use of an additional decoration, such as a mounting in a rim or granulation in the 4th century, in particular on multipla and medallions, and from the fifth century this use became more widespread.

The loops present great variety in details. The most commonly employed loops are gold bands with longitudinal ridges identical to the loops used for the bracteates and other locally produced pendants. There are few simple flat bands, and some examples of loops made of gold thread. In all cases the loop is attached to the coin without any visible use of glue or welding material, but plainly fastened by squeezing it around the rim. The aureus from the Varpelev burial is unique among the gold coins as the loop is made of a gold band riveted onto the coin, similar to the siliquae from Torstorp Vesterby and Hørup. Also the mountings and the occasional decoration in granulation technique around the loop are closely comparable to the ones used for the bracteates.

As noted there is some inconsistency in the position of the hole in the aurei: it is often placed above the portrait of the obverse, but a considerable number of coins have been pierced in front of or behind the head. Contrary to this, the loops are invariably placed above the head of the portrait of the obverse. The fixed position of the loop is clearly of importance. It contradicts the interpretation that the Roman medallions had "lost their symbolic value and become an anonymous piece of jewellery".[241] It is on the contrary clear that the image on the obverse had a great importance for the person who fitted the loops and/or carried the jewellery, and in particular the symbolic value of the portrait must have been immense.

6.8.4 Pierced or looped base metal coins

It has already been noted that Roman bronze coins are relatively rare among Danish finds, and only four

Fig. 95. Bækgård. Urbs Roma with loop eye. Reverse motif not recognizable. Photo HWH.

---

241 Andersson 1995, 44.

pierced Roman base metal coins and two mounted coins are known. All the pierced or mounted coins derive from contexts that are most likely deposited after the end of the Iron Age. One of the pierced coins came from an 8th century context in Ribe,[242] two have been found on detector sites where the majority of the other finds are dated within the range from Late Germanic Iron Age to Medieval period,[243] and a coin that was found in a courtyard in Frederiksberg was most likely lost there only a short time ago.[244] An *Urbs Roma* coin with a bronze loop was found on the Bækgård site in the Nørholm complex in northern Jutland (*Fig. 95*),[245] and another mounted coin struck by Constantine was found in a 12th century level at St. Villads Church.[246]

Two antoniniani have been reworked. One was found on a street with much traffic in central Copenhagen. It was pierced from the obverse above the top of the emperor's head. The other was found in a children's playground in Farum, one of the northern suburbs of Copenhagen. The antoninianus has been silver-plated and there are traces of a loop at the rim above the emperor's head. In neither of the cases the coin was found in an archaeological context, and in particular the reworking of the coin from Farum seems to be modern. This strongly indicates that Roman base metal coins were not regarded fitting to be used as jewellery/amulets during the Danish Iron Age.

6.8.5 Coin rings

A bronze coin mounted in a bronze fingering was once in the collection of the king Frederik VII (*Fig. 97*).[247] This coin ring is mentioned in archaeological literature together with a similar coin ring found in

Fig. 96. Renaissance ring mounted with imitation of Roman coin. GP 3266. Photo MLSS.

Holstein. The Holstein coin ring was found in the 1860's and handed in to the National Museum together with a bronze hand from a Roman statue (*Fig. 96*).[248] The two coin rings have played some role in research as both have been believed to be Roman, and as such they have been regarded as the northernmost finds of Roman coin rings. The view, however, must be revised. Although coin rings are quite common within the Empire,[249] neither of the rings in question, nor the coins mounted in them, is Roman. They are more probably to be dated in the 16th or 17th century. The "coins" are cast from ancient Roman coins: The Holstein coin has the impression of a Trajan laureate portrait to the right, with the legend: IMP CAES NERVA TRAIAN AVG GERM. The Holbæk ring has the portrait of Divus Trajanus draped and laureated to the right, with the legend: DIVO TRAIANO PARTH AVG PATRI.

Fig. 97. Renaissance ring mounted with imitation of Roman coin. NM II D 13312. After Lindahl 2003, 189.

---

242 190409 sb 50: FP 3727.33 a 4th century coin struck in Nicomedeia; Bendixen 1981, 97 no. 33; Horsnæs 2006a, cat.no. 99.
243 010504 sb 88: FP 6071 was struck by Constantius II in Trier and found at Meløse Gammeltofter; Horsnæs 2006a, cat. no. 82 and 180206 sb 143: FP 4560.2 was struck by Marcus Aurelius and found at Ryde Mølle; Horsnæs 2006a, cat.no. 28.
244 020306 sb 413: FP 2538; Horsnæs 2006a, cat.no. 62.
245 120508: FP 6700.
246 130815 sb 348: FP 2782; Horsnæs 2006a, cat.no. 69.
247 Now in the National Museum, Medieval and Renaissance inv.no. D 13312.

248 NM I inv.nos. 25497 and 25498. The ring is now in The Royal Coll. of Coins and Medals inv.no. GP 3266.
249 Beckmann 1969, in particular p. 40 with references; see also Bemmann 2006, 1 with further references.

6.8.6 Clipped coins

Among the siliquae there are a few examples of clipped coins. As noted several times, siliquae are rarely found Denmark, and again the uniqueness of the Gudme III Hoard and related siliquae should be underlined: Neither the Gudme siliquae, nor any of the related finds of siliquae from the middle of the 4th century are clipped.

On the contrary seven of the 21 siliquae found outside Funen have been clipped. Three are from Høsten Torp and one from Engelsborg, both in Sealand, and three from the Simmersted Moor in southern Jutland.[250] All the clipped coins belonged to the issues from the later part of the 4th century, but the hoards were deposited somewhat later, around or shortly after 500 AD.

The clipping of the edges is a common feature in the siliqua finds of Britain. In the enormous Hoxne Hoard 98.5 % of the siliquae were clipped, and this phenomenon received extensive treatment in the publication of the hoard.[251] The clipped coins from Britain belong to the issues of the second half of the 4th century, and the Danish material thus follow suit. Guest suggested that the clipping in Britain might have taken place both before and after the Roman withdrawal in AD 402, in the 5th century perhaps as a means to obtain silver for siliqua imitations, while Burnett was inclined to believe that the clipping was mainly a post-Roman phenomenon. It is noted that evidence of clipped siliquae are more rarely found in the Continent, but it is not unknown.[252]

6.8.7 Cut coins

Two of the siliquae from the Høsten Torp Hoard are intentionally cut and a third was attempted cut.[253] Two Late Roman solidi, both from Gudme, are clearly intentionally cut.[254] Cut solidi have been found also on Bornholm,[255] and an example of a quartered solidus is known from Czech Republic.[256] The cutting of coins should be no surprise in a cultural sphere where the cutting of objects made in valuable material is quite common, yet this phenomenon has not been discussed previously. It is quite suggestive that most of the cut solidi have been found recently. It is probable that the cutting of solidi may have been more common than what is seen in the material preserved today, but it is plausible that it has left little evidence in the coin cabinets, where cut coins may have been discarded as destroyed coins. It should be noted that the cut silver and gold coins were struck in the late 4th or 5th century, but the siliquae were not deposited until *c.* 500 AD.[257]

---

250 Furthermore two siliquae have been found on Bornholm, both are clipped. No siliquae are known from Swedish finds (personal information Lennart Lind).
251 Guest 2005, in particular chapter 7.
252 Burnett 1984, 168; Guest 2005, 110. See also Burnett 1984 for a discussion of Roman laws against clipping of coins.
253 FP 1830.8. Another coin: FP 1830.7, is fragmented, but it has not been possible to decide without doubt that they were intentionally cut.
254 090104 sb 107: FP 6792.11, Arcadius or Honorius struck in Milan 393-423 AD, halved, w. 2.12 g; 090104 sb 143: FP 4224.5, very small fragment of unidentified issue, w. 0.68 g. Horsnæs 2009, 267 fig. 3.36-37.
255 Horsnæs 2009.
256 Militký 2004.
257 An aureus struck by Vespasian has been tested by a cut in the edge, but there is clearly no attempt to cut the coin into pieces; Breitenstein 1946, 9 no. 4 and fig. 1.

CHAPTER 7

Find patterns in other parts of Barbaricum

It has been shown that the number of Roman coin finds decreased as distance to the Limes area increased.[1] But later and more specialized reviews of the material not only reveals that some parts of Barbaricum received many more Roman coins than other parts, no matter what the distance to the *Limes*, but also that there are differences in the denominations and striking periods represented in various parts of Barbaricum.

Studies of Roman coins in their non-Roman contexts have been undertaken by a large number of scholars, normally concentrating on their "own" area as defined by modern political borders. To get an overview of the material I will here summarize the most important characteristics of the find patterns from the non-Roman areas closest to modern Denmark. For the sake of clarity I will first summarize the finds from the areas south of Denmark, and then proceed to the northern areas.[2]

7.1 South of Denmark

The Netherlands

Van der Vin concluded in his studies of the finds from the Netherlands that four distinct areas could be seen.[3] The non-Roman part of northern Netherlands was divided into two areas: on the one hand the coastal area characterized by sea clay (Friesland and Groningen) and on the other the "higher sandy soils" of Drenthe-Overijssel. In the coastal area there are many finds, and the hoards are generally small. There is a considerable number of sestertii of the 2nd and 3rd century, and from the 4th century onwards a number of gold coins. Friesland also has a Julio-Claudian denarius hoard,[4] there is a considerable number of finds of Gallic antoniniani,[5] and there are several examples of gold coins from the 6th-7th century.[6]

The find density is smaller in the Drenthe-Overijssel area. There are large hoards, in particular of 1st-2nd century denarii – both Julio-Claudian hoards

---

1 Hedeager 1978 and 1988.
2 For recent in-depth analyses and references, see the articles in Bursche *et al.* 2008.
3 van der Vin 2000.
4 FMRN I, no. 86 from Fyns and perhaps no. 181 from Oudehorne(?); FMRN II, no. 1098 from Zoutkamp.
5 For example the hoards FMRN I, no. 51 from Driesum and no. 54 from Drieterpen, but also smaller hoards
6 For example FMRN I, no. 226.

with a significant number of Republican denarii and hoards with Flavian to Antonine denarii, while stray finds are few and with a prevalence for denarii; there are few gold coins and hardly any finds post-date *c.* 400 AD.

The southern part of the country was part of the Roman Empire. It was subject to a romanization process, and a large diversity of Roman coins occurs. Along the Limes more than 90 % of the coin finds are small change copper issues, the majority from the 1st and 2nd centuries. Recent research illuminates the huge differences in the distribution of denominations within the micro-regions along the Limes. In particular the differences in the find spectra between the Roman military installations along the Limes and the native sites south of the Limes, that is: within the Roman Empire, are striking. It clearly suggests that the forts were not the source of the coins found in native sites, while on the contrary the coin finds from the civic capital Forum Hadriani present similarities to the find from the native sites. The native sites north of the Limes have conspicuously few finds, but they present the same chronological distribution as the finds from the forts.[7] The material from the modern area of the Netherlands thereby stresses the variation in finds from one region to another and the importance of reading the finds within various levels.

Germany

The material from north-western Germany also reflects the different vicissitudes encountered by the various areas.[8] The Limes area again presents a relatively high number of bronze coinages and single finds of denarii that are interpreted as evidence of the use of coins as money in the area of Westfalen. Further away the finds are dominated by denarius hoards consisting of coins struck in the period between Vespasian and Septimius Severus. The finds related to the defeat of Varus at Kalkriese in particular, and in general to the Roman presence between the Rhine and the Elbe, of course take a special position.[9] Detector archaeology is responsible for a considerable number of new finds, mostly from the Wesermarch (Lower Weser: 87 coins of which 63 came from two sites). The recent finds to some degree differ from the earlier finds. Berger notes the relatively high number of bronze coins, and in particular the high incidence of reworking of the bronze coins: several have been deliberately fragmented or pierced. Also the southern part of Niedersachsen has yielded a number of new finds including 2nd century sestertii and antoniniani.[10]

Schleswig-Holstein is of course of major importance for the present study.[11] The overall find density is comparable to Denmark. There are some denarius hoards north of an imaginary line from the Elbe mouth to the Schlei, and a cluster of denarius finds around the Greater Plön Lake. Bronze coins are clustering at the urban areas of modern Hamburg, Neumünster and Kiel, in areas with relatively few denarius finds, and I suspect that many of these would turn out to be "modern" depositions in line with the Danish clusters of base metal coins at modern urban areas. Among the gold coins aurei are dominating. There are conspicuously many Early Imperial aurei, and two Barbarian imitations. Apart from a single solidus dated 394-395 AD from Hamburg, there are no Late Roman solidi.

The find density in Mecklenburg-Vorpommern and northern Brandenburg seems lower than what might be expected in comparison to Denmark and Schleswig-Holstein. Some finds from former Bezirk Rostock might have been lost, due to the transfer of the coins from Rostock to Schwerin and subsequent destruction of the collection in Schwerin,[12] but this can only be part of the explanation. Denarius hoards are not found in Mecklenburg-Vorpommern, and they are relatively rare in Brandenburg, but there are on the other hand as many single finds of denarii as of bronze coins and antoniniani. Among the gold coins there is a significant difference between on the one hand Sachsen (in particular the northern areas of former *Bezirke* Leipzig and Dresden), Sachsen-Anhalt, Thüringen, Schleswig-Holstein and the south-

---

7   Kemmers 2008.
8   Berger 1992, based on the coins published in the FMRD VII Niedersachsen and Bremen.
9   Berger 1996 on Kalkriese; Berger 1992, 47-121 on the finds from the period until AD 14 in general.

10   Berger 2008.
11   Find list in Balling 1962 includes part of the area north of the Eider River; updated find list in FMRD VIII Schleswig-Holstein.
12   Klüssendorf 1995.

ern part of Brandenburg with Berlin, where there is a considerably higher number of aurei than solidi, and on the other hand the areas close to the Baltic Sea, the northern part of Brandenburg and Mecklenburg-Vorpommern in Germany and Pommerania in Poland, where solidi by far outnumber aurei.

Poland

The general find density of Pomerania is slightly higher than in Mecklenburg-Vorpommern, and seems more easily comparable to the pattern in Schleswig and Denmark. But along the Vistula and at its estuary into the Gdansk Bay the number is far greater. This applies to all denominations, but there is a relatively smaller percentage of bronze coins and antoniniani in Pomerania than in the German regions. The number of aurei is far smaller than the number of solidi and among the latter, only three coins are dated in the 4th century, all the remaining are 5th century solidi. The gold coins are found mostly in the coastal areas, both on the Baltic Sea and in particular at the Gdansk Bay, while the denarii are also very commonly found in the whole area east of the Vistula.

Dense find patterns are also visible at the Upper Vistula and San in Little Poland[13] and in particular at the Upper Oder in the province of Silesia.[14] It is interesting to note the reversal of the chronological distribution of gold coins in comparison with Pomerania: the number of aureus finds in Silesia is twice the number of solidus finds, and among the latter only one find postdates 395 AD.

The eastern part of Poland (the Wielbark Culture)[15] presents smaller numbers of finds. This pattern is also visible in modern Belorussia, where c. 2550 Roman coins have been found. Many of them are not preserved to our days, but it is clear that the overwhelming majority of the finds were denarii from the 1st to the early 3rd centuries, and that these finds were concentrated in the western part of the country. Later coins (only late 3rd to early 4th century issues are mentioned) are extremely rare.[16]

Bohemia, Northern Austria and Slovakia

Denarii struck during the period from Vespasian to Commodus dominate the single finds in Bohemia. The number of finds drops in the 3rd and 4th centuries, but coins from these centuries are still more common than in Denmark, as are the finds of bronze coins and antoniniani. Aurei are rare, and the majority of gold coins derive from the second half of the 4th century and the 5th century (from Constantius II to Zeno). A recent rise in the number of new finds is due to detector archaeology, and among these a number of 3rd and 4th century coins have been found in settlements on high ground. Few coins are noted from burials from the Migration period.[17]

The southern border of modern Slovakia is partly following the Danube and thus the Limes. The lowlands north of the Limes is the area with the largest numbers of finds of Roman coins, while other finds have mostly been made along the river valleys. Considering the size of Slovakia and the position close to the Limes the number of sites is not large, but the average number of coins per site is considerably higher than in Denmark (278 sites with c. 5000 coins compared to Western Denmark 360+ sites with almost 2900 coins).[18]

The non-Roman part of Austria, along the March River that also forms the border towards modern Slovakia, presents a growing number of finds throughout the first four centuries AD. It is, however, suggested that there is a break in the continuity in the period after the reign of Commodus and into the first half of the 3rd century, and it is suggested that this break may have been caused by the Marcomannic wars. After the mid-3rd century the coin influx is growing and finds are outnumbering the preceding centuries. It is noted that base metal coins are rare among these finds. The high number of finds continues into the 4th century, but dies out from the Valentinian dynasty to disappear completely in the mid-5th century.[19]

---

13 Kunisz 1985 and Bursche 1996.
14 Bursche 1996. Unfortunately Ciołek's recent corpus of Roman coin finds from Silesia, Ciołek 2008, arrived too late to be fully considered.
15 Bursche 1996.
16 Sidorovič 2007.

17 Militký 2008.
18 Kolníková 2008. See also Beljak 2006 on finds from the Hron and Ipel' River basins.
19 Dembski 2008, referring to Jedlicka 2005 (not available for consultation).

7.2 North of Denmark

Norway

There are relatively few finds of Roman coins from Norway.[20] The denarii are particularly rare in comparison with other parts of Barbaricum, which means that the distribution of denominations is quite different from for example Denmark. Some gold coins have been found in contexts from the Early Germanic Iron Age, and they may together with the imitations of 4th century medallions and the Nordic bracteates from similar contexts be interpreted as evidence for connections with Southern Scandinavia/Denmark. Some Roman bronze coins have been found in securely dated Viking Age contexts as is also the case in Denmark, and there is an example of a Roman solidus in the Viking Age hoard from Hoen.[21]

Mainland Sweden

Sweden is distinguished by marked regionality in the material. The overall pattern is comparable to the general picture provided by the Danish material: the overwhelming majority of the finds are denarii from the period from Vesparian to Commodus. There are few aurei and early solidi.[22] Most of them are single finds, and gold hoards comparable to the ones from Funen are totally absent. The number of base metal coins is somewhat higher, but many of them have provenances that may be relatively recent.[23] Coins from the 3rd and 4th centuries are in general rare. There is a considerable number of Late Roman solidi.[24] The finds are, however, not evenly distributed within Sweden.

In southern part of mainland Sweden coins have mainly been found in coastal areas.[25] There are a number of single finds of denarii, one small and two large denarius hoards. The hoard from Flintarp on the western coast of Halland consists of 230 denarii with a relatively early composition and the end coin is struck during the reign of Septimius Severus. The hoard from Hagestadsborg on the south-eastern tip of Schonen consists of no less than 539 denarii with a somewhat later composition, but also ending with Septimius Severus. Three ensembles of bronze coins were noted, none of which have archaeological provenances.[26] Metal detector surveys have only been undertaken in connection with the archaeological investigation of the Uppåkra site. Here they have brought to light 45 denarii and three Roman bronze coins, making Uppåkra the most important site for finds of Roman coins in southern Sweden. The chronological distribution of the denarii, from Titus to Commodus, is closely comparable to the Danish finds. The bronze coins are somewhat later, one from each of the 3rd, 4th and 5th centuries. Uppåkra has also yielded more than 150 Kufic coins, as well as a number of Western European Viking Age and Medieval coins.[27]

Concentrations of finds can be seen in the three landscapes surrounding modern Stockholm: Västmanland, Uppland and Södermannland. There are some single finds of denarii from Uppland and a hoard (69 denarii) from Västmanland,[28] but the most important finds are the Late Roman solidi (73 coins)[29] from Helgö and other sites in the Mälaran lake area.

Öland, Gotland and Bornholm

Discussing the three large islands of the Baltic Sea under the same heading is only telling part of the story. The islands present a number of similarities, but there are great differences in the details. The islands are all characterized by high find density, and there are considerable numbers of finds of Late Roman solidi.[30] Still, on both Bornholm and Gotland

---

20 Skaare 1976. Håkon Ingvardsson generously informed me of some finds not included in Skaare's list. See also Gullbekk 2009; Simensen & Khazai 2008.
21 Fuglesang & Wilson 2006.
22 Lists of gold coins from Sweden: Westermark 1980 (aurei and early solidi); Fagerlie 1967 and Westermark 1983 (Late Roman solidi).
23 Lists of bronze coins from Sweden in Westermark & Wiséhn 1983, 1984, and 1989. Recent finds in Moesgaard 1998 and Lind 2007b.
24 Fagerlie 1967; Westermark 1983.
25 On Schonen, Halland and Blekinge see Balling 1966, with distribution map p. 76. Denarius finds updated in Lind 1981, finds nos. 182-192 who also enumerates denarius finds from the landscapes Södermanland, Västergötland and Småland, not included by Balling.
26 Balling 1966, "finds" no. 2, 11 and 15.
27 Silvegren 2002.
28 Lind 1981, finds nos. 163-170 and 171.
29 Number from Lind 1988, 26.
30 Fagerlie 1967; Metcalf 1995. Find list for Bornholm

huge numbers of denarii by far outnumber the solidi.[31]

Denarii have been found in 25 sites on the island Öland. There is a hoard consisting of 79 denarii from Hulterstad, and a settlement find comprising 14 coins from Bredsätra. Furthermore 10 denarii were part of the weapon sacrifice at Skedemosse. The remaining finds were single finds. Öland has, however, provided the largest number of Late Roman solidi from Sweden, a total of 306 coins.[32]

Gotland has the highest find density in Sweden. Among the 195 finds from all Sweden comprising a total of 7161 Roman coins, no less than 139 finds with 6077 coins derived from Gotland.[33] Hardly any base metal coins or early gold coins have been found. The material consists of almost exclusively denarii.[34] There are furthermore 274 Late Roman solidi.[35]

It has long been recognized that Bornholm has played its own particular role in history. The Roman coin finds from Bornholm also differ greatly from the finds from the remaining parts of modern Denmark (see Chapter 1: Introduction). As on Gotland denarii dominate the finds, but there is a considerable number of Late Roman solidi as well.[36]

Finland

The relatively few finds of Ancient coins from Finland have been thoroughly discussed.[37] The single finds of coins from Finland are of a varied nature (Talvio nos. 4, 7, 10, 11, 13, 18), and some of them I would regard as doubtful, based on the coin type. It is noted by Talvio that some of the finds were made in areas without Iron Age settlements. The late 1st-2nd century denarii so common in Southern Scandinavia are conspicuously rare in Finland. Four Late Roman solidi have been found in southern Österbotton. They are closely comparable to the solidi found on the islands of Gotland, Öland and Bornholm,[38] confirming Talvio's suggestion that they derive from this area.

There are two secure finds of Roman bronze coins from Roman Iron Age burials, and there are six single finds that Talvio argues may have an Iron Age context. In the West Balt culture large numbers of Roman bronze coins, notably sestertii, have been found in burials, whereas the silver and gold coins dominating the finds in most other parts of Barbaricum, are almost absent.[39] The two bronze coins from the Finnish burials are an aes and a sestertius, and they are comparable to the coins from the West Balt culture. Talvio noted the influences from the West Balt culture in the Roman Iron Age of Finland, and he is undoubtedly right when considering the two bronze coins from burials a reflection of this influence. Roman finds in general are extremely rare in Finland, and they are restricted to the areas with the two burials with bronze coins.

In spite of over-all similarities in the find patterns of Barbaricum here surveyed it is clear that the vast area consisted of numerous regions that received Roman coins at different paces and in different periods. As already stressed by Hedeager,[40] coins with a smaller intrinsic value than face value are rarely found outside the Limes zone, and even within this zone there are differences in the use of base metal coinage.[41] The vast number of denarius finds of coins struck in the period 69-193 AD is not only the largest group numerically, but probably also the one most difficult to handle, not only because they all derive ultimately from the same mint, Rome, but also because of their extremely long period of circulation, first within and later outside the Empire. The find patterns of 3rd-5th century coinages become much more kaleidoscopic, and it therefore seems possible to draw wider conclusions about routes, chronologies and functions of these coins, regardless their relative rarity.

(finds made until 2007 included) in Horsnæs 2009.
31 Lind 1981.
32 Figures from Lind 1988, 26. On Öland see also Herschend 1980.
33 Figures given by Lind 1988, 22. The number of coins find from Gotland is steadily growing. Lind 2006 mentions *c.* 6500 denarii from Gotland: *c.* 6000 from large hoards (+40 coins), *c.* 400 from smaller hoards (2 to 40 coins), and *c.* 100 from single finds.
34 In reality Lind 1988 may be seen as a study of denarii from Gotland, rather than a study of denarii from Sweden.
35 Number from Lind 1988, 26.
36 Horsnæs *forthcoming A*; Horsnæs 2009 on solidus finds.
37 Talvio 1982.

38 Horsnæs 2009.
39 Bursche 1996, 170-183 (coin list); Sisdrys 2001.
40 Hedeager 1978.
41 Kemmers 2008.

CHAPTER 8
Synthesis

Denarius Antonini Pii, quem teneo & servo, prope Viburgum in Jutiâ ex cespitum fodinis effossum Anno 1693 etiam illo referendus est: neque enim locus Romanis denariis in tam putido loco, ubi cespites effodiuntur, & in eiusmodi lacunis convenit, sed per turbines ac procellas ex alio loco in istas voragines delatum esse necesse est.[1]

During the 20th century much weight was put on the issue of "why". Why are Roman coins found in such large numbers outside the Roman Empire? Two explanatory models have prevailed: the economic model (trade) and the political model (payment of mercenaries and/or allies, or treasure lost as war booty), and modern scholars have discussed which explanation was the more important. No doubt the Romans traded with the peoples outside the Limes, but in fact it is difficult to prove whether they paid in cash. It is also well known that the Romans paid for peace. This is repeated in several literary sources, often in sources regarding the "bad" emperors as a way to illustrate their lack of *virtus*, but no doubt also the "good" emperors subsidized Germanic neighbours to keep them from raiding the Limes area. The amounts paid by the Romans are calculated in either coins or amounts of gold, but again it is less easy to prove that payments were actually made in coind. Although a debated issue, little progress has been made since the days of Bolin.

The two models mentioned share a Roman point of view, with the Roman as the acting force focussed on the "why export?". The question "why import?" from a non-Roman point of view has only been addressed in the last decades, and often as a negation: "why not import post-Severan denarii?".[2] It has been maintained that the Barbarian communities did not want bad money and therefore refused to receive 3rd century coinage. It is undoubtedly true that the non-monetarized communities never needed base metal coins as money, and therefore received them only in insignificant numbers or for reasons not connected with economy, as must be the explanation for the many sestertii found in the West Balt culture burials. Still, Berger and Bursche have both pointed out that a relatively large number of subaerati have been found in Barbaricum, and noted that the differences in silver content is not clearly visible when handling the individual coin. Thus the explanation that Barbarians wanted good silver is too simplistic. In particular the early antoniniani would in this case have been found more commonly. Berger's suggestion that the lack of 3rd century coin reflects a new way of handling the Barbarian problem from the Roman Empire is in-

---

1 "A denarius of Antoninus Pius that I have and preserve, and that was excavated in a peat ditch near Viborg in Jutland is also to be referred to this: because the place in this stinking area, where peats are being dug up, and in these holes is not fitting for Roman coins, but they must have been brought from another place to these abysses by whirlwinds and gusts." Otto Sperling: *De nummorum bracteatorum et cavorum nostræ ac superioris ætatis origine et progressu*, ad Jac. a Mellen epistola, Lubecæ 1700. Quoted after Galster 1936, 41 find no. 32 (English translation HWH).

2 A good example: Bursche 1993.

triguing. The finds of Roman coins from Denmark are, however, of little help to solve this question.

Let us instead look at the possible import routes to Southern Scandinavia and at the possible roles played by the Roman coins within the Iron Age societies of Denmark.

8.1 From mint to soil – how to get there?

The question addressed by Sperling in the quotation above was complicated. "How" did the coins travel so far from their point of origin? Today it is easy to laugh at Otto Sperling and his wind-blown denarius, but considering that he was arguing against a hundred years older belief that the coins found in the soil had been born out of the sun's shining on a rainbow, his way of explaining how Roman coins came to Denmark was a leap forward.

One would think that the mints would be the obvious starting point for a discussion of the routes that the Roman coins travelled. During the first three centuries of the Empire however, the vast majority of the coins were struck in the *Urbs*, Rome itself.[3] The modes and means of transport of coins within the Empire are not fully clarified, and as noted there is a complete silence in the literary sources about coin use outside the Limes. The best starting point is therefore the finds themselves.

There is as noted above only a small group of finds of denarii from the Republican and Julio-Claudian periods in Denmark. The three dated contexts for these finds are the Ginderup Hoard, probably deposited *c.* 100 AD, the Republican coin found in Dankirke, and the aureus from the Bæk burial dated in period B1/B2a, i.e. during the 1st century AD. With some caution it is possible to hypothesize that other Republican denarii from Denmark may have been deposited during the 1st or early 2nd century AD, but with such a small number and so little conclusive evidence at hand, earlier as well as later deposition dates cannot be ruled out. Also single finds of Flavian coins may belong to a small group of depositions from *c.* 100 AD.

The distribution of these few finds is interesting, as it corresponds with other finds indicating some particular contacts out of the local area. This geographical distribution also seems to continue an existing tradition for long distance contacts with exchange of elite objects going back to Bronze and Pre-Roman Iron Ages. The relatively few finds of Augustan – or more broadly Republican/Julio-Claudian – coins are striking in view of the Roman interests in the area between the Rhine and the Elbe in the generation leading up to the fatal blow to the Roman army with the defeat of Varus, and the expeditions in the years following this blow. While Varus' defeat had great importance for the Roman policy in the years to follow and enormous symbolical significance within Rome, the Roman presence so close to Denmark left no impact on the numismatic material from Denmark!

The major influx of denarii came later. The dendrochronological date of Illerup deposition A is of major importance as it tells us that the types sacrificed in Illerup were definitely in use in the early 3rd century. It is the earliest well-dated context for denarii of the late 1st and 2nd centuries from Denmark, but it should be kept in mind that it is commonly believed that the sacrificed objects did not belong to peoples living within the area of modern Denmark. Still, denarii have been found in burials dated in period C1b (210/20-250/60), and thus there is no reason to doubt that the Roman denarii struck *c.* 69-193 AD were first deposited in Denmark, and more broadly in Southern Scandinavia, during the 3th century.

Denarii from the same period were no doubt also available much later in Scandinavia. A clear example from Denmark is the worn denarius from the Gudme II bracteate hoard dated in the early 6th century, but it is also indicated by the mixed denarius and siliqua hoard from Gudme IV, the primary deposition of which must have taken place no earlier than the late 4th century. The suggested dates of the archaeological layers at Gudme and at the Lundeborg port-of-trade underline this evidence for continuous use of denarii in Denmark in a very long period. The many finds

---

3   Other official imperial mints were temporarily employed, e.g. during the reign of Vespasian (Tarraco), but the number of denarii from Denmark struck outside Rome is minimal. A few 3rd century coins come from the mints operated by usurpers, e.g. in the Gallic Empire (Lyons), and by Allectus (London). Few Roman Provincial coins are found in Denmark, and it is argued that they are from secondary contexts (cf. above). They will therefore not be considered here.

from detector surveys can be related to sites in use for an even longer period, and there are examples of denarii from Medieval contexts that may be interpreted as continued use and/or re-use of finds.

Denarii were found in most parts of the country, but they are not equally distributed. Single finds as well as hoards are more common in Sealand, where an easterly and a westerly group can be seen, and in Funen in particular in the south-eastern half island. The find density is far smaller in Jutland. Here the majority of denarii come from northern Jutland, and the sites along the Limfjord should be stressed, while a smaller number of single finds are found in the easten parts of Jutland.

After the reforms of Diocletian a larger number of mints were employed. The mints were moved away from Rome, and they were sometimes situated nearer to frontier zones. All the mints were not active all the time, and at times some of the mints only produced some of the denominations employed. The mint can almost always be identified, at least on well-preserved coins. The 4th century coins found in Denmark come from a variety of mints, but the mint distribution is not random. Throughout the century the combination of mints represented in the individual hoard signifies that the coins most likely came to Denmark in small batches. The best example is the siliquae from Gudme. Not only the coins from the Gudme III Hoard, but also the siliquae from the Gudme IV Hoard and the single finds of siliquae present a surprising unity in chronological as well as spatial distribution that is best explained as the result of a single batch of siliquae coming to Gudme and being redistributed within the Gudme area including Lundeborg. The coins are mainly struck during the third quarter of the 4th century and the vast majority are from eastern mints. The closest parallels for siliqua hoards with this composition are found in south-eastern Europe, mainly between the Danube and the Dnjestr.[4] Similar siliquae have been found in the Engelsborg Hoard and as a few single finds. The remaining siliquae finds are of slightly later types struck in western mints, and among them there are examples of clipped siliquae. This is normally regarded to be a British feature, although it is not clear when clipping of the siliquae begun, and whether it continued after the withdrawal of the Romans in the early 5th century.[5] We may with som caution see these coins as examples of contacts with Britain through northwest Germany and the Frisian areas.

The solidi from the numerically smaller gold hoards from Funen also indicate that the hoards were already composed when the coins arrived. The Gudme I Hoard for example consists of coins struck during the reigns of the sons of Constantine the Great, and the 5th century coins are never mixed with earlier issues, as evidenced by the two larger hoards from Funen, Rynkebygård (five solidi) and Elsehoved (eight solidi).

The two contemporary hoards from Brangstrup and Boltinggård present interesting differences. While the Brangstrup Hoard consists of coins from mainly eastern mints, and the jewellery and the Barbarian imitations of solidi also point towards present-day Hungary as area of origin, the smaller Boltinggård Hoard contains a larger proportion of coins from western mints. This may, however, be a coincidence. The relatively lower number of coins from Boltinggård (as well as the presence of coins from western mint in the Brangstrup Hoard) does not exclude the possibility that the two hoards originally constituted one assemblage of coins that arrived in Denmark at the same time, was split into two groups, and deposited very close to each other. The two depositions, however, need not be contemporary, as particularly the Constantinian coins from the Brangstrup Hoard in general seem to be more worn than the contemporary solidi from the Boltinggård Hoard.

Among the 5th century coins as a whole, there are 15 coins from eastern mints and no less than 10 coins (23,8 %) from western, non-Imperial mints. This is a relatively high proportion, compared with the material from the Baltic Islands, but another 10 solidi are un-assigned imitations of 5th century Imperial issues, and they constitute an even more important element. The geographical distribution in the un-assigned coins is not even. They make up more than a third of the solidi from Jutland, but only one sixth

---

4 Kromann 1988.

5 Richard Reece suggests that "at least som clipping was already going on in 370-390", personal communication.

of the coins from Funen and Sealand.: (5 of 13 Late Roman/Byzantine solidi from Jutland, 4 of 24 from Funen, 1 of 6 from Sealand). This pattern is in striking contrast to the composition of 5th century coins from the Baltic area.[6] It is evident that solidi from Western Denmark were not redistributed from the Baltic Islands, as suggested by Fagerlie. They came directly to Western Denmark, and they derived from other sources than the solidi that arrived in Bornholm and the Swedish islands.

The survey of the Roman coin finds from Barbaricum (Chapter 7) illustrates the great variation in the composition of the coin finds from one region to another. Some differences may be ascribed to variation in the aims of the scientific approach or to different survival rates and registration levels. Still, having these possible sources for errors in mind there are notable diversities in the absence or presence of certain denominations, and the relative amount of coins from various phases. The long recognized pattern of denarii from the late 1st and 2nd centuries dominating the finds still holds good, as does the overall view of a growing number of base metal coinages among the finds from areas close to the Limes. Of great interest are the newly reported detector finds of in particular base metal coinages in settlements in Bohemia and northeast Germany alike that may add new nuances to the interpretation of the coin use in these areas. Detector archaeology in Polish settlements on the other hand seems to augment mainly the number of denarii,[7] complying to the pattern from Denmark. The most obvious differences from one area to another can be seen among the finds of gold coins, where 5th century solidi struck in eastern mints dominate the finds in the Baltic area, while earlier gold coins are more common in Central Europe (along the Oder-Elbe axis), Southern Scandinavia, and Norway.

A most striking example of the differences in the coin finds from various areas of Barbaricum is the case of the West Balt Culture. It seems difficult to explain these differences from an analysis of the exporting community (*in casu* Rome). It must rather be seen as a response to a wish in the local market, and therefore an analysis of find distribution and find density must always be followed up by an analysis of the find circumstances and find contexts.

8.2 Romans in Southern Scandinavia?

How much did the Romans know about the peoples living north of the Limes and the geography of the area? Scholars dealing with the ethnology of the Germanic peoples today seem to agree that the Romans in fact knew precious little about most of the many Germanic tribes mentioned in Roman literature. Of course the tribes that repeatedly came into close contact with the Romans along the Limes were known, but as soon as the Roman authors venture into descriptions of peoples living at some distance of the Limes, information tends to become less precise. There is a striking lack of consistency among the Roman authors when describing the tribal hierarchies (which tribes are part of which larger groupings of peoples) and when defining the area(s) settled by particular tribes or peoples.[8] We do not encounter the same lack of consistency, when the Romans talk about peoples they were dealing with on a regular basis. Many of the statements about the barbarians living north of the Limes are general rather than specific, and they are often presented as *topoi*: the wild Barbarian behaving and dressing in a way that is in direct opposition to how a civilized Roman would (or *ought to*) do. A curious feature is the way the amazons, who in Greek myth lived in the Black Sea area, in Roman times have moved farther away to the Baltic Sea. Still, they retain the characteristics (wild female warriors raping male neighbours) that make them a negation of culture from a Roman point of view – the same characteristics that have continued to inwoke fear and fascination among men till our days.

While there are several – often contradicting – lists of Germanic tribes and their homelands, and many more interpretations of them, there seem to be only two specific stories relating to Romans travelling north.

---

6 Horsnæs 2009.
7 Personal information Mateusz Bogucki.

8 For a collection of literary sources on the ethnography of the Nordic tribes see Lund 1993; a more recent discussion of the literary sources in Grane 2003.

8.3 Sailing the North Sea?

In the *res gestae* Augustus boasted that his fleet had sailed east from the mouth of the Rhine to the land of the Cimbrians. Other authors have described the geography of the northern lands from a maritime point of view, still there is no consensus as to how much the Romans knew about Southern Scandinavia. How far the Augustan fleet actually came in relation to modern geography has long been a debated issue.

It seems, however, that one important factor is overlooked in the discussion of the Augustan expedition, namely the context of the story. The description is a part of the *Res Gestae*,[9] boasting the deeds accomplished by the divine Augustus. It strongly indicates that the northern expedition was a unique undertaking during the reign of Augustus. And in fact the text continues to explain that no Roman had been in the land of the Cimbrians before. It is hard to tell whether all subsequent descriptions of the northern seas go back to this singular event, but it is remarkable that no later expeditions along the Frisian coast (and further?) are ever mentioned, and even more remarkable that the geographer Strabo, writing in the period of maximum Roman expansion into the area between the Rhine and the Elbe, specificly stated that the areas beyond the Elbe were unknown.[10]

It is indeed hard to imagine a fleet of Roman ships sailing along the Frisian tidal area and the notoriously dangerous west coast of Jutland. The archaeological material certainly does not support any idea of a regularly used route along the west coast of Jutland, on the contrary both coins and other Roman objects are extremely rare in western Jutland south of the Limfjord. The distribution of the Roman finds from Roman Iron Age contexts in Denmark stresses that the majority of these objects must have come by other routes. It is well known that the Romans traded with the Frisian areas, and the coin finds from the coastal area of the non-Roman parts of the Netherlands support this view. It is most likely that any redistribution of a minor number of Roman goods would have been in the hands of the local inhabitants of the tidal areas, who would have had the knowledge to navigate in these particular waters. No doubt the North Sea route had already existed for a long time, but contacts via this route were not intensified during the shortlived Roman experience in the area between the Rhine and the Elbe.

It is, however, possible that Frisian based contacts intensified during the Early Germanic Iron Age, heralding the Viking Age contacts around the North Sea.[11] The displacement of the centre of gravity of the distribution of some of the particular artefacts and context types,[12] as well as the distribution of coin types into the Elbe/Weser area and the distribution of the clipped siliquae may point in this direction.[13]

8.4 The Amber Routes

It is commonly accepted that amber was traded from the Baltic Sea to the Mediterranean long before the Roman Empire came into existence. The Amber Route is the common denominator for routes along the large European river valleys from amber rich areas at the Baltic coast to the Adriatic Sea.

Pliny states that the Germani brought the amber to the province of Pannonia,[14] and he proceeds to relate that during the reign of Nero a Roman *eques* was sent out to collect it and that the coast where it was collected was situated 600 miles from Carnuntum in

---

9 *Res Gestae* 26.2.4.
10 Strabo, *Geographiká* 7.2.4.

11 Kramer, Stoumann & Greg 2000.
12 Bemmann 2006.
13 Segschneider 2002 suggested the existence of a route from the Rhine to the outlet of the Limfjord into the North Sea in the period around AD 500, pointing out the possible landing places at Amrum, Dankirke and Degbjerg before entering into the Limfjord with the many coastal sites. Both Dankirke and Degbjerg had at that time been settled for centuries and both sites have yielded impressive finds. While Dankirke has yielded a considerable number of Roman coins it is hard to find a place in Denmark more distant from finds of Roman coins than Degbjerg! So even if the suggested route was in use c. 500 AD, there is little evidence for the previous period.
14 Pliny NH 37.43: … adfertur a Germanis in Pannoniam maxime provinciam …

Pannonia.[15] Pliny unfortunately does not provide us with more specific information on the route travelled by the Roman *eques*. Although not explicitly stated, it is commonly assumed that he travelled from a point on the Danube Limes along the river routes. Still, the passage in Pliny gives important information. It is obvious that the amber trade was normally in the hands of Germani. The Roman travelling all the way to the amber coast was clearly a first time experience, and there is no evidence that it was ever repeated.

Both the *Res Gestae* and Strabo's *Geographica* belong to the early 1st century AD, Pliny's *Natural History* were composed in the 1st century AD, and the works of Tacitus were concluded before his death in *c.* 117 AD. These are the most commonly used literary sources when discussing Roman relations with Barbaricum. But, as we have seen, few Roman coins reached Denmark that early. Few later authors provide us with detailed information on Barbaricum. When dealing with routes in Barbaricum in the first six centuries AD we therefore have to rely mainly on the archaeological material, in practise the geographical distribution of particular types.

Certainly several routes must have co-existed. The Limes may be seen as the most important highway through Europe, and the Roman towns along the Limes would have acted as centres not only of Roman culture and military installations, but also for trade. Thus the Limes may be seen as a zone of intensive interaction, rather than an Iron Curtain through Europe. This is reflected in the find patterns where a broad band along the Limes presents distinct differences in the find material from the remaining parts of Barbaricum.[16] The Amber Route is breaking out of this zone of interaction. The "classic" Amber Route from Pannonia would have started (or ended!) at Carnuntum (between modern Vienna and Bratislava), where we have several recent finds of possible Roman camps in the valley towards Mušov. Another route seems to have started at Brigetio moving northwards, passing Trenčín where a Roman inscription tells us that a unit of 855 men wintered in 179/180 AD under the command of M. Valerius Maximianus.[17]

The existence of transverse routes between the provinces of Dacia and Pannonia passing through Barbarian areas has also been suggested, based on archaeological finds.

In addition to the traditional Amber Route the existence of an Eastern or "Pontic" Route has been suggested: A route leading from the Northern Black Sea littoral, along the Dnjestr towards the Middle Vistula and further north connected the Cernachov and Sintana de Mures cultures with the Baltic.[18] This route seems to have played a minor role in 20th century research. No doubt Bolin's neglect of the eastern routes may have played a part,[19] but also the political situation in Europe following The 2nd World War, and a general lack of knowledge among western scholars of Slavic languages and consequently the archaeological literature presenting the finds from these areas, may have caused the smaller awareness of this route.

Among eastern scholars there seems to be a better understanding of the importance of the Eastern route(s).[20] According to Kulakov the Eastern Route existed in period C2-C3, and perhaps also earlier. It broke down in the late 4th century AD when the Goths started moving west as a result of the pressure imposed upon them by the Huns.[21] Kulakov is interpreting the archaeological material in light of recorded historical events, and he believed that the Eastern Route was established as a response to the 10th Legion blocking the traditional Amber Route

---

15 Pliny NH 37.45: … DC M p. fere a Carnunto Pannoniae abesse litus id Germaniae, ex quo invehitur, percognitum nuper, vivitque eques R. ad id comparandum missus ab Iuliano curante gladiatorium munus Neronis principis.

16 Hedeager 1988. This observation has been repeated by numerous scholars.

17 Tejral 1997.

18 Lind 1988, 128-129 summing up the discussion between Almgren & Nerman 1923 and Bolin 1926.

19 See for example the discussion by Lind 1988, 160-183.

20 E.g. Wladyslaw Duczko organized a seminar on the Bug River route in 2006.

21 Kulakov 2001. Although marred by misunderstanding of some of the Northern material, and somewhat jumping to the conclusions, the basic idea presented seems to hold good. Kulakov's argumentation is based on the distribution of certain artefact types, and it is supported by the distribution of for example aureus imitations.

after the end of the Marcomannic Wars.[22] This, however, seems less likely. Even if the 10th Legion controlled the traditional Amber Route, there is no reason to believe that exchanges of goods, and in this case goods wanted by the Romans, via this route were blocked.

Most scholars dealing with Roman coins in Scandinavia have stressed the importance of the routes leading through modern Poland to the mouth of the Vistula, and no matter whether the point of departure was the Danubian Limes or the Black Sea Coast the Vistula plays an enormous role because of the density and distribution of coin finds.[23] The close contacts towards the Chernachov culture centered around Kiev and the gold finds with parallels in the Danubian area are indubitable. Yet, important finds from Denmark of periods C2-C3 comprise denominations that are not common in the Vistula area, but have some parallels in the material from a zone strechting from northern Bohemia and Silesia towards Schleswig-Holstein, and 5th century finds (Danish period D) may eventually derive from the areas of the growing Germanic kingdoms of West-central Europe and/or Britain.

8.5 The distribution of Roman coins in Western Denmark

The geographical distribution of the Roman coins in Denmark is in many aspects closely comparable to the distribution of Roman objects in general, as presented in the most comprehensive study of Roman imports, *Römischer Import in Norden* in 1987.[24]

Intensive archaeological activity on the modern centres of growth and along new communication lines, much in the form of rescue excavation necessitated by the construction works, has yielded a considerable amount of new finds from settlements. Re-investigations of old find spots have in some cases proved useful. In other cases, more or less systematic detecting undertaken on private initiative have yielded unexpected finds.

The many differences between Funen and Sealand tend to hide the topographical elements that these two areas have in common. Archaeological finds have revealed a central place on the south-eastern coast of both main islands. On Funen the Gudme/Lundeborg centre and on Sealand the slightly earlier Himlingøje centre. This may be seen as an opening towards the southeast. In both cases these centres have been interpreted as acting as a filter for the import and subsequent re-distribution of foreign goods, including Roman coins and luxury articles.

It is however important to note that the filter stopped most of the imported high status objects and kept them within the elite centres. The restricted re-distribution of Roman coins is evident in the case of Gudme. No Roman coins are found on the smaller islands south of Funen, and it is striking that only a quite restricted number of denarii have been found in Funen outside Gudme, the workshop sites having yielded the largest number of these. Based on the other types of Roman imports from Denmark, Lund Hansen suggested that Himlingøje in Stevns on eastern Sealand was a particularly important centre during period B-C1b. The coin finds do not support this view unequivocally: in fact few coins have been found in connection with Himlingøje. This may be due to the Himlingøje centre being defined mainly by burials, while Roman coins are rarely found in funerary contexts. Another explanation could be that the area had already peaked before the masses of Roman coins arrived. The denarius hoards from Sealand may belong to a period where Himlingøje had already faded: without external evidence the deposition date of the denarius hoards is hard to pinpoint, but it should be kept in mind that the denarius hoard from Lærkefryd may be one of the earliest depositions on this site, where material from Early Germanic period prevails. Apart from the large denarius hoards concentrating on Sealand, the majority of the denarii from Sealand derive from workshop areas that were active at least into the Germanic Iron Age.

A central place corresponding to Himlingøje or Gudme has not been identified in Jutland. There are on the other hand a number of minor sites with finds of several Roman coins in eastern and northern

---

22 Kulakov 2001, 49.
23 Lind 1988, 136 was convinced that the denarii from Gotland came directly from the mouth of the Vistula, while he was not sure whether the denarii from Mainland Sweden and Öland might have come from the northern coast of Germany.
24 See maps in Lund Hansen 1987.

Jutland, and these areas are currently presenting the largest growth in finds of denarii from settlements.

8.6 The period of influx

The coins did not come to Denmark as a result of one or a few historical events. Rather, the majority of the Roman coins seem to have come continuously over a long period. There is clear evidence that some coins arrived and were deposited before AD 200, but the main influx of denarii probably started in the 3rd century. Late Imperial coins came in smaller numbers from the 4th century and continued to arrive into the 6th century AD. It is well known that both Greek and Roman coins are still arriving today – and some depositions of Ancient coins are very recent indeed.

In spite of the great number of denarius finds, only a lamentably low number of depositions can be dated: few burials, the weapon sacrifices, and some finds from archaeologically dated layers in settlements, notably Gudme and Lundeborg. These finds show beyond doubt that denarii were deposited throughout the period from $c.$ 200/210 AD (the Illerup sacrifice) and into the 6th century AD (the Gudme I bracteate hoard). It has not been possible to maintain the sharp division between hoards with an early composition and a Marcus Aurelius issue as end coin, and hoards with a later composition and a Commodus issue as end coin. For example the Orup Hoard should be regarded as a hoard with an "early" composition, but the end coin was a Septimius Severus issue. When comparing the chronological distributions of a number of hoards and assemblages no unambiguous line can be drawn between "early" and "late" composition, and it seems that most hoards end with a single specimen of a 3rd century denarius, no matter whether the composition is "early" or "late". We may with some caution suggest that Antonine denarii become increasingly prominent the later the assemblage was deposited. This suggestion, however, will have to be tested against a larger group of dated depositions.

The arrival of the later coins is of course provided with a *t.p.q.* by the date of production. Many of the depositions are however still somewhat later than the production date of the coins. The hoards with gold coins struck in the perod 250-336 AD is dated in the middle or later 4th century, and the Hacksilber hoards containing 4th century siliquae is normally dated $c.$ AD 500. The hoards containing 5th and early 6th century solidi may on the other hand have been deposited not considerably later than the coins.

The period of deposition of Roman coins in Denmark may thus be defined as beginning in the early 3rd century and lasting into the 6th century. A smaller number of coins have been deposited (or lost) in the period from the 6th century to present day.

8.7 An international network

Rather than believing that in each archaeological period there was one route operating the south-north (or rather the southeast-northwest) connections, we have to imagine a much more complex web of routes, along which ideas, news and goods were transferred. The physical position of the routes were of course to a large degree dictated by topographical features such as rivers, mountain barriers etc. and therefore they were unlikely to travel in straight lines. The routes were most probably controlled by local or regional aristocracies, resident in important junctions (hubs, gateway communities), from which immaterial as well as material goods were reloaded for further transport or redistributed to the less important areas.[25] Gudme seems one obvious candidate for such a position in Southern Scandinavia, as south-eastern Funen clearly had a continuous inflow of goods over a long period of time, in particular from period C2 onwards, and the goods came from different areas in Barbaricum, both east and west. Other such centres may have existed at for example Ibsker (the cluster of sites at Sorte Muld) on Bornholm and Uppåkra in southern Sweden. The networks would have been dynamic in the sense that site hierarchies and routes must have been changing continuously during the half-millenium here discussed.

---

25 Sindbæk 2007 describes the complex network theory in a Viking Age context using the expressing "hub" for the centres controlling exchange, while Bursche 2008 specifically discussing Roman coins in Barbaricum is using the expressions "port of trade" and "gateway community".

8.8 The routes to Denmark

All the Roman coins did not come along the same route, not even during the main period of interest in the present study, 200-550 AD. There are no clear differences between denarius finds from the various parts of Barbaricum. The routes taken by the denarii, from the mint in Rome to Denmark, are therefore impossible to map simply by looking at the find distributions. Studies of the Barbarian imitations of denarii, however, seem to indicate that they were produced in a number of different areas and that they travelled widely. Considering the vast distribution as well as the longevity of the denarii in Barbaricum it is possible to suggest that they circulated for a long period within Barbaricum. The route to Denmark therefore is unlikely to have been a simple one-way travel.

In the 4th century AD, when Roman coins were struck in several mints, the mintmark provides us with clear evidence of the production area. The 4th century coins from Funen in general point towards the southeast: Coins from mints in south eastern Europe dominate in the first two thirds of the 4th century, the gold medallions of the mid-4th century have a marked distribution from the area north of Danube through Poland towards Denmark, while Barbarian imitations of Roman gold coins may have come from two distinct areas: modern Ukraine and modern Hungary. It is thus possible to suggest that these artefact groups reflect contacts between the centre on Funen and two distinct areas of south-eastern Europe.

The relatively smaller number of finds of siliquae struck in the last third of the 4th century most often derive from western mints, notably Trier, but the clipping of a relatively large number of these coins seems to indicate that some of them have been engaged in exchanges crossing the Channel, and it is suggested that the late 4th century siliquae found in Denmark may have arrived *via* Britain and that they should be interpreted in light of the relations between northern Germany (and southern Jutland) and Kent in the 5th century.

Among the Late Roman solidi of the 5th-6th centuries both eastern and western (official as well as non-imperial) issues are represented, but there is also a considerable number of unidentified imitations, the provenance of which would be of outmost interest to establish. It is likely that those imitations could have been made somewhere in west-central Europe. There are clear differences between on the one hand the Late Roman solidi found in the Baltic islands (Gotland, Öland and Bornholm)[26] and on the other those found in Denmark and southern Sweden, stressing the diversity in the contact routes. The particularly great payments in gold as well as in other valuables made by the Roman emperors to for example the Huns in the 430's and 440's are not reflected at all in the coin finds from Western Denmark.

Finds of 6th century coins are extremely rare, and should be seen in relation to the isolated single finds of Byzantine type gold coins throughout Europe, as reflections of contacts towards the Frankish/Merovingian area, in a period where an eastern contact towards the Byzantine Empire seems to have been cut off.[27]

Not only did the coins come at various times and from various areas. They also came to different parts of Denmark, and the changing distribution patterns reflect the changing centres of local power. The earliest Roman coins are few, but the distribution of them is on an overall level conspicuously similar to the map of the Roman imports from period B1/2[28] – and even to areas with southern imports from the Pre-Roman Iron Age.

The denarii are found spread over most of the country, and they were clearly deposited throughout the periods C1b-D1. It is therefore difficult to conclude anything about chronological changes based on the denarius finds. When looking a the distribution maps of aurei (mainly from the 3rd century), 4th century solidi, siliquae and medallions, as well as the Barbarian imitations of gold coins, there can be no doubt that the centre at Gudme has played a pivotal role during the 4th century. There is a strong concentration of these denominations at Gudme and Lundeborg in particular, but also in other sites in Funen and to some extent in the eastern part of Jutland directed towards Funen. In spite of the large

---

26 And there are differences, although less marked, between the finds from these three islands as well.
27 Wołoszyn 2009. Unfortunately this important volume on Byzantine coins in Europe arrived too late to be considered in the present work.
28 Lund Hansen 1987, Karte 2.

scale excavations of settlement areas in the Tåstrup area west of Copenhagen, where among other things also richly furnished burials from the late 3rd and 4th century have been uncovered, the number of coin finds from Sealand is extremely low in comparison to the Gudme area. The same applies to the greater part of Jutland.

The number of 5th century coins from Denmark is considerably lower than the number of 4th century coins. Gudme still plays an important role in the 5th-6th centuries, yet the single finds of the 5th and early 6th century coins are more broadly distributed than the coins from the earlier period. The lower influx of 5th-6th century coins is reflected in other areas of north-western Barbaricum, while the wider distribution of coins from the 5th-6th centuries within Denmark must reflect changes in the local communities. Although struck in the late 4th century, it is believed that the western siliquae should be seen as part of this development.

8.9 The meaning of the Roman coins in the Danish Iron Age context

Coin use among the Barbarians was not a point of Roman interest. Except for the famous note by Tacitus about the Barbarians' preference for "old money", a note that basically serves to tell other Romans that the less civilized Barbarians did not appreciate the concept of coin-based economy, the Roman authors leave us in the dark about this. The only means to explore this issue is an analysis of the Roman coin in the local context, *in casu* the Danish finds.

There is clear evidence for a monetary economy in the Roman establishments of the Limes area, and evidence of some degree of monetarization in the zone along the Limes. But the more distant parts of Barbaricum normally only imported coins in good silver and gold. Thus the Danish Iron Age communities were never an integrated part of the Roman monetary system. Until the early 4th century practically the only coins available in Danish areas were the denarii. The denarii may have functioned as "pre-weighed silver" in a barter trade economy, but their distribution in a relatively restricted number of Late Roman and Early Germanic Iron Age sites shows that they can only have played a role in those special sites.

The 4th century coins are concentrated in Gudme and sites related to Gudme, for example the gold hoards in central Funen. The combination of toponyms related to the sacred sphere, the very large hall, the port-of-trade at Lundeborg, the enormous amounts of finds, the particular types among the finds (gold bracteates, gold foil figurines etc.), and not least the many Roman coins all mark Gudme as a so far unique site in Western Denmark. The numismatic material (the siliquae, the hoards of aurei and early solidi and the Barbarian imitations of Roman coins) indicates that south-eastern Funen had continuous relations with south-eastern Europe.

Also in the last third of the 4th to the early 6th century the finds from Funen dominate the general picture with the hoards from Elsehoved and Rynkebygård, but both here and even more explicitly in the coins found in the remaining parts of Denmark there is a prevalence of material that indicates connections to the kingdoms in central and western Europe. A very large part of these coins are reworked in various manners: the gold coins are more often than not mounted to be used as jewellery, while the silver coins may be clipped or cut, and they are found in Hacksilber hoards. The coins are relatively few and they never served as money.

As noted by Bjerg,[29] it seems that coins belonged to the sphere of the living, while other exotic finds are more common in burials. There might, however, be an error in this assumption: Many of the large detector sites have been discovered since the publication of *Römischer Import in Norden* in 1987, while the majority of the richly furnished burials were already known then. It is true that on the settlements few exotic valuables have been found. Yet, we should consider that fragments of imported glass have indeed been found on a considerable number of settlement sites (Dankirke, Lundeborg, Østervang), and even in areas without coin finds as Dejbjerg in western Jutland. In the cases of Dankirke, Østervang and Dejbjerg it is clear that the glass fragments, often very small pieces, all come from a layer of material that was cleared away after the sudden destruction by fire of a building. We may therefore assume that these types of exotica are under-represented in the archaeological material from settlements because they would normally be cleared out together with other

---

29 Bjerg 2007, 122.

movables when re-structuring a building. When not moved deliberately, for example in emergency cases, they were much more fragile – and more likely to disintegrate completely – than the sturdy silver denarii and therefore more rarely found during excavations, except when the soil is sieved. There is on the other hand no reason to believe that more coins will turn up in burials with improved excavation techniques. Burials, in particular rich burials, have always been subject to the most careful excavation, and – again – the coins are quite durable and would not have been overlooked. So it is probably fair to say that coins and other objects, whether imported from the Roman Empire or from other areas of Barbaricum, came to the same areas and to the same sites within modern Denmark, but while a number of exotic types were serviceable in the local burial ritual, this was not the case with coins. Although they make up the numerically largest number of imports, they are conspicuously absent from the burials.

No evidence supports the theory that the coins functioned as coins in a monetary economy. Base metal coins are quite rarely found, and although an analysis of the contexts of the base metal coins clearly indicates that some bronze coins were available during the Late Roman and Early Germanic Iron Ages, a very large number of the base metal coins from Denmark must be ascribed to the activity of modern collectors. This is no surprise, as it has long been recognized that the Roman bronze coins rarely travelled far from the Limes, the most important exception from the rule being the prevalence for large Roman base metal coins as amulets in the West Balt culture. Yet, it is likely that the silver and gold coins may in some cases have been regarded as pre-weighed metal in a barter trade system. The coins found in connection with Hacksilber hoards, as well as examples of cut solidi, are clear indications that these coins were treated as metal, rather than as a particular type of object.

It has often been assumed that the denarii were *the* main supply of silver for a local production of jewellery and dress ornaments, yet the only – preliminary – analysis of the silver from denarii and local silver objects including ingots from a Danish site has shown no 1:1 relationship in the composition of the metal. No denarii but a few siliquae have been found along with the fragments of Roman as well as local objects in the Hacksilber hoards from the early 6th century. Seeing that at least *some* denarii were available into the 6th century, we may speculate whether the lack of denarii in Hacksilber hoards should indicate that denarii were considered not suitable as raw material?

The majority of the gold coins were reworked into pendants, and the evidence from the few coins found in funerary contexts clearly indicates that coins were used as jewellery, often as a quite prominent element of the necklace. The early coins were normally pierced from the obverse, but the hole is not always positioned above the head of the portrait. There is a change in the way of reworking coins into jewellery taking place probably in the early 4th century. After that period the coins are normally mounted with a loop eye, and during the 5th century mountings become more elaborate. The loops on the 5th century coins are invariably positioned above the head of the Imperial portrait stressing the importance of the image. In this way the coin was worn as a piece of jewellery comparable to the gold bracteates of the Early Germanic Iron Age, and these two artefact types seem to have been interchangeable in their use within the Nordic societies.

The greater part of the material here studied derives from metal detector surveys, and the coins are found bereaved of their original archaeological context. Therefore the deposition date can only be ascertained for a minority of the finds. Among the Roman coins found in archaeologically dated contexts there is a conspicuous number of base metal coins in Viking Age or later contexts, and this material is a clear warning against mechanical interpretations drawn from uncommented coin lists based on the date of issue.

Iron Age Denmark should be defined as peripheral in relation to the Roman Empire: In spite of the fact that the Roman coins were produced within the Empire, evidence for direct contact between the inhabitants of the two areas is hardly to be found in the numismatic material. On the contrary the Danish area seems to have been well integrated into a complicated network of connections within the so-called Barbarian areas. This is particularly visible in the Late Imperial Period where not only the coins themselves were produced in a variety of mints, but where also the secondary reworking of the coins provide us with interesting information of this network.

Indices

362 sites with Roman coins, in geographical order

Site no.	Sb	Name	Pages
010103	156	Esrum	166
010105	90	Græsted	117, 121
010301	15	Hillerød	-
010301	122	Fredensborg	166
010304	41	Egholm-Nord	64, 117
010306	1	Lærkefryd	107-8, 129, 130, 185
010306	34	Sperrestrup Mose	42, 83-4
010306	106	Sperrestrup	42, 83-4
010312	36	Hørup	42-3, 108, 116-7, 135, 140-1, 161, 167, 169-70
010410	142	Hørsholm, Møllevej	163
010504	88	Meløse, Gamle Tofter	116, 171
010505	71	Vangbækgård	-
010507	27	Jernedegård, Sigerslevøster	-
010601	87	Farum	165, 171
010602	115	Søtoftegård	164
020102	18	Birkede Mose	84, 122
020103	16	Østervang	44, 84, 107-9, 117, 129, 134-5, 188
020105	36	Ellebækgård	44, 108, 117
020201	44	Borupgård Gymnasium	-
020202		Vridsløselille Prison	43, 117
020202		Brøndbyøster, Kirkebjerg Allé	-
020202	24	Avedøre, Grænsevej	43
020203	23	Brøndbyvester Præstegård	-
020204	10	Vissinge Vest 2	43, 117
020205	19	Hyldager, Kongsholmsparken	43, 117
020208	29	Ishøj	43, 117
020209	28	Ledøje, Hellerne	43, 80, 84, 112, 125, 129-30
020209	34	Gersager	80, 117
020211	59	Katrinebjerg	-
020213	20	Torstorp Vesterby	58, 60, 66, 70-1, 140-1, 169-70
020213	41	Brøndsager	57-8, 66, 70-1, 146, 148-9, 158
020215	25	Vallensbæk Nordmark	43, 117
020216	184	Kirke Værløse	-

Site no.	Sb	Name	Pages
020216	185	Søndersø	-
020302		Gentofte, manor at Hvidøre	92
020302	120	Hellerup, Sundvænget	154
020303		Bagsværd Hoard	41, 80-1, 83-4, 125, 129-30
020303	48	Gladsakse Kirke	-
020303	76	Bagsværd	-
020306		Copenhagen, near H.C. Ørstedværket	-
020306		Copenhagen, Frihavn	-
020306		Copenhagen, Søerne, Planetariet	166
020306		Copenhagen, "behind Carlsberg"	-
020306		Copenhagen, Amaliegade,	165
020306	208	Christiania	-
020306	410	Husum, Slotsfruens Vænge	92, 154
020306	411	Copenhagen, Nørrevoldgade	166
020306	412	Brønshøj	44, 117
020306	413	Frederiksberg Bredegade	171
020307		Virum, Kaplevej 46	-
020307	202	Lyngby, Marienborg	-
020308		Rødovre, Grøntofte Allé	-
020310	410	Ørholm	-
020400		Roskilde, area	-
020402	22	Glim	43, 117
020402	24	Glim	43, 117
020402	41	Glim, east	43, 117
020402	43	Øm-Gammeltoft	43, 117
020409	18	Højbjerggård	43, 117
020410		Roskilde, Ternevej	-
020502	8	Gammel Havdrup	-
020510	28	Kirsebærhaven	44, 109-10, 118
020510	31	Lisagergård	118
020510	37	Ejrebækgård	44, 109-10, 118
020512	4	Stålmosegård, Vindinge	43, 58, 60, 65-6, 70, 168
020601		Lejre	43, 118,
020601	106	Ledreborg	43, 118
020601	115	Lejre	43, 118, 122

191

Crossing boundaries

Site no.	Sb	Name	Pages
020601	143	Lejre, Hestebjerggård	-
020603	80	Lindholm 2	43, 118
020605	55	Kirke Hyllinge/Stensgård	116, 162
020611	174	Vårkærgård east, Rye	116, 118
030000		Holbæk area	171
030106		Fugledegård, Tissø	116, 162, 167
030106		Tissø	-
030109	251	Udby	-
030110	215	Melbygård	-
030202		Selchausdal	43, 118, 192
030205	59	Råmose Hoard	15, 41-2, 76-8, 80, 84, 121, 123-5, 128-30, 132-3
030211		Laurvig, Ruds Vedby	46, 118
030405		'Holtegård', Højby west	-
030405	100	Nyrup, Højby south	46, 60, 70, 140
030407		Nykøbing Sjælland	-
030706		Jyderup, at Humlevej	-
030708		Mørkøv parish	46, 84
030709	137	Breidablik, Bybjerg, Orø	-
030710		Bennebo Mark	46, 60, 66-7, 70
040101	44	Engelsborg, Alsted	45, 115, 140-1, 172, 180
040108		Munke-Bjergby	-
040112	445	Assentorp, Stenlille	45, 92, 154
040203	2	Bringstrup	44, 63, 118
040205	5	Høsten Torp	45, 86-7, 115, 140-3, 169, 172
040206		Skee-Tåstrup	45, 118
040207		Haslev	-
040210		Kværkeby parish	45, 92, 147
040211	17	Nordrup	45, 60, 67, 70
040213	64	Cirkelhusene, Ringsted	44, 118
040213	69	Gl. Kærup	44-5, 110, 118
040214	25	Englerup, Sigersted	63
040223		Gettehøj/Jettehøj	90
040301	101	Neble	45, 110, 118
040301	105	Neble	45, 46, 110, 118
040302		Asbjergård	45, 118
040308		Storebælt (off Korsør)	-
040308	43	Storebælt (in sand from)	-
040312	58	Rollerup, Valdemarskilde Mark	45, 156
040313		Idagård	46, 110, 118
040506	4	Haldagerlille parish	45, 92, 147
040509	71	Klinteby	46, 92, 146
050103	16	Slimminge Mark	44-5, 118
050104		Herfølge	44, 92, 154
050104	58	Gunnerupgård Mark	44, 61, 70

Site no.	Sb	Name	Pages
050105		Himlingøje parish, 'old smithy'	
050105	25	Nytofte, Himlingøje	44
050105	29	Himlingøje	44, 59-60, 66, 70, 167
050110	16	St. Tårnby	44, 118
050111	36	Toftegård, Valløby	44, 110, 118
050206	215	Langebæk, Rødesbjergsvej	-
050210	75	Skibinge	-
050212	27	Skovgårde	46, 59-60, 66, 70, 167
050213	134	Knudshoved, Vordingborg	-
050302		Fakse parish	46, 92
050302	36	Tyrstrup III, Fakse	46, 118
050407	32	Søndergård, Brandelev	118
050503	17	Store-Lind	92, 146
050505	163	Færgegården, Lilledamme	46, 92, 155
050507		Magleby parish	46
050600		Stevns	118
050601	15	"Bakkely"	-
050604	51	Gjorslev	92, 147
050606	16	Rødvigsvej	114, 118
050610		Bjælkerup	44, 118
050613	8	Varpelev parish	44, 60-1, 66, 70-1, 146, 158, 170
050701	7	Assenhøj	45, 118
050704	48	Bøgevej, Glumsø	-
050707		Lille Næstved	14, 61
050707	29	Næstved, Farvergade	46, 110, 114, 118
050707	53	Næstved, Kompagnistræde	46, 146, 159
050707	129	Næstved, Riddergade	-
050711	26	Orup	36, 41, 45, 79-80, 84, 125-5, 129-33, 180
070000		Falster	46, 118, 121
070110	65	Strangegården, Sundby	46-7, 92, 154
070207		Ejegod, Nykøbing F	-
070309		Holeby Kirke	162
070309		Holeby Station	-
070321	19	Erikstrup	47, 84-5
070403		Halsted	-
070403	37	Kohave	47, 118, 122-3
070403	46	Sæbyholm, Halsted	-
070405	153	Store Tvedegård	-
070408	27	Nakskov, Vejlebrogade	-
070512		Søllested	47, 118
080102	14	Sjelleberg	-
080105		Kerteminde Nordstrand	-
080108	80	Midskov Skov	49, 92, 155
080112	137	Baes Banke east	111, 118

192

Indices

Site no.	Sb	Name	Pages
080201	9	Assens	50
080201	22	Assens (field at)	50
080301	3	Allese	49, 92, 149
080404	30	Dalum Klosterruin	50, 162
080405	35	Fangel parish	49-50, 81, 84
080406	1	Vimose	49, 71, 75, 161
080406	18	Næsby, Ågade	49, 92, 155
080407	206	Odense, Hunderupgade	50
080407	239	Odense Kanal	-
080409	51	Troelsegård Syd	49, 111, 118
080506	19	Roerslev/Rorslev	49, 118
080604	49	Gamby	49, 92, 147
080609	55	Moderup	50, 118
080703	63	Broskov/Åbanken	92, 149
080705	35	Fjeldsted parish	49, 70
080708		Gelsted parish	-
080710		Husby, Storegade	-
080710	37	Wedellsborg	50, 118
080712	62	Skrillinge Mark	49, 64, 70, 118
080717	19	Rørup, Vends herred	49, 92, 147
080803	8	Holmeløkken, Fraugdegård	64, 70
080803	153	Fraugde	116, 147
080806	18	Nørre Søby	48, 93, 147
080809	7	Seden Syd	48-9, 110-1, 119, 135
080810	73	Horsemosegaard	111, 119
080811	98	Lundsgård/Toruplund	48, 110-1, 119, 135, 168-9
090101	16	Nøddekroggård	111, 119
090104		Gudme parish	14, 34, 36, 38-9, 47, 49, 80, 83, 86, 88-90, 94-101, 105, 110, 115-6, 121, 125, 129-30, 133, 135-6, 138-43, 145-8, 154, 157-8, 161, 167-70, 172, 180-1
090105		Lundeborg, Hesselager parish	14, 21, 34, 38, 47, 89, 94, 100-105, 110-14, 116, 124-5, 133-6, 138, 140-1, 143, 146, 157, 161, 180-1, 185-88
090107	36	Grønneskovs Skole	-
090107	40	Broholm	14, 37, 89, 95, 105, 146, 154
090107	85	Elsehoved	88-90, 95, 105, 154, 158, 170, 181, 188
090107	170	Broholm	119
090108	7	Rynkebygård	47, 88-9, 154, 158, 170, 181, 188
090108	11	Bregentved	47, 49, 62, 65-6, 69-70, 168

Site no.	Sb	Name	Pages
090108	13	Boltinggård Skov	37, 47, 87-90, 145, 147, 157-8, 170, 181
090108	19	Brangstrup	37, 47, 63, 88-90, 145, 147, 149, 157-8, 167, 169-70, 181
090108	125	Ringe	47, 89, 93, 147
090108	160	Ringe Golfbane	48, 111, 119
090403	34	Hågerup	49, 62, 64, 69-70
090411	1	Sallinge	48, 93, 155
090411	74	Skelbo Lykkenssæde	119
090416	36	Tange	48, 93, 149
090426		Skerninggård	-
090506	7	Kværndrup	48, 93, 111, 149
090506	32	Trunderup	48, 93, 149-50
090506	51	Falle Mølle	48, 111, 119
090507	78	Vornæs Skov	49, 93, 149
090510		Nørremarken	-
090510	117	Øster Åby	84-5
090511	22	Hundtofte	48, 93, 147
090513		Svendborg, Sørup Kirkevej	166
090513	169	Svendborg, Kobberbæksvej	119
090601	78	Rabenslyst Nordøst, Avnslev	49, 119
090605	10	Rørbæk	49, 64, 70, 104, 146
090605	55	Flødstrup parish	50, 119
090610	152	Nyborg, Rævebakkevej	50, 140
090611	71	Slipshavn	49, 90, 146, 158
090618	39	Ørbæk parish	49, 93, 147
090619	4	Årslev	48, 63, 65-6, 69-71, 146, 148, 158
100000		Jyske hede	-
100106	183	Vester Mellerup	53, 111, 119
100111	20	Stenum	53, 119
100203	383	Hjallerup, Dronninglund	53, 84-6
100205	164	Stentinget, Klokkerholm	53, 111, 119
100214	150	Ejstrup, Volstrup	53, 111-12, 119
100215	50	Ørum parish	53, 119
100303	85	Apholm	50, 90
100304		Frederikshavn, area	-
100406	77	Torpet	52-3, 112, 119
100406	78	Lille Norge	53, 112, 119, 123,
100605		Hjørring	53, 119
100606		Hirtshals	-
100612	77	Gaarestrup	53, 119
100618	92	Ugilt	53, 119
100705	99	Lerup Kirke, south of	119
100707	96	Overgård	52, 119
110301	206	Gammel Råstrup	-
110414		Bjørndrup Stand	-

193

Crossing boundaries

Site no.	Sb	Name	Pages
110605	88	Ginderup	50, 52, 105-7, 121, 123-5, 129-30, 132, 134, 146, 157, 180
110612	419	Vestervig	52, 112, 119, 146, 157
120108		Aalborg, area	52, 164
120108	67	Kirkebakken, Nørre Tranders	57, 119
120113		Sønder Tranders Kirke	51-2, 162
120201	54	"Illerknoppen", Kaldalgård	119
120312		Ejstrup, St. Brøndum	54, 119, 125
120504	16	Oddershøjgård, Drastrup	51-2
120506	56	Aalborg, Bejsebakken/Skelagervej	51-2, 112, 119
120506	64	Aalborg, Bejsebakken/Stolpedalsvej	51-2, 112, 119
120508	51	Kærgård/Bækgård	112, 116, 120, 171
120508	54	Mellemholm	51, 112, 116, 140
120511	144	Sønderholm northeast	51, 112, 120
120607	14	Hvorup Nymark,	52, 120
120608	8	Lindholm Høje, Nørresundby	112, 120
120608	11	Lindholm Høje, Nørresundby	52, 112, 120
120707	67	Malle Langhøj south	53, 113, 120, 135
120814	152	Års mark	50, 90-1
130100		Limfjorden, 'close to'	-
130110	106	Toftum, Mønsted s.	54, 113, 120
130114	147-8	Kvosted	54, 94, 113, 116, 120, 135, 161
130606	39	Tangeværket	-
130702		Gudenåen, Bjerringbro	54, 120
130815		Viborg, area	14, 54, 179
130815	348	Viborg, St. Villads Church	162, 171
130815	349	Viborg	163
130816	157	Hjarbæk Strand	54, 120
140108		Grenå	-
140108	67	Grenå	54, 120
140309	62	Voldum	-
140313		Kinbjerg	14-5, 61, 93, 155
140313	25	Ølst	-
140509		Eeg	93, 155
140601		Jørgensminde	166
140704		Hvornum Kær	50, 54, 81-4, 125, 129-30
140706		Hou	93
140908		Randers, Middelgade/Tårngade	-
140908	104	Randers	-
141006	57	Stavnsager (Moeskær)	51, 116
141011	70	Ryomgård Skov	54-5, 120
141013		Blindmosevej	-
141103		Hjortshøj	93, 150-53

Site no.	Sb	Name	Pages
141109	188	Thorsager	39
150210		Rathlousdal	55, 120
150309	55	Risskov, Toftefaldet	-
150311		Århus, Skolebakken	-
150311	174	Århus, Helgolandsgade	-
150406	36	Testrup Teglværk, Mårslet	55, 82-4, 129-30
150407		Constantinsborg	-
150409		Tranbjerg	94, 113, 120
160115	198/199	Katrinelund	36, 54-5, 113, 120, 125
160202		Blegind	-
160203		Ry, Klostervej 81	120
160203	216	Simgårdsmark, Sim	55, 120
160208	141	Illerup	34, 50-1, 54, 67, 71-2, 75, 86, 124-5, 130, 134-5, 137-8, 161, 180, 186
160411	104	Hem Mark	120
160507		Fredens Hjem	55, 120
160514		"Markedsplads", Hovedgaard St.	-
170102		Barrit/Rosenvold	-
170202	61	Eltang	93, 155
170203	5	Ejstrup Mark	91, 170
170203	28	Ejstrup, Harte	120
170204		Herslev parish	-
170205		Kolding, "Godset" (ex-train station)	-
170205		Kolding	164
170205		Kolding Nørremark	120
170205		Kolding	-
170210		Kirstinelyst	-
170303		Fredericia, Kongens Have	-
170503		Grøndalshus	-
170504		Between Fredericia and Pjedsted	93, 155
170704		Sønder Stenderup, Brusk herred(?)	93
170704	153	Seljumshave	93, 147-8
170802		Harrildsgård	-
170816		Vester parish	-
170818		Kollemorten	-
170904		Jelling	120
170908		Frederikshåb	94, 152
180106		Øster Herborg	-
180206	143	Ryde Mølle	54, 113, 116, 120, 171
180320		Vildbjerg, Hammerum herred	-
180404	10	Sdr. Haurvig, Holmslands Klit	39, 56
180404	18	Nr. Haurvig (south of), Holmslands Klit	56, 120
180704	355	Gudum	-

Indices

Site no.	Sb	Name	Pages
180902		Engbjerg	-
190105		Jordrup	91, 170
190403	134	Kalvslund Kirke, south of	-
190406		Ribe	56
190407	8	Skanet Bro, Øster Vedsted	114, 120
190409	50	Ribe, Art Museum	116, 171
190409	50	Ribe, Post Office	116
190409	77	Ribe, Gasværksgrunden	162
190411	19	Dankirke, Vester Vedsted	21, 36, 50, 106-7, 114, 116, 120, 121, 125, 129-30, 162, 180, 183, 188
190411	26	Ulhøj, Vester Vedsted, north of	55, 114, 120
190411	127	Okholm, Vester Vedsted	51, 116
190502		Gjesting, northeast of town	94
190503		Esbjerg, Veldbæk	-
190503		Esbjerg, Vognsbølparken	-
190506		Hjerting	-
190507	117	Sjelborg Strand	-
190508		Kikkebjerg, Nordby, northwest of	-
190511	74	Sneumgård	-
190514		Lifstrup	-
190604	304	Vorbasse parish	-
190706		Lunde	94, 148
190708		Nymindegab	-

Site no.	Sb	Name	Pages
190712	90	Varde/Søndervarde, Åvænget	163
200205		Magstrup	55, 120
200205	38	Simmersted mose	50, 86-7, 115, 140-3, 172
200206	215	Bæk	63, 70
200208	0	Skrydstrup	-
200302	19	Ejsbøl sø	51, 55, 71, 74-5, 135-6, 138, 146, 161, 168-9
200507	60	Stepping	94, 155
210103	4	Hviding	64
210103	107	Gl. Hviding	114
210103	109	Gl. Hviding	56, 114, 120
210204		Højer	166
220102		Volmerstoft	55, 120
220106		Sønderhave	-
220107		Kliplev	164
220108		Kværs	165
220205		Åbenrå, area	-
230205	214	Bro (Brovold)	-
230304	30	Nydam	34, 50-1, 55, 71-4, 125, 130, 134, 137
- no.		In bus(!) between Silkeborg and Ans	-
- no.		Randers/Aalborg area	-
- no.		Said to be from Tissø	-

Indices

362 sites with Roman coins, in alphabetical order

Site no.	Sb	Name	Pages
080301	3	Allese	49, 92, 149
100303	85	Apholm	50, 90
040302		Asbjergård	45, 118
050701	7	Assenhøj	45, 118
080201	9	Assens	50
080201	22	Assens (field at)	50
040112	445	Assentorp, Stenlille	45, 92, 154
020202	24	Avedøre, Grænsevej	43
080112	137	Baes Banke east	111, 118
020303	76	Bagsværd	-
020303		Bagsværd Hoard	41, 80-1, 83-4, 125, 129-30
050601	15	"Bakkely"	-
170102		Barrit/Rosenvold	-
030710		Bennebo Mark	46, 60, 66-7, 70
170504		Between Fredericia and Pjedsted	93, 155
020102	18	Birkede Mose	84, 122
050610		Bjælkerup	44, 118
110414		Bjørndrup Stand	-
160202		Blegind	-
141013		Blindmosevej	-
090108	13	Boltinggård Skov	37, 47, 87-90, 145, 147, 157-8, 170, 181
020201	44	Borupgård Gymnasium	-
090108	19	Brangstrup	37, 47, 63, 88-90, 145, 147, 149, 157-8, 167, 169-70, 181
090108	11	Bregentved	47, 49, 62, 65-6, 69-70, 168
030709	137	Breidablik, Bybjerg, Orø	-
040203	2	Bringstrup	44, 63, 118
230205	214	Bro (Brovold)	-
090107	40	Broholm	14, 37, 89, 95, 105, 146, 154
090107	170	Broholm	119
080703	63	Broskov/Åbanken	92, 149
020203	23	Brøndbyvester Præstegård	-
020202		Brøndbyøster, Kirkebjerg Allé	-

Site no.	Sb	Name	Pages
020213	41	Brøndsager	57-8, 66, 70-1, 146, 148-9, 158
020306	412	Brønshøj	44, 117
200206	215	Bæk	63, 70
050704	48	Bøgevej, Glumsø	-
020306	208	Christiania	-
040213	64	Cirkelhusene, Ringsted	44, 118
150407		Constantinsborg	-
020306		Copenhagen, Amaliegade,	165
020306		Copenhagen, "behind Carlsberg"	-
020306	413	Copenhagen, Frederiksberg Bredegade 1	
020306		Copenhagen, Frihavn	-
020306		Copenhagen, near H.C. Ørsted-værket	-
020306	411	Copenhagen, Nørrevoldgade	166
020306		Copenhagen, Søerne, Planetariet	166
080404	30	Dalum Klosterruin	50, 162
190411	19	Dankirke, Vester Vedsted	21, 36, 50, 106-7, 114, 116, 120, 121, 125, 129-30, 162, 180, 183, 188
140509		Eeg	93, 155
010304	41	Egholm-Nord	64, 117
070207		Ejegod, Nykøbing F	-
020510	37	Ejrebækgård	44, 109-10, 118
200302	19	Ejsbøl sø	51, 55, 71, 74-5, 135-6, 138, 146, 161, 168-9
170203	5	Ejstrup Mark	91, 170
170203	28	Ejstrup, Harte	120
120312		Ejstrup, St. Brøndum	54, 119, 125
100214	150	Ejstrup, Volstrup	53, 111-12, 119
090107	85	Elsehoved	88-90, 95, 105, 154, 158, 170, 181, 188
020105	36	Ellebækgård	44, 108, 117
170202	61	Eltang	93, 155
180902		Engbjerg	-
040101	44	Engelsborg, Alsted	45, 115, 140-1, 172, 180

197

Crossing boundaries

Site no.	Sb	Name	Pages
040214	25	Englerup, Sigersted	63
070321	19	Erikstrup	47, 84-5
190503		Esbjerg, Veldbæk	-
190503		Esbjerg, Vognsbølparken	-
010103	156	Esrum	166
050302		Fakse parish	46, 92
090506	51	Falle Mølle	48, 111, 119
070000		Falster	46, 118, 121
080405	35	Fangel parish	49-50, 81, 84
010601	87	Farum	165, 171
080705	35	Fjeldsted parish	49, 70
090605	55	Flødstrup parish	50, 119
080803	153	Fraugde	116, 147
160507		Fredens Hjem	55, 120
010301	122	Fredensborg	166
170303		Fredericia, Kongens Have	-
020306	413	Frederiksberg Bredegade	171
100304		Frederikshavn, area	-
170908		Frederikshåb	94, 152
030106		Fugledegård, Tissø	116, 162, 167
050505	163	Færgegården, Lilledamme	46, 92, 155
080604	49	Gamby	49, 92, 147
020502	8	Gammel Havdrup	-
110301	206	Gammel Råstrup	-
210103	107	Gl. Hviding	114
210103	109	Gl. Hviding	56, 114, 120
040213	69	Gl. Kærup	44-5, 110, 118
080708		Gelsted parish	-
020302		Gentofte, manor at Hvidøre	92
020209	34	Gersager	80, 117
040223		Gettehøj/Jettehøj	90
110605	88	Ginderup	50, 52, 105-7, 121, 123-5, 129-30, 132, 134, 146, 157, 180
190502		Gjesting, northeast of town	94
050604	51	Gjorslev	92, 147
020303	48	Gladsakse Kirke	-
020402	22	Glim	43, 117
020402	24	Glim	43, 117
020402	41	Glim, east	43, 117
140108		Grenå	-
140108	67	Grenå	54, 120
010105	90	Græsted	117, 121
170503		Grøndalshus	-
090107	36	Grønneskovs Skole	-
130702		Gudenåen, Bjerringbro	54, 120

Site no.	Sb	Name	Pages
090104		Gudme parish	14, 34, 36, 38-9, 47, 49, 80, 83, 86, 88-90, 94-101, 105, 110, 115-6, 121, 125, 129-30, 133, 135-6, 138-43, 145-8, 154, 157-8, 161, 167-70, 172, 180-1
180704	355	Gudum	-
050104	58	Gunnerupgård Mark	44, 61, 70
100612	77	Gaarestrup	53, 119
040506	4	Haldagerlille parish	45, 92, 147
070403		Halsted	-
170802		Harrildsgård	-
040207		Haslev	-
020302	120	Hellerup, Sundvænget	154
160411	104	Hem Mark	120
050104		Herfølge	44, 92, 154
170204		Herslev parish	-
050105	29	Himlingøje	44, 59-60, 66, 70, 167
050105		Himlingøje parish, "old smithy"	
010301	15	Hillerød	-
100606		Hirtshals	-
100203	383	Hjallerup, Dronninglund	53, 84-6
130816	157	Hjarbæk Strand	54, 120
190506		Hjerting	-
141103		Hjortshøj	93, 150-53
100605		Hjørring	53, 119
030000		Holbæk area	171
070309		Holeby Kirke	162
070309		Holeby Station	-
080803	8	Holmeløkken, Fraugdegård	64, 70
030405		"Holtegård", Højby west	-
080810	73	Horsemosegaard	111, 119
140706		Hou	93
090511	22	Hundtofte	48, 93, 147
080710		Husby, Storegade	-
020306	410	Husum, Slotsfruens Vænge	92, 154
210103	4	Hviding	64
140704		Hvornum Kær	50, 54, 81-4, 125, 129-30
120607	14	Hvorup Nymark	52, 120
020205	19	Hyldager, Kongsholmsparken	43, 117
020409	18	Højbjerggård	43, 117
210204		Højer	166
010312	36	Hørup	42-3, 108, 116-7, 135, 140-1, 161, 167, 169-70
010410	142	Hørsholm, Møllevej	163

Indices

Site no.	Sb	Name	Pages
040205	5	Høsten Torp	45, 86-7, 115, 140-3, 169, 172
090403	34	Hågerup	49, 62, 64, 69-70
040313		Idagård	46, 110, 118
120201	54	"Illerknoppen", Kaldalgård	119
160208	141	Illerup	34, 50-1, 54, 67, 71-2, 75, 86, 124-5, 130, 134-5, 137-8, 161, 180, 186
020208	29	Ishøj	43, 117
170904		Jelling	120
010507	27	Jernedegård, Sigerslevøster	-
190105		Jordrup	91, 170
030706		Jyderup, at Humlevej	-
100000		Jyske hede	-
140601		Jørgensminde	166
190403	134	Kalvslund Kirke, south of	-
020211	59	Katrinebjerg	-
160115	198/199	Katrinelund	36, 54-5, 113, 120, 125
080105		Kerteminde Nordstrand	-
190508		Kikkebjerg, Nordby, northwest of	-
140313		Kinbjerg	14-5, 61, 93, 155
020605	55	Kirke Hyllinge/Stensgård	116, 162
020216	184	Kirke Værløse	-
120108	67	Kirkebakken, Nørre Tranders	57, 119
020510	28	Kirsebærhaven	44, 109-10, 118
170210		Kirstinelyst	-
040509	71	Klinteby	46, 92, 146
220107		Kliplev	164
050213	134	Knudshoved, Vordingborg	-
070403	37	Kohave	47, 118, 122-3
170205		Kolding	164
170205		Kolding Nørremark	120
170205		Kolding, "Godset" (ex-train station)	-
170205		Kolding	-
170818		Kollemorten	-
130114	147-8	Kvosted	54, 94, 113, 116, 120, 135, 161
040210		Kværkeby parish	45, 92, 147
090506	7	Kværndrup	48, 93, 111, 149
220108		Kværs	165
120508	51	Kærgård/Bækgård	112, 116, 120, 171
050206	215	Langebæk, Rødesbjergsvej	-
030211		Laurvig, Ruds Vedby	46, 118
020601	106	Ledreborg	43, 118
020209	28	Ledøje, Hellerne	43, 80, 84, 112, 125, 129-30
020601		Lejre	43, 118

Site no.	Sb	Name	Pages
020601	115	Lejre	43, 118, 122
020601	143	Lejre, Hestebjerggård	-
100705	99	Lerup Kirke, south of	119
190514		Lifstrup	-
100406	78	Lille Norge	53, 112, 119, 123
050707		Lille Næstved	14, 61
130100		Limfjorden, "close to"	-
120608	8	Lindholm Høje, Nørresundby	112, 120
120608	11	Lindholm Høje, Nørresundby	52, 112, 120
020603	80	Lindholm 2	43, 118
020510	31	Lisagergård	118
190706		Lunde	94, 148
090105		Lundeborg, Hesselager parish	14, 21, 34, 38, 47, 89, 94, 100-105, 110-14, 116, 124-5, 133-6, 138, 140-1, 143, 146, 157, 161, 180-1, 185-88
080811	98	Lundsgård/Toruplund	48, 110-1, 119, 135, 168-9
020307	202	Lyngby, Marienborg	-
010306	1	Lærkefryd	107-8, 129, 130, 185
050507		Magleby parish	46
200205		Magstrup	55, 120
120707	67	Malle Langhøj south	53, 113, 120, 135
160514		"Markedsplads", Hovedgaard St.	-
030110	215	Melbygård	-
120508	54	Mellemholm	51, 112, 116, 140
010504	88	Meløse, Gamle Tofter	116, 171
080108	80	Midskov Skov	49, 92, 155
080609	55	Moderup	50, 118
040108		Munke-Bjergby	-
030708		Mørkøv parish	46, 84
070408	27	Nakskov, Vejlebrogade	-
040301	101	Neble	45, 110, 118
040301	105	Neble	45, 46, 110, 118
040211	17	Nordrup	45, 60, 67, 70
090610	152	Nyborg, Rævebakkevej	50, 140
230304	30	Nydam	34, 50-1, 55, 71-4, 125, 130, 134, 137
030407		Nykøbing Sjælland	-
190708		Nymindegab	-
030405	100	Nyrup, Højby south	46, 60, 70, 140
050105	25	Nytofte, Himlingøje	44
080406	18	Næsby, Ågade	49, 92, 155
050707	29	Næstved, Farvergade	46, 110, 114, 118
050707	53	Næstved, Kompagnistræde	46, 146, 159
050707	129	Næstved, Riddergade	-
090101	16	Nøddekroggård	111, 119

199

Crossing boundaries

Site no.	Sb	Name	Pages
180404	18	Nr. Haurvig (south of), Holmslands Klit	56, 120
080806	18	Nørre Søby	48, 93, 147
090510		Nørremarken	-
120504	16	Oddershøjgård, Drastrup	51-2
080407	206	Odense, Hunderupgade	50
080407	239	Odense Kanal	-
190411	127	Okholm, Vester Vedsted	51, 116
050711	26	Orup	36, 41, 45, 79-80, 84, 125-5, 129-33, 180
100707	96	Overgård	52, 119
090601	78	Rabenslyst Nordøst, Avnslev	46, 119
140908	104	Randers	-
140908		Randers, Middelgade/Tårngade	-
150210		Rathlousdal	55, 120
190406		Ribe	56
190409	50	Ribe, Art Museum	116, 171
190409	77	Ribe, Gasværksgrunden	162
190409	50	Ribe, Post Office	116
090108	125	Ringe	47, 89, 93, 147
090108	160	Ringe Golfbane	48, 111, 119
150309	55	Risskov, Toftefaldet	-
080506	19	Roerslev/Rorslev	49, 118
040312	58	Rollerup, Valdemarskilde Mark	45, 156
020400		Roskilde, area	-
020410		Roskilde, Ternevej	-
160203		Ry, Klostervej 81	120
180206	143	Ryde Mølle	54, 113, 116, 120, 171
090108	7	Rynkebygård	47, 88-9, 154, 158, 170, 181, 188
141011	70	Ryomgård Skov	54-5, 120
020308		Rødovre, Grøntofte Allé	-
050606	16	Rødvigsvej	114, 118
090605	10	Rørbæk	49, 64, 70, 104, 146
080717	19	Rørup, Vends herred	49, 92, 147
030205	59	Råmose Hoard	15, 41-2, 76-8, 80, 84, 121, 123-5, 128-30, 132-3
090411	1	Sallinge	48, 93, 155
080809	7	Seden Syd	48-9, 110-1, 119, 135
030202		Selchausdal	43, 118, 192
170704	153	Seljumshave	93, 147-8
160203	216	Simgårdsmark, Sim	55, 120
200205	38	Simmersted mose	50, 86-7, 115, 140-3, 172
190507	117	Sjelborg Strand	-
080102	14	Sjelleberg	-

Site no.	Sb	Name	Pages
190407	8	Skanet Bro, Øster Vedsted	114, 120
040206		Skee-Tåstrup	45, 118
090411	74	Skelbo Lykkenssæde	119
090426		Skerninggård	-
050210	75	Skibinge	-
050212	27	Skovgårde	46, 59-60, 66, 70, 167
080712	62	Skrillinge Mark	49, 64, 70, 118
200208	0	Skrydstrup	-
050103	16	Slimminge Mark	44-5, 118
090611	71	Slipshavn	49, 90, 146, 158
190511	74	Sneumgård	-
010306	106	Sperrestrup	42, 83-4
010306	34	Sperrestrup Mose	42, 83-4
141006	57	Stavnsager/Moeskær	51, 116
100205	164	Stentinget, Klokkerholm	53, 111, 119
100111	20	Stenum	53, 119
200507	60	Stepping	94, 155
050600		Stevns	118
050503	17	Store-Lind	92, 146
070405	153	Store Tvedegård	-
050110	16	St. Tårnby	44, 118
040308	43	Storebælt (in sand from)	-
040308		Storebælt (off Korsør)	-
070110	65	Strangegården, Sundby	46-7, 92, 154
020512	4	Stålmosegård, Vindinge	43, 58, 60, 65-6, 70, 168
090513	169	Svendborg, Kobberbæksvej	119
090513		Svendborg, Sørup Kirkevej	166
070403	46	Sæbyholm, Halsted	-
070512		Søllested	47, 118
180404	10	Sdr. Haurvig, Holmslands Klit	39, 56
170704		Sønder Stenderup, Brusk herred(?)	93
120113		Sønder Tranders Kirke	51-2, 162
050407	32	Søndergård, Brandelev	118
220106		Sønderhave	-
120511	144	Sønderholm northeast	51, 112, 120
020216	185	Søndersø	-
010602	115	Søtoftegård	164
090416	36	Tange	48, 93, 149
130606	39	Tangeværket	-
150406	36	Testrup Teglværk, Mårslet	55, 82-4, 129-30
141109	188	Thorsager	39
030106		Tissø	-
050111	36	Toftegård, Valløby	44, 110, 118
130110	106	Toftum, Mønsted s.	54, 113, 120
100406	77	Torpet	52-3, 112, 119

200

Indices

Site no.	Sb	Name	Pages
020213	20	Torstorp Vesterby	58, 60, 66, 70-1, 140-1, 169-70
150409		Tranbjerg	94, 113, 120
080409	51	Troelsegård Syd	49, 111, 118
090506	32	Trunderup	48, 93, 149-50
050302	36	Tyrstrup III, Fakse	46, 118
030109	251	Udby	-
100618	92	Ugilt	53, 119
190411	26	Ulhøj, Vester Vedsted, north of	55, 114, 120
020215	25	Vallensbæk Nordmark	43, 117
010505	71	Vangbækgård	-
190712	90	Varde/Søndervarde, Åvænget	163
050613	8	Varpelev parish	44, 60-1, 66, 70-1, 146, 158, 170
100106	183	Vester Mellerup	53, 111, 119
170816		Vester parish	-
110612	419	Vestervig	52, 112, 119, 146, 157
130815	349	Viborg	163
130815		Viborg, area	14, 54, 179
130815	348	Viborg, St. Villads Church	162, 171
180320		Vildbjerg, Hammerum herred	-
080406	1	Vimose	49, 71, 75, 161
020307		Virum, Kaplevej 46	-
020204	10	Vissinge Vest 2	43, 117
140309	62	Voldum	-
220102		Volmerstoft	55, 120
190604	304	Vorbasse parish	-

Site no.	Sb	Name	Pages
090507	78	Vornæs Skov	49, 93, 149
020202		Vridsløselille Prison	43, 117
020611	174	Vårkærgård east, Rye	116, 118
080710	37	Wedellsborg	50, 118
140313	25	Ølst	-
020402	43	Øm-Gammeltoft	43, 117
090618	39	Ørbæk parish	49, 93, 147
020310	410	Ørholm	-
100215	50	Ørum parish	53, 119
180106		Øster Herborg	-
090510	117	Øster Åby	84-5
020103	16	Østervang	44, 84, 107-9, 117, 129, 134-5, 188
220205		Åbenrå, area	-
120108		Aalborg, area	52, 164
120506	56	Aalborg, Bejsebakken/ Skelagervej	51-2, 112, 119
120506	64	Aalborg, Bejsebakken/ Stolpedalsvej	51-2, 112, 119
150311	174	Århus, Helgolandsgade	-
150311		Århus, Skolebakken	-
120814	152	Års mark	50, 90-1
090619	4	Årslev	48, 63, 65-6, 69-71, 146, 148, 158
- no.		In bus(!) between Silkeborg and Ans	-
- no.		Randers/Aalborg area	-
- no.		Said to be from Tissø	-

201

Abbreviations

AUD	*Arkæologiske Udgravninger i Danmark*, 1984-2001
RIC	*Roman Imperial Coinage*, London
BMC	*Coins of the Roman Empire in The British Museum*, London
FMRN	*Die Fundmünzen der Römischen Zeit in den Niederlanden*
FMRD	*Die Fundmünzen der Römischen Zeit in Deutschland*
NNÅ	*Nordisk Numismatisk Årsskrift/Nordic Numismatic Journal*, Copenhagen/Stockholm/Oslo
NNUM	*Nordisk Numismatisk Unions Medlemsblad*, Copenhagen
RRC	Crawford, M.: *Roman Republican Coinage*

Bibliography

Aarsleff, E. 2006: Single finds of Viking Age coins in Kirke Hyllige and Vester Egesborg, in: Horsnæs & Moesgaard 2006, 173-189.

Albrectsen, E. 1968: *Fynske Jernaldergrave III, Yngre romersk jernalder*, Odense.

Albrectsen, E. 1971: *Fynske Jernaldergrave IV, Gravpladsen på Møllegårdsmarken ved Broholm*, Fynske Studier IX, Odense.

Alföldi, A. 1928/29: Materialien zur Klassifizierung der gleichzeitigen Nachahmungen von römischen münzen aus Ungarn und den Nachbarländern, Teil II, *Numizmatikai Közlöny* XXVI/XXVII, (1931), 59-671.

Alföldi, M.R. 1958: Die constantinische Goldprägung in Trier, *Jahr. für Num. und Geldgesch.* 9, 99-139.

Alföldi, M. 1968: Le trésor de Wiesbaden-Kastel (IVe-Ve siècle), *Bulletin du Cercle d'Études Numismatiques*, Brussels, vol. 5 no. 4, 95-102.

Andersen, H. Chr. H. 2003: New investigations in Ejsbøl Bog, in: Jørgensen *et al.*, 246-255.

Andersson, K. 1995: *Romartida guldsmide i Norden 3, Övriga smycken, teknisk analys och verkstadsgrupper*, Uppsala.

Andrcasen, Ø. (ed.) 1967: *Georg Zoëga, Briefe und Dokumente im Auftrage der Gesellschaft für Dänische Sprache und Literatur* I, 1755-1785, Copenhagen.

Axboe, M. 1982: The Scandinavian gold bracteates. Studies on their regional variations, *Acta Achaeologica* 52 (1981), 1-87.

Axboe, M. 2001: Om forholdet mellem medaillonefterligninger og brakteater, eller: Hvad var der i Gudmes guldrum?, in: B. Magnus *et al.* (eds.): *Vi får tacka Lamm*. Studies of the Museum of National Antiquities, 10, Stockholm, 39-46.

Axboe, M. 2004: *Die Goldbrakteaten der Völkerwanderungszeit. Herstellungsprobleme und Chronologie*, Reallexikon der Germanischen Altertumskunde – Ergänzungsbände 38, Berlin – N.Y.

Axboe, M. 2007: *Brakteatstudier*, Nordiske Fortidminder, serie B, vol. 25, København.

Balling, J. 1962: De romerske møntfund fra Jylland, *NNÅ*, 5-78.

Balling, J. 1966: De romerske møntfund fra Skåne, Halland og Blekinge, *NNÅ*, 5-81.

Bazelmans, J. 2003: *De romeinse muntvonsten uit de drie nordelijke provincies. Methodische kanttekeningen bij én niewwe periodisering der ralties*. Tweede Van Gelder-lezing, Leiden.

Becker, C.J. 1972: Mosepotter fra Danmarks jernalder. Problemer omkring mosefundne lerkar og deres tolkning, *Aarbøger for Nordisk Oldkyndighed og Historie* 1971, 5-60.

Beckmann, C. 1969: Metallfingerringe der römischen Kaiserzeit im Freien Germanien, *Saalburg Jahrbuch* XXVI, 5-106.

Beljak, J. 2006: A few comments on occurrence of Roman cins in the Hron and Ipel' River basins, *Slovenská numizmatika* XVIII, 187-202.

Bemmann, J. 2003: Romanisierte Barbaren oder erfolgreiche Plünderer? Anmerkungen zur Intensität, Form und Dauer des provinzialrömischen Einflußes auf Mitteldeutschland während der jüngeren Römischen Kaiserzeit und der Völkerwanderungszeit, in: A. Bursche & R. Ciołek (eds.), *Antyk i Barbarzyńcy. Księga dedykowana Profesorowi Jerzemu Kolendo w siedemdziesiątą rocznicę urodzin (Festschr. J. Kolendo)*, Warszawa, 53-108.

Bemmann, J. 2006: Zur Münz- und Münzerstazbeigabe in Gräbern der Römischen Kaiserzeit und Völkerwanderungszeit des mittel- und nordwesteuropäischen Barbaricums, *Studien zur Sachsenforschung* 15, 1-62.

Bemmann, G. & Bemmann, J. (eds.) 1998: *Der Opferplatz von Nydam. Die Funde aus dem älteren grabungen. Nydam-I und Nydam-II*. Neumünster.

Benassai, R. 1998: Monete da contesti funerari in Campania tra IV e III sec. A.C.: ideologia o rito?, *Annali dell'Istituto Italiano di Numismatica* 45, 97-123.

Bendixen, K. 1972: Mønterne fra Dankirke, *Nationalmuseets Arbejdsmark*, 61-66.

Bendixen, K. 1981: Sceattas and Other Coin Finds, in: M. Bencard (ed.), *Ribe Excavations 1970-76*. 1. Esbjerg, 63-101.

Bendixen, K. *et al.* 1990: En vikingetidsskat fra Neble, Sjælland, *Nationalmuseets Arbejdsmark*, 208-223.

Berger, F. 1992: *Untersuchungen zu Römerzeitlichen Münzfunden in Nordwestdeutschland*, Studien zu Fundmünzen der Antike (SFMA) 9, Berlin.

Berger, F. 1996: *Kalkriese 1. Die römischen Fundmünzen*, Römische-Germanischen Forschungen 55, Mainz.

Berger, F. 2008: Die römishcen Fundmünzen in Niedersachsen und Westfalen. Kontext und Funktion, in: Bursche, Ciołek & Wolters (eds.), 105-112.

Birkebæk, F. 1997: *Tidernes Samling*, Roskilde Museum.

Bjerg, L.M.H. 2007: *Romerske denarfund fra jyske jernalderbopladser. En arkæologisk kulegravning*; Aarhus.

Bolin, S. 1926: *Fynden av romerska mynt i det Fria Germanien*, Lund.

Bolin, S. 1958: *State and Currency in the Roman Empire to 300 A.D* Stockholm.

Boye, L. 2002a: Glas i mund, *Skalk* 5, 5-9.

Boye, L. 2002b: Glasskår i munden – en upåagtet gravskik i yngre romersk jernalder, in: J. Pind *et al.* (eds.) 2002, 203-210.

Boye, L. 2004: Two rich cemeteries from the Late Roman Iron Age in Høje-Taastrup, West of Copenhagen", in: Lodewijckx 2004, 47-56.

Boye, L. 2008: Bosættelsesmønstre på Østsjælland, in: Carlie 2008, 15-32.

Breitenstein, N. 1936: Denar-Fundet fra Hvornum Kær, *NNÅ*, 89-94.

Breitenstein, N. 1942: De romerske Møntfund fra Gudme Herred, *NNÅ*, 69-98.

Breitenstein, N. 1943: De romerske Møntfund fra Fyen udenfor Gudme Herred, *NNÅ*, 1-20.

Breitenstein, N. 1943b: En nyfunden romersk guldmedaillon, *Nationalmuseets Arbejdsmark*, 91-94.

Breitenstein, N. 1944: De romerske Møntfund fra Bornholm, *NNÅ*, 1-85.

Breitenstein, N. 1946: De romerske Møntfund fra den sjællandske Øgruppe, *NNÅ*, 1-34.

Burnett, A.M. 1984: Clipped siliquae and the end of Roman Britain, *Britannia* 15, 163-168.

Bursche, A. 1993: Pourquoi les denarii frappés après 194 etaient absent dans le Barbaricum?, in: Moucharte, G. & Hackens, T.: *Proceedings of the 11th International Numismatic Congress, Bruxelles 1991,2*, Louvain-la-Neuve, 297-303.

Bursche, A. 1994: Celtic, Roman and merovingian coins in North-West Germany: remarks on Frank Berger's Untersuchugen, Review of: Untersuchungen zu römerzeitlichen Münzfunden in Nordwestdeutschland / Frank Berger Berlin, 1992, *Numismatic Chronicle* 154, 225-241.

Bursche, A. 1996: *Later Roman-Barbarian Contacts in Central Europe, numismatic evidence. Spätrömische Münzfunde aus Mitteleuropa. Ein Beitrag zur Geschichte der Beziehungen zwischen Rom und den Barbaricum in 3. und 4. Jh. N. Chr.*, Studien zu Fundmünzen der Antike (SFMA), Band 11, Berlin.

Bursche, A. 1998: *Złote medaiony rzymskie w Barbaricum. Geneza symbolika prestiżu i władzy społeczeństw barbarzyńskich u schyłku starożytności*,

Światowit Supplement Series A, Antiquity vol II, Warszawa.

Bursche, A. 1999: Die Rolle römischer Goldmedaillone in der Spätantike, in: Seipel 1999, 39-53.

Bursche, A. 2001: Roman Gold Medallions as Power Symbols, in: B. Magnus (ed.): *Roman Gold and the Development of the Early Germanic Kingdoms*, Kungl. Vitterhets Historie och Antikvitets Akademin Konferenser 51, Stockholm, 83-102.

Bursche, A. 2002: Roman coins in Scandinavia. Some remarks from the Continental perspective, in: Pind 2002, 69-78.

Bursche, A. 2003: The Victoria Sarmatica of AD 340 and three gold medallions from Barbaricum, in: C. von Carnap-Bornheim (ed.): *Kontakt – Kooperation – Konflikt: Germanen und Sarmaten zwischen dem 1. und dem 4. Jahrh. N.Chr.*, Neumünster, 407-413.

Bursche, A. 2007: Two Scandinavian bracteates from the Württembergisches Landesmuseum Stuttgart, in: M. Andersen *et al.* (eds.): *Magister Monetae, Studies in Honour of Jørgen Stehen Jensen*, Publications of the National Museum 13, København, 59-79.

Bursche, A. 2008: Function of Roman coins in Barbaricum of Later Antiquity. An Anthropological Essay, in: Bursche, Ciołek & Wolters (eds.), 395-416.

Bursche, A., Coiłek, R. & Wolters, R. (eds.). 2008: *Roman coins outside the Empire. Way and Phases, Contexts and Functions. Proceedings of the ESF/SCH Exploratory Workshop Radziwill Palace, Nieborów (Poland) 3-6 September 2005*, Collection Moneta 82, Wetteren.

Böhme, H. 1974: Germanische Grabfunde des 4.-5. Jahrhunderts zwischen unterer Elbe und Loire, *Münchener Beiträge zur Vor- und Frühgeschichte* 19, 149-150.

Carlie, A. (ed.) 2008: *Öresund – Barriär eller bro?*, Center för Danmarksstudier 18, Göteborg – Stockholm.

Carnap-Bornheim, C. von 2003: The ornamental belts from Ejsbøl Bog and Neudorf-Bornstein, in: Jørgensen *et al.* (eds.), 240-245.

Carnap-Bornheim, C. von 2007: Thorsberg. Archäologisch. *Reallexikon der Germanischen Altertumskunde. 2. erweiterte Auflage Band 35*, Berlin, 123-127.

Carnap-Bornheim, C. von & Matešić, S. 2007: The Thorsberg Bog Find: Some Remarks on Roman-Germanic Relationships Regarding Early Third Century Militaria, in: A. Bliujiene (ed.), *Weapons, Weaponry and Man. Archaeologia Baltica* 8, 133-140.

Caronte. Un obolo per l'aldilá, Parola del Passato 282-285, 1995.

Christoffersen, J. 1987: Møllegårdsmarken –Struktur und Belegung eines Gräberfeldes, *Frühmittelalterliche Studien* 21, 85-100.

Ciołek, R. 2001: *Katalog znalezisk monet rzymskich na Pomorzu*, Swiatowit Supplement Series A: Antiquity, vol. VI, Warszawa.

Ciołek, R. 2003: Die römischen Münzfunde in Pommern, *Wiadomosci Numizmatyczne* XLVII, 25-39.

Ciołek, R. 2007: *Die Fundmünzen der römischen Zeit in Polen. Pommern*, Wetteren.

Ciołek, R. 2008: Ein Beitrag zur Funktion römischer Münzen in the Wielbark und in der Przworks-Kultur, in: Bursche, Ciołek & Wolters (eds.), 157-170.

Crawford, M. 1974: *Roman Republican Coinage*, Cambridge.

Crumlin Petersen, O. 1991: *Bådgrave og gravbåde, Slusegårdgravpladsen III*, 93-263.

Dembski, G. 2008: Die römischen Fundmünzen aus Österreich ausserhalb des Imperium Romanum, in: Bursche, Coiłek & Wolters (eds.), 227-230.

Depeyrot, G. 1996: Les médaillons d'or unifaces du quatrième siècle (318-340), in: *Italiam fato profvgi. Numismatic studies dedicated to Vladimir and Elvira Eliza Clain-Stefanelli*, Numismatica Lovaniensia 12, Louvain, 163-170.

Dumez, T. *et al.* 1999: Les monnaies de la nécropole du Bas-Empire de Sierentz (Haut-Rhin), in: Dubuis *et al.* (eds.), 229-246.

Duncan-Jones, R.P. 2005: Implications of Roman coinage: debates and differences, *Klio* 87, 459-487.

Duncan-Jones, R.P. 2006: Crispina and the Coinage of the Empresses, *NC* 166, 223-228.

Dubuis, O.F. *et al.* (eds.) 1999: *Trouvailles monétaires des tombes, Actes du deuxième colloque international du Groupes suisse pour l'étude des trouvailles monétaires (Neuchâtel, 3-4 mars 1995)*, Lausanne.

Engelhardt, C. 1863: *Thorsbjerg Mosefund*, Kjöbenhavn. (*Sønderjyske og fynske mosefund I*. Photographic re-edition with introduction by Mogens Ørsnes, København 1969)

Engelhardt, C. 1865: *Nydam Mosefund*, Kjøbenhavn. (*Sønderjyske og fynske mosefund II*. Photographic re-edition with introduction by Mogens Ørsnes, København 1970)

Engelhardt, C. 1869: *Vimose Fundet*, Kjøbenhavn. (*Sønderjyske og fynske mosefund III part 2*. Photographic re-edition with introduction by Mogens Ørsnes, København 1970)

Engelhardt, C. 1877: Skeletgrave paa Sjælland og i det øvrige Danmark, *Aarbøger for Nordisk Oldkyndighed og Historie*, 347-402.

Eriksen, P. 2000: Guldkysten, *FRAM – Fra Ringkøbing Amts Museer*, 73-84.

Ethelberg, P. 2000: *Skovgårde. Ein Bestattungsplatz mit reichen Frauengräbern des 3. Jhs.n.Chr. auf Seeland*, Nordiske Fortidsminder, Serie B bd. 19. København.

Fabech, C. & Ringtved, J. 1991: *Samfundsorganisation og regional variation: Norden i romersk jernalder og folkevandringstid: beretning fra 1. nordiske jernaldersymposium på Sandbjerg Slot 11.-15. april 1989*, Jysk Arkæologisk Selskabs Skrifter 27, Århus.

Fabech, C. & Ringtved, J. 1999: *Settlement and landscape: proceedings of a conference in Århus, Denmark, May 4-7 1998*, Århus.

Faber, C.G.V. 1868: Efterretninger om „Nordisk Museum" i Odense, *Aarbøger for nordisk Oldkyndighed og Historie (Annual of the Royal Society of Northern Antiquaries)*, 334-351.

Fagerlie, J. 1967: *Late Roman and Byzantine Solidi Found in Sweden and Denmark*, ANS Numismatic Notes and Monographs 157, New York.

Feveile, C. 2001: Okholm – en plads med håndværksspor og grubehuse fra 8.-9. årh., *By, Marsk og Geest*, 5,32.

Feveile, C. 2006: Sceattaerne fra Dankirke – skatte eller enkeltfund?, *NNUM* 1, 2006, 3-9.

Fischer, S. 2008: The Udovice solidus pendents, *Fornvännen* 103, 81-88.

Fonnesbech-Sandberg, E. 1987: Vægtsystemer i ældre germansk jernalder, *Aarbøger for nordisk oldkyndighed og historie*, 139-160.

Fonnesbech-Sandberg, E. 1989: Münzfunktionen in der Kaiserzeit und Völkerwanderungszeit Dänemarks, *Frühmittelalterliche Studien* 23, 420-452.

Fonnesbech-Sandberg, E. 1990: Anvendelsen af mønter i romersk og ældre germansk jernalder, in: Thrane (ed.), 75-87.

Fonnesbech-Sandberg, E. 1990b: De arkæologiske undersøgelser i Torstorp, *Høje Taastrup Kommunes Lokalhistoriske Arkiv, Årsskrift*, 45-63.

Fonnesbech-Sandberg, E. 2004 (✝): Brøndsager: Rige grave og bebyggelse i Yngre romersk jernalder i Høje-Tåstrup, Københavns amt, Danmark, in: Gudmundsson, G. (ed.): *Current Issues in Archaeology. Proceedings of the 21st Conference of Nordic Archaeologists, 6-9 September 2001, Akureyri, Iceland*, Reykjavik, 59-62.

Fonnesbech-Sandberg, E. 2004b (✝): Brøndsager: A Small cemetery with roman imports in Høje-Taastrup, County of Copenhagen, in: Lodewijckx (ed.), 97-102.

Fonnesbech-Sandberg, E. 2006 (✝): Torstorp Vesterby. A cemetery from the Late Roman Iron Age, *JDA* 14, 109-125.

Friis Johansen, K. 1923: Hoby-fundet, *Nordiske Fortidsminder 2,3*, 119-164 (French summary).

Fuglesang, S.H. & Wilson, D.M. (eds.) 2006: *The Hoen hoard, a Viking gold treasure of the ninth century*, Acta ad archaeologiam et artium historiam pertinentia 14, Oslo.

Galster, G. 1924: Romerske Mønter, fundne i Danmark og indgaaede efter 1893, *NFM* VII, 187-189.

Galster, G. 1936: *Den kgl. Mønt- og Medaillesamling i Finansaaret 1934-1935, Tillæg: Møntfund fra Danmark og Norge 1670-1700*, København.

Galster, G. 1937: Møntfund i Danmark og Norge 1739-1780, *NNÅ*, 39-96.

Galster, G. 1938: Møntfund i Danmark 1780-1800, *NNÅ*, 53-88.

Gnecchi, F. 1912: *I medaglioni romani*, Milano.

Gorecki, J. 1975: Studien zur Sitte der Münzbeigabein römerzeitlichen Körpergräbern zwischen Rhein, Mosel und Somme, *Bericht der Römisch-Germanischen Kommission Band* 56, 179-468.

Grane, T. 2003: Roman sources for the geography and ethnography of Germania, in: Jørgensen *et al.* (eds.), 126-146.

Grane, T. 2007: *The Roman Empire and southern Scandinavia – a northern connection! : a re-eva-

luation of military-political relations between the Roman Empire and the Barbaricum in the first three centuries AD with a special emphasis on southern Scandinavia, unpublished ph.d. dissertation Copenhagen University.

Grinder-Hansen, K. 1991: Charon's fee in Ancient Greece? – some remarks on a well-known death rite, *Acta Hyperborea* 3, 207-218.

Grønnegård, T. 1997: *Yngre jernalders centralpladser – indfaldsvinkler til et helhedsbillede*, unpublished mag.art. thesis Copenhagen University.

Guest, P. 2005: *The late Roman gold and silver coins from the Hoxne treasure*, London.

Gullbekk, S. 2009: Kejser Claudius i Gokstadhaugen – romerske mynter i vikingtidskontekst, *Viking*, 169-182.

Gundestrup, B. 2001: From the Royal Kunstkammer to the Modern Museums of Copenhagen, in: Impey, O. & MacGregor, A. (eds.): *The Origins of Museums*, Oxford 1985, 128-134. Second edition, London 2001, 176-185.

Hagberg, U.E. et al. 1967-1977: *The Archaeology of Skedemosse*, vols. 1-4. Stockholm.

Hatt, G. 1935: Jernalderbopladsen ved Ginderup i Thy, *Nationalmuseets Arbejdsmark*, 37-51.

Hatt, G. 1938: Jernalders bopladser i Himmerland, *Aarbøger for Nordisk Oldkyndighed og Historie*, 119-126. [French summary]

Hauberg, P. 1894: Skandinaviens Fund af romersk Guld- og Sølvmønt før Aar 500, *Aarbøger for nordisk Oldkyndighed og Historie*, 326-377.

Hässler, H.-J. 2001: *Das sächsische Gräberfeld von Issendorf*, Studien zur Sachsenforschung 9.3.

Hedeager, L. 1978: A Quantitative Analysis of Roman Imports in Europe North of the Limes (0-400 A.D.), and the Question of Roman-Germanic Exchange, in: K. Kristiansen & C. Paludan-Müller (eds.): *New directions in Sacndinavian Archaeology, Studies in Scandinavian Prehistory and Early History* vol. 1, 191-216.

Hedeager, L. 1988: Pengeøkonomi og prestigeøkonomi i romersk jernalder, in: Mortensen & Rasmussen 1988, 117-122 [English summary: Monetary and Prestige Economy in the Roman Iron Age].

Hedeager, L. 1990: *Danmarks jernalder – mellem stamme og stat*, Århus.

Henriksen, M.B. 1989: Bregentved I – en gravplads ved Ringe Sø med våbendeponeringer fra yngre romersk jernalder, *Fynske Minder*, 67-76 (German summary: Bregentved I – ein Grabplatz am Ringe-See mit Waffenlagern aus der späten römischen Eisenzeit).

Henriksen, M.B. 1992a: Brangstrupfundet. En guldskat fra slutningen af romersk jernalder, *Fynske Minder*, 43-73.

Henriksen, M.B. 1992b: Brand- og jordfæstegrave samt våbendeponeringer ved Ringe Sø, *Fynske Minder*, 157-159.

Henriksen, M.B. 1994a: Vikinger på Fyns Hoved, *Fynske Minder*, 181-191.

Henriksen, M.B. 1994b: Parcelhushavearkæologi – eller: om at finde danefæ i baghaven, *Fynboer og Arkæologi*, nr. 2 maj, 11-18.

Henriksen, M.B. 1998: Fynske jernalderbopladser – et publikationsprojekt, in: M.B. Henriksen (ed.): *Bebyggelseshistoriske projekter, deres betydning, bearbejdning og* publikation, Skrifter fra Odense Bys Museer vol. 3, 7-19.

Henriksen, M.B. 2000: Lundsgård, Seden Syd og Hjulby. Tre fynske bopladsområder med detektorfund, in: M.B. Henriksen (ed.): *Detektorfund – hvad skal vi med dem?*, Skrifter fra Odense Bys Museer, vol. 5, 17-60.

Henriksen, M.B. 2006: The Metal Detector – Friend or Foe, in: K. Møller Hansen & K. Buck Pedersen: *Across the Western Baltic, Proceedings from an archaeological conference in Vordingborg*, Sydsjællands Museums Publikationer vol. 1, Vordingborg, 217-226.

Henriksen, M.B. & Horsnæs, H.W. 2004: Guldskatten fra Boltinggård Skov på Midtfyn, *Fynske Minder*, 123-151.

Henriksen, M.B. & Horsnæs, H.W. 2006: Boltinggård Skov: A Hoard of Roman gold coins of Constantinian period from Funen, Denmark, *Revue Numismatique* 162, 259-271.

Herschend, F. 1980: Två studier i ölandska guldfynd. I. Det myntade guldet, II. Det omyntade guldet, *TOR Tidsskrift för nordisk fornkundskap* XVIII (1978-1979), 33-294.

Herschend, F. 1983: Solidusvikt, *Numismatiska Meddelanden* XXXIV, 49-74.

Hertz, J. 1987: *Danmarks længste udgravning. Arkæologi på naturgassens vej 1979-86*, København.

Holmes, N.M.McQ. 2004: A uniface gold medallion of Constantine II, *NC*, 233-235.

Holst, H. 1929: Numismatica IV. Three unpublished Roman and Byzantine Silver Coins found in Norway. *Symbolae Osloensis* VIII, 114-119.

Horsnæs, H.W. 2000: Den romerske denarskat fra Præstemosen, Gudme, *NNUM* 6, september, 127-131.

Horsnæs, H.W. 2002a: Nye romerfund fra Bornholm, *NNUM* 1, februar 2002, 6-8.

Horsnæs, H.W. 2002b: Lidt om Ole Worm og nogle barbariske guldmønter, in: L.K. Jacobsen & A.M. Carstens: *(Festskrift) Til Jens Erik Skydsgaard, Meddelelser fra Klassisk Arkæologisk Forening, supplement 1*, 29-39.

Horsnæs, H.W. 2003a: The coins in the bogs, in: Jørgensen *et al.* (eds.), 330-340.

Horsnæs, H.W. 2003b: Fund af romerske mønter i Danmark – nogle tanker i utide, *Meddelelser fra Klassisk Arkæologisk Forening* 54, marts, 21-33.

Horsnæs, H.W. 2004: Endnu en detektorfunden guldmønt fra Brangstrup-skatten, *NNUM* 3, august, 94-95.

Horsnæs, H.W. 2005: Når mønter ikke er penge – et eksempel på postmodernistisk numismatik, *META medeltidsarkeologisk tidskrift* 3, 2005, 11-20.

Horsnæs, H.W. 2006a: Roman bronze coins from Barbaricum – Denmark as a case study, in: Horsnæs & Moesgaard (eds.), 63-99.

Horsnæs, H.W. 2006b: Many coins from one site. Towards a method to distinguish between single finds and hoards in detector material, in: Horsnæs & Moesgaard (eds.), 100-108.

Horsnæs, H.W. 2008a: Danske fund af romerske bronzemønter – og det der ligner, *NNUM* 1, 8-13.

Horsnæs, H.W. 2008b: Roman coins and their contexts in Denmark, in: Bursche, Ciołek & Wolters (eds.), 135-145.

Horsnæs, H.W. 2009: Late Roman and Byzantine coins found in Denmark, in: Wołoszyn (ed.), 231-270.

Horsnæs, H.W. 2009b: Johannes Wiedewelt – designer of exhibitions, in: Nielsen, M. & Rathje, A. (eds.): *Johannes Wiedewelt. A Danish Artist in Search of the Past, Shaping the Future, Acta Hyperborea* 11, 259-274.

Horsnæs, H.W. 2010: Et grænseoverskridende fund, in: Andersen, M. & Nielsen, P.O. (eds.): *Danefæ. Skatte fra den danske muld*, København, 105-110.

Horsnæs, H.W. *forthcoming A*: Roman Coins from Bornholm – a preliminary overview, in: Bitner-Wroblewska, A. & Lund Hansen, U. (eds.): *Papers from the 'Network Denmark – Poland, Archaeology and Heritage. Contatcs across the Baltic Sea during the Iron Age (500 BC to AD 1000)'*, Warszawa.

Horsnæs, H.W. *forthcoming B*: Imitations in gold, in: N. Holmes: *Proceedings of the XIV International Numismatic Congress, Glasgow Monday 31st August to Friday 4th September 2009*.

Horsnæs, H.W. *forthcoming C*: Gold imitations of Roman coins produced in Outer Barbaricum, in: L. Bjerg, J. Lind & S. Sindbæk: *From Goths to Varangians. Communication and Cultural Exchange between the Baltic and the Black Sea*, Black Sea Studies vol. 20, Århus 2010.

Horsnæs, H.W., Gottlieb. B., Schnell, U. & Tornbjerg, Sv.Å. 2005: Sølvanalyser og romerske denarer fra Østervang, *NNUM* 4, august, 119-125.

Horsnæs, H.W. & Ingvardson, G.T. 2010: Detektortræf i Thy, in: Andersen, M. & Nielsen, P.O. (eds.): *Danefæ. Skatte fra den danske muld*, København, 100-104.

Horsnæs, H.W. & Moesgaard, J.Chr. (eds.) 2006: *Single Finds – the Nordic Perspective. Proceedings of the Seminar in Copenhagen 23-24 November 2001*, NNÅ (2000-2002), Copenhagen.

Horsnæs, H.W. & Schilling, H. 2002: En tidlig romersk mønt fra Kohave ved Halsted, *Lolland-Falsters Historiske Samfund, Årbog* (90. årg.), 22-28.

Hässler, H.-J. 2001: *Das sächsische Gräberfeld von Issendorf*, Studien zur Sachsenforschung 9.3. Oldenburg.

Høilund Nielsen, K. & Fiedel, R. 2001: Stavnsager: spredte glimt af et jernaldersamfund gennem mere end 7000 år – fra 400 til 1100 e.Kr.f., *Kulturhistorisk Museum Randers* 2001, 71-89.

Høilund Nielsen, K. & Loveluck, C.P. 2006: Fortid og fremtid på Stavnsager – om de britiske undersøgelser august 2005 og de foreløbige resultater, *Kulturhistorisk Museum Randers Årbog*, 63-79.

Høj, M. 2005: Bygherrerapport for arkæologisk udgravning af gravplads fra 300-tallet, *ROMU*.

Årsskrift fra Roskilde Museum 2004 (2005), 180-190.

Hårdh, B. & Larsson, L. (eds.) 2002: *Central places in the Migration and Merovingian Periods*, Papers from the 52nd Sachsensymposium Lund, August 2001 = Uppåkrastudier 6, Stockholm.

Ilkjær, J. 1993: *Illerup Ådal 3-4. Die Gürtel. Bestandteile und Zubehör*, Jysk Arkæologisk Selskabs Skrifter 25, Højbjerg.

Ilkjær, J. 2000: *Illerup Ådal – Et arkæologisk tryllespejl*, Højbjerg (also in Norwegian, German and English versions).

Ilkjær, J. 2003: Danish war booty sacrifices, in: Jørgensen *et al.* (eds.), 44-65.

Imer, L.M. 2007: Latin og græsk i romersk jernalder – Fremmed indflydelse på Nordens tidligste skrift, *Aarbøger for nordisk Oldkyndighed og Historie* 2004, 63-105 (English summary: Latin and Greek in the Roman Iron Age).

Jedlicka, F. 2005: *Ein Stück Bernsteinstraße im nordöstlichen Weinviertel. Münzgeld in keltischer und römisch-germanischer Zeit*, Haugsdorf – Wien.

Jensen, S. 1991: *Ribes vikinger*, Ribe.

Jensen, S. 1998: *Marsk, land og bebyggelse – Ribeegnen gennem 10.000 år*, Jysk Arkæologisk Selskabs Skrifter XXXV.

Jørgensen, E. & Petersen, P.V. 2003: Nydam Bog – new finds and observations, in: Jørgensen *et al.* (eds.), 258-284.

Jørgensen, L. 1987: En bornholmerpige fra 700-årene, *Nationalmuseets Arbejdsmark*, 75-86.

Jørgensen, L. 1994: The Find Material from the Settlement of Gudme II – Composition and Interpretation, in: Nielsen, P.O. *et al.* (eds.), 53-63.

Jørgensen, L. 1995: Stormandssæde og skattefund i 3.-12. århundrede, *Fortid og nutid*, 81-110.

Jørgensen, L. 1998: Fra nutidens pløjelag til jernalderens samfund – stormænd og håndværkere i Gudme, *Årbog fra Svendborg & Omegns Museum*, 8-21.

Jørgensen, L. & Petersen, P.V. 1998: *Guld, magt og tro – Danske guldskatte fra oldtid og middelalder/ Gold, Power and Belief – Danish gold treasures from Prehistory and the Middle Ages*, København.

Jørgensen, L., Storgaard, B. & Thomsen, L. Gebauer (eds.) 2003: *The spoils of victory. The North in the shadow of the Roman Empire*, Copenhagen (also published in Danish and German).

Kaul, F. 2003: The bog – the gateway to another world, in: Jørgensen *et al.* (eds.), 2003, 18-43.

Kaczanowski, P. & Rodzińska-Nowak, J. 1999: Die römischen Fundmünzen aus der Siedlung der Przeworsk-Kultur in Opatkowice (Gemeinde Proszowice, Woiwodschaft Kraków), *Notae Numismaticae* III/IV, 183-199 (Polish summary).

Kemmers, F. 2008: Interaction or indifference? The Roman coin finds from the Lower Rhine delta, in: Bursche, Ciołek & Wolters (eds.), 93-104.

Kent, J.P.C. 1994: *The Roman Imperial Coinage, Vol. X, The Divided Empire and the Fall of the Western Parts 395-491*, London.

Klindt-Jensen, O. 1978: *Slusegårdgravpladsen II*, Jysk Arkæologisk Selskabs Skrifter 14.

Klüssendorf, N. 1995: Das akademische Münzkabinet der Universität Rostock (1794-1944), in: W. Buchholz & G. Mangelsdorf (eds.): *Land am Meer, Pommern in Spiegel seiner Geschichte, Roderick Schmiedt zum 70. Geburtstag*, Köln – Weimar – Wien, 725-757.

Kolníková, E. 2008: Die römischen Fundmünzen in der Slowakei – Kontext und Funktion, in: Bursche, Ciołek & Wolters (eds.), 245-254.

Komnick, H. 1994: *Die Fundmünzen der römischen Zeit, Abteilung VIII. Schleswig—Holstein und Hamburg*, Berlin.

Korthauer, C. 1995-96: En ældre romertidsgrav med guldmønt fra Jylland samt nogle iagttagelser om møntomløb og –funktion i jernalderens Danmark, *KUML*, 113-134 (English summary: An Early Roman Iron Age Grave containing a Roman Gold Coin).

Korthauer, C. 1998: *Römischen Münzen im nordwestlichen Barbaricum, (Funktion und Umlauf)*, unpublished „Magisterarbeit", Philosophical Faculty, University of Münster.

Kousgård Sørensen, J. 1985: Gudhem, *Frühmittelalterliche Studien* 19, 131-138.

Kramer, E., Stoumann, I. & Greg, A. (eds.) 2000: Kings of the North Sea, AD 250-850. Leeuwarden.

Kromann, A. 1970: En nyfunden solidus fra Jylland, *NNUM*, 97.

Kromann, A. 1983-84: Recent Roman coin finds from Denmark, Supplement to Breitenstein and Balling, *NNÅ*, 59-122.

Kromann, A. 1987: Die römischen Münzen von Gudme, *Frühmittelalterliche Studien* 21, 61-73.

Kromann, A. 1988: A Fourth Century Hoard from Denmark, *Rivista Italiana di Numismatica* XC, 239-261.

Kromann, A. 1989: Romerske denarer fundne i Sverige, review of Lind 1988, *NNUM* 4, 81-82.

Kromann, A. 1990: Recent Roman coin finds from Denmark, *Proceedings of the 10th International Congress of Numismatics, London, September 1986*, Maastricht, 263-274.

Kromann, A. 1991: The denarii from the moor of Illerup, *NNÅ*, 45-54.

Kromann, A. 1994: Gudme and Lundeborg – The Coins, in: Nielsen, P.O. et al. (eds.), 64-67.

Kromann, A. 1995: Die römische Münzfunde von Sjælland, in: Lund Hansen 1995, 347-363.

Kromann, A. 1999 (✝): Har romerske mønter cirkuleret i Danmark?, *NNUM* 7, nov., 130-135.

Kromann, A. 2003 (✝): Gallienus fra Koldingegnen. En romersk guldmønt fundet ved Sønder Stenderup, *NNUM* 5-6, 79-82.

Kromann, A. & Jensen, J. 1993: Guldfundet fra Lundeborg 1585, *NNUM*, 104-108.

Kromann, A. & Watt, M. 1984: Skattefundet fra Smørenge; en nedgravet skat fra folkevandringstid på Bornholm, *Nationalmuseets Arbejdsmark*, 29-41.

Kropotkin, V.V. 1961/2005: *Les trouvailles de monnaies romaines en U.R.S.S.*, Collection Moneta 49, Wetteren (French edition by G. Depeyrot).

Kropotkin, V.V. 1976: Варварские лодажания римским золотым моиетам в восточиой европе (German summary: Barbarische Imitationen römischer Goldmünzen in Osteuropa), *Slovenska numizmatika* IV, 11-35.

Kubiak, S. 1979: *Znaleziska monet rzymskich z Mazowsza i Podlasia*, Wrocław.

Kulakov, V.I. 2001: Jütland – Dobrudscha: Die Rochade der „Barbaren" vom 2. bis 4. Jh.n.Chr., *Archaeologica Bulgarica* V.2, 45-58 (Summary: Ютланя – Добружа: Рокада на "варварите" през" II-IV век).

Kunisz, A. 1985: *Znalesiska monet rzymskich z Małopolski*, Wrocław.

Kyhlberg, O. 1980: *Vikt och värde. Arkeologiske studier i värdemätning, betalingsmedel och metrologi under yngre järnålder. I Helgö, II Birka*, Stockholm Studies in Archaeology 1, Stockholm.

Kyhlberg, O. 1983: Aureus solidus. Metodologiska studier i 400- och 500-talens myntskatter, *Numismatiska Meddelanden* XXXIV, 5-48.

Kyhlberg, O. 1986: Late Roman and Byzantine Solidi, An archaeological analysis of coins and hoards, in: *Excavations at Helgö X. Coins, Iron and Gold*, Stockholm, 13-126.

Larsen, L.K. 1996: Ved Kompagnistræde – fra Næstveds middelalderlige havnekvarter, *Liv & Levn* 10, 18-23.

Laser, R. 1980: *Die römischen und frühbyzantinischen Fundmünzen auf dem Gebiet der DDR*, Schriften zur Ur- und Frühgeschichte 28, Berlin.

Lind, L. 1981: *Roman denarii found in Sweden 2, catalogue, text*, Acta Universitas Stockholmiensis, Stockhom Studies in Classica Archaeology 11:2, Stockholm.

Lind, L. 1988: *Romerska denarer funna i Sverige*, Stockholm.

Lind, L. 2006: Roman denarii found on Gotland: single finds, in: Horsnæs & Moesgaard (eds.), 44-52.

Lind, L. 2007: A group of barbarous Roman denarii represented in Sweden and Hungary (and Germany and Britain?), in: Andersen, M. et al. (eds.): *Magister Monetae, Studies in Honour of Jørgen Steen Jensen*, Publications of the National Museum 13, Copenhagen 2007, 53-58.

Lind, L. 2007b: Fynd av romerska sestertier på Gotland, *Myntstudier* 3, 13-16.

Lind, L. 2008: En ny grupp imitationer av romerska denarer representerad på Gotland, *Myntstudier* http://www.myntstudier.se/myntstudier_low/0802lag.pdf, 9-13.

Lodewijckx, M. (ed.) 2004: *BRUC EALLES WELL, Archaeological Essays Concerning the Peoples of North-West Europe in the First Millennium A.D. Acta Archaeologica Lovaniensia, Monographiae* 15, Leuven.

Lund, J. 1973: Ginderup, *Hoops Reallexikon der Germanische Altertumskunde*, 114-118.

Lund Hansen, U. 1976: En af de ypperste – en rig romertidsgrav fra Bennebo Mark, *Fra Holbæk Amt*, 63-76.

Lund Hansen, U. 1987: *Römischer Import im Norden. Warenaustausch zwischen dem Römischen Reich und dem freien Germanien*, Nordiske Fortidsminder, Serie B, Bind 10, København.

Lund Hansen, U. 1995: *Himlingøje – Seeland – Eur-

opa. Ein Gräberfeld der jüngeren römischen Kaiserzeit auf Seeland, seine Bedeutung und Internationale Beziehungen, Nordiske Fortidsminder, Serie B, Band 13, København.

Mackeprang, M.B. 1940: Aarslev-fundet. Et rigt fynsk Gravudstyr fra 4. Aarh. e.Kr., *Nationalmuseets Arbejdsmark*, 87-96.

Mackeprang, M.B. 1952: *De nordiske guldbrakteater*, Jysk Arkæologisk Selskabs Skrifter II, Aarhus.

Madsen, C. & Michaelsen, K.K. 1998: Penge lugter ikke… og dog, *Fynske Minder*, 65-76.

Madsen, C. & Thrane, H. 1995: Møllegårdsmarkens veje og huse, *Fynske Minder*, 77-91.

Mahler, D.L. (ed.) 1999: *Høje Tåstrup før buerne*, Københavns Amtsmuseumsråd, Høje-Taastrup.

Metcalf, D.M. 1995: Viking-Age Numismatics 1. Late Roman and Byzantine Gold in the Northern Lands, *NC*, 413-441.

Michaelsen, K.K. 1989-90: Ejstrup – en landsby fra yngre germansk jernalder og vikingetid ved Sæby, *Vendsyssel nu & da*, 38-59

Michaelsen K.K. & Thomsen P.O. 1991: Broholmskatten: historien om et guldfund, *Årbog fra Svendborg og Omegns Museum*, 8-23

Mielczarek, M. 1989: *Ancient Greek coins found in Central, Eastern and Northern Europe*, Bibliotheca Antiqua vol. XXI, Academia Scientiarum Polona.

Militký, J. 2004: Import zlatých římských a raně byzantských mincí do českých zemí v době římské až raném středověku, *Archeologie ve středních Čechách* 8, 505-536 (English summary: Imported Roman and Early Byzantine gold coins on the Czech territory between Roman and Early Medieval times).

Militký, J. 2008: Die römischen Fundmünzen in Böhmen – Kontexte und Funktionen. Notizen zu dem heutigen Stand der Forschung, in: Bursche, Ciołek & Wolters (eds.), 231-244.

Moesgaard, J.C. 1998: To antikke kobbermønter fundne nær Göteborg?, *Nordisk Numismatisk Unions Medlemsblad*, 39.

Moesgaard, J.C. 2002: The Law and Practice Concerning Coin Finds in Denmark, *Compte Rendu*, 27-33. (reprint from *Compte Rendu* 1999, 74-80)

Montelius, O. 1869: *Från jernåldern*, Stockholm.

Mortensen, P. & Rasmussen, B.M. 1988: *Fra stamme til stat i Danmark 1, Jernalderens Stammesamfund*, Jysk Arkæologisk Selskabs Skrifter XXII.

Mouchmov, N.A. 1934: *Le trésor numismatique de Réka-Devnia (Marcianopolis)*, Édition du Musée Naltional Bulgare 31, Sofia.

Munksgaard, E. 1955: Late-antique scrap-silver found in Denmark. The Hardenberg, Høstentorp and Simmersted Hoards, *Acta Archaeologica* 26, 31-69.

Møller Hansen, K. & Staal, B. 1996: Enkeltgård og landsby fra jernalderen: de arkæologiske undersøgelser på Fakse Lossceplads, *Kulturhistoriske Studier* 1996, 60-66.

Mørkholm, O. 1982: A history of the study of Greek numismatics. III. C. 1870-1940. The scientific organization, *NNÅ*, 7-26.

Nielsen, H. 1997: Et regionalt rigdomscenter i Sydvestsjælland, „…*Gick Grendel att söka det höga huset..*" *Arkeologiska källor till aristokratiska miljöer i Skandinavien under yngre järnålder. Rapport från ett seminarium i Falkenberg 16-17 november 1995. Hallands Länsmuseers Skriftserie* No. 9 / *GOTARC c. Akeologiska Skrifter* No. 17, 55 –70.

Nielsen, J. 1980: Jernalderbopladsen ved Malle Degnegård i Himmerland, *Museerne i Viborg Amt*, 62-73.

Nielsen, J.N. 2002: Bejsebakken: a central site near Aalborg in northern Jutland, in: Hårdh & Larsson (eds.), 197-213.

Nielsen, P.O. et al. (eds.) 1994: *The Archaeology of Gudme and Lundeborg. Papers presented at a conference at Svendborg 1991*, København.

Nielsen, S. 1986: Denarerne fra romersk jernalder – funktion og udbredelse, *Aarbøger for Nordisk Oldkyndighed og Historie*, 147-164 (German summary: Denare der römischen Eisenzeit – Funktion und Verbreitung).

Nielsen, S. 1987-88: Roman Denarii in Denmark – an Archaeological Approach, *NNÅ*, 147-169 (Danish summary: Romerske denarer i Danmark – en arkæologisk tolkning).

Nielsen, S. 1989: Roman denarii and Iron Age Denmark, in: H. Clarke & E. Schia (eds.): *Coins and Archaeology, Medieval Archaeology Research Group, Proceedings of the First Meeting at Isegran, Norway 1988*, BAR International Series 556, 29-36.

Nilsson, T. 1990: Stentinget, en indlandsbebyggelse med handel og håndværk fra yngre jernalder og vikingetid, *Kuml*, 119-132.

Nilsson, T. 1992: Stentinget, en indlandsbebyggelse med handel og håndværk fra yngre jernalder og vikingetid, *Skalk* 4, 3-9.

Norling-Christensen, H. 1942: Une trouvaille de parures de l'ancien age du fer romain faite à Vester Mellerup, Vendsyssel, *Acta Archaeologica* 13, 332-355.

Norling-Christensen, H. 1956: Haraldstedgravpladsen og ældre germansk jernalder i Danmark, *Aarbøger for Nordisk Oldkyndighed og Historie*, 14-143.

Paulsson, J. 1999: Metalldetektering och Uppåkra. Att förhålla sig till ett detektormaterial, in: Hårdh, B. (ed.): *Fynden i centrum. Keramik, glass och metall från Uppåkra*, Acta Archaeologica Lundensia, series in 8°, no. 30 = Uppåkrastudier 2, Lund, 41-58.

Pauli Jensen, X. 2003: The Vimose Find, in: Jørgensen *et al.* (eds.), 224-239.

Pauli Jensen, X. 2008: *Våben fra Vimose – bearbejdning og tolkning af et gammelkendt fund*. Ph.d. dissertation, University of Copenhagen.

Pentz, P. 2007: Krystalkugler og kristen mystik, *Sfinx* 30.1, 4-9.

Peter, M. 1990: *Eine Werkstätte zur Herstellung von subaeraten Denaren in Augusta Raurica*, Studien zu Fundmunzen der Antike 7, Berlin.

Peter, M. 2008: Imitations of Roman coins in non-Roman contexts, in: Bursche, Ciołek & Wolters (eds.), 389-394.

Petersen, H. 1890: Gravpladsen fra den ældre Jernalder paa Nordrup Mark ved Ringsted, *Nordiske Fortidsminder* I, 1-18 (French summary: Polyandre de l'ancient age de fer a Nordrup en Selande).

Petersen, J.E. 1987: Farvergade i Næstved. Arkæologiske fund fra germansk jernalder og middelalder, *Aarbøger for Nordisk Oldkyndighed og Historie*, København (1988), 171-209.

Petersen, P.V. 1987: Zwei Schatzfunde mit römischer Münzen in Gudme – archäologische Untersuchungen, *Frühmittelalterliche Studien* 21, 51-60.

Petersen, P.V. 1988: Gudme II, en guldskat i hus!, *Årbog for Svendborg og Omegns Museer*, 42-51.

Petersen, P.V. 1994: Excavations at Sites with Treasure Trove Finds at Gudme, in: Nielsen, P.O. *et al.* (eds.), 30-40.

Pind, J. *et al.* (eds.) 2002: *Drik – og du vil leve skønt. Festskrift til Ulla Lund Hansen*, Publications from the National Museum, Studies in Archaeology and History Vol. 7, Copenhagen.

Poulsen, P. 1987: Der Brakteaten-Fund von Gudme 1982, *Frühmittelalterliche Studien* 21, 74-75.

Poulsen, Th.G. 2008: Tolkning af enkeltfundne mønter. Hvor meget er mange mønter?, *Nordisk Numismatisk Unions Medlemsblad* 4, 151-165.

Ramskou, Th. 1976: *Lindholm Høje Gravpladsen*, Nordiske Fortidsminder, Ser. B in quarto, vol. 2, Copenhagen.

Ramus, C. 1816: *Catalogus numorum veterum græcorum et latinorum musei regis Daniæ*, Hafniæ (Copenhagen).

Rasbach, G. 1999: Zur Münzbeigabe in Brandgräbern des 1. und 2. Jh. am Beispiel der Gräberfelder von *Asciburgium*, in Dubuis *et al.* (eds.), 215-227.

Riis, P.J. 1959: The Danish bronze vessels of Greek, Early Campanian and Etruscan manufactures, *Acta Archaeologica* 30, 2-50.

Rindel, P.O. 2002: Regional Settlement Patterns and Central Places on Late Iron Age Zealand, Denmark, in: Hårdh & Larsson (eds.), 185-196.

Roland, Th. & Horsnæs, H.W. 2004: Orup-skatten – romerske mønter og sjællandske stormænd, *Liv & Levn* 18, 9-20.

Runge, M. 2007: Guldsmedens skrot, *Skalk* 2007.4, 3-7.

Segschneider, M. 2002: Trade and Centrality between the Rhine and the Limfjord around 500 AD. The Beachmarket on the Northfrisian Island Amrum and its Context, in: Hårdh & Larsson (eds.), 247-256.

Sehested, F. 1878: *Fortidsminder og Oldsager fra Egnen omkring Broholm*, København.

Sehested, F. 1884: *Archæologiske Undersøgelser 1878-1881*, København.

Seipel, W. (ed.) 1999: *Barbarenschmuck und Römergold. Der Schatz von Szilágysomlyó*, Wien.

Sidorovič, V. 2007: Findings of Roman coins from the second half of the 3rd and the first half of the 4th century from territory of Belarus [trilingual text], in: *Iconography of money in Central and East Europe, International numismatic symposium – lecture summaries*, Slovak Numismatic Society, Humenné 13.-16.9. 2007, 40-41. (download from http://www.muenzgeschichte.ch/downloads/symposium_hummene.pdf)

Silvegren, U. 1999: Mynten från Uppåkra, in: B. Hårdh (ed): Fynden i centrum: keramik, glas och metall från Uppåkra, Uppåkrastudier 2 = Acta Archaeologica Lundensia, series in 8° no. 30, 95-112.

Silvegren, U. 2002: Mynten från Uppåkra, *Svensk Numismatisk Tidsskrift* 3, 52-57 and 4, 2002, 76-80.

Simensen, C.J. & Khazai, H. 2008: Funn av en kobbermynt i Sarpsborg, *NNF-Nytt* 2, 14-19.

Sindbæk, S.M. 2007: The Small World of the Vikings: Networks in Early Medieval Communication and Exchange, *Norwegian Archaeological Review* vol. 40.1, 59-74.

Sisdrys, R.V. 2001: Roman imports among the West Balt: commerce or „beads for the natives", in: A. Butrimas (ed.): *Baltic Amber*, Vilnius, 157-169.

Skaare, K. 1976: *Coins and Coinage in Viking Age Norway*. Oslo.

Skaare, K. 1993: Roman gold medallions and their imitations in Scandinavia, *RIN* 95, 473-486.

Staal, B. 1997: Etagebyggeri?, *Skalk* 1997.1, 30-32.

Stenalt, P. 2000: Fund med perspektiv, *Skalk* 2000.2, 14-17.

Stevens, S.T. 1991: Charon's obol and other coins in ancient funerary practise, *Phoenix* 45, 215-229.

Stjernquist, B. 1983: Ett nytt fynd av guldmynt från Skåne, *Ale, Historisk tidskrift för Skåne* 3, 3-9.

Storgaard, B. 1990: Årslev-fundet – et fynsk gravfund fra slutningen af yngre romersk jernalder, *Aarbøger for Nordisk Oldkyndighed og Historie*, 23-58 (German summary: Årslev – ein Grabfund von Fünen vom Ende der jüngeren römischen Kaiserzeit)

Storgaard, B. 1997: *Forbindelserne mellem Sydskandinavien og Sydøsteuropa i tiden ca. 250 til 475 e.Kr. – belyst ved en nybearbejdning af Brangstrup-depotet og en undersøgelse af Sösdala- og Nydam-stilenes kontinentale relationer*, unpubl. ph.d. diss. University of Copenhagen.

Streefkerk, M. 1994: Diep in het veen van Diepenveen, *Westerheem* 43-46, 245-253.

Stribrny, K. 2003: *Funktionsanalyse barbarisierter, barbarischer Denare mittels numismatischer und metallurgische Metoden. Zur Erforschung der sarmatisch-germanischen Kontakte im 3. Jahrhundert n.Chr.*, Studien zu Fundmünzen der Antike Band 18, Mainz am Rhein.

Sørensen, P.Ø. 1994a: Gudmehallerne. Kongeligt byggeri fra jernalderen, *Nationalmuseets Arbejdsmark*, 25-39.

Sørensen, P.Ø. 1994b: Houses, Farmsteads and Settlement Pattern in the Gudme Area, in: Nielsen, P.O. et al. (eds.), 41-52.

Sørensen, P.Ø. 2000: Bebyggelsen på Gudme III – Tre skattefund og en langvarig historie, *Årbog for Svendborg & Omegns Museum*, 24-35.

Sørensen, S.A. 1993: Skattefund fra Lærkefryd ved Jørlunde, *Arkæologi i Frederiksborg Amt 1983-1993*, Frederiksborg Amts Museumsråd, 107-113.

Sørensen, S.A. 2000: *Hørup: en sjællandsk værkstedsplads fra romersk jernalder*, Museet Færgegården.

Sørensen, S.A. 2006a: Hørup – a specialised workshop site from the Roman Iron Age and Early Migration Period on Zealand, *JDA* 14, 169-178.

Sørensen, S.A. 2006b: Metal detector finds from Lærkefryd, Zealand. Votive offerings from the Late Roman Iron Age – Viking Period, *JDA* 14, 179-186.

Talvio, T. 1982: Romerske myntfund i Finland, *Nordisk Numismatisk Årsskrift* 1979-1980, 34-54.

Talvio, T. 1992: Some reflections on the Roman denarii in northern finds, *Florilegium Numismaticum, Studies in honorem U. Westermark edita, NM* 38, 323-326.

Thomsen, P.O. 1994: Lundeborg – an Early Port of Trade in South-East Funen, in: Nielsen et al. 1994, 23-29

Thomsen, P.O. 1998: Metalværksteder fra romersk jernalder i Kværndrup – en foreløbig præsentation, *Årbog for Svendborg & Omegns Museer*, 22-32.

Thrane, H. (ed.) 1990: *Gudme-rapport. Beretning fra det 3. Gudme-symposium, Hollufgård den 2. juni 1989*. Skrifter fra Historisk Institut, Odense Universitet nr. 38.

Thrane, H. 1994: Gudme – a Focus of Archaeological Research 1833-1987, in: Nielsen, P.O. et al. (eds.), 8-15.

Thüry, G.E. 1999: Charon und die Funktion der Münzen in römischen Gräber der Kaiserzeit, in: Dubuis et al. (eds.), 17-30.

Tomasini, W.J. 1964: *The Barbaric Tremissis in Spain and Southern France. Anastasius to Leovigild*,

Numismatic Notes and Monographs 152, New York. [Rev. by J. Lafaurie in Revue Numismatique, Ser. 6, Vol. 8 (1966), pp. 336-338.]

Tornbjerg, Sv.Å. 1997: Fra gubbernes verden, *Skalk* 3, 6-10.

Tornbjerg, Sv.Å. 2002: Skrot og godt fra Østervang – en værkstedsplads ved Ejby nær Køge, in: Pind (ed.), 149-158.

Tornbjerg, Sv.Å. 2003: Ellebækgård – Ølbys forgænger?, *Årbog for Køge Museum*, 7-22.

Ulriksen, J. 1998: En ejendommelig sag, *ROMU Årsskrift fra Roskilde Museum*, 7-28.

Van der Vin, J.P.A. 1996: Roman coins in the Dutch province of Friesland, in: King, C.E. & Wigg, D.G.: *Coin finds and coin use in the Roman World, the thirteenth Oxford Symposium on Coinage and Monetary History, Studien zu Fundmünzen der Antike (SFMA)* 10, 357-371.

Van der Vin, J.P.A. 2000: Roman coins in the Northern Netherlands, *Proceedings of the 12th International Congress of Numismatics 1997*, Berlin, 635-638.

Voss, O. 1954: The Høstentorp silver hoard and its period. A study of a Danish find of scrap silver from about 500 a.d., *Acta Archaeologica* XXV, 171-219.

Weber, M. 1998: Das Gräberfeld von Issendorf, Niedersachsen. Ausgangspunkt für Wanderungen nach Britannien?, *Studien zur Sachsenforschung* 11, 1998, 199- 212

Werner, J. 1989: Zu den römischen Mantelfibeln zweier Kriegergräber von Leuna, *Jahresschrift für mitteldeutschen Vorgeschichte* 72, 121-134.

Westermark, U. 1980: Fynn av äldre romerska guldmynt i Kungl. Myntkabinettets samling, *Nordisk Numismatisk Unions Medlemsblad*, 99-104.

Westermark, U. 1983: Solidi found in Sweden and Denmark after 1967, *Numismatiska Meddelanden* XXXIII, 29-40.

Westermark, U. & Wiséhn, I. 1983: Romerska bronsmynt funna i Sverige 1, *NNUM* 8, 162-170.

Westermark, U. & Wiséhn, I. 1984: Romerska bronsmynt funna i Sverige 2, *NNUM* 8, 148-153.

Westermark, U. & Wiséhn, I. 1989: Romerska bronsmynt funna i Sverige 3, *NNUM* 9, 205-209.

Wiell, S. 2003: Denmark's bog find pioneer. The archaeologist Conrad Engelhardt and his work, in: Jørgensen *et. al.* (eds.) 66-83.

Wiker, G. 1999: Gullbrakteaterne og deres funnsteder, *Nicolay* 77, 12-20.

Wiker, G. 2001: Om konstruktion av ny menneskelig identitet i jernalderen, *Primitive tider*, 51-72.

Wołoszyn, M. 2008: Byzantine coins from the 6th and the 7th c. from Poland and their East-Central European context. Ways and phases, contexts and functions, in: Bursche, Ciołek & Wolters (eds.), 195-224.

Wołoszyn, M. (ed.) 2009: *Byzantine Coins in Central Europe between the 5th and the 10th century*, (Congress Polish Academy of Arts and Sciences Krakow April 23rd to 26th 2007), *Moravia Magna* seria Polona vol. III, Krakow.

Wolters, R. & Stoess, Ch. 1985: Die römischen Münzschatzfunde im Westteil des freien Germanien – Ein Beitrag zur Beurteilung des ‚Geldumlaufs im Gebiet zwischen Rhein, Donau und Oder während der ersten beiden Jahrhunderte n. Chr., *Münsterische Beiträge zur Antiken Handelsgeschichte* IV.2, 3-41.

Zapolska, A. 2007: Denary rzymskie znajdowane w kontekstach wczesnośredniowiecznych naziemiach Polskich (English summary: Roman denarii found in Early Medieval contexts in Polish lands), *Wiadomości Numizmatyczne* LI, zeszyt 2 (184), 149-178.

Zedelius, V. 1974: *Spätkaiserzeitlich-völkerwanderungszeitliche Keramik und römische Münzen von Laatzen, Ldkr. Hannover*, Münstersche Beiträge zur Vor- und Frühgeschichte 8, Hildesheim.

Zedelius, V. 1980: Zwei Funden römischer Denare aus dem freien Germanien: Middels-Osterloog und Fickmühlen (Bederkesa), *Studien zur Sachsenforschung* 2, 489-514.

Zedelius, V. 1982: Der grosse römische Denarschatz von Jever (1850), Niedersachsen, *Studien zur Sachsenforschung* 3, 315-355.

Ørsnes, M. 1988: *Ejsbøl I. Waffenopferfunde des 4.-5. Jahrh. nach Chr.*, Nordiske Fortidsminder, serie B, 11. København.

Östergren, M. 1981: *Gotlandska fynd av solidi och denarer. En undersökning af fyndplatserna*, RAGU Arkeologiska skrifter 1, Stockholm.